CORE STATUTES ON
CONTRACT, TORT & RESTITUTION 2017–18

The *Palgrave Core Statutes* series

CORE STATUTES ON CONTRACT, TORT & RESTITUTION 2017–18

Graham Stephenson

This edition first published 2017 by
PALGRAVE

Palgrave in the UK is an imprint of Macmillan Publishers Limited, registered in England, company number 785998, of 4 Crinan Street, London, N1 9XW.

Palgrave® and Macmillan® are registered trademarks in the United States, the United Kingdom, Europe and other countries.

ISBN: 978–1–352–00053–5 paperback

This book is printed on paper suitable for recycling and made from fully managed and sustained forest sources. Logging, pulping and manufacturing processes are expected to conform to the environmental regulations of the country of origin.

A catalogue record for this book is available from the British Library.

A catalog record for this book is available from the Library of Congress.

PREFACE

The main changes to this new edition include alterations to the Nuclear Installations Act 1965, new rules on liability for errant horses incorporated into the Animals Act 1971, the tardy coming into force of the Third Parties (Rights against Insurers) Act 2010 and some minor amendments to the Misrepresentation Act 1967 and the Consumer Contracts (Information, Cancellation and Additional Charges) Regulations 2013. For the future, when and how we leave the European Union is going to prove highly interesting for this and other volumes in the series!

Thanks once again for the invaluable help from all those involved at the publishers.

Graham Stephenson
June 2017

CONTENTS

ALPHABETICAL LIST OF CONTENTS

PART I
STATUTES

STATUTE OF FRAUDS 1677
(29 Chas. II, c. 3)

4   **No action against executors, etc. upon a special promise, or upon any agreement, or contract for sale of lands, etc. unless agreement, etc. be in writing and signed**
No action shall be brought ... whereby to charge the defendant upon any special promise to answere for the debt default or miscarriages of another person ... unlesse the agreement upon which such action shall be brought or some memorandum or note thereof shall be in writeing and signed by the partie to be charged therewith or some other person thereunto by him lawfully authorised.

FIRES PREVENTION (METROPOLIS) ACT 1774
(14 Geo. III, c. 78)

86   **No action to lie against a person where the fire accidentally begins**
And no action, suit or process whatever shall be had, maintained or prosecuted against any person in whose house, chamber, stable, barn or other building, or on whose estate any fire shall ... accidentally begin, nor shall any recompence be made by such person for any damage suffered thereby, any law, usage or custom to the contrary notwithstanding; ... provided that no contract or agreement made between landlord and tenant shall be hereby defeated or made void.

STATUTE OF FRAUDS AMENDMENT ACT 1828
(9 Geo. IV, c. 14)

6   **Action not maintainable on representations of character, etc., unless they be in writing signed by the party chargeable**
No action shall be brought whereby to charge any person upon or by reason of any representation or assurance made or given concerning or relating to the character, conduct, credit, ability, trade, or dealings of any other person, to the intent or purpose that such other person may obtain credit, money, or goods upon, unless such representation or assurance be made in writing, signed by the party to be charged therewith.

PARLIAMENTARY PAPERS ACT 1840
(3 & 4 Vict., c. 9)

1   **Proceedings, criminal or civil, against persons for publication of papers printed by order of Parliament, to be stayed upon delivery of a certificate and affidavit to the effect that such publication is by order of either House of Parliament**
It shall and may be lawful for any person or persons who now is or are, or hereafter shall be, a defendant or defendants in any civil or criminal proceeding commenced or prosecuted in any manner soever, for or on account or in respect of the publication of any such report, paper, votes, or proceedings by such person or persons, or by his, her, or their servant or servants, by or under the authority of either House of Parliament, to bring before the court in which such proceeding shall have been or shall be so commenced or prosecuted, or before any judge of the same (if one of the superior courts at the Royal Courts of Justice), first giving twenty-four hours notice of his intention so to do to the prosecutor or plaintiff in

such proceeding, a certificate under the hand of ... the speaker of the House of Lords ...,
or of the clerk of the Parliaments, or of the speaker of the House of Commons, or of the
clerk of the same house, stating that the report, paper, votes, or proceedings, as the case
may be, in respect whereof such civil or criminal proceeding shall have been commenced
or prosecuted, was published by such person or persons, or by his, her, or their servant
or servants, by order or under the authority of the House of Lords or of the House of
Commons, as the case may be, together with an affidavit verifying such certificate; and
such court or judge shall thereupon immediately stay such civil or criminal proceeding; and
the same, and every writ or process issued therein, shall be and shall be deemed and taken
to be finally put an end to, determined, and superseded by virtue of this Act.

2   Proceedings to be stayed when commenced in respect of a copy of an authenticated report, etc.

In case of any civil or criminal proceeding hereafter to be commenced or prosecuted for
or on account or in respect of the publication of any copy of such report, paper, votes,
or proceedings, it shall be lawful for the defendant or defendants at any stage of the
proceedings to lay before the court or judge such report, paper, votes, or proceedings,
and such copy, with an affidavit verifying such report, paper, votes, or proceedings, and
the correctness of such copy, and the court or judge shall immediately stay such civil or
criminal proceedings; and the same, and every writ or process issued therein, shall be and
shall be deemed and taken to be finally put an end to, determined, and superseded by
virtue of this Act.

3   In proceedings for printing any extract or abstract of a paper, it may be shewn that such extract was bona fide made

It shall be lawful in any civil or criminal proceeding to be commenced or prosecuted for
printing any extract from or abstract of such report, paper, votes, or proceedings, to give
in evidence ... such report, paper, votes, or proceedings, and to show that such extract or
abstract was published bona fide and without malice; and if such shall be the opinion of the
jury, a verdict of not guilty shall be entered for the defendant or defendants.

4   Act not to affect the privileges of Parliament

Provided always that nothing herein contained shall be deemed or taken, or held or
construed, directly or indirectly, by implication or otherwise, to affect the privileges of
Parliament in any manner whatsoever.

LIBEL ACT 1843
(6 & 7 Vict., c.96)

1   Offer of an apology admissible in evidence of mitigation of damages in action for defamation

In any action for defamation it shall be lawful for the defendant (after notice in writing of
his intention so to do, duly given to the plaintiff at the time of filing or delivering the plea
in such action,) to give in evidence, in mitigation of damages, that he made or offered an
apology to the plaintiff for such defamation before the commencement of the action, or as
soon afterwards as he had an opportunity of doing so, in case the action shall have been
commenced before there was an opportunity of making or offering such apology.

2   In an action against a newspaper for libel, the defendant may plead that it was inserted without malice and without neglect and may pay money into court as amends

In an action for libel contained in any public newspaper or other periodical publication it
shall be competent to the defendant to plead that such libel was inserted in such newspaper
or other periodical publication without actual malice, and without gross negligence, and
that before the commencement of the action, or at the earliest opportunity afterwards,
he inserted in such newspaper or other periodical publication a full apology for the said
libel, or, if the newspaper or periodical publication in which the said libel appeared should

be ordinarily published at intervals exceeding one week, had offered to publish the said apology in any newspaper or periodical publication to be selected by the plaintiff in such action; ... and to such plea to such action it shall be competent to the plaintiff to reply generally, denying the whole of such plea.

LIBEL ACT 1845
(8 & 9 Vict., c. 75)

2   Defendant not to file such plea without paying money into court by way of amends

It shall not be competent to any defendant in such action, whether in England or Ireland, to file any such plea, without at the same time making a payment of money into court by way of amends ... , but every such plea so filed without payment of money into court shall be deemed a nullity, and may be treated as such by the plaintiff in the action.

OFFENCES AGAINST THE PERSON ACT 1861
(24 & 25 Vict., c. 100)

44   If the magistrates dismiss the complaint, they shall make out a certificate to that effect

If the Justices, upon the Hearing of any ... Case of Assault or Battery upon the Merits, where the Complaint was preferred by or on the Behalf of the Party aggrieved, ... shall deem the Offence not to be proved, or shall find the Assault or Battery to have been justified, or so trifling as not to merit any Punishment, and shall accordingly dismiss the Complaint, they shall forthwith make out a Certificate ... stating the Fact of such Dismissal, and shall deliver such Certificate to the Party against whom the Complaint was preferred.

45   Certificate or conviction shall be a bar to any other proceedings

If any Person, against whom any such Complaint as is mentioned in section 44 of this Act shall have been preferred by or on the Behalf of the Party aggrieved, shall have obtained such Certificate, or, having been convicted, shall have paid the whole Amount adjudged to be paid, or shall have suffered the Imprisonment awarded, in every such Case he shall be released from all further or other Proceedings, Civil or Criminal, for the same Cause.

FACTORS ACT 1889
(52 & 53 Vict., c. 45)

1   Definitions

For the purposes of this Act—

(1)   The expression "mercantile agent" shall mean a mercantile agent having in the customary course of his business as such agent authority either to sell goods or to consign goods for the purpose of sale, or to buy goods, or to raise money on the security of goods:

(2)   A person shall be deemed to be in possession of goods or of the documents of title to goods, where the goods or documents are in the actual custody or are held by any other person subject to his control or for him or on his behalf:

(3)   The expression "goods" shall include wares and merchandise:

(4)   The expression "document of title" shall include any bill of lading, dock warrant, warehouse-keeper's certificate, and warrant or order for the delivery of goods, and any other document used in the ordinary course of business as proof of the possession or control of goods, or authorising or purporting to authorise, either by endorsement or by delivery, the possessor of the document to transfer or receive goods thereby represented:

(5)   The expression "pledge" shall include any contract pledging, or giving a lien or security on, goods, whether in consideration of an original advance or of any further or continuing advance or of any pecuniary liability:

(6)   The expression "person" shall include any body of persons corporate or unincorporate.

2   Powers of mercantile agent with respect to disposition of goods

(1)   Where a mercantile agent is, with the consent of the owner, in possession of goods or of the documents of title to goods, any sale, pledge, or other disposition of the goods, made by him when acting in the ordinary course of business of a mercantile agent, shall, subject to the provisions of this Act, be as valid as if he were expressly authorised by the owner of the goods to make the same; provided that the person taking under the disposition acts in good faith, and has not at the time of the disposition notice that the person making the disposition has not authority to make the same.

(2)   Where a mercantile agent has, with the consent of the owner, been in possession of goods or of the documents of title to goods, any sale, pledge, or other disposition, which would have been valid if the consent had continued, shall be valid notwithstanding the determination of the consent; provided that the person taking under the disposition has not at the time thereof notice that the consent has been determined.

(3)   Where a mercantile agent has obtained possession of any documents of title to goods by reason of his being or having been, with the consent of the owner, in possession of the goods represented thereby, or of any other documents of title to the goods, his possession of the first-mentioned documents shall, for the purposes of this Act, be deemed to be with the consent of the owner.

(4)   For the purposes of this Act the consent of the owner shall be presumed in the absence of evidence to the contrary.

MARINE INSURANCE ACT 1906
(6 Edw. VII, c. 41)

22   Contract must be embodied in policy

Subject to the provisions of any statute, a contract of marine insurance is inadmissible in evidence unless it is embodied in a marine policy in accordance with this Act. The policy may be executed and issued either at the time when the contract is concluded, or afterwards.

33   Nature of warranty

(1)   A warranty, in the following sections relating to warranties, means a promissory warranty, that is to say, a warranty by which the assured undertakes that some particular thing shall or shall not be done, or that some condition shall be fulfilled, or whereby he affirms or negatives the existence of a particular state of facts.

(2)   A warranty may be express or implied.

(3)   A warranty, as above defined, is a condition which must be exactly complied with, whether it be material to the risk or not. If it be not so complied with, then, subject to any express provision in the policy, the insurer is discharged from liability as from the date of the breach of warranty, but without prejudice to any liability incurred by him before that date.

35   Express warranties

(1)   An express warranty may be in any form of words from which the intention to warrant is to be inferred.

(2)   An express warranty must be included in, or written upon, the policy, or must be contained in some document incorporated by reference into the policy.

(3)   An express warranty does not exclude an implied warranty, unless it be inconsistent therewith.

49   Excuses for deviation or delay

(1)   Deviation or delay in prosecuting the voyage contemplated by the policy is excused—

    (a)   where authorised by any special term in the policy; or

(b)   where caused by circumstances beyond the control of the master and his employer; or

(c)   where reasonably necessary in order to comply with an express or implied warranty; or

(d)   where reasonably necessary for the safety of the ship or subject-matter insured; or

(e)   for the purpose of saving human life, or aiding a ship in distress where human life may be in danger; or

(f)   where reasonably necessary for the purpose of obtaining medical or surgical aid for any person on board the ship; or

(g)   where caused by the barratrous conduct of the master or crew, if barratry be one of the perils insured against.

(2)   When the cause excusing the deviation or delay ceases to operate, the ship must resume her course, and prosecute her voyage, with reasonable dispatch.

82   Enforcement of return

Where the premium or a proportionate part thereof is, by this Act, declared to be returnable, —

(a)   If already paid, it may be recovered by the assured from the insurer; and

(b)   If unpaid, it may be retained by the assured or his agent.

83   Return by agreement

Where the policy contains a stipulation for the return of the premium, or a proportionate part thereof, on the happening of a certain event, and that event happens, the premium, or, as the case may be, the proportionate part thereof, is thereupon returnable to the assured.

84   Return for failure of consideration

(1)   Where the consideration for the payment of the premium totally fails, and there has been no fraud or illegality on the part of the assured or his agents, the premium is thereupon returnable to the assured.

(2)   Where the consideration for the payment of the premium is apportionable and there is a total failure of any apportionable part of the consideration, a proportionate part of the premium is, under the like conditions, thereupon returnable to the assured.

(3)   In particular—

(a)   Where the policy is void, or is avoided by the insurer as from the commencement of the risk, the premium is returnable, provided that there has been no fraud or illegality on the part of the assured; but if the risk is not apportionable, and has once attached, the premium is not returnable;

(b)   Where the subject-matter insured, or part thereof, has never been imperilled, the premium, or, as the case may be, a proportionate part thereof, is returnable: Provided that where the subject-matter has been insured "lost or not lost" and has arrived in safety at the time when the contract is concluded, the premium is not returnable unless, at such time, the insurer knew of the safe arrival.

(c)   Where the assured has no insurable interest throughout the currency of the risk, the premium is returnable, provided that this rule does not apply to a policy effected by way of gaming or wagering;

(d)   Where the assured has a defeasible interest which is terminated during the currency of the risk, the premium is not returnable;

(e)   Where the assured has over-insured under an unvalued policy, a proportionate part of the premium is returnable;

(f)   Subject to the foregoing provisions, where the assured has over-insured by double insurance, a proportionate part of the several premiums is returnable: Provided that, if the policies are effected at different times, and any earlier policy has at any time borne the entire risk, or if a claim has been paid on the policy in respect of the full sum insured thereby, no premium is returnable in respect of that policy, and when the double insurance is effected knowingly by the assured no premium is returnable.

87   Implied obligations varied by agreement or usage

(1)   Where any right, duty, or liability would arise under a contract of marine insurance by implication of law, it may be negatived or varied by express agreement, or by usage, if the usage be such as to bind both parties to the contract.

RESERVOIRS (SAFETY PROVISIONS) ACT 1930
(20 & 21 Geo. V, c. 51)

7   Liability for damage and injury

Where damage or injury is caused by the escape of water from a reservoir constructed after the year 1930 or under statutory powers granted after July 1930, the fact that the reservoir was so constructed shall not exonerate the undertakers from any indictment, action or other proceedings to which they would otherwise have been liable.

LAW REFORM (MISCELLANEOUS PROVISIONS) ACT 1934
(24 & 25 Geo. V, c. 41)

1   Effect of death on certain causes of action

(1)   Subject to the provisions of this section, on the death of any person after the commencement of this Act all causes of action subsisting against or vested in him shall survive against, or, as the case may be, for the benefit of, his estate. Provided that this subsection shall not apply to causes of action for defamation ...

(1A) The right of a person to claim under section 1A of the Fatal Accidents Act 1976 (bereavement) shall not survive for the benefit of his estate on his death.

(2)   Where a cause of action survives as aforesaid for the benefit of the estate of a deceased person, the damages recoverable for the benefit of the estate of that person:—

    (a)   shall not include—
       (i)   any exemplary damages;
       (ii)   any damages for loss of income in respect of any period after that person's death;

    (b)   ...

    (c)   where the death of that person has been caused by the act or omission which gives rise to the cause of action, shall be calculated without reference to any loss or gain to his estate consequent on his death, except that a sum in respect of funeral expenses may be included.

(4)   Where damage has been suffered by reason of any act or omission in respect of which a cause of action would have subsisted against any person if that person had not died before or at the same time as the damage was suffered, there shall be deemed, for the purposes of this Act, to have been subsisting against him before his death such cause of action in respect of that act or omission as would have subsisted if he had died after the damage was suffered.

(5)   The rights conferred by this Act for the benefit of the estates of deceased persons shall be in addition to and not in derogation of any rights conferred on the dependants of deceased persons by the Fatal Accidents Act 1976 ... and so much of this Act as relates to causes of action against the estates of deceased persons shall apply in relation to causes of action under the said Act as it applies in relation to other causes of action not expressly excepted from the operation of subsection (1) of this section.

(6)   In the event of the insolvency of an estate against which proceedings are maintainable by virtue of this section, any liability in respect of the cause of action in respect of which the proceedings are maintainable shall be deemed to be a debt provable in the administration of the estate, notwithstanding that it is a demand in the nature of unliquidated damages arising otherwise than by a contract, promise or breach of trust.

LAW REFORM (MARRIED WOMEN AND TORTFEASORS) ACT 1935
(25 & 26 Geo. V, c. 30)

3   Abolition of husband's liability for wife's torts and ante-nuptial contracts, debts and obligations

Subject to the provisions of this Part of this Act, the husband of a married woman shall not, by reason only of his being her husband, be liable—

(a)   in respect of any tort committed by her whether before or after the marriage, or in respect of any contract entered into, or debt or obligation incurred, by her before the marriage; or

(b)   to be sued, or made a party to any legal proceeding brought, in respect of any such tort, contract, debt, or obligation.

4   Savings

(2)   For the avoidance of doubt it is hereby declared that nothing in this Part of this Act—

(a)   renders the husband of a married woman liable in respect of any contract entered into, or debt or obligation incurred, by her after the marriage in respect of which he would not have been liable if this Act had not been passed;

(b)   exempts the husband of a married woman from liability in respect of any contract entered into, or debt or obligation (not being a debt or obligation arising out of a commission of a tort) incurred, by her after the marriage in respect of which he would have been liable if this Act had not been passed;

(c)   prevents a husband and wife from acquiring, holding, and disposing of, any property jointly or as tenants in common, or from rendering themselves, or being rendered, jointly liable in respect of any tort, contract, debt or obligation, and of suing and being sued either in tort or in contract or otherwise, in like manner as if they were not married;

(d)   prevents the exercise of any joint power given to a husband and wife.

LAW REFORM (FRUSTRATED CONTRACTS) ACT 1943
(6 & 7 Geo. VI, c. 40)

1   Adjustment of rights and liabilities of parties to frustrated contracts

(1)   Where a contract governed by English law has become impossible of performance or been otherwise frustrated, and the parties thereto have for that reason been discharged from the further performance of the contract, the following provisions of this section shall, subject to the provisions of section two of this Act, have effect in relation thereto.

(2)   All sums paid or payable to any party in pursuance of the contract before the time when the parties were so discharged (in this Act referred to as "the time of discharge") shall, in the case of sums so paid, be recoverable from him as money received by him for the use of the party by whom the sums were paid, and, in the case of sums so payable, cease to be so payable:

Provided that, if the party to whom the sums were so paid or payable incurred expenses before the time of discharge in, or for the purpose of, the performance of the contract, the court may, if it considers it just to do so having regard to all the circumstances of the case, allow him to retain or, as the case may be, recover the whole or any part of the sums so paid or payable, not being an amount in excess of the expenses so incurred.

(3)   Where any party to the contract has, by reason of anything done by any other party thereto in, or for the purpose of, the performance of the contract, obtained a valuable benefit (other than a payment of money to which the last foregoing subsection applies) before the time of discharge there shall be recoverable from him by the said other party such sum (if any), not exceeding the value of the said benefit to the party obtaining it, as the court considers just, having regard to all the circumstances of the case and, in particular,—

(a)   the amount of any expenses incurred before the time of discharge by the benefited party in, or for the purpose of, the performance of the contract, including any sums paid or payable by him to any other party in pursuance of the contract and retained or recoverable by that party under the last foregoing subsection, and

(b)   the effect, in relation to the said benefit, of the circumstances giving rise to the frustration of the contract.

(4)   In estimating, for the purposes of the foregoing provisions of this section, the amount of any expenses incurred by any party to the contract, the court may, without prejudice to the generality of the said provisions, include such sum as appears to be reasonable in respect of overhead expenses and in respect of any work or services performed personally by the said party.

(5)   In considering whether any sum ought to be recovered or retained under the foregoing provisions of this section by any party to the contract, the court shall not take into account any sums which have, by reason of the circumstances giving rise to the frustration of the contract, become payable to that party under any contract of insurance unless there was an obligation to insure imposed by an express term of the frustrated contract or by or under any enactment.

(6)   Where any person has assumed obligations under the contract in consideration of the conferring of a benefit by any other party to the contract upon any other person, whether a party to the contract or not, the court may, if in all the circumstances of the case it considers it just to do so, treat for the purposes of subsection (3) of this section any benefit so conferred as a benefit obtained by the person who has assumed the obligations as aforesaid.

2   Provision as to application of this Act

(1)   This Act shall apply to contracts, whether made before or after the commencement of this Act, as respects which the time of discharge is on or after the first day of July, nineteen hundred and forty-three, but not to contracts as respects which the time of discharge is before the said date.

(2)   This Act shall apply to contracts to which the Crown is a party in like manner as to contracts between subjects.

(3)   Where any contract to which this Act applies contains any provision which, upon the true construction of the contract, is intended to have effect in the event of circumstances arising which operate, or would but for the said provision operate, to frustrate the contract, or is intended to have effect whether such circumstances arise or not, the court shall give effect to the said provision and shall only give effect to the foregoing section of this Act to such extent, if any, as appears to the court to be consistent with the said provision.

(4)   Where it appears to the court that a part of any contract to which this Act applies can properly be severed from the remainder of the contract, being a part wholly performed before the time of discharge, or so performed except for the payment in respect of that part of the contract of sums which are or can be ascertained under the contract, the court shall treat that part of the contract as if it were a separate contract and had not been frustrated and shall treat the foregoing section of this Act as only applicable to the remainder of that contract.

(5)   This Act shall not apply—

     (a)   to any charterparty, except a time charterparty or a charterparty by way of demise, or to any contract (other than a charterparty) for the carriage of goods by sea; or

     (b)   to any contract of insurance, save as is provided by subsection (5) of the foregoing section; or

     (c)   to any contract to which section 7 of the Sale of Goods Act 1979 (which avoids contracts for the sale of specific goods which perish before the risk has passed to the buyer) applies, or to any other contract for the sale, or for the sale and delivery, of specific goods, where the contract is frustrated by reason of the fact that the goods have perished.

3   Short title and interpretation

(1)   This Act may be cited as the Law Reform (Frustrated Contracts) Act, 1943.

(2)   In this Act the expression "court" means, in relation to any matter, the court or arbitrator by or before whom the matter falls to be determined.

LAW REFORM (CONTRIBUTORY NEGLIGENCE) ACT 1945
(8 & 9 Geo. VI, c. 28)

1   Apportionment of liability in case of contributory negligence

(1)   Where any person suffers damage as the result partly of his own fault and partly of the fault of any other person or persons, a claim in respect of that damage shall not be defeated by reason of the fault of the person suffering the damage, but the damages

recoverable in respect thereof shall be reduced to such extent as the court thinks just and equitable having regard to the claimant's share in the responsibility of the damage: Provided that—

(a)   this subsection shall not operate to defeat any defence arising under a contract;

(b)   where any contract or enactment providing for the limitation of liability is applicable to the claim, the amount of damages recoverable by the claimant by virtue of this subsection shall not exceed the maximum limit so applicable.

(2)   Where damages are recoverable by any person by virtue of the foregoing subsection subject to such reduction as is therein mentioned, the court shall find and record the total damages which would have been recoverable if the claimant had not been at fault.

(5)   Where, in any case to which subsection (1) of this section applies, one of the persons at fault avoids liability to any other such person or his personal representative by pleading the Limitation Act, 1939, or any other enactment limiting the time within which proceedings may be taken, he shall not be entitled to recover any damages … from that other person or representative by virtue of the said subsection.

(6)   Where any case to which subsection (1) of this section applies is tried with a jury, the jury shall determine the total damages which would have been recoverable if the claimant had not been at fault and the extent to which those damages are to be reduced.

4   Interpretation

The following expressions have the meanings hereby respectively assigned to them, that is to say—

"court" means, in relation to any claim, the court or arbitrator by or before whom the claim falls to be determined;

"damage" includes loss of life and personal injury;

…

"fault" means negligence, breach of statutory duty or other act or omission which gives rise to liability in tort or would, apart from this Act, give rise to the defence of contributory negligence.

CROWN PROCEEDINGS ACT 1947
(10 & 11 Geo. VI, c. 44)

2   Liability of the Crown in tort

(1)   Subject to the provisions of this Act, the Crown shall be subject to all those liabilities in tort to which, if it were a private person of full age and capacity, it would be subject:—

(a)   in respect of torts committed by its servants or agents;

(b)   in respect of any breach of those duties which a person owes to his servants or agents at common law by reason of being their employer; and

(c)   in respect of any breach of the duties attaching at common law to the ownership, occupation, possession or control of property:

Provided that no proceedings shall lie against the Crown by virtue of paragraph (a) of this subsection in respect of any act or omission of a servant or agent of the Crown unless the act or omission would apart from the provisions of this Act have given rise to a cause of action in tort against that servant or agent or his estate.

(2)   Where the Crown is bound by a statutory duty which is binding also upon persons other than the Crown and its officers, then, subject to the provisions of this Act, the Crown shall, in respect of a failure to comply with that duty, be subject to all those liabilities in tort (if any) to which it would be so subject if it were a private person of full age and capacity.

LAW REFORM (PERSONAL INJURIES) ACT 1948
(11 & 12 Geo. VI, c. 41)

1   Common employment

(1)   It shall not be a defence to an employer who is sued in respect of personal injuries caused by the negligence of a person employed by him, that that person was at the time the injuries were caused in common employment with the person injured.

(3)   Any provision contained in a contract of service or apprenticeship, or in an agreement collateral thereto, (including a contract or agreement entered into before the commen-cement of this Act) shall be void in so far as it would have the effect of excluding or limiting any liability of the employer in respect of personal injuries caused to the person employed or apprenticed by the negligence of persons in common employment with him.

2   Measure of damages

(4)   In an action for damages for personal injuries (including any such action arising out of a contract), there shall be disregarded, in determining the reasonableness of any expenses, the possibility of avoiding those expenses or part of them by taking advantage of facilities available under the National Health Service Act 2006 of the National Health Service (Wales) Act 2006 or the National Health Service (Scotland) Act, 1978, or of any corresponding facilities in Northern Ireland.

3   Definition of "personal injury"

In this Act the expression "personal injury" includes any disease and any impairment of a person's physical or mental condition, and the expression "injured" shall be construed accordingly.

NATIONAL PARKS AND ACCESS TO THE COUNTRYSIDE ACT 1949
(12, 13 & 14 Geo. VI, c. 97)

60   Rights of public where access agreement or order in force

(1)   Subject to the following provisions of this Part of this Act, where an access agreement or order is in force as respects any land a person who enters upon land comprised in the agreement or order for the purpose of open-air recreation without breaking or damaging any wall, fence, hedge or gate, or who is on such land for that purpose after having so entered thereon, shall not be treated as a trespasser on that land or incur any other liability by reason only of so entering or being on the land:
Provided that this subsection shall not apply to land which for the time being is excepted land as hereinafter defined.

(2)   Nothing in the provisions of the last foregoing subsection shall entitle a person to enter or be on any land, or to do anything thereon, in contravention of any prohibition contained in or having effect under any enactment.

(3)   An access agreement or order may specify or provide for imposing restrictions subject to which persons may enter or be upon land by virtue of subsection (1) of this section, including in particular, but without prejudice to the generality of this subsection, restrictions excluding the land or any part thereof at particular times from the operation of the said subsection (1); and that subsection shall not apply to any person entering or being on the land in contravention of any such restriction or failing to comply therewith while he is on the land.

66   Effect of access agreement or order on rights and liabilities of owners

(1)   A person interested in any land comprised in an access agreement or order, not being excepted land, shall not carry out any work thereon whereby the area to which the public are able to have access by virtue of the agreement or order is substantially reduced: Provided that nothing in this subsection shall affect the doing of anything whereby any land becomes excepted land.

(2)   The operation of subsection (1) of section sixty of this Act in relation to any land shall not increase the liability, under any enactment not contained in this Act or under any rule of law, of a person interested in that land or adjoining land in respect of the state thereof or of things done or omitted thereon.

RESERVE AND AUXILIARY FORCES (PROTECTION OF CIVIL INTERESTS) ACT 1951
(14 & 15 Geo. VI, c. 65)

13   Effect of failure to observe restrictions under Part I

(2)   In any action for damages for conversion or other proceedings which lie by virtue of any such omission, failure or contravention, the court may take account of the conduct of the defendant with a view, if the court thinks fit, to awarding exemplary damages in respect of the wrong sustained by the plaintiff.

DEFAMATION ACT 1952
(15 & 16 Geo. VI & 1 Eliz. II, c. 66)

2   Slander affecting official, professional or business reputation

In an action for slander in respect of words calculated to disparage the plaintiff in an office, profession, calling, trade or business held or carried on by him at the time of the publication, it shall not be necessary to allege or prove special damage, whether or not the words are spoken of the plaintiff in the way of his office, profession, calling, trade or business.

3   Slander of title, etc.

(1)   In an action for slander of title, slander of goods or other malicious falsehood, it shall not be necessary to allege or prove special damage—

    (a)   if the words upon which the action is founded are calculated to cause pecuniary damage to the plaintiff and are published in writing or other permanent form; or

    (b)   if the said words are calculated to cause pecuniary damage to the plaintiff in respect of any office, profession, calling, trade or business held or carried on by him at the time of the publication.

(2)   Section one of this Act shall apply for the purposes of this section as it applies for the purposes of the law of libel and slander.

9   Extension of certain defences to broadcasting

(1)   Section three of the Parliamentary Papers Act, 1840 (which confers protection in respect of proceedings for printing extracts from or abstracts of parliamentary papers) shall have effect as if the reference to printing included a reference to broadcasting by means of wireless telegraphy.

10   Limitation on privilege at elections

A defamatory statement published by or on behalf of a candidate in any election to local government authority, to the National Assembly for Wales, to the Scottish Parliament or to Parliament shall not be deemed to be published on a privileged occasion on the ground that it is material to a question in issue in the election, whether or not the person by whom it is published is qualified to vote at the election.

11   Agreements for indemnity

An agreement for indemnifying any person against civil liability for libel in respect of the publication of any matter shall not be unlawful unless at the time of the publication that person knows that the matter is defamatory, and does not reasonably believe that there is a good defence to any action brought upon it.

12   Evidence of other damages recovered by plaintiff

In any action for libel or slander the defendant may give evidence in mitigation of damages that the plaintiff has recovered damages, or has brought actions for damages, for libel or slander in respect of the publication of words to the same effect as the words on which the action is founded, or has received or agreed to receive compensation in respect of any such publication.

16   Interpretation

(1)   Any reference in this Act to words shall be construed as including a reference to pictures, visual images, gestures and other methods of signifying meaning.

OCCUPIERS' LIABILITY ACT 1957
(5 & 6 Eliz. II, c. 31)

1   Preliminary

(1)   The rules enacted by the two next following sections shall have effect, in place of the rules of the common law, to regulate the duty which an occupier of premises owes to his visitors in respect of dangers due to the state of the premises or to things done or omitted to be done on them.

(2)   The rules so enacted shall regulate the nature of the duty imposed by law in consequence of a person's occupation or control of premises and of any invitation or permission he gives (or is to be treated as giving) to another to enter or use the premises, but they shall not alter the rules of the common law as to the persons on whom a duty is so imposed or to whom it is owed; and accordingly for the purpose of the rules so enacted the persons who are to be treated as an occupier and as his visitors are the same (subject to subsection (4) of this section) as the persons who would at common law be treated as an occupier and as his invitees or licensees.

(3)   The rules so enacted in relation to an occupier of premises and his visitors shall also apply, in like manner and to the like extent as the principles applicable at common law to an occupier of premises and his invitees or licensees would apply, to regulate—
  (a)   the obligations of a person occupying or having control over any fixed or moveable structure, including any vessel, vehicle or aircraft; and
  (b)   the obligations of a person occupying or having control over any premises or structure in respect of damage to property, including the property of persons who are not themselves his visitors.

(4)   A person entering any premises in exercise of rights conferred by virtue of—
  (a)   section 2(1) of the Countryside and Rights of Way Act 2000, or
  (b)   an access agreement or order under the National Parks and Access to the Countryside Act 1949,
  is not, for the purposes of this Act, a visitor of the occupier of those premises.

2   Extent of occupier's ordinary duty

(1)   An occupier of premises owes the same duty, the "common duty of care", to all his visitors, except in so far as he is free to and does extend, restrict, modify or exclude his duty to any visitor or visitors by agreement or otherwise.

(2)   The common duty of care is a duty to take such care as in all the circumstances of the case is reasonable to see that the visitor will be reasonably safe in using the premises for the purposes for which he is invited or permitted by the occupier to be there.

(3)   The circumstances relevant for the present purposes include the degree of care, and of want of care, which would ordinarily be looked for in such a visitor, so that (for example) in proper cases—
  (a)   an occupier must be prepared for children to be less careful than adults; and
  (b)   an occupier may expect that a person, in the exercise of his calling, will appreciate and guard against any special risks ordinarily incident to it, so far as the occupier leaves him free to do so.

(4)   In determining whether the occupier of premises has discharged the common duty of care to a visitor, regard is to be had to all the circumstances, so that (for example)—
  (a)   where damage is caused to a visitor by a danger of which he had been warned by the occupier, the warning is not to be treated without more as absolving the occupier from liability, unless in all the circumstances it was enough to enable the visitor to be reasonably safe; and
  (b)   where damage is caused to a visitor by a danger due to the faulty execution of any work of construction, maintenance or repair by an independent contractor employed by the occupier, the occupier is not to be treated without more as

answerable for the danger if in all the circumstances he had acted reasonably in entrusting the work to an independent contractor and had taken such steps (if any) as he reasonably ought in order to satisfy himself that the contractor was competent and that the work had been properly done.

(5) The common duty of care does not impose on an occupier any obligation to a visitor in respect of risks willingly accepted as his by the visitor (the question whether a risk was so accepted to be decided on the same principles as in other cases in which one person owes a duty of care to another).

(6) For the purposes of this section, persons who enter premises for any purpose in the exercise of a right conferred by law are to be treated as permitted by the occupier to be there for that purpose, whether they in fact have his permission or not.

3   Effect of contract on occupier's liability to third party

(1) Where an occupier of premises is bound by contract to permit persons who are strangers to the contract to enter or use the premises, the duty of care which he owes to them as his visitors cannot be restricted or excluded by that contract, but (subject to any provision of the contract to the contrary) shall include the duty to perform his obligations under the contract, whether undertaken for their protection or not, in so far as those obligations go beyond the obligations otherwise involved in that duty.

(2) A contract shall not by virtue of this section have the effect, unless it expressly so provides, of making an occupier who has taken all reasonable care answerable to strangers to the contract for dangers due to the faulty execution of any work of construction, maintenance or repair or other like operation by persons other than himself, his servants and persons acting under his direction and control.

(3) In this section, "stranger to the contract" means a person not for the time being entitled to the benefit of the contract as a party to it or as the successor by assignment or otherwise of a party to it, and accordingly includes a party to the contract who has ceased to be so entitled.

(4) Where by the terms or conditions governing any tenancy (including a statutory tenancy which does not in law amount to a tenancy) either the landlord or the tenant is bound, though not by contract, to permit persons to enter or use premises of which he is the occupier, this section shall apply as if the tenancy were a contract between the landlord and the tenant.

(5) This section, in so far as it prevents the common duty of care from being restricted or excluded, applies to contracts entered into and tenancies created before the commencement of this Act, as well as to those entered into or created after its commencement; but, in so far as it enlarges the duty owed by an occupier beyond the common duty of care, it shall have effect only in relation to obligations which are undertaken after the commencement or which are renewed by agreement (whether express or implied) after that commencement.

5   Implied term in contracts

(1) Where persons enter or use, or bring or send goods to, any premises in exercise of a right conferred by contract with a person occupying or having control of the premises, the duty he owes them in respect of dangers due to the state of the premises or to things done or omitted to be done by them, in so far as the duty depends on a term to be implied in the contract by reason of its conferring that right, shall be the common duty of care.

(2) The foregoing subsection shall apply to fixed and moveable structures as it applies to premises.

(3) This section does not affect the obligations imposed on a person by or by virtue of any contract for the hire of, or for the carriage for reward of persons or goods in, any vehicle, vessel, aircraft or other means of transport, or by virtue of any contract of bailment.

(4) This section does not apply to contracts entered into before the commencement of this Act.

OCCUPIERS' LIABILITY (SCOTLAND) ACT 1960
(8 & 9 Eliz. II, c. 30)

1   Variation of rules of common law as to duty of care owed by occupiers

(1)   The provisions of the next following section of this Act shall have effect, in place of the rules of the common law, for the purpose of determining the care which a person occupying or having control of land or other premises (in this Act referred to as an "occupier of premises") is required, by reason of such occupation or control, to show towards persons entering on the premises in respect of dangers which are due to the state of the premises or to anything done or omitted to be done on them and for which he is in law responsible.

(2)   Nothing in those provisions shall be taken to alter the rules of the common law which determine the person on whom in relation to any premises a duty to show care as aforesaid towards persons entering thereon is incumbent.

(3)   Those provisions shall apply, in like manner and to the same extent as they do in relation to an occupier of premises and to persons entering thereon,—

(a)   in relation to a person occupying or having control of any fixed or moveable structure, including any vessel, vehicle or aircraft, and to persons entering thereon; and

(b)   in relation to an occupier of premises or a person occupying or having control of any such structure and to property thereon, including the property of persons who have not themselves entered on the premises or structure.

2   Extent of occupier's duty to show care

(1)   The care which an occupier of premises is required, by reason of his occupation or control of the premises, to show towards a person entering thereon in respect of dangers which are due to the state of the premises or to anything done or omitted to be done on them and for which the occupier is in law responsible shall, except in so far as he is entitled to and does extend, restrict, modify or exclude by agreement his obligations towards that person, be such care as in all the circumstances of the case is reasonable to see that that person will not suffer injury or damage by reason of any such danger.

(2)   Nothing in the foregoing subsection shall relieve an occupier of premises of any duty to show in any particular case any higher standard of care which in that case is incumbent on him by virtue of any enactment or rule of law imposing special standards of care on particular classes of persons.

(3)   Nothing in the foregoing provisions of this Act shall be held to impose on an occupier any obligation to a person entering on his premises in respect of risks which that person has willingly accepted as his; and any question whether a risk was so accepted shall be decided on the same principles as in other cases in which one person owes to another a duty to show care.

3   Landlord's liability by virtue of responsibility for repairs

(1)   Where premises are occupied or used by virtue of a tenancy under which the landlord is responsible for the maintenance or repair of the premises, it shall be the duty of the landlord to show towards any persons who or whose property may from time to time be on the premises the same care in respect of dangers arising from any failure on his part in carrying out his responsibility aforesaid as is required by virtue of the foregoing provisions of this Act to be shown by an occupier of premises towards persons entering on them.

(2)   Where premises are occupied or used by virtue of a sub-tenancy, the foregoing subsection shall apply to any landlord who is responsible for the maintenance or repair of the premises comprised in the sub-tenancy.

(3)   Nothing in this section shall relieve a landlord of any duty which he is under apart from this section.

(4)   For the purposes of this section, any obligation imposed on a landlord by any enactment by reason of the premises being subject to a tenancy shall be treated as if it were an obligation imposed on him by the tenancy, "tenancy" includes a statutory tenancy which does not in law amount to a tenancy and includes also any contract conferring a right of occupation, and "landlord" shall be construed accordingly.

(5)   This section shall apply to tenancies created before the commencement of this Act as well as to tenancies created after its commencement.

4   Application to Crown

This Act shall bind the Crown, but as regards the liability of the Crown for any wrongful or negligent act or omission giving rise to liability in reparation shall not bind the Crown any further than the Crown is made liable in respect of such acts or omissions by the Crown Proceedings Act, 1947, and that Act and in particular section two thereof shall apply in relation to duties under section two or section three of this Act as statutory duties.

PUBLIC BODIES (ADMISSION TO MEETINGS) ACT 1960
(8 & 9 Eliz. Ii, c. 67)

1   Admission to public meetings of local authorities and other bodies

(5)   Where a meeting of a body is required by this Act to be open to the public during the proceedings or any part of them, and there is supplied to a member of the public attending the meeting, or in pursuance of paragraph (b) of subsection (4) above there is supplied for the benefit of a newspaper, any such copy of the agenda as is mentioned in that paragraph, with or without further statements or particulars for the purpose of indicating the nature of any item included in the agenda, the publication thereby of any defamatory matter contained in the agenda or in the further statements or particulars shall be privileged, unless the publication is proved to be made with malice.

LAW REFORM (HUSBAND AND WIFE) ACT 1962
(10 & 11 Eliz. II, c. 48)

1   Actions in tort between husband and wife

(1)   Subject to the provisions of this section, each of the parties to a marriage shall have the like right of action in tort against the other as if they were not married.

(2)   Where an action in tort is brought by one of the parties to a marriage against the other during the subsistence of the marriage, the court may stay the action if it appears—

(a)   that no substantial benefit would accrue to either party from the continuation of the proceedings; or

(b)   that the question or questions in issue could more conveniently be disposed of on an application made under section seventeen of the Married Women's Property Act 1882 (determination of questions between husband and wife as to the title to or possession of property);

and without prejudice to paragraph (b) of this subsection the court may, in such an action, either exercise any power which could be exercised on an application under that said section seventeen, or give such directions as it thinks fit for the disposal under that section of any question arising in the proceedings.

NUCLEAR INSTALLATIONS ACT 1965
(1965, c. 57)

7   Duty of licensee of licensed site

(1)   Subject to subsection (4), where a nuclear site licence has been granted in respect of a site, the licensee has the duties set out in subsections (1A), (1C) and (1E).

(1A) It is the duty of the licensee to secure that no occurrence involving nuclear matter falling within subsection (1B) causes—

(a)   injury to any person,

(b)   damage to any property of any person other than the licensee, or

(c)   significant impairment of the environment,

being injury, damage or impairment that arises out of or results from the radioactive properties, or a combination of those and any toxic, explosive or other hazardous properties, of that nuclear matter.

(1B) The occurrences referred to in subsection (1A) are—
  (a)   any occurrence on the licensed site involving nuclear matter during the period of the licensee's responsibility;
  (b)   any occurrence elsewhere than on the licensed site involving nuclear matter that is not excepted matter and which, at the time of the occurrence, satisfies the requirement in section 7A(1).
(1C) It is the duty of the licensee to secure that no occurrence involving the emission of ionising radiations falling within subsection (1D) causes—
  (a)   injury to any person,
  (b)   damage to any property of any person other than the licensee, or
  (c)   significant impairment of the environment,
being injury, damage or impairment that arises out of or results from the radioactive properties, or a combination of those and any toxic, explosive or other hazardous properties, of the source of the emissions.
(1D) The occurrences referred to in subsection (1C) are—
  (a)   an emission of ionising radiations during the period of the licensee's responsibility from anything caused or suffered by the licensee to be on the site which is not nuclear matter,
  (b)   a discharge on or from the site of waste, being waste (of any form) that emits ionising radiations but is not nuclear matter, during the period of the licensee's responsibility.
(1E) It is the duty of the licensee to secure that no event happens that creates a grave and imminent threat of a breach of duty under subsection (1A) or (1C).

9   Duty of Crown in respect of certain sites
If a government department uses any site for any purpose which, if section 1 of this Act applied to the Crown, would require the authority of a nuclear site licence in respect of that site, sections 7 and 7A of this Act shall apply in like manner as if—
  (a)   the Crown were the licensee under a nuclear site licence in respect of that site; and
  (b)   any reference to the period of the licensee's responsibility were a reference to any period during which the department occupies this site.

12   Right to compensation
(1)   Where any injury or damage has been caused in breach of a duty imposed by section 7, 7B, 8, 9 or 10, compensation is payable in accordance with section 16 wherever the injury or damage was incurred.
(1A) Where any significant impairment of the environment has been caused in breach of a duty imposed by section 7,7B, 8, 9 or 10, such compensation as may be claimed by virtue of section 11A(1) or 11G(1) or paragraph 1 of Schedule 1A is payable in accordance with section 16 wherever the impairment arises.
(1B) Where preventive measures are taken after a breach of duty imposed by section 7, 7B, 8, 9, or 10, such compensation as may be claimed by virtue of section 11H(1) is payable in accordance with section 16 wherever the preventive measures are taken.
(1C) Where any injury to a person or damage to property is caused by preventive measures taken after a breach of duty imposed by section 7, 7B, 8, 9 or 10, such compensation as may be claimed by virtue of section 11H(2) is payable in accordance with section 16 wherever the injury or damage was incurred.
(1E) No liability other than that imposed by subsections (1) to (1C) may be incurred by any person in respect of—
  (a)   injury, damage or significant impairment of the environment caused or threatened in breach of a duty imposed by section 7, 7B, 8, 9 or 10,
  (b)   preventive measures taken after a breach of duty imposed by section 7, 7B, 8, 9 or 10, or
  (c)   injury or damage caused by preventive measures taken after a breach of duty imposed by section 7, 7B, 8, 9 or 10.
(2)   Subject to subsection (3), any injury, damage or significant impairment of the environment which, though not caused in breach of a duty imposed by section 7, 7B, 8, 9 or 10, is not reasonably separable from injury, damage or significant impairment so caused, is to be deemed for the purposes of subsections (1) to (1C) to have been so caused.

(3)   Where any injury, damage or significant impairment of the environment is caused partly in breach of such a duty as aforesaid and partly by an emission of ionising radiations which does not constitute such a breach, subsection (2) of this section shall not affect any liability of any person in respect of that emission apart from this Act, but a claimant shall not be entitled to recover compensation in respect of the same injury, damage or significant impairment of the environment both under this Act and otherwise than under this Act.

15   Time for bringing claims under ss. 7 to 11

(1)   A claim by virtue of section 7, 7B, 8, 9, 10 or 11 of this Act may be made at any time before, but is not to be entertained if made at any time after, the expiration of 10 years from the relevant date.

(1A)   Subsection (1) is subject to subsections (3), (4) and (6).

(2)   ...

(3)   A claim in respect of injury caused by a breach of duty under section 7, 7B, 8, 9, 10 or 11 may be made at any time before, but is not to be entertained if made at any time after, the expiration of 30 years from the relevant date.

(4)   A claim in respect of injury where—

(a)   that injury is caused by ionising radiations, and

(b)   exposure to those ionising radiations is the result of preventive measures having been taken after a breach of duty under section 7, 7B, 8, 9 or 10,

may be made at any time before, but is not to be entertained if made at any time after, the expiration of 30 years from the relevant date.

(5)   Subsections (3) and (4) are subject to subsection (6).

(6)   A claim made after the expiration of the period that applies to it because of subsection (1), (3) or (4) may be entertained if—

(a)   the European Nuclear Energy Tribunal has determined that a court in the United Kingdom has jurisdiction in respect of that claim, and

(b)   the claim is brought—

(i)   within the period specified by the Tribunal, or

(ii)   if the Tribunal does not specify a period, within the period of 28 days beginning with the day after the day on which the Tribunal made its determination.

(7)   This section has effect notwithstanding provision in any other enactment about the period of time for the bringing of proceedings.

(8)   A reference in this section to the relevant date is—

(a)   in the case of a claim in respect of an occurrence which constitutes a breach of a person's duty under section 7(1A) or (1C), 7B, 8, 9, 10(1) or 11, a reference to—

(i)   the date of the occurrence,

(ii)   where the occurrence is a continuing one, the date of the last thing to happen in the course of that occurrence,

(iii)   where the occurrence is one of a succession of occurrences, all of which are attributable to a particular happening on a particular relevant site or to the carrying out from time to time on a relevant site of a particular operation, the date of the last thing to happen in the course of that succession of occurrences,

(iv)   where the occurrence is one of a succession of occurrences, all of which are attributable to a particular happening and take place in one course of carriage, the date of the last thing to happen in the course of that succession of occurrences;

(b)   in the case of a claim in respect of an event which constitutes a breach of a person's duty under section 7(1E), 7B, 8, 9 or 10(1A) because it created a grave and imminent threat of a breach of another duty imposed by section 7, 7B, 8, 9 or 10, a reference to—

(i)   the date of the event,

(ii)   where the event is a continuing one, the date of the last thing to happen in the course of that event,

(iii)   where the event is one of a succession of events, all of which are attributable to a particular happening on a particular relevant site, the date of the last thing to happen in the course of that succession of events, or

(iv) where the event is one of a succession of occurrences, all of which are attributable to a particular happening and take place during one course of carriage, the date of the last thing to happen in the course of that succession of events.

16   Satisfaction of claims by virtue of ss. 7 to 10

(1) The liability of person to pay compensation under this Act by virtue of a duty imposed on that person by section 7, 7B, 8 or 9 does not require that person to make in respect of any one occurrence or event constituting a breach of that duty payments by way of compensation exceeding in the aggregate, apart from payments in respect of interest and costs—

(a) the equivalent in sterling of 70 million euros, where the person is the licensee of a licensed site that is prescribed for the purposes of this paragraph and the breach of duty is a breach of duty by that person as licensee of that licensed site that consists of—

(i) an occurrence or event on the licensed site, or

(ii) an occurrence or event elsewhere than on the licensed site involving nuclear matter other than excepted matter, where the nuclear matter in question satisfies the condition in section 7A(8) in relation to the licensee, without also satisfying any of the conditions in section 7A(2) to (7);

(b) the equivalent in sterling of 70 million euros, where the person is the operator of a relevant disposal site that is a site prescribed for the purposes of this paragraph and the breach of duty is a breach of duty by that person as the operator of that relevant disposal site that consists of—

(i) an occurrence or event on the relevant disposal site, or

(ii) an occurrence or event elsewhere than on the relevant disposal site involving nuclear matter other than excepted matter, where the nuclear matter in question satisfies the condition in section 7A(8) (as applied by section 7B) in relation to the operator, without also satisfying any of the conditions in section 7A(2) to (7) (as applied by section 7B);

(c) the equivalent in sterling of 160 million euros, where the person is the licensee of a licensed that is prescribed for the purposes of this paragraph and the breach of duty is a breach of duty by the person as licensee of that licensed site that consists of—

(i) an occurrence or event on the licensed site, or

(ii) an occurrence or event elsewhere than on the licensed site involving nuclear matter other than excepted matter, where the nuclear matter in question satisfies the condition in 7A(8) in relation to the licensee, without also satisfying any of the conditions in section 7A(2) to (7);

(d) the equivalent in sterling of 80 million euros, in the case of an occurrence or event involving nuclear matter which is not excepted matter and which is either in the course of such carriage as is described section 7A(2)(a), (3)(a), (4)(a), (5)(a) or (7)(a) or in such case as is described in section 7A(6)(c) (7)(b), where—

(i) the nuclear matter in question meets such conditions as are prescribed for the purposes of this paragraph or such condition specific to the means of carriage used as are prescribed for the purposes of this paragraph, and

(ii) the occurrence or event constitutes a breach of duty by a licensee as licensee of a licensed site;

(e) the equivalent in sterling of 80 million euros, in the case of an occurrence or event involving nuclear matter which is not excepted matter and which is either in the course of such carriage as is described in section 7A(2)(a), (3)(a), (4)(a), (5)(a) or (7)(a) (as applied by section 7B) or in such case as is described in section 7A(6)(c) or (7)(b) (as applied by section 7B), where—

(i) the nuclear matter in question meets such conditions as are prescribed for the purposes of this paragraph or such conditions specific to the means of carriage used as are prescribed for the purposes of this paragraph, and

(ii) that occurrence or event constitutes a breach of duty by the operator of a relevant disposal site in that capacity;

(f) subject to section 16B, the equivalent in sterling of 1,200 million euros, in any other case.

CRIMINAL LAW ACT 1967
(1967, c. 58)

3   Use of force in making arrest, etc.

(1)   A person may use such force as is reasonable in the circumstances in the prevention of crime, or in effecting or assisting in the lawful arrest of offenders or suspected offenders or of persons unlawfully at large.

14   Civil rights in respect of maintenance and champerty

(1)   No person shall, under the law of England and Wales, be liable in tort for any conduct on account of its being maintenance or champerty as known to the common law, except in the case of a cause of action accruing before this section has effect.

(2)   The abolition of criminal and civil liability under the law of England and Wales for maintenance and champerty shall not affect any rule of that law as to the cases in which a contract is to be treated as contrary to public policy or otherwise illegal.

MISREPRESENTATION ACT 1967
(1967, c. 7)

1   Removal of certain bars to rescission for innocent misrepresentation

Where a person has entered into a contract after a misrepresentation has been made to him, and—

(a)   the misrepresentation has become a term of the contract; or

(b)   the contract has been performed;

or both, then, if otherwise he would be entitled to rescind the contract without alleging fraud, he shall be so entitled, subject to the provisions of this Act, notwithstanding the matters mentioned in paragraphs (a) and (b) of this section.

2   Damages for misrepresentation

(1)   Where a person has entered into a contract after a misrepresentation has been made to him by another party thereto and as a result thereof he has suffered loss, then, if the person making the misrepresentation would be liable to damages in respect thereof had the misrepresentation been made fraudulently, that person shall be so liable notwithstanding that the misrepresentation was not made fraudulently, unless he proves that he had reasonable ground to believe and did believe up to the time the contract was made that the facts represented were true.

(2)   Where a person has entered into a contract after a misrepresentation has been made to him otherwise than fraudulently, and he would be entitled, by reason of the misrepresentation, to rescind the contract, then, if it is claimed, in any proceedings arising out of the contract, that the contract ought to be or has been rescinded, the court or arbitrator may declare the contract subsisting and award damages in lieu of rescission, if of opinion that it would be equitable to do so, having regard to the nature of the misrepresentation and the loss that would be caused by it if the contract were upheld, as well as to the loss that rescission would cause to the other party.

(3)   Damages may be awarded against a person under subsection (2) of this section whether or not he is liable to damages under subsection (1) thereof, but where he is so liable any award under the said subsection (2) shall be taken into account in assessing his liability under the said subsection (1).

3   Avoidance of provision excluding liability for misrepresentation

(1)   If a contract contains a term which would exclude or restrict—

(a)   any liability to which a party to a contract may be subject by reason of any misrepresentation made by him before the contract was made; or

(b)   any remedy available to another party to the contract by reason of such a misrepresentation,

that term shall be of no effect except in so far as it satisfies the requirement of reasonableness as stated in section 11(1) of the Unfair Contract Terms Act 1977; and it is for those claiming that the term satisfies that requirement to show that it does.

(2)   This section does not apply to a term in a consumer contract within the meaning of Part 2 of the Consumer Rights Act 2015 (but see the provision made about such contracts in section 62 of that Act).

(4)   This section does not entitle a person to be paid damages in respect of a misrepresentation if the person has a right to redress under Part 4A of the Consumer Protection from Unfair Trading Regulations 2008 (SI 2008/1277) in respect of the conduct constituting the misrepresentation.

(5)   Subsection (4) does not prevent a debtor from bringing a claim under section 75(1) of the Consumer Credit Act 1974 against a creditor under a debtor-creditor-supplier agreement where, but for subsection (4), the debtor would have a claim against the supplier in respect of a misrepresentation (and, where section 75 would otherwise apply, it accordingly applies as if the debtor had a claim against the supplier).

PARLIAMENTARY COMMISSIONER ACT 1967
(1967, c. 13)

10   Reports by Commissioner

(5)   For the purposes of the law of defamation, any such publication as is hereinafter mentioned shall be absolutely privileged, that is to say—

    (a)   the publication of any matter by the Commissioner in making a report to either House of Parliament for the purposes of this Act;

    (b)   the publication of any matter by a member of the House of Commons in communicating with the Commissioner or his officers for those purposes or by the Commissioner or his officers in communicating with such a member for those purposes;

    (c)   the publication by such a member to the person by whom a complaint was made under this Act of a report or statement sent to the member in respect of the complaint in pursuance of subsection (1) of this section;

    (d)   the publication by the Commissioner to such a person as is mentioned in subsection (2) or (2A) of this section of a report sent to that person in pursuance of that subsection.

CIVIL EVIDENCE ACT 1968
(1968, c. 64)

11   Convictions as evidence in civil proceedings

(1)   In any civil proceedings the fact that a person has been convicted of an offence by or before any court in the United Kingdom or of a service offence anywhere shall (subject to subsection (3) below) be admissible in evidence for the purpose of proving where to do so is relevant to any issue in those proceedings, that he committed that offence, whether he was so convicted upon a plea of guilty or otherwise and whether or not he is a party to the civil proceedings; but no conviction other than a subsisting one shall be admissible in evidence by virtue of this section.

(2)   In any civil proceedings in which by virtue of this section a person is proved to have been convicted of an offence by or before any court in the United Kingdom of a service offence anywhere—

    (a)   he shall be taken to have committed that offence unless the contrary is proved; and

    (b)   without prejudice to the reception of any other admissible evidence for the purpose of identifying the facts on which the conviction was based, the contents of any documents which is admissible as evidence of the conviction, and the contents of the information, complaint, indictment or charge-sheet on which the person in question was convicted, shall be admissible in evidence for that purpose.

(3)   Nothing in this section shall prejudice the operation of section 13 of this Act or any other enactment whereby a conviction or a finding of fact in any criminal proceedings is for the purposes of any other proceedings made conclusive evidence of any fact.

(4)   Where in any civil proceedings the contents of any document are admissible in evidence by virtue of subsection (2) above, a copy of that document, or of the material

part thereof, purporting to be certified or otherwise authenticated by or on behalf of the court or authority having custody of that document shall be admissible in evidence and shall be taken to be a true copy of that document or part unless the contrary is shown.

13 Conclusiveness of convictions for purposes of defamation actions

(1) In an action for libel or slander in which the question whether the plaintiff did or did not commit a criminal offence is relevant to an issue arising in the action, proof that at the time when that issue falls to be determined, he stands convicted of that offence shall be conclusive evidence that he committed that offence; and his conviction thereof shall be admissible in evidence accordingly.

(2) In any such action as aforesaid in which by virtue of this section the plaintiff is proved to have been convicted of an offence, the contents of any document which is admissible as evidence of the conviction, and the contents of the information, complaint, indictment or charge-sheet on which he was convicted, shall, without prejudice to the reception of any other admissible evidence for the purpose of identifying the facts on which the conviction was based, be admissible in evidence for the purpose of identifying those facts.

(2A) In the case of an action for libel or slander in which there is more than one plaintiff—
    (a) the references in subsections (1) and (2) above to the plaintiff shall be construed as references to any of the plaintiffs, and
    (b) proof that any of the plaintiffs stands convicted of an offence shall be conclusive evidence that he committed that offence so far as that fact is relevant to any issue arising in relation to his cause of action or that of any other plaintiff.

(3) For the purposes of this section a person shall be taken to stand convicted of an offence if but only if there subsists against him a conviction of that offence by or before a court in the United Kingdom or (in the case of a service offence) a conviction (anywhere) of that service offence.

(4) Subsections (4) to (6) of section 11 of this Act shall apply for the purposes of this section as they apply for the purposes of that section, but as if in the said subsection (4) the reference to subsection (2) were a reference to subsection (2) of this section.

THEATRES ACT 1968
(1968, c. 54)

4 Amendment of law of defamation

(1) For the purposes of the law of libel and slander ... the publication of words in the course of a performance of a play shall, subject to section 7 of this Act, be treated as publication in permanent form.

(2) The foregoing subsection shall apply for the purposes of section 3 (slander of title, etc.) of the Defamation Act 1952 as it applies for the purposes of the law of libel and slander.

(3) In this section "words" includes pictures, visual images, gestures and other methods of signifying meaning.

7 Exceptions for performances given in certain circumstances

(1) Nothing in sections 2 to 4 of this Act shall apply in relation to a performance of a play given on a domestic occasion in a private dwelling.

EMPLOYERS' LIABILITY (COMPULSORY INSURANCE) ACT 1969
(1969, c. 57)

1 Insurance against liability for employees

(1) Except as otherwise provided by this Act, every employer carrying on any business in Great Britain shall insure, and maintain insurance, under one or more approved policies with an authorised insurer or insurers against liability for bodily injury or disease sustained by his employees, and arising out of and in the course of their employment in Great Britain in that business, but except in so far as regulations otherwise provide not including injury or disease suffered or contracted outside Great Britain.

(2) Regulations may provide that the amount for which an employer is required by this Act to insure and maintain insurance shall, either generally or in such cases or classes of case as may be prescribed by the regulations, be limited in such manner as may be so prescribed.

2 Employees to be covered

(1) For the purposes of this Act the term "employee" means an individual who has entered into or works under a contract of service or apprenticeship with an employer whether by way of manual labour, clerical work or otherwise, whether such contract is expressed or implied, oral or in writing.

(2) This Act shall not require an employer to insure—

(a) in respect of an employee of whom the employer is the husband, wife, civil partner, father, mother, grandfather, grandmother, step-father, step-mother, son, daughter, grandson, granddaughter, stepson, stepdaughter, brother, sister, half-brother, half-sister; or

(b) except as otherwise provided by regulations, in respect of employees not ordinarily resident in Great Britain.

EMPLOYER'S LIABILITY (DEFECTIVE EQUIPMENT) ACT 1969
(1969, c. 37)

1 Extension of employer's liability for defective equipment

(1) Where after the commencement of this Act—

(a) an employee suffers personal injury in the course of his employment in consequence of a defect in equipment provided by his employer for the purposes of the employer's business; and

(b) the defect is attributable wholly or partly to the fault of a third party (whether identified or not), the injury shall be deemed to be also attributable to negligence on the part of the employer (whether or not he is liable in respect of the injury apart from this subsection), but without prejudice to the law relating to contributory negligence and to any remedy by way of contribution or in contract or otherwise which is available to the employer in respect of the injury.

(2) In so far as any agreement purports to exclude or limit any liability of an employer arising under subsection (1) of this section, the agreement shall be void.

(3) In this section—

"business" includes the activities carried on by any public body;

"employee" means a person who is employed by another person under a contract of service or apprenticeship and is so employed for the purposes of a business carried on by that other person, and "employer" shall be construed accordingly;

"equipment" includes any plant and machinery, vehicle, aircraft and clothing;

"fault" means negligence, breach of statutory duty or other act or omission which gives rise to liability in tort in England and Wales or which is wrongful and gives rise to liability in damages in Scotland; and

"personal injury" includes loss of life, any impairment of a person's physical or mental condition and any disease.

(4) This section binds the Crown, and persons in the service of the Crown shall accordingly be treated for the purposes of this section as employees of the Crown if they would not be so treated apart from this subsection.

ANIMALS ACT 1971
(1971, c. 22)

1 New provisions as to strict liability for damage done by animals

(1) The provisions of sections 2 to 5 of this Act replace—

(a) the rules of the common law imposing a strict liability in tort for damage done by an animal on the ground that the animal is regarded as ferae naturae or that its vicious or mischievous propensities are known or presumed to be known;

    (b)   subsections (1) and (2) of section 1 of the Dogs Act 1906 as amended by the Dogs (Amendment) Act 1928 (injury to cattle or poultry); and

    (c)   the rules of the common law imposing a liability for cattle trespass.

(2)   Expressions used in those sections shall be interpreted in accordance with the provisions of section 6 (as well as those of section 11) of this Act.

2   Liability for damage done by dangerous animals

(1)   Where any damage is caused by an animal which belongs to a dangerous species, any person who is a keeper of the animal is liable for the damage, except as otherwise provided by this Act.

(2)   Where damage is caused by an animal which does not belong to a dangerous species, a keeper of the animal is liable for the damage, except as otherwise provided by this Act, if—

    (a)   the damage is of a kind which the animal, unless restrained, was likely to cause or which, if caused by the animal, was likely to be severe; and

    (b)   the likelihood of the damage or of its being severe was due to characteristics of the animal which are not normally found in animals of the same species or are not normally so found except at particular times or in particular circumstances; and

    (c)   those characteristics were known to that keeper or were at any time known to a person who at that time had charge of the animal as that keeper's servant or, where that keeper is the head of a household, were known to another keeper of the animal who is a member of that household and under the age of sixteen.

3   Liability for injury done by dogs to livestock

Where a dog causes damage by killing or injuring livestock, any person who is a keeper of the dog is liable for the damage, except as otherwise provided by this Act.

4   Liability for damage and expenses due to trespassing livestock

(1)   Where livestock belonging to any person strays on to land in the ownership or occupation of another and—

    (a)   damage is done by the livestock to the land or to any property on it which is in the ownership or possession of the other person; or

    (b)   any expenses are reasonably incurred by that other person in keeping the livestock while it cannot be restored to the person to whom it belongs or while it is detained in pursuance of **section** 7 of this Act, or in ascertaining to whom it belongs;

the person to whom the livestock belongs is liable for the damage or expenses, except as otherwise provided by this Act.

(2)   For the purposes of this section any livestock belongs to the person in whose possession it is.

4A   Liability for damage and expenses due to horses on land in England without lawful authority

(1)   This section applies where a horse is on any land in England without lawful authority.

(2)   The person to whom the horse belongs is liable for—

    (a)   any damage done by the horse to—

        (i)   the land,

        (ii)   any property on it which is in the ownership or possession of the freeholder or occupier of the land, and

    (b)   any expenses which are reasonably incurred by a person detaining the horse under section 7A or 7B of this Act—

        (i)   in keeping the horse while it cannot be restored to the person to whom it belongs or while it is detained under section 7A or 7B of this Act, or

        (ii)   in ascertaining to whom it belongs.

This is subject to the other provisions of this Act.

(3)   For the purposes of this section a horse belongs to the person in whose possession it is.

5   Exceptions from liability under sections 2 to 4A

(1) A person is not liable under sections 2 to 4A of this Act for any damage which is due wholly to the fault of the person suffering it.

(2) A person is not liable under section 2 of this Act for any damage suffered by a person who has voluntarily accepted the risk thereof.

(3) A person is not liable under section 2 of this Act for any damage caused by an animal kept on any premises or structure to a person trespassing there, if it is proved either—

   (a)   that the animal was not kept there for the protection of persons or property; or

   (b)   (if the animal was kept there for the protection of persons or property) that keeping it there for that purpose was not unreasonable.

(4) A person is not liable under section 3 of this Act if the livestock was killed or injured on land on to which it had strayed and either the dog belonged to the occupier or its presence on the land was authorised by the occupier.

(5A) A person is not liable under section 4 of this Act in respect of a horse which strays from a highway and its presence there was a lawful use of the highway.

(5) A person is not liable under section 4 of this Act where the livestock strayed from a highway and its presence there was a lawful use of the highway.

(6) In determining whether any liability for damage under section 4 of this Act, or under section 4A of this Act so far as relating to a straying horse in England, is excluded by subsection (1) of this section the damage shall not be treated as due to the fault of the person suffering it by reason only that he could have prevented it by fencing; but a person is not liable under that section where it is proved that the straying of the livestock on to the land would not have occurred but for a breach by any other person, being a person having an interest in the land, of a duty to fence.

6   Interpretation of certain expressions used in sections 2 to 5

(1) The following provisions apply to the interpretation of sections 2 to 5 of this Act.

(2) A dangerous species is a species—

   (a)   which is not commonly domesticated in the British Islands; and

   (b)   whose fully grown animals normally have such characteristics that they are likely, unless restrained, to cause severe damage or that any damage they may cause is likely to be severe.

(3) Subject to subsection (4) of this section, a person is a keeper of an animal if—

   (a)   he owns the animal or has it in his possession; or

   (b)   he is the head of a household of which a member under the age of sixteen owns the animal or has it in his possession;

   and if at any time an animal ceases to be owned by or to be in the possession of a person, any person who immediately before that time was a keeper thereof by virtue of the preceding provisions of this subsection continues to be a keeper of the animal until another person becomes a keeper thereof by virtue of those provisions.

(4) Where an animal is taken into and kept in possession for the purpose of preventing it from causing damage or of restoring it to its owner, a person is not a keeper of it by virtue only of that possession.

(5) Where a person employed as a servant by a keeper of an animal incurs a risk incidental to his employment he shall not be treated as accepting it voluntarily.

7   Detention and sale of trespassing livestock

(1) The right to seize and detain any animal by way of distress damage feasant is hereby abolished.

(2) Where any livestock strays on to any land and is not then under the control of any person the occupier of the land may detain it, subject to subsection (3) of this section, unless ordered to return it by a court.

(3) Where any livestock is detained in pursuance of this section the right to detain it ceases—

   (a)   at the end of a period of forty-eight hours, unless within that period notice of the detention has been given to the officer in charge of a police station and also, if the person detaining the livestock knows to whom it belongs, to that person; or

   (b)   when such amount is tendered to the person detaining the livestock as is sufficient to satisfy any claim he may have under section 4 of this Act in respect of the livestock; or,

(c)   if he has no such claim, when the livestock is claimed by a person entitled to its possession.

(4)   Where livestock has been detained in pursuance of this section for a period of not less than fourteen days the person detaining it may sell it at a market or by public auction, unless proceedings are then pending for the return of the livestock or for any claim under section 4 of this Act in respect of it.

(5)   Where any livestock is sold in the exercise of the right conferred by this section and the proceeds of the sale, less the costs thereof and any costs incurred in connection with it, exceed the amount of any claim under section 4 of this Act which the vendor had in respect of the livestock, the excess shall be recoverable from him by the person who would be entitled to the possession of the livestock but for the sale.

(6)   A person detaining any livestock in pursuance of this section is liable for any damage caused to it by a failure to treat it with reasonable care and supply it with adequate food and water while it is so detained.

(7)   References in this section to a claim under section 4 of this Act in respect of any livestock do not include any claim under that section for damage done by or expenses incurred in respect of the livestock before the straying in connection with which it is detained under this section.

(8)   Subsections (2) to (7) do not apply to horses on land In England (as to which, see sections 7A to 7C).

7A   Power of local authorities in England to detain horses

(1)   A local authority in England may detain a horse which is in any public place in its area, if the conditions in subsection (2) are met.

(2)   The conditions are—
    (a)   the local authority has reasonable grounds for believing that the horse is there without lawful authority, and
    (b)   if the land is lawfully occupied by a person—
        (i)   that person consents to the detention of the horse, or
        (ii)   the local authority has reasonable grounds for believing that that person would consent to the detention of the horse (but this does not require the authority to seek consent).

(3)   Section 7C contains further provision about detention under this section.

(4)   In this section "local authority" means—
    (a)   a county council,
    (b)   a district council,
    (c)   a London borough council
    (d)   the Common Council of the City of London, and
    (e)   the Council of the Isles of Scilly.

7B   Powers of freeholders and occupiers in England to detain horses

(1)   This section applies where a horse is on any land in England without lawful authority.

(2)   The horse may be detained—
    (a)   in any case, by the occupier of the land, and
    (b)   if the freeholder is not the occupier, by the freeholder with the occupier's consent.

(3)   Section 7C contains further provision about detention under this section.

7C   Detention of horses under sections 7A and 7B

(1)   This section applies where a horse is detained under section 7A or 7B.

(2)   The right to detain the horse ceases at the end of the period of 24 hours beginning with the time when it was first detained unless, within that period, the person detaining the horse gives notice of the detention to—
    (a)   the officer in charge of a police station, and
    (b)   if the person detaining the horse knows to whom the horse belongs, that person.

(3)   Where notice is given under subsection (2), the right to detain the horse ceases if, within the period of 96 hours beginning with the time when it is first detained, the person entitled to possession of the horse—
    (a)   claims it, and
    (b)   complies with the condition in subsection (4).

(4)   The condition is that the person tenders to each person with a claim under section 4A in respect of the horse such amount as is sufficient to satisfy the claim.

(5)   If by the end of the 96 hour period referred to in subsection (3) the right to detain the horse has not ceased under this section—
   (a)   ownership of the horse passes to the person detaining the horse, and
   (b)   accordingly, the person detaining the horse may dispose of it by selling it, arranging for it to be destroyed or in any other way.

(6)   Where a horse is sold under this section and the proceeds of sale, less the costs of sale and any costs incurred in connection with it, exceed the amount of any claims under section 4A in respect of the horse, the excess is recoverable from the person detaining the horse by the person who would have been entitled to possession of the horse but for this section.

(7)   A person detaining a horse under this section is liable for any damage caused to it by a failure to treat it with reasonable care and supply it with adequate food and water while it is so detained.

(8)   References in this section to a claim under section 4A do not include a claim under that section for damage done by or expenses incurred in respect of the horse before it was on the land without lawful authority.

(9)   In calculating a period of 96 hours for the purposes of this section, disregard any time falling on—
   (a)   a Saturday or Sunday,
   (b)   Good Friday or Christmas Day, or
   (c)   a day which is a bank holiday in England and Wales under the Banking and Financial Dealings Act 1971.

8   Duty to take care to prevent damage from animals straying on to the highway

(1)   So much of the rules of the common law relating to liability for negligence as excludes or restricts the duty which a person might owe to others to take such care as is reasonable to see that damage is not caused by animals straying on to a highway is hereby abolished.

(2)   Where damage is caused by animals straying from unfenced land to a highway a person who placed them on the land shall not be regarded as having committed a breach of the duty to take care by reason only of placing them there if—
   (a)   the land is common land, or is land situated in an area where fencing is not customary, or is a town or village green; and
   (b)   he had a right to place the animals on that land.

9   Killing of or injury to dogs worrying livestock

(1)   In any civil proceedings against a person (in this section referred to as the defendant) for killing or causing injury to a dog it shall be a defence to prove—
   (a)   that the defendant acted for the protection of any livestock and was a person entitled to act for the protection of that livestock; and
   (b)   that within forty-eight hours of the killing or injury notice thereof was given by the defendant to the officer in charge of a police station.

(2)   For the purposes of this section a person is entitled to act for the protection of any livestock if, and only if—
   (a)   the livestock or the land on which it is belongs to him or to any person under whose express or implied authority he is acting; and
   (b)   the circumstances are not such that liability for killing or causing injury to the livestock would be excluded by section 5(4) of this Act.

(3)   Subject to subsection (4) of this section, a person killing or causing injury to a dog shall be deemed for the purposes of this section to act for the protection of any livestock if, and only if, either—
   (a)   the dog is worrying or is about to worry the livestock and there are no other reasonable means of ending or preventing the worrying; or
   (b)   the dog has been worrying livestock, has not left the vicinity and is not under the control of any person and there are no practicable means of ascertaining to whom it belongs.

(4)   For the purposes of this section the condition stated in either of the paragraphs of the preceding subsection shall be deemed to have been satisfied if the defendant believed that it was satisfied and had reasonable ground for that belief.

(5)   For the purposes of this section—

(a)   an animal belongs to any person if he owns it or has it in his possession; and

(b)   land belongs to any person if he is the occupier thereof.

10   Application of certain enactments to liability under sections 2 to 4

For the purposes of the Fatal Accidents Act 1976, the Law Reform (Contributory Negligence) Act 1945 and the Limitation Act 1980 any damage for which a person is liable under sections 2 to 4 of this Act shall be treated as due to his fault.

11   General interpretation

In this Act—

"common land" means—

(a)   land registered as common land in a register of common land kept under Part 1 of the Commons Act 2006;

(b)   land to which Part 1 of that Act does not apply and which is subject to rights of common within the meaning of that Act;

"town or village green" means land registered as a town or village green in a register of town or village greens kept under Part 1 of the Commons Act 2006;

"damage" includes the death of, or injury to, any person (including any disease and any impairment of physical or mental condition);

"fault" has the same meaning as in the Law Reform (Contributory Negligence) Act 1945;

"fencing" includes the construction of any obstacle designed to prevent animals from straying;

"horse" includes an ass, mule or hinny;

"livestock" means cattle, sheep, pigs, goats and poultry, and also deer not in the wild state and, in section 3 and 9 also, while in captivity, pheasants, partridges and grouse;

"poultry" means the domestic varieties of the following, that is to say, fowls, turkeys, geese, ducks, guinea-fowls, pigeons, peacocks and quails; and

"public place" includes—

(a)   any common land or town or village green;

(b)   any highway (and the verges of any highway);

"species" includes sub-species and variety.

12   Application to Crown

(1)   This Act binds the Crown, but nothing in this section shall authorise proceedings to be brought against Her Majesty in her private capacity.

(2)   Section 38(3) of the Crown Proceedings Act 1947 (interpretation of references to Her Majesty in her private capacity) shall apply as if this section were contained in that Act.

DEFECTIVE PREMISES ACT 1972
(1972, c. 35)

1   Duty to build dwellings properly

(1)   A person taking on work for or in connection with the provision of a dwelling (whether the dwelling is provided by the erection or by the conversion or enlargement of a building) owes a duty—

(a)   if the dwelling is provided to the order of any person, to that person; and

(b)   without prejudice to paragraph (a) above, to every person who acquires an interest (whether legal or equitable) in the dwelling;

to see that the work which he takes on is done in a workmanlike or, as the case may be, professional manner, with proper materials and so that as regards that work the dwelling will be fit for habitation when completed.

(2)   A person who takes on any such work for another on terms that he is to do it in accordance with instructions given by or on behalf of that other shall, to the extent

to which he does it properly in accordance with those instructions, be treated for the purposes of this section as discharging the duty imposed on him by subsection (1) above except where he owes a duty to that other to warn him of any defects in the instructions and fails to discharge that duty.

(3) A person shall not be treated for the purposes of subsection (2) above as having given instructions for the doing of work merely because he has agreed to the work being done in a specified manner, with specified materials or to a specified design.

(4) A person who—

    (a) in the course of a business which consists of or includes providing or arranging for the provision of dwellings or installations in dwellings; or

    (b) in the exercise of a power of making such provision or arrangements conferred by or by virtue of any enactment;

arranges for another to take on work for or in connection with the provision of a dwelling shall be treated for the purposes of this section as included among the persons who have taken on the work.

(5) Any cause of action in respect of a breach of the duty imposed by this section shall be deemed, for the purposes of the Limitation Act 1980, to have accrued at the time when the dwelling was completed, but if after that time a person who has done work for or in connection with the provision of the dwelling does further work to rectify the work he has already done, any such cause of action in respect of that further work shall be deemed for those purposes to have accrued at the time when the further work was finished.

2 Cases excluded from the remedy under section 1

(1) Where—

    (a) in connection with the provision of a dwelling or its first sale or letting for habitation any rights in respect of defects in the state of the dwelling are conferred by an approved scheme to which this section applies on a person having or acquiring an interest in the dwelling; and

    (b) it is stated in a document of a type approved for the purposes of this section that the requirements as to design or construction imposed by or under the scheme have, or appear to have, been substantially complied with in relation to the dwelling;

no action shall be brought by any person having or acquiring an interest in the dwelling for breach of the duty imposed by section 1 above in relation to the dwelling.

(2) A scheme to which this section applies—

    (a) may consist of any number of documents and any number of agreements or other transactions between any number of persons; but

    (b) must confer, by virtue of agreements entered into with persons having or acquiring an interest in the dwellings to which the scheme applies, rights on such persons in respect of defects in the state of the dwellings.

(3) In this section "approved" means approved by the Secretary of State, and the power of the Secretary of State to approve a scheme or document for the purposes of this section shall be exercisable by order, except that any requirements as to construction or design imposed under a scheme to which this section applies may be approved by him without making any order or, if he thinks fit, by order.

(4) The Secretary of State—

    (a) may approve a scheme or document for the purposes of this section with or without limiting the duration of his approval; and

    (b) may by order revoke or vary a previous order under this section or, without such an order, revoke or vary a previous approval under this section given otherwise than by order.

(5) The production of a document purporting to be a copy of an approval given by the Secretary of State otherwise than by order and certified by an officer of the Secretary of State to be a true copy of the approval shall be conclusive evidence of the approval, and without proof of the handwriting or official position of the person purporting to sign the certificate.

(6) The power to make an order under this section shall be exercisable by statutory instrument which shall be subject to annulment in pursuance of a resolution by either House of Parliament.

(7) Where an interest in a dwelling is compulsorily acquired—

(a) no action shall be brought by the acquiring authority for breach of the duty imposed by section 1 above in respect of the dwelling; and

(b) if any work for or in connection with the provision of the dwelling was done otherwise than in the course of a business by the person in occupation of the dwelling at the time of the compulsory acquisition, the acquiring authority and not that person shall be treated as the person who took on the work and accordingly as owing that duty.

3 Duty of care with respect to work done on premises not abated by disposal of premises

(1) Where work of construction, repair, maintenance or demolition or any other work is done on or in relation to premises, any duty of care owed, because of the doing of the work, to persons who might reasonably be expected to be affected by defects in the state of the premises created by the doing of the work shall not be abated by the subsequent disposal of the premises by the person who owed the duty.

(2) This section does not apply—

(a) in the case of premises which are let, where the relevant tenancy of the premises commenced, or the relevant tenancy agreement of the premises was entered into, before the commencement of this Act;

(b) in the case of premises disposed of in any other way, when the disposal of the premises was completed, or a contract for their disposal was entered into, before the commencement of this Act; or

(c) in either case, where the relevant transaction disposing of the premises is entered into in pursuance of an enforceable option by which the consideration for the disposal was fixed before the commencement of this Act.

4 Landlord's duty of care in virtue of obligation or right to repair premises demised

(1) Where premises are let under a tenancy which puts on the landlord an obligation to the tenant for the maintenance or repair of the premises the landlord owes to all persons who might reasonably be expected to be affected by defects in the state of the premises a duty to take such care as is reasonable in all the circumstances to see that they are reasonably safe from personal injury or from damage to their property caused by a relevant defect.

(2) The said duty is owed if the landlord knows (whether as the result of being notified by the tenant or otherwise) or if he ought in all the circumstances to have known of the relevant defect.

(3) In this section "relevant defect" means a defect in the state of the premises existing at or after the material time and arising from, or continuing because of, an act or omission by the landlord which constituted or would if he had had notice of the defect, have constituted a failure by him to carry out his obligation to the tenant for the maintenance or repair of the premises; and for the purposes of the foregoing provision "the material time" means—

(a) where the tenancy commenced before this Act, the commencement of this Act; and

(b) in all other cases, the earliest following times, that is to say—

(i) the time when the tenancy commences;

(ii) the time when the tenancy agreement is entered into;

(iii) the time when possession is taken of the premises in contemplation of the letting.

(4) Where premises are let under a tenancy which expressly or impliedly gives the landlord the right to enter the premises to carry out any description of maintenance or repair of the premises, then, as from the time when he first is, or by notice or otherwise can put himself, in a position to exercise the right and so long as he is or can put himself in that

position, he shall be treated for the purposes of subsections (1) to (3) above (but for no other purpose) as if he were under an obligation to the tenant for that description of maintenance or repair of the premises; but the landlord shall not owe the tenant any duty by virtue of this subsection in respect of any defect in the state of the premises arising from, or continuing because of, a failure to carry out an obligation expressly imposed on the tenant by the tenancy.

(5)　For the purposes of this section obligations imposed or rights given by any enactment in virtue of a tenancy shall be treated as imposed or given by the tenancy.

(6)　This section applies to a right of occupation given by contract or any enactment and not amounting to a tenancy as if the right were a tenancy, and "tenancy" and cognate expressions shall be construed accordingly.

5　Application to Crown

This Act shall bind the Crown, but as regards the Crown's liability in tort shall not bind the Crown further than the Crown is made liable in tort by the Crown Proceedings Act 1947.

6　Supplemental

(1)　In this Act: "disposal", in relation to premises, includes a letting, and an assignment or surrender of a tenancy, of the premises and the creation by contract of any other right to occupy the premises, and "dispose" shall be construed accordingly;

"personal injury" includes any disease and any impairment of a person's physical or mental condition;

...

(2)　Any duty imposed by or enforceable by virtue of any provision of this Act is in addition to any duty a person may owe apart from that provision.

(3)　Any term of an agreement which purports to exclude or restrict, or has the effect of excluding or restricting, the operation of any of the provisions of this Act, or any liability arising by virtue of any such provision, shall be void.

SUPPLY OF GOODS (IMPLIED TERMS) ACT 1973
(1973, c. 13)

8　Implied terms as title

(1)　In every relevant hire-purchase agreement, other than one to which subsection (2) below applies, there is—

(a)　an implied term on the part of the creditor that he will have a right to sell the goods at the time when the property is to pass; and

(b)　an implied term that—

(i)　the goods are free, and will remain free until the time when the property is to pass, from any charge or encumbrance not disclosed or known to the person to whom the goods are bailed or (in Scotland) hired before the agreement is made, and

(ii)　that person will enjoy quiet possession of the goods except so far as it may be disturbed by any person entitled to the benefit of any charge or encumbrance so disclosed or known.

(2)　In a relevant hire-purchase agreement, in the case of which there appears from the agreement or is to be inferred from the circumstances of the agreement an intention that the creditor should transfer only such title as he or a third person may have, there is—

(a)　an implied term that all charges or encumbrances known to the creditor and not known to the person to whom the goods are bailed or hired have been disclosed to that person before the agreement is made; and

(b)　an implied term that neither—

(i)　the creditor; nor

(ii)　in a case where the parties to the agreement intend that any title which may be transferred shall be only such title as a third person may have, that person; nor

      (iii)   anyone claiming through or under the creditor or that third person otherwise than under a charge or encumbrance disclosed or known to the person to whom the goods are bailed or hired, before the agreement is made;

    will disturb the quiet possession of the person to whom the goods are bailed or hired.

(3)   As regards England and Wales and Northern Ireland, the term implied by subsection (1)(a) above is a condition and the terms implied by subsections (1)(b), (2)(a) and (2)(b) above are warranties.

9   Bailing or hiring by description

(1)   Where under a relevant hire-purchase agreement goods are bailed or (in Scotland) hired by description, there is an implied term that the goods will correspond with the description, and if under the agreement the goods are bailed or hired by reference to a sample as well as a description, it is not sufficient that the bulk of the goods corresponds with the sample if the goods do not also correspond with the description.

(1A)   As regards England and Wales and Northern Ireland, the term implied by subsection (1) above is a condition.

(2)   Goods shall not be prevented from being bailed or hired by description by reason only that, being exposed for sale, bailment or hire, they are selected by the person to whom they are bailed or hired.

10   Implied undertakings as to quality or fitness

(1)   Except as provided by this section and section 11 below and subject to the provisions of any other enactment, including any enactment of the Parliament of Northern Ireland or the Northern Ireland Assembly, there is no implied term as to the quality or fitness for any particular purpose of goods bailed or (in Scotland) hired under a relevant hire-purchase agreement.

(2)   Where the creditor bails or hires goods under a relevant hire purchase agreement in the course of a business, there is an implied term that the goods supplied under the agreement are of satisfactory quality.

(2A)   For the purposes of this Act, goods are of satisfactory quality if they meet the standard that a reasonable person would regard as satisfactory, taking account of any description of the goods, the price (if relevant) and all the other relevant circumstances.

(2B)   For the purposes of this Act, the quality of goods includes their state and condition and the following (among others) are in appropriate cases aspects of the quality of goods—

    (a)   fitness for all the purposes for which goods of the kind in question are commonly supplied,

    (b)   appearance and finish,

    (c)   freedom from minor defects,

    (d)   safety, and

    (e)   durability.

(2C)   The term implied by subsection (2) above does not extend to any matter making the quality of goods unsatisfactory—

    (a)   which is specifically drawn to the attention of the person to whom the goods are bailed or hired before the agreement is made,

    (b)   where that person examines the goods before the agreement is made, which that examination ought to reveal, or

    (c)   where the goods are bailed or hired by reference to a sample, which would have been apparent on a reasonable examination of the sample.

(3)   Where the creditor bails or hires goods under a relevant hire-purchase agreement in the course of a business and the person to whom the goods are bailed or hired, expressly or by implication, makes known—

    (a)   to the creditor in the course of negotiations conducted by the creditor in relation to the making of the relevant hire-purchase agreement, or

    (b)   to a credit-broker in the course of negotiations conducted by that broker in relation to goods sold by him to the creditor before forming the subject matter of the relevant hire-purchase agreement, any particular purpose for which the goods are being bailed or hired, there is an implied term that the goods supplied under the agreement are reasonably fit for that purpose, whether or not that is a purpose for which such goods are commonly supplied, except where the circumstances show that the person to whom the goods are bailed or hired does not rely, or that it is unreasonable for him to rely, on the skill or judgment of the creditor or credit-broker.

(4) An implied term as to quality or fitness for a particular purpose may be annexed to a relevant hire-purchase agreement by usage.

(5) The preceding provisions of this section apply to a relevant hire-purchase agreement made by a person who in the course of a business is acting as agent for the creditor as they apply to an agreement made by the creditor in the course of a business, except where the creditor is not bailing or hiring in the course of a business and either the person to whom the goods are bailed or hired knows that fact or reasonable steps are taken to bring it to the notice of that person before the agreement is made.

(6) In subsection (3) above and this subsection—
    (a) "credit-broker" means a person acting in the course of a business of credit brokerage;
    (b) "credit brokerage" means the effecting of introductions of individuals desiring to obtain credit—
        (i) to persons carrying on any business so far as it relates to the provision of credit, or
        (ii) to other persons engaged in credit brokerage.

(7) As regards England and Wales and Northern Ireland, the terms implied by subsections (2) and (3) above are conditions.

11 Samples

(1) Where under a relevant hire-purchase agreement goods are bailed or (in Scotland) hired by reference to a sample, there is an implied term—
    (a) that the bulk will correspond with the sample in quality; and
    (b) that the person to whom the goods are bailed or hired will have a reasonable opportunity of comparing the bulk with the sample; and
    (c) that the goods will be free from any defect, making their quality unsatisfactory, which would not be apparent on reasonable examination of the sample.

(2) As regards England and Wales and Northern Ireland, the term implied by subsection (1) above is a condition.

11A Modification of remedies for breach of statutory condition in nonconsumer cases

(1) Where in the case of a relevant hire purchase agreement—
    (a) the person to whom goods are bailed would, apart from this subsection, have the right to reject them by reason of a breach on the part of the creditor of a term implied by section 9, 10 or 11(1)(a) or (c) above, but
    (b) the breach is so slight that it would be unreasonable for him to reject them,
the breach is not to be treated as a breach of condition but may be treated as a breach of warranty.

(2) This section applies unless a contrary intention appears in, or is to be implied from, the agreement.

(3) It is for the creditor to show—
    (a) that a breach fell within subsection (1)(b) above, and
    (b) that the agreement was a relevant hire-purchase agreement.

(5) This section does not apply to Scotland.

12 Exclusion of implied terms and conditions

An express term does not negative a term implied by this Act unless inconsistent with it.

15 Supplementary

(1) In sections 8 to 14 above and this section—
"business" includes a profession and the activities of any government department (including a Northern Ireland department), or local or public authority;

"buyer"and"seller" includes a person to whom rights and duties under a conditional sale agreement have passed by assignment or operation of law;

"conditional sale agreement" means an agreement for the sale of goods under which the purchase price or part of it is payable by instalments, and the property in the goods is to remain in the seller (notwithstanding that the buyer is to be in possession of the goods) until such conditions as to the payment of instalments or otherwise as may be specified in the agreement are fulfilled;

"consumer sale" has the same meaning as in section 55 of the Sale of Goods Act 1979 (as set out in paragraph 11 of Schedule 1 to that Act);

"creditor" means the person by whom the goods are bailed or (in Scotland) hired under a relevant hire-purchase agreement or the person to whom his rights and duties under the agreement have passed by assignment or operation of law; and

"hire-purchase agreement" means an agreement, other than conditional sale agreement, under which—

(a) goods are bailed or (in Scotland) hired in return for periodical payments by the person to whom they are bailed or hired, and

(b) the property in the goods will pass to that person if the terms of the agreement are complied with and one or more of the following occurs—

    (i) the exercise of an option to purchase by that person,

    (ii) the doing of any other specified act by any party to the agreement,

    (iii) the happening of any other specified event and a hire-purchase agreement is relevant if it is not a contract to which Chapter 2 of Part 1 of the Consumer Rights Act 2015 applies;.

(4) Nothing in sections 8 to 13 above shall prejudice the operation of any other enactment including any enactment of the Parliament of Northern Ireland or the Northern Ireland Assembly or any rule of law whereby any term, other than one relating to quality or fitness, is to be implied in any relevant hire-purchase agreement.

HEALTH AND SAFETY AT WORK ACT 1974
(1974, c. 37)

2   General duties of employers to their employees

(1) It shall be the duty of every employer to ensure, so far as is reasonably practicable, the health, safety and welfare at work of all his employees.

3   General duties of employers and self-employed to persons other than their employees

(1) It shall be the duty of every employer to conduct his undertaking in such a way as to ensure, so far as is reasonably practicable, that persons not in his employment who may be affected thereby are not thereby exposed to risks to their health or safety.

(2) It shall be the duty of every self-employed person who conducts an undertaking of a prescribed description to conduct the undertaking in such a way as to ensure, so far as is reasonably practicable, that he and other persons (not being his employees) who may be affected thereby are not thereby exposed to risks to their health or safety.

(2A) A description of undertaking included in regulations under subsection (2) may be framed by reference to—

(a) the type of activities carried out by the undertaking, where those activities are carried out or any other feature of the undertaking;

(b) whether persons who may be affected by the conduct of the undertaking, other than the self-employed person (or his employees), may therefore be exposed to risks to their health or safety.

(3) In such cases as may be prescribed, it shall be the duty of every employer and every self-employed person, in the prescribed circumstances and in the prescribed manner, to give to persons (not being his employees) who may be affected by the way in which he conducts his undertaking the prescribed information about such aspects of the way in which he conducts his undertaking as might affect their health or safety.

4   General duties of persons concerned with premises to persons other than their employees

(1)   This section has effect for imposing on persons duties in relation to those who—

    (a)   are not their employees; but

    (b)   use non-domestic premises made available to them as a place of work or as a place where they may use plant or substances provided for their use there,

and applies to premises so made available and other non-domestic premises used in connection with them.

(2)   It shall be the duty of each person who has, to any extent, control of premises to which this section applies or of the means of access thereto or egress therefrom or of any plant or substance in such premises to take such measures as it is reasonable for a person in his position to take to ensure, so far as is reasonably practicable, that the premises, all means of access thereto or egress therefrom available for use by persons using the premises, and any plant or substance in the premises or, as the case may be, provided for use there, is or are safe and without risks to health.

(3)   Where a person has, by virtue of any contract or tenancy, an obligation of any extent in relation to—

    (a)   the maintenance or repair of any premises to which this section applies or any means of access thereto or egress therefrom; or

    (b)   the safety of or the absence of risks to health arising from plant or substances in any such premises;

that person shall be treated, for the purposes of subsection (2) above, as being a person who has control of the matters to which his obligation extends.

(4)   Any reference in this section to a person having control of any premises or matter is a reference to a person having control of the premises or matter in connection with the carrying on by him of a trade, business or other undertaking (whether for profit or not).

17   Use of approved codes of practice in criminal proceedings

(1)   A failure on the part of any person to observe any provision of an approved code of practice shall not of itself render him liable to any civil or criminal proceedings; but where in any criminal proceedings a party is alleged to have committed an offence by reason of a contravention of any requirement or prohibition imposed by or under any such provision as is mentioned in section 16(1) being a provision for which there was an approved code of practice at the time of the alleged contravention, the following subsection shall have effect with respect to that code in relation to those proceedings.

47   Civil liability

(1)   Nothing in this Part shall be construed—

    (a)   as conferring a right of action in any civil proceedings in respect of any failure to comply with any duty imposed by sections 2 to 7 or any contravention of section 8; or

    ...

    (c)   as affecting the operation of section 12 of the Nuclear Installations Act 1965 (right to compensation by virtue of certain provisions of that Act).

(2)   Breach of a duty imposed by a statutory instrument containing (whether alone or with other provision) health and safety regulations shall not be actionable except to the extent that regulations under this section so provide.

(2A) Breach of a duty imposed by an existing statutory provision shall not be actionable except to the extent that regulations under this section so provide (including by modifying any of the existing statutory provisions).

(2B) Regulations under this section may provide for—

    (a)   a defence to be available in any action for breach of the duty mentioned in subsection (2) or (2A);

    (b)   any term of an agreement which purports to exclude or restrict any liability for such a breach to be void.

(3)   No provision made by virtue of section 15(6)(b) shall afford a defence in any civil proceedings.

(4) Subsections (1)(a), (2) and (2A) above are without prejudice to any right of action which exists apart from the provisions of this Act, and subsection (2B)(a) above is without prejudice to any defence which may be available apart from the provisions of the regulations there mentioned.

(5) ...

(6) ...

(7) The power to make regulations under this section shall be exercisable by the Secretary of State.

REHABILITATION OF OFFENDERS ACT 1974
(1974, c. 53)

4 Effect of rehabilitation

(1) Subject to sections 7 and 8 below, a person who has become a rehabilitated person for the purposes of this Act in respect of a conviction shall be treated for all purposes in law as a person who has not committed or been charged with or prosecuted for or convicted of or sentenced for the offence or offences which were the subject of that conviction; ...

8 Defamation actions

(1) This section applies to any action for libel or slander begun after the commencement of this Act by a rehabilitated person and founded upon the publication of any matter imputing that the plaintiff has committed or been charged with or prosecuted for or convicted of or sentenced for an offence which was the subject of a spent conviction.

(2) Nothing in section 4(1) above shall affect an action to which this section applies where the publication complained of took place before the conviction in question became spent, and the following provisions of this section shall not apply in any such case.

(3) Subject to subsections (5) and (6) below, nothing in section 4(1) above shall prevent the defendant in an action to which this section applies from relying on any defence under section 2 or 3 of the Defamation Act 2013 which is available to him or any defence of absolute or qualified privilege which is available to him, or restrict the matters he may establish in support of any such defence.

(4) Without prejudice to the generality of subsection (3) above, where in any such action malice is alleged against a defendant who is relying on a defence of qualified privilege, nothing in section 4(1) above shall restrict the matters he may establish in rebuttal of the allegation.

(5) A defendant in any such action shall not by virtue of subsection (3) above be entitled to rely upon a defence under section 2 of the Defamation Act 2013 if the publication is proved to have been made with malice.

(6) Subject to subsection (7) below a defendant in any such action shall not, by virtue of subsection (3) above, be entitled to rely on any matter or adduce or require any evidence for the purpose of establishing (whether under section 14 of the Defamation Act 1996 or otherwise) the defence that the matter published constituted a fair and accurate report of judicial proceedings if it is proved that the publication contained a reference to evidence which was ruled to be inadmissible in the proceedings by virtue of section 4(1) above.

(7) Subsection (3) above shall apply without the qualifications imposed by subsection (6) above in relation to—

(a) any report of judicial proceedings contained in any bona fide series of law reports which does not form part of any other publication and consists solely of reports of proceedings in courts of law, and

(b) any report or account of judicial proceedings published for bona fide educational, scientific or professional purposes or given in the course of any lecture, class or discussion given or held for any of those purposes.

(7A) Nothing in section 4(1) above shall restrict the evidence that may be adduced in mitigation of damages under section 13(2) of the Defamation Act 1996.

CONGENITAL DISABILITIES (CIVIL LIABILITY) ACT 1976
(1976, c. 28)

1   Civil liability to child born disabled

(1)   If a child is born disabled as the result of such an occurrence before its birth as is mentioned in subsection (2) below, and a person (other than the child's own mother) is under this section answerable to the child in respect of the occurrence, the child's disabilities are to be regarded as damage resulting from the wrongful act of that person and actionable accordingly at the suit of the child.

(2)   An occurrence to which this section applies is one which—

     (a)   affected either parent of the child in his or her ability to have a normal, healthy child; or

     (b)   affected the mother during her pregnancy, or affected her or the child in the course of its birth, so that the child is born with disabilities which would not otherwise have been present.

(3)   Subject to the following subsections, a person (here referred to as "the defendant") is answerable to the child if he was liable in tort to the parent or would, if sued in due time, have been so; and it is no answer that there could not have been such liability because the parent suffered no actionable injury, if there was a breach of legal duty which, accompanied by injury, would have given rise to the liability.

(4)   In the case of an occurrence preceding the time of conception, the defendant is not answerable to the child if at that time either or both of the parents knew the risk of their child being born disabled (that is to say, the particular risk created by the occurrence); but should it be the child's father who is the defendant, this subsection does not apply if he knew of the risk and the mother did not.

(4A)   In the case of a child who has a parent by virtue of section 42 or 43 of the Human Fertilisation and Embryology Act 2008, the reference in subsection (4) to the child's father includes a reference to the woman who is a parent by virtue of that section.

(5)   The defendant is not answerable to the child, for anything he did or omitted to do when responsible in a professional capacity for treating or advising the parent, if he took reasonable care having due regard to then received professional opinion applicable to the particular class of case; but this does not mean that he is answerable only because he departed from received opinion.

(6)   Liability to the child under this section may be treated as having been excluded or limited by contract made with the parent affected, to the same extent and subject to the same restrictions as liability in the parent's own case; and a contract term which could have been set up by the defendant in an action by the parent, so as to exclude or limit his liability to him or her, operates in the defendant's favour to the same, but no greater, extent in an action under this section by the child.

(7)   If in the child's action under this section it is shown that the parent affected shared the responsibility for the child being born disabled, the damages are to be reduced to such extent as the court thinks just and equitable having regard to the extent of the parent's responsibility.

1A   Extension of section 1 to cover infertility treatments

(1)   In any case where—

     (a)   a child carried by a woman as the result of the placing in her of an embryo or of sperm and eggs or her artificial insemination is born disabled,

     (b)   the disability results from an act or omission in the course of the selection, or the keeping or use outside the body, of the embryo carried by her or of the gametes used to bring about the creation of the embryo, and

     (c)   a person is under this section answerable to the child in respect of the act or omission,

the child's disabilities are to be regarded as damage resulting from the wrongful act of that person and actionable accordingly at the suit of the child.

(2)   Subject to subsection (3) below and the applied provisions of section 1 of this Act, a person (here referred to as "the defendant") is answerable to the child if he was liable in tort to one or both of the parents (here referred to as "the parent or parents concerned") or would, if sued in due time, have been so; and it is no answer that there

could not have been such liability because the parent or parents concerned suffered no actionable injury, if there was a breach of legal duty which, accompanied by injury, would have given rise to the liability.

(3) The defendant is not under this section answerable to the child if at the time the embryo, or the sperm and eggs, are placed in the woman or the time of her insemination (as the case may be) either or both of the parents knew the risk of their child being born disabled (that is to say, the particular risk created by the act or omission).

(4) Subsections (5) to (7) of section 1 of this Act apply for the purposes of this section as they apply for the purposes of that but as if references to the parent or the parent affected were references to the parent or parents concerned.

2 Liability of woman driving while pregnant

A woman driving a motor vehicle when she knows (or ought reasonably to know) herself to be pregnant is to be regarded as being under the same duty to take care for the safety of her unborn child as the law imposes on her with respect to the safety of other people; and if in consequence of her breach of that duty her child is born with disabilities which would not otherwise have been present, those disabilities are to be regarded as damage resulting from her wrongful act and actionable accordingly at the suit of the child.

3 Disabled birth due to radiation

(1) Section 1 of this Act does not affect the operation of the Nuclear Installations Act 1965 as to liability for, and compensation in respect of, injury or damage caused by occurrences involving nuclear matter or the emission of ionising radiations.

(2) For the avoidance of doubt anything which—
    (a) affects a man in his ability to have a normal, healthy child; or
    (b) affects a woman in that ability, or so affects her when she is pregnant that her child is born with disabilities which would not otherwise have been present, is an injury for the purposes of that Act.

(3) If a child is born disabled as the result of an injury to either of its parents caused in breach of a duty imposed by any of sections 7 to 11 of that Act (nuclear site licensees and others to secure that nuclear incidents do not cause injury to persons, etc.), the child's disabilities are to be regarded under the subsequent provisions of that Act (compensation and other matters) as injuries caused on the same occasion, and by the same breach of duty, as was the injury to the parent.

(4) As respects compensation to the child, section 13(6) of that Act (contributory fault of person injured by radiation) is to be applied as if the reference there to fault were to the fault of the parent.

(5) Compensation is not payable in the child's case if the injury to the parent preceded the time of the child's conception and at that time either or both of the parents knew the risk of their child being born disabled (that is to say, the particular risk created by the injury).

4 Interpretation and other supplementary provisions

(1) References in this Act to a child being born disabled or with disabilities are to its being born with any deformity, disease or abnormality, including predisposition (whether or not susceptible or immediate prognosis) to physical or mental defect in the future.

(2) In this Act—
    (a) "born" means born alive (the moment of a child's birth being when it first has a life separate from its mother), and "birth" has a corresponding meaning; and
    (b) "motor vehicle" means a mechanically propelled vehicle intended or adapted for use on roads.
    and references to embryos shall be construed in accordance with section 1(1) of the Human Fertilisation and Embryology Act 1990 and any regulations under section 1(6) of that Act.

(3) Liability to a child under section 1, 1A or 2 of this Act is to be regarded—
    (a) as respects all its incidents and any matters arising or to arise out of it; and
    (b) subject to any contrary context or intention, for the purpose of construing references in enactments and documents to personal or bodily injuries and cognate matters,
    as liability for personal injuries sustained by the child immediately after its birth.

(4)   No damages shall be recoverable under any of those sections in respect of any loss of expectation of life, nor shall any such loss be taken into account in the compensation payable in respect of a child under the Nuclear Installations Act 1965 as extended by section 3, unless (in either case) the child lives for at least 48 hours.

(4A) In any case where a child carried by a woman as the result of the placing in her of an embryo or of sperm and eggs or her artificial insemination is born disabled, any reference in section 1 of this Act to a parent includes a reference to a person who would be a parent but for sections 27 to 29 of the Human Fertilisation and Embryology Act 1990 or sections 33 to 47 of the Human Fertilisation and Embryology Act 2008.

(5)   This Act applies in respect of births after (but not before) its passing, and in respect of any such birth it replaces any law in force before its passing, whereby a person could be liable to a child in respect of disabilities with which it might be born; but in section 1(3) of this Act the expression "liable in tort" does not include any reference to liability by virtue of this Act or to liability by virtue of any such law.

5   Crown application
This Act binds the Crown.

FATAL ACCIDENTS ACT 1976
(1976, c. 30)

1   Right of action for wrongful act causing death

(1)   If death is caused by any wrongful act, neglect or default which is such as would (if death had not ensued) have entitled the person injured to maintain an action and recover damages in respect thereof, the person who would have been liable if death had not ensued shall be liable to an action for damages, notwithstanding the death of the person injured.

(2)   Subject to section 1A(2) below, every such action shall be for the benefit of the dependants of the person ("the deceased") whose death has been so caused.

(3)   In this Act "dependant" means—
   (a)   the wife or husband or former wife or husband of the deceased;
   (aa)   the civil partner or former civil partner of the deceased;
   (b)   any person who—
          (i)   was living with the deceased in the same household immediately before the date of the death; and
          (ii)   had been living with the deceased in the same household for at least two years before that date; and
          (iii) was living during the whole of that period as the husband or wife or civil partner of the deceased;
   (c)   any parent or other ascendant of the deceased;
   (d)   any person who was treated by the deceased as his parent;
   (e)   any child or other descendant of the deceased;
   (f)   any person (not being a child of the deceased) who, in the case of any marriage to which the deceased was at any time a party, was treated by the deceased as a child of the family in relation to that marriage;
   (fa)   any person (not being a child of the deceased) who in the case of any civil partnership in which the deceased was at any time a civil partner, was treated by the deceased as a child of the family in relation to that civil partnership;
   (g)   any person who is, or is the issue of, a brother, sister, uncle or aunt of the deceased.

(4)   The reference to the former wife or husband of the deceased in subsection (3)(a) above includes a reference to a person whose marriage to the deceased has been annulled or declared void as well as a person whose marriage to the deceased has been dissolved.

(4A) The reference to the former civil partner of the deceased in subsection (3)(aa) above includes a reference to a person whose civil partnership with the deceased has been annulled as well as a person whose civil partnership with the deceased has been dissolved.

(5) In deducing any relationship for the purposes of subsection (3) above—
   (a) any relationship by marriage or civil partnership shall be treated as a relationship of consanguinity, any relationship of the half blood as a relationship of the whole blood, and the stepchild of any person as his child, and
   (b) an illegitimate person shall be treated as—
      (i) the legitimate child of his mother and reputed father, or
      (ii) in the case of a person who has a female parent by virtue of section 43 of the Human Fertilisation and Embryology Act 2008, the legitimate child of his mother and that female parent.
(6) Any reference in this Act to injury includes any disease and any impairment of a person's physical or mental condition.

1A Bereavement

(1) An action under this Act may consist of or include a claim for damages for bereavement.
(2) A claim for damages for bereavement shall only be for the benefit—
   (a) of the wife or husband or civil partner of the deceased; and
   (b) where the deceased was a minor who was never married or a civil partner—
      (i) of his parents, if he was legitimate; and
      (ii) of his mother, if he was illegitimate.
(3) Subject to subsection (5) below, the sum to be awarded as damages under this section shall be £12,980.
(4) Where there is a claim for damages under this section for the benefit of both the parents of the deceased, the sum awarded shall be divided equally between them (subject to any deduction falling to be made in respect of costs not recovered from the defendant).
(5) The Lord Chancellor may by order made by statutory instrument, subject to annulment in pursuance of a resolution of either House of Parliament, amend this section by varying the sum for the time being specified in subsection (3) above.

2 Persons entitled to bring the action

(1) The action shall be brought by and in the name of the executor or administrator of the deceased.
(2) If—
   (a) there is no executor or administrator of the deceased, or
   (b) no action is brought within six months after the death by and in the name of an executor or administrator of the deceased,
   the action may be brought by and in the name of all or any of the persons for whose benefit an executor or administrator could have brought it.
(3) Not more than one action shall lie for and in respect of the same subject matter of complaint.
(4) The plaintiff in the action shall be required to deliver to the defendant or his solicitor full particulars of the persons for whom and on whose behalf the action is brought and of the nature of the claim in respect of which damages are sought to be recovered.

3 Assessment of damages

(1) In the action such damages, other than damages for bereavement, may be awarded as are proportioned to the injury resulting from the death to the dependants respectively.
(2) After deducting the costs not recovered from the defendant any amount recovered otherwise than as damages for bereavement shall be divided among the dependants in such shares as may be directed.
(3) In an action under this Act where there fall to be assessed damages payable to a widow in respect of the death of her husband there shall not be taken into account the re-marriage of the widow or her prospects of re-marriage.
(4) In an action under this Act where there fall to be assessed damages payable to a person who is a dependant by virtue of section 1(3)(b) above in respect of the death of the person with whom the dependant was living as husband or wife or civil partner there shall be taken into account (together with any other matter that appears to the court to be relevant to the action) the fact that the dependant had no enforceable right to financial support by the deceased as a result of their living together.

(5) If the dependants have incurred funeral expenses in respect of the deceased, damages may be awarded in respect of those expenses.

(6) Money paid into court in satisfaction of a cause of action under this Act may be in one sum without specifying any person's share.

4   Assessment of damages: disregard of benefits

In assessing damages in respect of a person's death in an action under this Act, benefits which have accrued or will or may accrue to any person from his estate or otherwise as a result of his death shall be disregarded.

5   Contributory negligence

Where any person dies as the result partly of his own fault and partly of the fault of any other person or persons, and accordingly if an action were brought for the benefit of the estate under the Law Reform (Miscellaneous Provisions) Act 1934 the damages recoverable would be reduced under section 1(1) of the Law Reform (Contributory Negligence) Act 1945, any damages recoverable in an action … under this Act shall be reduced to a proportionate extent.

TORTS (INTERFERENCE WITH GOODS) ACT 1977
(1977, c. 32)

1   Definition of "wrongful interference with goods"

In this Act "wrongful interference", or "wrongful interference with goods", means—
- (a) conversion of goods (also called trover),
- (b) trespass to goods,
- (c) negligence so far as it results in damage to goods or to an interest in goods,
- (d) subject to section 2, any other tort so far as it results in damage to goods or to an interest in goods.

and references in this Act (however worded) to proceedings for wrongful interference or to a claim or right to claim for wrongful interference shall include references to proceedings by virtue of Part I of the Consumer Protection Act 1987 or Part II of the Consumer Protection (Northern Ireland) Order 1987 (product liability) in respect of any damage to goods or to an interest in goods or, as the case may be, to a claim or right to claim by virtue of that Part in respect of any such damage.

2   Abolition of detinue

(1) Detinue is abolished.

(2) An action lies in conversion for loss or destruction of goods which a bailee has allowed to happen in breach of his duty to his bailor (that is to say it lies in a case which is not otherwise conversion, but would have been detinue before detinue was abolished).

3   Forms of judgment where goods are detained

(1) In proceedings for wrongful interference against a person who is in possession or in control of the goods relief may be given in accordance with this section, so far as appropriate.

(2) The relief is—
- (a) an order for delivery of the goods, and for payment of any consequential damages, or
- (b) an order for delivery of the goods, but giving the defendant the alternative of paying damages by reference to the value of the goods, together in either alternative with payment of any consequential damages, or
- (c) damages.

(3) Subject to rules of court—
- (a) relief shall be given under only one of paragraphs (a), (b) and (c) of subsection (2),
- (b) relief under paragraph (a) of subsection (2) is at the discretion of the court, and the claimant may choose between the others.

(4) If it is shown to the satisfaction of the court that an order under subsection (2)(a) had not been complied with, the court may—
- (a) revoke the order, or the relevant part of it, and
- (b) make an order for payment of damages by reference to the value of the goods.

(5)   Where an order is made under subsection (2)(b) the defendant may satisfy the order by returning the goods at any time before execution of judgment, but without prejudice to liability to pay any consequential damages.

(6)   An order for delivery of the goods under subsection (2)(a) or (b) may impose such conditions as may be determined by the court, or pursuant to rules of court, and in particular, where damages by reference to the value of the goods would not be the whole of the value of the goods, may require an allowance to be made by the claimant to reflect the difference.

For example, a bailor's action against the bailee may be one in which the measure of damages is not the full value of the goods, and then the court may order delivery of the goods, but require the bailor to pay the bailee a sum reflecting the difference.

(7)   Where under subsection (1) or subsection (2) of section 6 an allowance is to be made in respect of an improvement of the goods, and an order is made under subsection (2)(a) or (b), the court may assess the allowance to be made in respect of the improvement, and by the order require, as a condition for delivery of the goods, that allowance to be made by the claimant.

(8)   This section is without prejudice—

     (a)   to the remedies afforded by section 133 of the Consumer Credit Act 1974, or

     ...

     (c)   to any jurisdiction to afford ancillary or incidental relief.

4   Interlocutory relief where goods are detained

(1)   In this section "proceedings" means proceedings for wrongful interference.

(2)   On the application of any person in accordance with rules of court, the High Court shall, in such circumstances as may be specified in the rules, have power to make an order providing for the delivery up of any goods which are or may become the subject matter of subsequent proceedings in the court, or as to which any question may arise in proceedings.

(3)   Delivery shall be, as the order may provide, to the claimant or to a person appointed by the court for the purpose, and shall be on such terms and conditions as may be specified in the order.

5   Extinction of title on satisfaction of claim for damages

(1)   Where damages for wrongful interference are, or would fall to be, assessed on the footing that the claimant is being compensated—

     (a)   for the whole of his interest in the goods, or

     (b)   for the whole of his interest in the goods subject to a reduction for contributory negligence,

payment of the assessed damages (under all heads), or as the case may be settlement of a claim for damages for the wrong (under all heads), extinguishes the claimant's title to that interest.

(2)   In subsection (1) the reference to the settlement of the claim includes—

     (a)   where the claim is made in court proceedings, and the defendant has paid a sum into court to meet the whole claim, the taking of that sum by the claimant, and

     (b)   where the claim is made in court proceedings, and the proceedings are settled or compromised, the payment of what is due in accordance with the settlement or compromise, and

     (c)   where the claim is made out of court and is settled or compromised, the payment of what is due in accordance with the settlement or compromise.

(3)   It is hereby declared that subsection (1) does not apply where damages are assessed on the footing that the claimant is being compensated for the whole of his interest in the goods, but the damages paid are limited to some lesser amount by virtue of any enactment or rule of law.

(4)   Where under section 7(3) the claimant accounts over to another person (the "third party") so as to compensate (under all heads) the third party for the whole of his interest in the goods, the third party's title to that interest is extinguished.

(5)   This section has effect subject to any agreement varying the respective rights of the parties to the agreement, and where the claim is made in court proceedings has effect subject to any order of the court.

6   Allowance for improvement of the goods

(1) If in proceedings for wrongful interference against a person (the "improver") who has improved the goods, it is shown that the improver acted in the mistaken but honest belief that he had a good title to them, an allowance shall be made for the extent to which, at the time as at which the goods fall to be valued in assessing damages, the value of the goods is attributable to the improvement.

(2) If, in proceedings for wrongful interference against a person ("the purchaser") who has purported to purchase the goods —

     (a) from the improver, or

     (b) where after such a purported sale the goods passed by a further purported sale on one or more occasions, on any such occasion,

it is shown that the purchaser acted in good faith, an allowance shall be made on the principle set out in subsection (1).

For example, where a person in good faith buys a stolen car from the improver and is sued in conversion by the true owner the damages may be reduced to reflect the improvement, but if the person who bought the stolen car from the improver sues the improver for failure of consideration, and the improver acted in good faith, subsection (3) below will ordinarily make a comparable reduction in the damages he recovers from the improver.

(3) If in a case within subsection (2) the person purporting to sell the goods acted in good faith, then in proceedings by the purchaser for recovery of the purchase price because of failure of consideration, or in any other proceedings founded on that failure of consideration, an allowance shall, where appropriate, be made on the principle set out in subsection (1).

(4) This section applies, with the necessary modifications, to a purported bailment or other disposition of goods as it applies to a purported sale of goods.

7   Double liability

(1) In this section "double liability" means the double liability of the wrongdoer which can arise —

     (a) where one of two or more rights of action for wrongful interference is founded on a possessory title, or

     (b) where the measure of damages in an action for wrongful interference founded on a proprietary title is or includes the entire value of the goods, although the interest is one of two or more interests in the goods.

(2) In proceedings to which any two or more claimants are parties, the relief shall be such as to avoid double liability of the wrongdoer as between those claimants.

(3) On satisfaction, in whole or in part, of any claim for an amount exceeding that recoverable if subsection (2) applied, the claimant is liable to account over to the other person having a right to claim to such extent as will avoid double liability.

(4) Where, as the result of enforcement of a double liability, any claimant is unjustly enriched to an extent, he shall be liable to reimburse the wrongdoer to that extent.

For example, if a converter of goods pays damages first to a finder of the goods, and then to the true owner, the finder is unjustly enriched unless he accounts over to the true owner under subsection (3); and then the true owner is unjustly enriched and becomes liable to reimburse the converter of the goods.

8   Competing rights to the goods

(1) The defendant in an action for wrongful interference shall be entitled to show, in accordance with rules of court, that a third party has a better right than the plaintiff as respects all or any part of the interest claimed by the plaintiff, or in right of which he sues, and any rule of law (sometimes called jus tertii) to the contrary is abolished.

(2) Rules of court relating to proceedings for wrongful interference may —

     (a) require the plaintiff to give particulars of his title,

     (b) require the plaintiff to identify any person who, to his knowledge, has or claims any interest in the goods,

     (c) authorise the defendant to apply for directions as to whether any person should be joined with a view to establishing whether he has a better right than the plaintiff, or has a claim as a result of which the defendant might be doubly liable,

(d)   where a party fails to appear on an application within paragraph (c), or to comply with any direction given by the court on such an application, authorise the court to deprive him of any right of action against the defendant for the wrong either unconditionally, or subject to such terms or conditions as may be specified.

(3)   Subsection (2) is without prejudice to any other power of making rules of court.

9   Concurrent actions

(1)   This section applies where goods are the subject of two or more claims for wrongful interference (whether or not the claims are founded on the same wrongful act, and whether or not any of the claims relates also to other goods).

(2)   Where the goods are the subject of two or more claims under section 6 this section shall apply as if any claim under section 6(3) were a claim for wrongful interference.

(3)   If proceedings have been brought in England and Wales in the county court and in Northern Ireland on one of those claims, rules of court may waive, or allow a court to waive, any limit (financial or territorial) on the jurisdiction of county courts in the County Courts Act 1984 or the County Courts Act (Northern Ireland) Order 1980 so as to allow another of those claims to be brought in the same court.

(4)   If proceedings are brought on one of the claims in the High Court, and proceedings on any other are brought in England and Wales in a county court or in Northern Ireland, whether prior to the High Court proceedings or not, the High Court may, on the application of the defendant, after notice has been given to the claimant in the county court proceedings—
(a)   order that the county court proceedings be transferred to the High Court, and
(b)   order security for costs or impose such other terms as the court thinks fit.

10   Co-owners

(1)   Co-ownership is no defence to an action founded on conversion or trespass to goods where the defendant without the authority of the other co-owner—
(a)   destroys the goods, or disposes of the goods in a way giving a good title to the entire property in the goods, or otherwise does anything equivalent to the destruction of the other's interest in the goods, or
(b)   purports to dispose of the goods in a way which would give a good title to the entire property in the goods if he was acting with the authority of all co-owners of the goods.

(2)   Subsection (1) shall not affect the law concerning execution or enforcement of judgments, or concerning any form of distress.

(3)   Subsection (1)(a) is by way of restatement of existing law so far as it relates to conversion.

11   Minor amendments

(1)   Contributory negligence is no defence in proceedings founded on conversion, or on intentional trespass to goods.

(2)   Receipt of goods by way of pledge is conversion if the delivery of the goods is conversion.

(3)   Denial of title is not of itself conversion.

12   Bailee's power of sale

(1)   This section applies to goods in the possession or under the control of a bailee where—
(a)   the bailor is in breach of an obligation to take delivery of the goods or, if the terms of the bailment so provide, to give directions as to their delivery, or
(b)   the bailee could impose such an obligation by giving notice to the bailor, but is unable to trace or communicate with the bailor, or
(c)   the bailee can reasonably expect to be relieved of any duty to safeguard the goods on giving notice to the bailor, but is unable to trace or communicate with the bailor.

(2)   In the cases of Part I of Schedule 1 to this Act a bailee may, for the purposes of subsection (1), impose an obligation on the bailor to take delivery of the goods, or as the case may be to give directions as to their delivery, and in those cases the said Part I sets out the method of notification.

(3) If the bailee—
   (a) has in accordance with Part II of Schedule 1 to this Act given notice to the bailor of his intention to sell the goods under this subsection, or
   (b) has failed to trace or communicate with the bailor with a view to giving him such a notice, after having taken reasonable steps for the purpose,
   and is reasonably satisfied that the bailor owns the goods, he shall be entitled, as against the bailor, to sell the goods.

(4) Where subsection (3) applies but the bailor did not in fact own the goods, a sale under this section, or under section 13, shall not give a good title as against the owner, or as against a person claiming under the owner.

(5) A bailee exercising his powers under subsection (3) shall be liable to account to the bailor for the proceeds of sale, less any cost of sale, and—
   (a) the account shall be taken on the footing that the bailee should have adopted the best method of sale reasonably available in the circumstances, and
   (b) where subsection (3)(a) applies, any sum payable in respect of the goods by the bailor to the bailee which accrued due before the bailee gave notice of intention to sell the goods shall be deductible from the proceeds of sale.

(6) A sale duly made under this section gives a good title to the purchaser as against the bailor.

(7) In this section, section 13, and Schedule 1 to this Act,
   (a) "bailor" and "bailee" include their respective successors in title, and
   (b) references to what is payable, paid or due to the bailee in respect of the goods include references to what would be payable by the bailor to the bailee as a condition of delivery of the goods at the relevant time.

(8) This section, and Schedule 1 to this Act, have effect subject to the terms of the bailment.

(9) This section shall not apply where the goods were bailed before the commencement of this Act.

13   Sale authorised by the court

(1) If a bailee of the goods to which section 12 applies satisfies the court that he is entitled to sell the goods under section 12, or that he would be so entitled if he had given any notice required in accordance with Schedule 1 to this Act, the court—
   (a) may authorise the sale of the goods subject to such terms and conditions, if any, as may be specified in the order, and
   (b) may authorise the bailee to deduct from the proceeds of sale any costs of sale and any amount due from the bailor to the bailee in respect of the goods, and
   (c) may direct the payment into court of the net proceeds of sale, less any amount deducted under paragraph (b), to be held to the credit of the bailor.

(2) A decision of the court authorising a sale under this section shall, subject to any right of appeal, be conclusive, as against the bailor, of the bailee's entitlement to sell the goods, and gives a good title to the purchaser as against the bailor.

(3) In this section "the court", in relation to England and Wales, means the High Court or the county court, and, in relation to Northern Ireland, means the High Court or a county court save that a county court in Northern Ireland has jurisdiction in proceedings only if the value of the goods does not exceed the county court limit mentioned in Article 10(1) of the County Courts (Northern Ireland) Order 1980.

14   Interpretation

(1) In this Act, unless the context otherwise requires—
   ...
   "goods" includes all chattels personal other than things in action and money ...

16   Extent and application to the Crown

(3) This Act shall bind the Crown, but as regards the Crown's liability in tort shall not bind the Crown further than the Crown is made liable in tort by the Crown Proceedings Act 1947.

SCHEDULES

SCHEDULE 1
UNCOLLECTED GOODS

PART I
POWER TO IMPOSE OBLIGATION TO COLLECT GOODS

1.　(1)　For the purposes of section 12(1) a bailee may, in the circumstances specified in this Part of this Schedule, by notice given to the bailor impose on him an obligation to take delivery of the goods.

　　(2)　The notice shall be in writing, and may be given either—
　　　(a)　by delivering it to the bailor, or
　　　(b)　by leaving it at his proper address, or
　　　(c)　by post.

　　(3)　The notice shall—
　　　(a)　specify the name and address of the bailee, and give sufficient particulars of the goods and the address or place where they are held, and
　　　(b)　state that the goods are ready for delivery to the bailor, or where combined with a notice terminating the contract of bailment, will be ready for delivery when the contract is terminated, and
　　　(c)　specify the amount, if any, which is payable by the bailor to the bailee in respect of the goods and which became due before the giving of the notice.

　　(4)　Where the notice is sent by post it may be combined with a notice under Part II of this Schedule if the notice is sent by post in a way complying with paragraph 6(4).

　　(5)　References in this Part of this Schedule to taking delivery of the goods include, where the terms of the bailment admit, references to giving directions as to their delivery.

　　(6)　This Part of this Schedule is without prejudice to the provisions of any contract requiring the bailor to take delivery of the goods.

Goods accepted for repair or other treatment

2.　If a bailee has accepted goods for repair or other treatment on the terms (expressed or implied) that they will be re-delivered to the bailor when the repair or other treatment has been carried out, the notice may be given at any time after the repair or other treatment has been carried out.
Goods accepted for valuation or appraisal

3.　If a bailee has accepted goods in order to value or appraise them, the notice may be given at any time after the bailee has carried out the valuation or appraisal.

Storage, warehousing, etc.

4.　(1)　If a bailee is in possession of goods which he has held as custodian, and his obligation as custodian has come to an end, the notice may be given at any time after the -ending of the obligation, or may be combined with any notice terminating his obligation as custodian.

　　(2)　This paragraph shall not apply to goods held by a person as mercantile agent, that is to say by a person having in the customary course of his business as a mercantile agent authority either to sell goods or to consign goods for the purpose of sale, or to buy goods, or to raise money on the security of goods.

Supplemental

5.　Paragraphs 2, 3 and 4 apply whether or not the bailor has paid any amount due to the bailee in respect of the goods, and whether or not the bailment is for reward, or in the course of business, or gratuitous.

PART II

NOTICE OF INTENTION TO SELL GOODS

6.   (1)   A notice under section 12(3) shall—
      (a)   specify the name and address of the bailee, and give sufficient particulars of the goods and the address or place where they are held, and
      (b)   specify the date on or after which the bailee proposes to sell the goods, and
      (c)   specify the amount, if any, which is payable by the bailor to the bailee in respect of the goods, and which became due before the giving of the notice.
      (2)   The period between giving of the notice and the date specified in the notice as that on or after which the bailee proposes to exercise the power of sale shall be such as will afford the bailor a reasonable opportunity of taking delivery of the goods.
      (3)   If any amount is payable in respect of the goods by the bailor to the bailee, and becomes due before giving of the notice, the said period shall be not less than three months.
      (4)   The notice shall be in writing and shall be sent by post in a registered letter, or by the recorded delivery service.

7.   (1)   The bailee shall not give a notice under section 12(3), or exercise his right to sell the goods pursuant to such a notice, at a time when he has notice that, because of a dispute concerning the goods, the bailor is questioning or refusing to pay all or any part of what the bailee claims to be due to him in respect of the goods.
      (2)   This paragraph shall be left out of account in determining under section 13(1) whether a bailee of goods is entitled to sell the goods under section 12, or would be so entitled if he had given any notice required in accordance with this Schedule.

UNFAIR CONTRACT TERMS ACT 1977
(1977, c. 50)

PART I

1   Scope of Part I

(1)   For the purposes of this Part of this Act, "negligence" means the breach—
      (a)   of any obligation, arising from the express or implied terms of a contract, to take reasonable care or exercise reasonable skill in the performance of the contract;
      (b)   of any common law duty to take reasonable care or exercise reasonable skill (but not any stricter duty);
      (c)   of the common duty of care imposed by the Occupiers' Liability Act 1957 or the Occupier's Liability Act (Northern Ireland) 1957.

(2)   This Part of this Act is subject to Part III; and in relation to contracts, the operation of sections 2, 3 and 7 is subject to the exceptions made by Schedule I.

(3)   In the case of both contract and tort, sections 2 to 7 apply (except where the contrary is stated in section 6(4)) only to business liability, that is liability for breach of obligations or duties arising—
      (a)   from things done or to be done by a person in the course of a business (whether his own business or another's); or
      (b)   from the occupation of premises used for business purposes of the occupier;
      and references to liability are to be read accordingly but liability of an occupier of premises for breach of an obligation or duty towards a person obtaining access to the premises for recreational or educational purposes, being liability for loss or damage suffered by reason of the dangerous state of the premises, is not a business liability of the occupier unless granting that person such access for the purposes concerned falls within the business purposes of the occupier.

(4)   In relation to any breach of duty or obligation, it is immaterial for any purpose of this Part of this Act whether the breach was inadvertent or intentional, or whether liability for it arises directly or vicariously.

2   Negligence liability

(1)   A person cannot by reference to any contract term or to a notice given to persons generally or to particular persons exclude or restrict his liability for death or personal injury resulting from negligence.

(2)   In the case of other loss or damage, a person cannot so exclude or restrict his liability for negligence except in so far as the term or notice satisfies the requirement of reasonableness.

(3)   Where a contract term or notice purports to exclude or restrict liability for negligence a person's agreement to or awareness of it is not of itself to be taken as indicating his voluntary acceptance of any risk.

(4)   This section does not apply to—
(a)   a term in a consumer contract, or
(b)   a notice to the extent that it is a consumer notice,
(but see the provision made about such contracts and notices in sections 62 and 65 of the Consumer Rights Act 2015).

3   Liability arising in contract

(1)   This section applies as between contracting parties where one of them deals on the other's written standard terms of business.

(2)   As against that party, the other cannot by reference to any contract term—
(a)   when himself in breach of contract, exclude or restrict any liability of his in respect of the breach; or
(b)   claim to be entitled—
(i)   to render a contractual performance substantially different from that which was reasonably expected of him, or
(ii)   in respect of the whole or any part of his contractual obligation, to render no performance at all,
except in so far as (in any of the cases mentioned above in this subsection) the contract term satisfies the requirement of reasonableness.

(3)   This section does not apply to a term in a consumer contract (but see the provision made about such contracts in section 62 of the Consumer Rights Act 2015).

6   Sale and hire-purchase

(1)   Liability for breach of the obligations arising from—
(a)   section 12 of the Sale of Goods Act 1979 (seller's implied undertakings as to title, etc.);
(b)   section 8 of the Supply of Goods (Implied Terms) Act 1973 (the corresponding thing in relation to hire-purchase),
cannot be excluded or restricted by reference to any contract term.

(1A)   Liability for breach of the obligations arising from—
(a)   section 13, 14 or 15 of the 1979 Act (seller's implied undertakings as to conformity of goods with description or sample, or as to their quality or fitness for a particular purpose);
(b)   section 9, 10 or 11 of the 1973 Act (the corresponding provisions in relation to hire purchase),
cannot be excluded or restricted by reference to a contract term except in so far as the term satisfies the requirement of reasonableness.

(4)   The liabilities referred to in this section are not only the business liabilities defined by section 1(3), but include those arising under any contract of sale of goods or hirepurchase agreement.

(5)   This section does not apply to a consumer contract (but see the provision made about such contracts in section 31 of the Consumer Rights Act 2015).

7   Miscellaneous contracts under which goods pass

(1)   Where the possession or ownership of goods passes under or in pursuance of a contract not governed by the law of sale of goods or hire-purchase, subsections (2) to (4) below apply as regards the effect (if any) to be given to contract terms excluding or restricting liability for breach of obligation arising by implication of law from the nature of the contract.

(1A)   Liability in respect of the goods' correspondence with description or sample, or their quality or fitness for any particular purpose, cannot be excluded or restricted by reference to such a term except in so far as the term satisfies the requirement of reasonableness.

(3A) Liability for breach of the obligations arising under section 2 of the Supply of Goods and Services Act 1982 (implied terms about title etc. in certain contracts for the transfer of the property in goods) cannot be excluded or restricted by reference to any such term.

(4) Liability in respect of—
 (a) the right to transfer ownership of the goods, or give possession; or
 (b) the assurance of quiet possession to a person taking goods in pursuance of the contract,

cannot (in a case to which subsection (3A) above does not apply) be excluded or restricted by reference to any such term except in so far as the term satisfies the requirement of reasonableness.

(4A) This section does not apply to a consumer contract (but see the provision made about such contracts in section 31 of the Consumer Rights Act 2015).

10 Evasion by means of secondary contract

A person is not bound by any contract term prejudicing or taking away rights of his which arise under, or in connection with the performance of, another contract, so far as those rights extend to the enforcement of another's liability which this Part of this Act prevents that other from excluding or restricting.

11 The "reasonableness" test

(1) In relation to a contract term, the requirement of reasonableness for the purposes of this Part of this Act, section 3 of the Misrepresentation Act 1967 and section 3 of the Misrepresentation Act (Northern Ireland) 1967 is that the term shall have been a fair and reasonable one to be included having regard to the circumstances which were, or ought reasonably to have been, known to or in the contemplation of the parties when the contract was made.

(2) In determining for the purposes of section 6 or 7 above whether a contract term satisfies the requirement of reasonableness, regard shall be had in particular to the matters specified in Schedule 2 to this Act; but this subsection does not prevent the court or arbitrator from holding, in accordance with any rule of law, that a term which purports to exclude or restrict any relevant liability is not a term of the contract.

(3) In relation to a notice (not being a notice having contractual effect), the requirement of reasonableness under this Act is that it should be fair and reasonable to allow reliance on it, having regard to all the circumstances obtaining when the liability arose or (but for the notice) would have arisen.

(4) Where by reference to a contract term or notice a person seeks to restrict liability to a specified sum of money, and the question arises (under this or any other Act) whether the term or notice satisfies the requirement of reasonableness, regard shall be had in particular (but without prejudice to subsection (2) above in the case of contract terms) to—
 (a) the resources which he could expect to be available to him for the purpose of meeting the liability should it arise; and
 (b) how far it was open to him to cover himself by insurance.

(5) It is for those claiming that a contract term or notice satisfies the requirement of reasonableness to show that it does.

13 Varieties of exemption clause

(1) To the extent that this Part of this Act prevents the exclusion or restriction of any liability it also prevents—
 (a) making the liability or its enforcement subject to restrictive or onerous conditions;
 (b) excluding or restricting any right or remedy in respect of the liability, or subjecting a person to any prejudice in consequence of his pursuing any such right or remedy;
 (c) excluding or restricting rules of evidence or procedure;

and (to that extent) sections 2 , 6 and 7 also prevent excluding or restricting liability by reference to terms and notices which exclude or restrict the relevant obligation or duty.

(2) But an agreement in writing to submit present or future differences to arbitration is not to be treated under this Part of this Act as excluding or restricting any liability.

14   Interpretation of Part I

In this Part of the Act—

"business" includes a profession and the activities of any government department or local or public authority;

"consumer contract" has the same meaning as in the Consumer Rights Act 2015 (see section 61);

"consumer notice" has the same meaning as in the Consumer Rights Act 2015 (see section 61);

"goods" has the same meaning as in the Sale of Goods Act 1979;

"hire-purchase agreement" has the same meaning as in the Consumer Credit Act 1974;

"negligence" has the meaning given by section 1(1);

"notice" includes an announcement, whether or not in writing, and any other communication or pretended communication; and

"personal injury" includes any disease and any impairment of physical or mental condition.

PART III

26   International supply contracts

(1)   The limits imposed by this Act on the extent to which a person may exclude or restrict liability by reference to a contract term do not apply to liability arising under such a contract as is described in subsection (3) below.

(2)   The terms of such a contract are not subject to any requirement of reasonableness under section 3: and nothing in Part II of this Act shall require the incorporation of the terms of such a contract to be fair and reasonable for them to have effect.

(3)   Subject to subsection (4), that description of contract is one whose characteristics are the following—

(a)   either it is a contract of sale of goods or it is one under or in pursuance of which the possession or ownership of goods passes; and

(b)   it is made by parties whose places of business (or, if they have none, habitual residences) are in the territories of different States (the Channel Islands and the Isle of Man being treated for this purpose as different States from the United Kingdom).

(4)   A contract falls within subsection (3) above only if either—

(a)   the goods in question are, at the time of the conclusion of the contract, in the course of carriage, or will be carried, from the territory of one State to the territory of another; or

(b)   the acts constituting the offer and acceptance have been done in the territories of different States; or

(c)   the contract provides for the goods to be delivered to the territory of a State other than that within whose territory those acts were done.

27   Choice of law clauses

(1)   Where the law applicable to a contract is the law of any part of the United Kingdom only by choice of the parties (and apart from that choice would be the law of some country outside the United Kingdom) sections 2 to 7 and 16 to 21 of this Act do not operate as part of the law applicable to the contract.

(2)   This Act has effect notwithstanding any contract term which applies or purports to apply the law of some country outside the United Kingdom, where—

(a)   the term appears to the court, or arbitrator or arbiter to have been imposed wholly or mainly for the purpose of enabling the party imposing it to evade the operation of this Act;

(b)   ...

29   Saving for other relevant legislation

(1)   Nothing in this Act removes or restricts the effect of, or prevents reliance upon, any contractual provision which—

(a)   is authorised or required by the express terms or necessary implication of an enactment; or

      (b)   being made with a view to compliance with an international agreement to which the United Kingdom is a party, does not operate more restrictively than is contemplated by the agreement.

   (2)   A contract term is to be taken—

      (a)   for the purposes of Part I of this Act, as satisfying the requirement of reasonableness ...

      if it is incorporated or approved by, or incorporated pursuant to a decision or ruling of, a competent authority acting in the exercise of any statutory jurisdiction or function and is not a term in a contract to which the competent authority is itself a party.

   (3)   In this section—

      "competent authority" means any court, arbitrator or arbiter, government department or public authority;

      "enactment" means any legislation (including subordinate legislation) of the United Kingdom or Northern Ireland and any instrument having effect by virtue of such legislation; and "statutory" means conferred by an enactment.

SCHEDULES

Section 1(2)   ## SCHEDULE 1

SCOPE OF SECTIONS 2, 3 AND 7

1.   Sections 2 and 3 of this Act do not extend to—

      (a)   any contract of insurance (including a contract to pay an annuity on human life);

      (b)   any contract so far as it relates to the creation or transfer of an interest in land, or to the termination of such an interest, whether by extinction, merger, surrender, forfeiture or otherwise;

      (c)   any contract so far as it relates to the creation or transfer of a right or interest in any patent, trade mark, copyright, design right, registered design, technical or commercial information or other intellectual property, or relates to the termination of any such right or interest;

      (d)   any contract so far as it relates—

         (i)   to the formation or dissolution of a company (which means any body corporate or unincorporated association and includes a partnership), or

        (ii)   to its constitution or the rights or obligations of its corporators or members;

      (e)   any contract so far as it relates to the creation or transfer of securities or of any right or interest in securities;

      (f)   anything that is governed by Article 6 of Regulation (EU) no 181/2011 of the European Parliament and of the Council of the 16th of February 2011 concerning the rights of passengers in bus and coach transport amending Regulation (EC) no 2006/2004.

2.   Section 2(1) extends to—

      (a)   any contract of marine salvage or towage;

      (b)   any charterparty of a ship or hovercraft; and

      (c)   any contract for the carriage of goods by ship or hovercraft;

    but subject to this sections 2, 3 and 7 do not extend to any such contract.

3.   Where goods are carried by ship or hovercraft in pursuance of a contract which either—

      (a)   specifies that as the means of carriage over part of the journey to be covered, or

      (b)   makes no provision as to the means of carriage and does not exclude that means,

    then sections 2(2) and 3 do not extend to the contract as it operates for and in relation to the carriage of the goods by that means.

4.   Section 2(1) and (2) do not extend to a contract of employment, except in favour of the employee.

5.   Section 2(1) does not affect the validity of any discharge and indemnity given by a person, on or in connection with an award to him of compensation for pneumoconiosis attributable to employment in the coal industry, in respect of any further claim arising from his contracting that disease.

Sections 11(2) and 24(2)   SCHEDULE 2
"GUIDELINES" FOR APPLICATION OF REASONABLENESS TEST

The matters to which regard is to be had in particular for the purposes of sections 6(1A), 7(1A) and (4), 20 and 21 are any of the following which appear to be relevant—

(a)   the strength of the bargaining positions of the parties relative to each other, taking into account (among other things) alternative means by which the customer's requirements could have been met;

(b)   whether the customer received an inducement to agree to the term, or in accepting it had an opportunity of entering into a similar contract with other persons, but without having to accept a similar term;

(c)   whether the customer knew or ought reasonably to have known of the existence and extent of the term (having regard, among other things, to any custom of the trade and any previous course of dealing between the parties);

(d)   where the term excludes or restricts any relevant liability if some condition is not complied with, whether it was reasonable at the time of the contract to expect that compliance with that condition would be practicable;

(e)   whether the goods were manufactured, processed or adapted to the special order of the customer.

CIVIL LIABILITY (CONTRIBUTION) ACT 1978
(1978, c. 47)

1   Entitlement to contribution

(1)   Subject to the following provisions of this section, any person liable in respect of any damage suffered by another person may recover contribution from any other person liable in respect of the same damage (whether jointly with him or otherwise).

(2)   A person shall be entitled to recover contribution by virtue of subsection (1) above notwithstanding that he has ceased to be liable in respect of the damage in question since the time when the damage occurred, provided that he was so liable immediately before he made or was ordered or agreed to make the payment in respect of which the contribution is sought.

(3)   A person shall be liable to make contribution by virtue of subsection (1) above notwithstanding that he has ceased to be liable in respect of the damage in question since the time when the damage occurred, unless he ceased to be liable by virtue of the expiry of a period of limitation or prescription which extinguished the right on which the claim against him in respect of the damage was based.

(4)   A person who has made or agreed to make any payment in bona fide settlement or compromise of any claim made against him in respect of any damage (including a payment into court which has been accepted) shall be entitled to recover contribution in accordance with this section without regard to whether or not he himself is or ever was liable in respect of the damage, provided, however, that he would have been liable assuming that the factual basis of the claim against him could be established.

(5)   A judgment given in any action brought in any part of the United Kingdom by or on behalf of the person who suffered the damage in question against any person from whom contribution is sought under this section shall be conclusive in the proceedings for contribution as to any issue determined by that judgment in favour of the person from whom the contribution is sought.

(6)   References in this section to a person's liability in respect of any damage are references to any such liability which has been or could be established in an action brought against him in England and Wales by or on behalf of the person who suffered the damage; but it is immaterial whether any issue arising in any such action was or would be determined (in accordance with the rules of private international law) by reference to the law of a country outside England and Wales.

2   Assessment of contribution

(1)   Subject to subsection (3) below, in any proceedings for contribution under section 1 above the amount of the contribution recoverable from any person shall be such as may be found by the court to be just and equitable having regard to the extent of that person's responsibility for the damage in question.

(2)   Subject to subsection (3) below, the court shall have power in any such proceedings to exempt any person from liability to make contribution or to direct that the contribution to be recovered from any person shall amount to a complete indemnity.

(3)   Where the amount of the damages which have or might have been awarded in respect of the damage in question in any action brought in England and Wales by or on behalf of the person who suffered it against the person from whom the contribution is sought was or would have been subject to—

     (a)   any limit imposed by or under any enactment or by any agreement made before the damage occurred;

     (b)   any reduction by virtue of section 1 of the Law Reform (Contributory Negligence) Act 1945 or section 5 of the Fatal Accidents Act 1976; or

     (c)   any corresponding limit or reduction under the law of a country outside England and Wales;

     the person from whom the contribution is sought shall not by virtue of any contribution awarded under section 1 above be required to pay in respect of the damage a greater amount than the amount of those damages as so limited or reduced.

3   Proceedings against persons jointly liable for the same debt or damage

Judgment recovered against any person liable in respect of any debt or damage shall not be a bar to an action, or to the continuance of an action, against any other person who is (apart from any such bar) jointly liable with him in respect of the same debt or damage.

4   Successive actions against persons liable (jointly or otherwise) for the same damage

If more than one action is brought in respect of any damage by or on behalf of the person by whom it was suffered against persons liable in respect of the damage (whether jointly or otherwise) the plaintiff shall not be entitled to costs in any of those actions, other than that in which judgment is first given, unless the court is of the opinion that there was reasonable ground for bringing the action.

5   Application to the Crown

Without prejudice to section 4(1) of the Crown Proceedings Act 1947 (indemnity and contribution), this Act shall bind the Crown, but nothing in this Act shall be construed as in any way affecting Her Majesty in Her private capacity (including in right of Her Duchy of Lancaster) or the Duchy of Cornwall.

6   Interpretation

(1)   A person is liable in respect of any damage for the purposes of this Act if the person who suffered it (or anyone representing his estate or dependants) is entitled to recover compensation from him in respect of that damage (whatever the legal basis of his liability, whether tort, breach of contract, breach of trust or otherwise).

(2)   References in this Act to an action brought by or on behalf of the person who suffered any damage include references to an action brought for the benefit of his estate or dependants.

(3)   In this Act "dependants" has the same meaning as in the Fatal Accidents Act 1976.

(4)   In this Act, except in section 1(5) above, "action" means an action brought in England and Wales.

7   Savings

(3)   The right to recover contribution in accordance with section 1 above supersedes any right, other than an express contractual right, to recover contribution (as distinct from

indemnity) otherwise than under this Act in corresponding circumstances; but nothing in this Act shall affect—

(a)   any express or implied contractual or other right to indemnity; or

(b)   any express contractual provision regulating or excluding contribution;

which would be enforceable apart from this Act (or render enforceable any agreement for indemnity or contribution which would not be enforceable apart from this Act).

STATE IMMUNITY ACT 1978
(1978, c. 33)

1   General immunity from jurisdiction

(1)   A State is immune from the jurisdiction of the courts of the United Kingdom except as provided in the following provisions of this Part of this Act.

(2)   A court shall give effect to the immunity conferred by this section even though the State does not appear in the proceedings in question.

3   Commercial transactions and contracts to be performed in United Kingdom

(1)   A State is not immune as respects proceedings relating to—

(a)   a commercial transaction entered into by the State; or

(b)   an obligation of the State which by virtue of a contract (whether a commercial transaction or not) falls to be performed wholly or partly in the United Kingdom.

(2)   This section does not apply if the parties to the dispute are States or have otherwise agreed in writing; and subsection (1)(b) above does not apply if the contract (not being a commercial transaction) was made in the territory of the State concerned and the obligation in question is governed by its administrative law.

5   Personal injuries and damage to property

A State is not immune as respects proceedings in respect of—

(a)   death or personal injury; or

(b)   damage to or loss of tangible property, caused by an act or omission in the United Kingdom.

PNEUMOCONIOSIS ETC. (WORKERS' COMPENSATION) ACT 1979
(1979, c. 41)

1   Lump sum payments

(1)   If, on a claim by a person who is disabled by a disease to which this Act applies, the Secretary of State is satisfied that the conditions of entitlement mentioned in section 2(1) below are fulfilled, he shall in accordance with this Act make to that person a payment of such amount as may be prescribed by regulations.

(2)   If, on a claim by the dependant of a person who, immediately before he died, was disabled by a disease to which this Act applies, the Secretary of State is satisfied that the conditions of entitlement mentioned in section 2(2) below are fulfilled, he shall in accordance with this Act make to that dependant a payment of such amount as may be so prescribed.

(3)   The diseases to which this Act applies are pneumoconiosis, byssinosis and diffuse mesothelioma and any other disease which is specified by the Secretary of State for the purpose of this Act by order made by statutory instrument.

2   Conditions of entitlement

(1)   In the case of a person who is disabled by a disease to which this Act applies, the conditions of entitlement are—

(a)   that disablement benefit is payable to him in respect of the disease or, subject to subsection (3A) below, would be payable to him in respect of it but for his disablement amounting to less than the appropriate percentage;

(b)   that every relevant employer of his has ceased to carry on business;

(ba)   that no application has been made for a payment under the Diffuse Mesothelioma Payment Scheme in respect of the disease (for the scheme, see the Mesothelioma Act 2014); and

(c)   that he has not brought any action, or compromised any claim, for damages in respect of the disablement.

(2)   In the case of the dependant of a person who, immediately before he died, was disabled by a disease to which this Act applies, the conditions of entitlement are—

     (a)   that no payment under this Act has been made to the deceased in respect of the disease;

     (b)   that disablement benefit was payable to the deceased in respect of the disease immediately before he died or, subject to subsection (3A) below, would have been so payable to him—

          (i)   but for his disablement amounting to less than the appropriate percentage; or

          (ii)   but for his not having claimed the benefit; or

          (iii)   but for his having died before he had suffered from the disease for the appropriate period;

     (c)   that every relevant employer of the deceased has ceased to carry on business;

     (ca)   that no application has been made by the deceased, or any dependant, for a payment under the Diffuse Mesothelioma Payment Scheme in respect of the disease (for the scheme, see the Mesothelioma Act 2014); and

     (d)   that neither the deceased nor his personal representatives nor any relative of his has brought any action, or compromised any claim, for damages in respect of the disablement or death.

(3A)   No amount is payable under this Act in respect of disablement amounting to less than 1 per cent.

(4)   For the purposes of this section any action which has been dismissed otherwise than on the merits (as for example for want of prosecution or under any enactment relating to the limitation of actions) shall be disregarded.

5   Reconsideration of determinations

(1)   Subject to subsection (2) below, the Secretary of State may reconsider a determination that a payment should not be made under this Act on the ground—

     (a)   that there has been a material change of circumstances since the determination was made; or

     (b)   that the determination was made in ignorance of, or was based on a mistake as to, some material fact;

and the Secretary of State may, on the ground set out in paragraph (b) above, reconsider a determination that such a payment should be made.

(4)   If, whether fraudulently or otherwise, any person misrepresents or fails to disclose any material fact and in consequence of the misrepresentation or failure a payment is made under this Act, the person to whom the payment was made shall be liable to repay the amount of that payment to the Secretary of State unless he can show that the misrepresentation or failure occurred without his connivance or consent.

SALE OF GOODS ACT 1979
(1979, c. 54)

PART I
CONTRACTS TO WHICH ACT APPLIES

1   Contracts to which Act applies

(1)   This Act applies to contracts of sale of goods made on or after (but not to those made before) 1 January 1894.

(2)   In relation to contracts made on certain dates, this Act applies subject to the modification of certain of its sections as mentioned in Schedule 1 below.

(3) Any such modification is indicated in the section concerned by a reference to Schedule 1 below.

(4) Accordingly, where a section does not contain such a reference, this Act applies in relation to the contract concerned without such modification of the section.

(5) Certain sections or subsections of this Act do not apply to a contract to which Chapter 2 of Part 1 of the Consumer Rights Act 2015 applies.

(6) Where that is the case it is indicated in the section concerned.

PART II
FORMATION OF THE CONTRACT

Contract of Sale

2 Contract of sale

(1) A contract of sale of goods is a contract by which the seller transfers or agrees to transfer the property in goods to the buyer for a money consideration, called the price.

(2) There may be a contract of sale between one part owner and another.

(3) A contract of sale may be absolute or conditional.

(4) Where under a contract of sale the property in the goods is transferred from the seller to the buyer the contract is called a sale.

(5) Where under a contract of sale the transfer of the property in the goods is to take place at a future time or subject to some condition later to be fulfilled the contract is called an agreement to sell.

(6) An agreement to sell becomes a sale when the time elapses or the conditions are fulfilled subject to which the property in the goods is to be transferred.

3 Capacity to buy and sell

(1) Capacity to buy and sell is regulated by the general law concerning capacity to contract and to transfer and acquire property.

(2) Where necessaries are sold and delivered to a minor or to a person who by reason of … drunkenness is incompetent to contract, he must pay a reasonable price for them.

(3) In subsection (2) above "necessaries" means goods suitable to the condition in life of the minor or other person concerned and to his actual requirements at the time of the sale and delivery.

4 How contract of sale is made

(1) Subject to this and any other Act, a contract of sale may be made in writing (either with or without seal), or by word of mouth, or partly in writing and partly by word of mouth, or may be implied from the conduct of the parties.

(2) Nothing in this section affects the law relating to corporations.

5 Existing or future goods

(1) The goods which form the subject of a contract of sale may be either existing goods, owned or possessed by the seller, or goods to be manufactured or acquired by him after the making of the contract of sale, in this Act called future goods.

(2) There may be a contract for the sale of goods the acquisition of which by the seller depends on a contingency which may or may not happen.

(3) Where by a contract of sale the seller purports to effect a present sale of future goods, the contract operates as an agreement to sell the goods.

6 Goods which have perished

Where there is a contract for the sale of specific goods, and the goods without the knowledge of the seller have perished at the time when the contract is made, the contract is void.

7 Goods perishing before sale but after agreement to sell

Where there is an agreement to sell specific goods and subsequently the goods, without any fault on the part of the seller or buyer, perish before the risk passes to the buyer, the agreement is avoided.

8   Ascertainment of price

(1)   The price in a contract of sale may be fixed by the contract, or may be left to be fixed in a manner agreed by the contract, or may be determined by the course of dealing between the parties.

(2)   Where the price is not determined as mentioned in subsection (1) above the buyer must pay a reasonable price.

(3)   What is a reasonable price is a question of fact dependent on the circumstances of each particular case.

9   Agreement to sell at valuation

(1)   Where there is an agreement to sell goods on the terms that the price is to be fixed by the valuation of a third party, and he cannot or does not make the valuation, the agreement is avoided; but if the goods or any part of them have been delivered to and appropriated by the buyer he must pay a reasonable price for them.

(2)   Where the third party is prevented from making the valuation by the fault of the seller or buyer, the party not at fault may maintain an action for damages against the party at fault.

Implied terms etc.

10   Stipulations about time

(1)   Unless a different intention appears from the terms of the contract, stipulations as to time of payment are not of the essence of a contract of sale.

(2)   Whether any other stipulation as to time is or is not of the essence of the contract depends on the terms of the contract.

(3)   In a contract of sale "month" prima facie means calendar month.

11   When condition to be treated as warranty

(1)   This section does not apply to Scotland.

(2)   Where a contract of sale is subject to a condition to be fulfilled by the seller, the buyer may waive the condition, or may elect to treat the breach of the condition as a breach of warranty and not as a ground for treating the contract as repudiated.

(3)   Whether a stipulation in a contract of sale is a condition, the breach of which may give rise to a right to treat the contract as repudiated, or a warranty, the breach of which may give rise to a claim for damages but not to a right to reject the goods and treat the contract as repudiated, depends in each case on the construction of the contract; and a stipulation may be a condition, though called a warranty in the contract.

(4)   Subject to section 35A below where a contract of sale is not severable and the buyer has accepted the goods or part of them, the breach of a condition to be fulfilled by the seller can only be treated as a breach of warranty, and not as a ground for rejecting the goods and treating the contract as repudiated, unless there is an express or implied term of the contract to that effect.

(4A)   Subsection (4) does not apply to a contract to which Chapter 2 of Part 1 of the Consumer Rights Act 2015 applies (but see the provision made about such contracts in sections 19 to 22 of that Act).

(6)   Nothing in this section affects a condition or warranty whose fulfilment is excused by law by reason of impossibility or otherwise.

(7)   Paragraph 2 of Schedule 1 below applies in relation to a contract made before 22 April 1967 or (in the application of this Act to Northern Ireland) 28 July 1967.

12   Implied terms about title, etc.

(1)   In a contract of sale, other than one to which subsection (3) below applies, there is an implied term on the part of the seller that in the case of a sale he has a right to sell the goods, and in the case of an agreement to sell he will have such a right at the time when the property is to pass.

(2)   In a contract of sale, other than one to which subsection (3) below applies, there is also an implied term that—

(a) the goods are free, and will remain free until the time when the property is to pass, from any charge or encumbrance not disclosed or known to the buyer before the contract is made, and

(b) the buyer will enjoy quiet possession of the goods except so far as it may be disturbed by the owner or other person entitled to the benefit of any charge or encumbrance so disclosed or known.

(3) This subsection applies to a contract of sale in the case of which there appears from the contract or is to be inferred from its circumstances an intention that the seller should transfer only such title as he or a third person may have.

(4) In a contract to which subsection (3) above applies there is an implied term that all charges or encumbrances known to the seller and not known to the buyer have been disclosed to the buyer before the contract is made.

(5) In a contract to which subsection (3) above applies there is also an implied term that none of the following will disturb the buyer's quiet possession of the goods, namely—

(a) the seller;

(b) in a case where the parties to the contract intend that the seller should transfer only such title as a third person may have, that person;

(c) anyone claiming through or under the seller or that third person otherwise than under a charge or encumbrance disclosed or known to the buyer before the contract is made.

(5A) As regards England and Wales and Northern Ireland, the term implied by subsection (1) above is a condition and the terms implied by subsections (2), (4) and (5) above are warranties.

(6) Paragraph 3 of Schedule 1 below applies in relation to a contract made before 18 May 1973.

(7) This section does not apply to a contract to which Chapter 2 of Part 1 of the Consumer Rights Act 2015 applies (but see the provision made about such contracts in section 17 of that Act).

13 Sale by description

(1) Where there is a contract for the sale of goods by description, there is an implied term that the goods will correspond with the description.

(1A) As regards England and Wales and Northern Ireland, the term implied by subsection (1) above is a condition.

(2) If the sale is by sample as well as by description it is not sufficient that the bulk of the goods corresponds with the sample if the goods do not also correspond with the description.

(3) A sale of goods is not prevented from being a sale by description by reason only that, being exposed for sale or hire, they are selected by the buyer.

(4) Paragraph 4 of Schedule 1 below applies in relation to a contract made before 18 May 1973.

(5) This section does not apply to a contract to which Chapter 2 of Part 1 of the Consumer Rights Act 2015 applies (but see the provision made about such contracts in section 11 of that Act).

14 Implied terms about quality or fitness

(1) Except as provided by this section and section 15 below and subject to any other enactment, there is no implied term about the quality or fitness for any particular purpose of goods supplied under a contract of sale.

(2) Where the seller sells goods in the course of a business, there is an implied term that the goods supplied under the contract are of satisfactory quality.

(2A) For the purposes of this Act, goods are of satisfactory quality if they meet the standard that a reasonable person would regard as satisfactory, taking account of any description of the goods, the price (if relevant) and all the other relevant circumstances.

(2B) For the purposes of this Act, the quality of goods includes their state and condition and the following (among others) are in appropriate cases aspects of the quality of goods—

(a) fitness for all the purposes for which goods of the kind in question are commonly supplied,

(b) appearance and finish,

> (c)   freedom from minor defects,
>
> (d)   safety, and
>
> (e)   durability.

(2C) The term implied by subsection (2) above does not extend to any matter making the quality of goods unsatisfactory—

> (a)   which is specifically drawn to the buyer's attention before the contract is made,
>
> (b)   where the buyer examines the goods before the contract is made, which that examination ought to reveal, or
>
> (c)   in the case of a contract for sale by sample, which would have been apparent on a reasonable examination of the sample.

(3)   Where the seller sells goods in the course of a business and the buyer, expressly or by implication, makes known—

> (a)   to the seller, or
>
> (b)   where the purchase price or part of it is payable by instalments and the goods were previously sold by a credit-broker to the seller, to that credit-broker,

any particular purpose for which the goods are being bought, there is an implied term that the goods supplied under the contract are reasonably fit for that purpose, whether or not that is a purpose for which such goods are commonly supplied, except where the circumstances show that the buyer does not rely, or that it is unreasonable for him to rely, on the skill or judgment of the seller or credit-broker.

(4)   An implied term about quality or fitness for a particular purpose may be annexed to a contract of sale by usage.

(5)   The preceding provisions of this section apply to a sale by a person who in the course of a business is acting as agent for another as they apply to a sale by a principal in the course of a business, except where that other is not selling in the course of a business and either the buyer knows that fact or reasonable steps are taken to bring it to the notice of the buyer before the contract is made.

(6)   As regards England and Wales and Northern Ireland, the terms implied by subsections (2) and (3) above are conditions.

(7)   Paragraph 5 of Schedule 1 below applies in relation to a contract made on or after 18 May 1973 and before the appointed day, and paragraph 6 in relation to one made before 18 May 1973.

(8)   In subsection (7) above and paragraph 5 of Schedule 1 below references to the appointed day are to the day appointed for the purposes of those provisions by an order of the Secretary of State made by statutory instrument.

(9)   This section does not apply to a contract to which Chapter 2 of Part 1 of the Consumer Rights Act 2015 applies (but see the provision made about such contracts in sections 9, 10 and 18 of that Act).

Sale by sample

15   Sale by sample

(1)   A contract of sale is a contract for sale by sample where there is an express or implied term to that effect in the contract.

(2)   In the case of a contract for sale by sample there is an implied term—

> (a)   that the bulk will correspond with the sample in quality;
>
> (b)   ...
>
> (c)   that the goods will be free from any defect, making their quality unsatisfactory which would not be apparent on reasonable examination of the sample.

(3)   As regards England and Wales and Northern Ireland, the term implied by subsection (2) above is a condition.

(4)   Paragraph 7 of Schedule 1 below applies in relation to a contract made before 18 May 1973.

(5)   This section does not apply to a contract to which Chapter 2 of Part 1 of the Consumer Rights Act applies (but see the provision made about such contracts in sections 13 and 18 of that Act).

Miscellaneous

15A   Modification of remedies for breach of condition in non-consumer cases

(1)   Where in the case of a contract of sale—
    (a)   the buyer would, apart from this subsection, have the right to reject goods by reason of a breach on the part of the seller of a term implied by section 13, 14 or 15 above, but
    (b)   the breach is so slight that it would be unreasonable for him to reject them,
the breach is not to be treated as a breach of condition but may be treated as a breach of warranty.

(2)   This section applies unless a contrary intention appears in, or is to be implied from, the contract.

(3)   It is for the seller to show that a breach fell within subsection (1)(b) above.

(4)   This section does not apply to Scotland.

15B   Remedies for breach of contract as respects Scotland

(1)   Where in a contract of sale the seller is in breach of any term of the contract (express or implied), the buyer shall be entitled—
    (a)   to claim damages, and
    (b)   if the breach is material, to reject any goods delivered under the contract and treat it as repudiated.

(1A)   Subsection (1) does not apply to a contract to which Chapter 2 of Part 1 of the Consumer Rights Act 2015 applies (but see the provision made about such contracts in sections 19 to 22 of that Act).

(3)   This section applies to Scotland only.

PART III
EFFECTS OF THE CONTRACT

Transfer of property as between seller and buyer

16   Goods must be ascertained

Subject to section (20A) below where there is a contract for the sale of unascertained goods no property in the goods is transferred to the buyer unless and until the goods are ascertained.

17   Property passes when intended to pass

(1)   Where there is a contract for the sale of specific or ascertained goods the property in them is transferred to the buyer at such time as the parties to the contract intend it to be transferred.

(2)   For the purpose of ascertaining the intention of the parties regard shall be had to the terms of the contract, the conduct of the parties and the circumstances of the case.

18   Rules for ascertaining intention

Unless a different intention appears, the following are rules for ascertaining the intention of the parties as to the time at which the property in the goods is to pass to the buyer.

Rule 1.—Where there is an unconditional contract for the sale of specific goods in a deliverable state the property in the goods passes to the buyer when the contract is made, and it is immaterial whether the time of payment or the time of delivery, or both, be postponed.

Rule 2.—Where there is a contract for the sale of specific goods and the seller is bound to do something to the goods for the purpose of putting them into a deliverable state, the property does not pass until the thing is done and the buyer has notice that it has been done.

Rule 3.—Where there is a contract for the sale of specific goods in a deliverable state but the seller is bound to weigh, measure, test, or do some other act or thing with reference to the goods for the purpose of ascertaining the price, the property does not pass until the act or thing is done and the buyer has notice that it has been done.

Rule 4.—When goods are delivered to the buyer on approval or on sale or return or other similar terms the property in the goods passes to the buyer—

(a)   when he signifies his approval or acceptance to the seller or does any other act adopting the transaction;

(b)   if he does not signify his approval or acceptance to the seller but retains the goods without giving notice of rejection, then, if a time has been fixed for the return of the goods, on the expiration of that time, and, if no time has been fixed, on the expiration of a reasonable time.

Rule 5.—(1) Where there is a contract for the sale of unascertained or future goods by description, and goods of that description and in a deliverable state are unconditionally appropriated to the contract, either by the seller with the assent of the buyer or by the buyer with the assent of the seller, the property in the goods then passes to the buyer; and the assent may be express or implied, and may be given either before or after the appropriation is made.

(2)   Where, in pursuance of the contract, the seller delivers the goods to the buyer or to a carrier or other bailee or custodier (whether named by the buyer or not) for the purpose of transmission to the buyer, and does not reserve the right of disposal, he is to be taken to have unconditionally appropriated the goods to the contract.

(3)   Where there is a contract for the sale of a specified quantity of unascertained goods in a deliverable state forming part of a bulk which is identified either in the contract or by subsequent agreement between the parties and the bulk is reduced to (or to less than) that quantity, then, if the buyer under that contract is the only buyer to whom goods are then due out of the bulk—

(a)   the remaining goods are to be taken as appropriated to that contract at the time when the bulk is so reduced; and

(b)   the property in those goods then passes to that buyer.

(4)   Paragraph (3) above applies also (with the necessary modifications) where a bulk is reduced to (or to less than) the aggregate of the quantities due to a single buyer under separate contracts relating to that bulk and he is the only buyer to whom goods are then due out of that bulk.

19   Reservation of right of disposal

(1)   Where there is a contract for the sale of specific goods or where goods are subsequently appropriated to the contract, the seller may, by the terms of the contract or appropriation, reserve the right of disposal of the goods until certain conditions are fulfilled; and in such a case, notwithstanding the delivery of the goods to the buyer, or to a carrier or other bailee or custodier for the purpose of transmission to the buyer, the property in the goods does not pass to the buyer until the conditions imposed by the seller are fulfilled.

(2)   Where goods are shipped, and by the bill of lading the goods are deliverable to the order of the seller or his agent, the seller is prima facie to be taken to reserve the right of disposal.

(3)   Where the seller of goods draws on the buyer for the price, and transmits the bill of exchange and bill of lading to the buyer together to secure acceptance or payment of the bill of exchange, the buyer is bound to return the bill of lading if he does not honour the bill of exchange, and if he wrongfully retains the bill of lading the property in the goods does not pass to him.

20   Passing of risk

(1)   Unless otherwise agreed, the goods remain at the sellers's risk until the property in them is transferred to the buyer, but when the property in them is transferred to the buyer the goods are at the buyer's risk whether delivery has been made or not.

(2)   But where delivery has been delayed through the fault of either buyer or seller the goods are at the risk of the party at fault as regards any loss which might not have occurred but for such fault.

(3)   Nothing in this section affects the duties or liabilities of either seller or buyer as a bailee or custodier of the goods of the other party.

(4)   This section does not apply to a contract to which Chapter 2 of Part 1 of the Consumer Rights Act 2015 applies (but see the provision made about such contracts in section 29 of that Act).

20A Undivided shares in goods forming part of a bulk

(1) This section applies to a contract for the sale of a specified quantity of unascertained goods if the following conditions are met—
  (a) the goods or some of them form part of a bulk which is identified either in the contract or by subsequent agreement between the parties; and
  (b) the buyer has paid the price for some or all of the goods which are the subject of the contract and which form part of the bulk.

(2) Where this section applies, then (unless the parties agree otherwise), as soon as the conditions specified in paragraphs (a) and (b) of subsection (1) above are met or at such later time as the parties may agree—
  (a) property in an undivided share in the bulk is transferred to the buyer; and
  (b) the buyer becomes an owner in common of the bulk.

(3) Subject to subsection (4) below, for the purposes of this section, the undivided share of a buyer in a bulk at any time shall be such share as the quantity of goods paid for and due to the buyer out of the bulk bears to the quantity of goods in the bulk at that time.

(4) Where the aggregate of the undivided shares of buyers in a bulk determined under subsection (3) above would at any time exceed the whole of the bulk at that time, the undivided share in the bulk of each buyer shall be reduced proportionately so that the aggregate of the undivided shares is equal to the whole bulk.

(5) Where a buyer has paid the price for only some of the goods due to him out of a bulk, any delivery to the buyer out of the bulk shall, for the purposes of this section, be ascribed in the first place to the goods in respect of which payment has been made.

(6) For the purpose of this section payment of part of the price for any goods shall be treated as payment for a corresponding part of the goods.

20B Deemed consent by co-owner to dealings in bulk goods

(1) A person who has become an owner in common of a bulk by virtue of section 20A above shall be deemed to have consented to—
  (a) any delivery of goods out of the bulk to any other owner in common of the bulk, being goods which are due to him under his contract;
  (b) any removal, dealing with, delivery or disposal of goods in the bulk by any other person who is an owner in common of the bulk in so far as the goods fall within that co-owner's undivided share in the bulk at the time of the removal, dealing, delivery or disposal.

(2) No cause of action shall accrue to anyone against a person by reason of that person having acted in accordance with paragraph (a) or (b) of subsection (1) above in reliance on any consent deemed to have been given under that subsection.

(3) Nothing in this section or section 20A above shall—
  (a) impose an obligation on a buyer of goods out of a bulk to compensate any other buyer of goods out of that bulk for any shortfall in the goods received by that other buyer;
  (b) affect any contractual arrangement between buyers of goods out of a bulk for adjustments between themselves; or
  (c) affect the rights of any buyer under his contract.

Transfer of title

21 Sale by person not the owner

(1) Subject to this Act, where goods are sold by a person who is not their owner, and who does not sell them under the authority or with the consent of the owner, the buyer acquires no better title to the goods than the seller had, unless the owner of the goods is by his conduct precluded from denying the seller's authority to sell.

(2) Nothing in this Act affects—
  (a) the provisions of the Factors Acts or any enactment enabling the apparent owner of goods to dispose of them as if he were their true owner;
  (b) the validity of any contract of sale under any special common law or statutory power of sale or under the order of a court of competent jurisdiction.

22　Market overt

(2)　This section does not apply to Scotland.

(3)　Paragraph 8 of Schedule 1 below applies in relation to a contract under which goods were sold before 1 January 1968 or (in the application of this Act to Northern Ireland) 29 August 1967.

23　Sale under voidable title

When the seller of goods has a voidable title to them, but his title has not been avoided at the time of the sale, the buyer acquires a good title to the goods, provided he buys them in good faith and without notice of the seller's defect of title.

24　Seller in possession after sale

Where a person having sold goods continues or is in possession of the goods, or of the documents of title to the goods, the delivery or transfer by that person, or by a mercantile agent acting for him, of the goods or documents of title under any sale, pledge, or other disposition thereof, to any person receiving the same in good faith and without notice of the previous sale, has the same effect as if the person making the delivery or transfer were expressly authorised by the owner of the goods to make the same.

25　Buyer in possession after sale

(1)　Where a person having bought or agreed to buy goods obtains, with the consent of the seller, possession of the goods or the documents of title to the goods, the delivery or transfer by that person, or by a mercantile agent acting for him, of the goods or documents of title, under any sale, pledge, or other disposition thereof, to any person receiving the same in good faith and without notice of any lien or other right of the original seller in respect of the goods, has the same effect as if the person making the delivery or transfer were a mercantile agent in possession of the goods or documents of title with the consent of the owner.

(2)　For the purposes of subsection (1) above—

(a)　the buyer under a conditional sale agreement is to be taken not to be a person who has bought or agreed to buy goods, and

(b)　"conditional sale agreement" means an agreement for the sale of goods which is a consumer credit agreement within the meaning of the Consumer Credit Act 1974 under which the purchase price or part of it is payable by instalments, and the property in the goods is to remain in the seller (notwithstanding that the buyer is to be in possession of the goods) until such conditions as to the payment of instalments or otherwise as may be specified in the agreement are fulfilled.

(3)　Paragraph 9 of Schedule 1 below applies in relation to a contract under which a person buys or agrees to buy goods and which is made before the appointed day.

(4)　In subsection (3) above and paragraph 9 of Schedule 1 below references to the appointed day are to the day appointed for the purposes of those provisions by an order of the Secretary of State made by statutory instrument.

26　Supplementary to sections 24 and 25

In sections 24 and 25 above "mercantile agent" means a mercantile agent having in the customary course of his business as such agent authority either—

(a)　to sell goods, or

(b)　to consign goods for the purpose of sale, or

(c)　to buy goods, or

(d)　to raise money on the security of goods.

PART IV
PERFORMANCE OF THE CONTRACT

27　Duties of seller and buyer

It is the duty of the seller to deliver the goods, and of the buyer to accept and pay for them, in accordance with the terms of the contract of sale.

28   Payment and delivery are concurrent conditions

Unless otherwise agreed, delivery of the goods and payment of the price are concurrent conditions, that is to say, the seller must be ready and willing to give possession of the goods to the buyer in exchange for the price and the buyer must be ready and willing to pay the price in exchange for possession of the goods.

29   Rules about delivery

(1)   Whether it is for the buyer to take possession of the goods or for the seller to send them to the buyer is a question depending in each case on the contract, express or implied, between the parties.

(2)   Apart from any such contract, express or implied, the place of delivery is the seller's place of business if he has one, and if not, his residence; except that, if the contract is for the sale of specific goods, which to the knowledge of the parties when the contract is made are in some other place, then that place is the place of delivery.

(3)   Where under the contract of sale the seller is bound to send the goods to the buyer, but no time for sending them is fixed, the seller is bound to send them within a reasonable time.

(3A)   Subsection (3) does not apply to a contract to which Chapter 2 of Part 1 of the Consumer Rights Act 2015 applies (but see the provision about such contracts made in section 28 of that Act).

(4)   Where the goods at the time of sale are in the possession of a third person, there is no delivery by seller to buyer unless and until the third person acknowledges to the buyer that he holds the goods on his behalf; but nothing in this section affects the operation of the issue or transfer of any document of title to goods.

(5)   Demand or tender of delivery may be treated as ineffectual unless made at a reasonable hour; and what is a reasonable hour is a question of fact.

(6)   Unless otherwise agreed, the expenses of and incidental to putting the goods into a deliverable state must be borne by the seller.

30   Delivery of wrong quantity

(1)   Where the seller delivers to the buyer a quantity of goods less than he contracted to sell, the buyer may reject them, but if the buyer accepts the goods so delivered he must pay for them at the contract rate.

(2)   Where the seller delivers to the buyer a quantity of goods larger than he contracted to sell, the buyer may accept the goods included in the contract and reject the rest, or he may reject the whole.

(2A)   A buyer may not—

(a)   where the seller delivers a quantity of goods less than he contracted to sell, reject the goods under subsection (1) above, or

(b)   where the seller delivers a quantity of goods larger than he contracted to sell, reject the whole under subsection (2) above,

if the shortfall or, as the case may be, excess is so slight that it would be unreasonable for him to do so.

(2B)   It is for the seller to show that a shortfall or excess fell within subsection (2A) above.

(2C)   Subsections (2A) and (2B) above do not apply to Scotland.

(3)   Where the seller delivers to the buyer a quantity of goods larger than he contracted to sell and the buyer accepts the whole of the goods so delivered he must pay for them at the contract rate.

(5)   This section is subject to any usage of trade, special agreement, or course of dealing between the parties.

(6)   This section does not apply to a contract to which Chapter 2 of Part 1 of the Consumer Rights Act 2015 applies (but see the provision made about such contracts in section 25 of that Act).

31   Instalment deliveries

(1)   Unless otherwise agreed, the buyer of goods is not bound to accept delivery of them by instalments.

(2)   Where there is a contract for the sale of goods to be delivered by stated instalments, which are to be separately paid for, and the seller makes defective deliveries in respect of one or more instalments, or the buyer neglects or refuses to take delivery of or pay

for one or more instalments, it is a question in each case depending on the terms of the contract and the circumstances of the case whether the breach of contract is a repudiation of the whole contract or whether it is a severable breach giving rise to a claim for compensation but not to a right to treat the whole contract as repudiated.

(3)   This section does not apply to a contract to which Chapter 2 of Part 1 of the Consumer Rights Act 2015 applies (but see the provision made about such contracts in section 26 of that Act).

32   Delivery to carrier

(1)   Where, in pursuance of a contract of sale, the seller is authorised or required to send the goods to the buyer, delivery of the goods to a carrier (whether named by the buyer or not) for the purpose of transmission to the buyer is prima facie deemed to be delivery of the goods to the buyer.

(2)   Unless otherwise authorised by the buyer, the seller must make such contract with the carrier on behalf of the buyer as may be reasonable having regard to the nature of the goods and the other circumstances of the case; and if the seller omits to do so, and the goods are lost or damaged in course of transit, the buyer may decline to treat the delivery to the carrier as a delivery to himself or may hold the seller responsible in damages.

(3)   Unless otherwise agreed, where goods are sent by the seller to the buyer by a route involving sea transit, under circumstances in which it is usual to insure, the seller must give such notice to the buyer as may enable him to insure them during their sea transit, and if the seller fails to do so, the goods are at his risk during such sea transit.

(4)   This section does not apply to a contract to which Chapter 2 of Part 1 of the Consumer Rights Act 2015 applies (but see the provision made about such contracts in section 29 of that Act).

33   Risk where goods are delivered at distant place

(1)   Where the seller of goods agrees to deliver them at his own risk at a place other than that where they are when sold, the buyer must nevertheless (unless otherwise agreed) take any risk of deterioration in the goods necessarily incident to the course of transit.

(2)   This section does not apply to a contract to which Chapter 2 of Part 1 of the Consumer Rights Act 2015 applies (but see the provision made about such contracts in section 29 of that Act).

34   Buyer's right of examining the goods

(1)   Unless otherwise agreed, when the seller tenders delivery of goods to the buyer, he is bound on request to afford the buyer a reasonable opportunity of examining the goods for the purpose of ascertaining whether they are in conformity with the contract and, in the case of a contract for sale by sample, of comparing the bulk with the sample .

(2)   Nothing in this section affects the operation of section 22 (time limit for short-term right to reject) of the Consumer Rights Act 2015.

35   Acceptance

(1)   The buyer is deemed to have accepted the goods subject to subsection (2) below—
    (a)   when he intimates to the seller that he has accepted them, or
    (b)   when the goods have been delivered to him and he does any act in relation to them which is inconsistent with the ownership of the seller.

(2)   Where goods are delivered to the buyer, and he has not previously examined them, he is not deemed to have accepted them under subsection (1) above until he has had areasonable opportunity of examining them for the purpose—
    (a)   of ascertaining whether they are in conformity with the contract, and
    (b)   in the case of a contract for sale by sample, of comparing the bulk with the sample.

(4)   The buyer is also deemed to have accepted the goods when after the lapse of a reasonable time he retains the goods without intimating to the seller that he has rejected them.

(5)   The questions that are material in determining for the purposes of subsection (4) above whether a reasonable time has elapsed include whether the buyer has had a reasonable opportunity of examining the goods for the purpose mentioned in subsection (1) above.

(6) The buyer is not by virtue of this section deemed to have accepted the goods merely because—
    (a)   he asks for, or agrees to, their repair by or under an arrangement with the seller, or
    (b)   the goods are delivered to another under a sub-sale or other disposition.
(7) Where the contract is for the sale of goods making one or more commercial units, a buyer accepting any goods included in a unit is deemed to have accepted all the goods making the unit; and in this subsection "commercial unit" means a unit division of which would materially impair the value of the goods or the character of the unit.
(8) Paragraph 10 of Schedule 1 below applies in relation to a contract made before 22 April 1967 or (in the application of this Act to Northern Ireland) 28 July 1967.
(9) This section does not apply to a contract to which Chapter 2 of Part 1 of the Consumer Rights Act 2015 applies (but see the provision made about such contracts in section 21 of that Act).

35A Right of partial rejection

(1) If the buyer—
    (a)   has the right to reject the goods by reason of a breach on the part of the seller that affects some or all of them, but
    (b)   accepts some of the goods, including, where there are any goods unaffected by the breach, all such goods,
he does not by accepting them lose his right to reject the rest.
(2) In the case of a buyer having the right to reject an instalment of goods, subsection (1) above applies as if references to the goods were references to the goods comprised in the instalment.
(3) For the purposes of subsection (1) above, goods are affected by a breach if by reason of the breach they are not in conformity with the contract.
(4) This section applies unless a contrary intention appears in, or is to be implied from, the contract.
(5) This section does not apply to a contract to which Chapter 2 of Part 1 of the Consumer Rights Act 2015 applies (but see the provision made about such contracts in section 21 of that Act).

36 Buyer not bound to return rejected goods

(1) Unless otherwise agreed, where goods are delivered to the buyer, and he refuses to accept them, having the right to do so, he is not bound to return them to the seller, but it is sufficient if he intimates to the seller that he refuses to accept them.
(2) This section does not apply to a contract to which Chapter 2 of Part 1 of the Consumer Rights Act 2015 applies (but see the provision made about such contracts in section 20 of that Act).

37 Buyer's liability for not taking delivery of goods

(1) When the seller is ready and willing to deliver the goods, and requests the buyer to take delivery, and the buyer does not within a reasonable time after such request take delivery of the goods, he is liable to the seller for any loss occasioned by his neglect or refusal to take delivery, and also for a reasonable charge for the care and custody of the goods.
(2) Nothing in this section affects the rights of the seller where the neglect or refusal of the buyer to take delivery amounts to a repudiation of the contract.

PART V
RIGHTS OF UNPAID SELLER AGAINST THE GOODS

Preliminary

38 Unpaid seller defined

(1) The seller of goods is an unpaid seller within the meaning of this Act—
    (a)   when the whole of the price has not been paid or tendered;
    (b)   when a bill of exchange or other negotiable instrument has been received as conditional payment, and the condition on which it was received has not been fulfilled by reason of the dishonour of the instrument or otherwise.

(2)   In this Part of this Act "seller" includes any person who is in the position of a seller, as, for instance, an agent of the seller to whom the bill of lading has been indorsed, or a consignor or agent who has himself paid (or is directly responsible for) the price.

39   Unpaid seller's rights

(1)   Subject to this and any other Act, notwithstanding that the property in the goods may have passed to the buyer, the unpaid seller of goods, as such, has by implication of law—
   (a)   a lien on the goods or right to retain them for the price while he is in possession of them;
   (b)   in the case of the insolvency of the buyer, a right of stopping the goods in transit after he has parted with the possession of them; (c) a right of re-sale as limited by this Act.
(2)   Where the property in goods has not passed to the buyer, the unpaid seller has (in addition to his other remedies) a right of withholding delivery similar to and coextensive with his rights of lien or retention and stoppage in transit where the property has passed to the buyer.

Unpaid seller's lien

41   Seller's lien

(1)   Subject to this Act, the unpaid seller of goods who is in possession of them is entitled to retain possession of them until payment or tender of the price in the following cases:—
   (a)   where the goods have been sold without any stipulation as to credit;
   (b)   where the goods have been sold on credit but the term of credit has expired;
   (c)   where the buyer becomes insolvent.
(2)   The seller may exercise his lien or right of retention notwithstanding that he is in possession of the goods as agent or bailee or custodier for the buyer.

42   Part delivery

Where an unpaid seller has made part delivery of the goods, he may exercise his lien or right of retention on the remainder, unless such part delivery has been made under such circumstances as to show an agreement to waive the lien or right of retention.

43   Termination of lien

(1)   The unpaid seller of goods loses his lien or right of retention in respect of them—
   (a)   when he delivers the goods to a carrier or other bailee or custodier for the purpose of transmission to the buyer without reserving the right of disposal of the goods;
   (b)   when the buyer or his agent lawfully obtains possession of the goods;
   (c)   by waiver of the lien or right of retention.
(2)   An unpaid seller of goods who has a lien or right of retention in respect of them does not lose his lien or right of retention by reason only that he has obtained judgment or decree for the price of the goods.

Stoppage in transit

44   Right of stoppage in transit

Subject to this Act, when the buyer of goods becomes insolvent the unpaid seller who has parted with the possession of the goods has the right of stopping them in transit, that is to say, he may resume possession of the goods as long as they are in course of transit, and may retain them until payment or tender of the price.

45   Duration of transit

(1)   Goods are deemed to be in course of transit from the time when they are delivered to a carrier or other bailee or custodier for the purpose of transmission to the buyer, until the buyer or his agent in that behalf takes delivery of them from the carrier or other bailee or custodier.

(2) If the buyer or his agent in that behalf obtains delivery of the goods before their arrival at the appointed destination, the transit is at an end.

(3) If, after the arrival of the goods at the appointed destination, the carrier or other bailee or custodier acknowledges to the buyer or his agent that he holds the goods on his behalf and continues in possession of them as bailee or custodier for the buyer or his agent, the transit is at an end, and it is immaterial that a further destination for the goods may have been indicated by the buyer.

(4) If the goods are rejected by the buyer, and the carrier or other bailee or custodier continues in possession of them, the transit is not deemed to be at an end, even if the seller has refused to receive them back.

(5) When goods are delivered to a ship chartered by the buyer it is a question depending on the circumstances of the particular case whether they are in the possession of the master as a carrier or as agent to the buyer.

(6) Where the carrier or other bailee or custodier wrongfully refuses to deliver the goods to the buyer or his agent in that behalf, the transit is deemed to be at an end.

(7) Where part delivery of the goods has been made to the buyer or his agent in that behalf, the remainder of the goods may be stopped in transit, unless such part delivery has been made under such circumstances as to show an agreement to give up possession of the whole of the goods.

46   How stoppage in transit is effected

(1) The unpaid seller may exercise his right of stoppage in transit either by taking actual possession of the goods or by giving notice of his claim to the carrier or other bailee or custodier in whose possession the goods are.

(2) The notice may be given either to the person in actual possession of the goods or to his principal.

(3) If given to the principal, the notice is ineffective unless given at such time and under such circumstances that the principal, by the exercise of reasonable diligence, may communicate it to his servant or agent in time to prevent a delivery to the buyer.

(4) When notice of stoppage in transit is given by the seller to the carrier or other bailee or custodier in possession of the goods, he must re-deliver the goods to, or according to the directions of, the seller; and the expenses of the re-delivery must be borne by the seller.

Resale etc. by buyer

47   Effect of sub-sale etc. by buyer

(1) Subject to this Act, the unpaid seller's right of lien or retention or stoppage in transit is not affected by any sale or other disposition of the goods which the buyer may have made, unless the seller has assented to it.

(2) Where a document of title to goods has been lawfully transferred to any person as buyer or owner of the goods, and that person transfers the document to a person who takes it in good faith and for valuable consideration, then—

   (a) if the last-mentioned transfer was by way of sale the unpaid seller's right of lien or retention or stoppage in transit is defeated; and

   (b) if the last-mentioned transfer was made by way of pledge or other disposition for value, the unpaid seller's right of lien or retention of stoppage in transit can only be exercised subject to the rights of the transferee.

Rescission: and re-sale by seller

48   Rescission: and re-sale by seller

(1) Subject to this section, a contract of sale is not rescinded by the mere exercise by an unpaid seller of his right of lien or retention or stoppage in transit.

(2) Where an unpaid seller who has exercised his right of lien or retention or stoppage in transit re-sells the goods, the buyer acquires a good title to them as against the original buyer.

(3)   Where the goods are of a perishable nature, or where the unpaid seller gives notice to the buyer of his intention to re-sell, and the buyer does not within a reasonable time pay or tender the price, the unpaid seller may re-sell the goods and recover from the original buyer damages for any loss occasioned by his breach of contract.

(4)   Where the seller expressly reserves the right of re-sale in case the buyer should make default, and on the buyer making default re-sells the goods, the original contract of sale is rescinded but without prejudice to any claim the seller may have for damages.

PART VI
ACTIONS FOR BREACH OF THE CONTRACT
Seller's remedies

49   Action for price

(1)   Where, under a contract of sale, the property in the goods has passed to the buyer and he wrongfully neglects or refuses to pay for the goods according to the terms of the contract, the seller may maintain an action against him for the price of the goods.

50   Damages for non-acceptance

(1)   Where the buyer wrongfully neglects or refuses to accept and pay for the goods, the seller may maintain an action against him for damages for non-acceptance.

(2)   The measure of damages is the estimated loss directly and naturally resulting, in the ordinary course of events, from the buyer's breach of contract.

(3)   Where there is an available market for the goods in question the measure of damages is prima facie to be ascertained by the difference between the contract price and the market or current price at the time or times when the goods ought to have been accepted or (if no time was fixed for acceptance) at the time of the refusal to accept.

51   Damages for non-delivery

(1)   Where the seller wrongfully neglects or refuses to deliver the goods to the buyer, the buyer may maintain an action against the seller for damages for non-delivery.

(2)   The measure of damages is the estimated loss directly and naturally resulting, in the ordinary course of events, from the seller's breach of contract.

(3)   Where there is an available market for the goods in question the measure of damages is prima facie to be ascertained by the difference between the contract price and the market or current price of the goods at the time or times when they ought to have been delivered or (if no time was fixed) at the time of the refusal to deliver.

(4)   This section does not apply to a contract to which Chapter 2 of Part 1 of the Consumer Rights Act 2015 applies (but see the provision made about such contracts in section 19 of that Act).

52   Specific performance

(1)   In any action for breach of contract to deliver specific or ascertained goods the court may, if it thinks fit, on the plaintiff's application, by its judgment or decree direct that the contract shall be performed specifically, without giving the defendant the option of retaining the goods on payment of damages.

(3)   The judgment or decree may be unconditional, or on such terms and conditions as to damages, payment of the price and otherwise as seem just to the court.

(5)   This section does not apply to a contract to which Chapter 2 of Part 1 of the Consumer Rights Act 2015 applies (but see the provision made about such contracts in section 19 of that Act).

53   Remedy for breach of warranty

(1)   Where there is a breach of warranty by the seller, or where the buyer elects (or is compelled) to treat any breach of a condition on the part of the seller as a breach of warranty, the buyer is not by reason only of such breach of warranty entitled to reject the goods; but he may—

(a) set up against the seller the breach of warranty in diminution or extinction of the price, or

(b) maintain an action against the seller for damages for the breach of warranty.

(2) The measure of damages for breach of warranty is the estimated loss directly and naturally resulting, in the ordinary course of events, from the breach of warranty.

(3) In the case of breach of warranty of quality such loss is prima facie the difference between the value of the goods at the time of delivery to the buyer and the value they would have had if they had fulfilled the warranty.

(4) The fact that the buyer has set up the breach of warranty in diminution or extinction of the price does not prevent him from maintaining an action for the same breach of warranty if he has suffered further damage.

(4A) This section does not apply to a contract to which Chapter 2 of Part 1 of the Consumer Rights Act 2015 applies (but see the provision made about such contracts in section 19 of that Act).

(5) This section does not apply to Scotland.

53A Measure of damages as respects Scotland

(1) The measure of damages for the seller's breach of contract is the estimated loss directly and naturally resulting, in the ordinary course of events, from the breach.

(2) Where the seller's breach consists of the delivery of goods which are not of the quality required by the contract and the buyer retains the goods, such loss as aforesaid is prima facie the difference between the value of the goods at the time of delivery to the buyer and the value they would have had if they had fulfilled the contract.

(2A) This section does not apply to a contract to which Chapter 2 of Part 1 of the Consumer Rights Act 2015 applies (but see the provision made about such contracts in section 19 of that Act).

(3) This section applies to Scotland only.

54 Interest, etc.

(1) Nothing in this Act affects the right of the buyer or the seller to recover interest or special damages in any case where by law interest or special damages may be recoverable, or to recover money paid where the consideration for the payment of it has failed.

(2) This section does not apply to a contract to which Chapter 2 of Part 1 of the Consumer Rights Act 2015 applies (but see the provision made about such contracts in section 19 of that Act).

PART VII
SUPPLEMENTARY

55 Exclusion of implied terms

(1) Where a right, duty or liability would arise under a contract of sale of goods by implication of law, it may (subject to the Unfair Contract Terms Act 1977) be negatived or varied by express agreement, or by the course of dealing between the parties, or by such usage as binds both parties to the contract.

(1A) Subsection (1) does not apply to a contract to which Chapter 2 of Part 1 of the Consumer Rights Act 2015 applies (but see the provision made about such contracts in section 31 of that Act).

(2) An express term does not negative a term implied by this Act unless inconsistent with it.

(3) Paragraph 11 of Schedule 1 below applies in relation to a contract made on or after 18 May 1973 and before 1 February 1978, and paragraph 12 in relation to one made before 18 May 1973.

56 Conflict of laws

Paragraph 13 of Schedule 1 below applies in relation to a contract made on or after 18 May 1973 and before 1 February 1978, so as to make provision about conflict of laws in relation to such a contract.

57   Auction sales

(1)   Where goods are put up for sale by auction in lots, each lot is prima facie deemed to be the subject of a separate contract of sale.

(2)   A sale by auction is complete when the auctioneer announces its completion by the fall of the hammer, or in other customary manner; and until the announcement is made any bidder may retract his bid.

(3)   A sale by auction may be notified to be subject to a reserve or upset price, and a right to bid may also be reserved expressly by or on behalf of the seller.

(4)   Where a sale by auction is not notified to be subject to a right to bid by or on behalf of the seller, it is not lawful for the seller to bid himself or to employ any person to bid at the sale, or for the auctioneer knowingly to take any bid from the seller or any such person.

(5)   A sale contravening subsection (4) above may be treated as fraudulent by the buyer.

(6)   Where, in respect of a sale by auction, a right to bid is expressly reserved (but not otherwise) the seller or any one person on his behalf may bid at the auction.

58   Payment into court in Scotland

(1)   In Scotland where a buyer has elected to accept goods which he might have rejected, and to treat a breach of contract as only giving rise to a claim for damages, he may, in an action by the seller for the price, be required, in the discretion of the court before which the action depends, to consign or pay into court the price of the goods, or part of the price, or to give other reasonable security for its due payment.

(2)   This section does not apply to a contract to which Chapter 2 of Part 1 of the Consumer Rights Act 2015 applies (but see the provision made about such contracts in section 27 of that Act).

59   Reasonable time a question of fact

Where a reference is made in this Act to a reasonable time the question what is a reasonable time is a question of fact.

60   Rights etc. enforceable by action

Where a right, duty or liability is declared by this Act, it may (unless otherwise provided by this Act) be enforced by action.

61   Interpretation

(1)   In this Act, unless the context or subject matter otherwise requires,—

"action" includes counterclaim and set-off, and in Scotland condescendence and claim and compensation; "bulk" means a mass or collection of goods of the same kind which—

(a)   is contained in a defined space or area; and

(b)   is such that any goods in the bulk are interchangeable with any other goods therein of the same number or quantity;

"business" includes a profession and the activities of any government department including a Northern Ireland department) or local or public authority;

"buyer" means a person who buys or agrees to buy goods;

"contract of sale" includes an agreement to sell as well as a sale;

"credit-broker" means a person acting in the course of a business of credit brokerage carried on by him, that is a business of effecting introductions of individuals desiring to obtain credit—

(a)   to persons carrying on any business so far as it relates to the provision of credit, or

(b)   to other persons engaged in credit brokerage;

"defendant" includes in Scotland defender, respondent, and claimant in a multiplepoinding;

"delivery" means voluntary transfer of possession from one person to another; except that in relation to sections 20A and 20B above it includes such appropriation of goods to the contract as results in property in the goods being transferred to the buyer;

"document of title to goods" has the same meaning as it has in the Factors Acts;

"Factors Acts" means the Factors Act 1889, the Factors (Scotland) Act 1890, and any enactment amending or substituted for the same;

"fault" means wrongful act or default;

"future goods" means goods to be manufactured or acquired by the seller after the making of the contract of sale;

"goods" includes all personal chattels other than things in action and money, and in Scotland all corporeal moveables except money; and in particular "goods" includes emblements, industrial growing crops, and things attached to or forming part of the land which are agreed to be severed before sale or under the contract of sale; and includes an undivided share in goods;

"plaintiff" includes pursuer, complainer, claimant in a multiplepoinding and defendant or defender counter-claiming;

"property" means the general property in goods, and not merely a special property;

"sale" includes a bargain and sale as well as a sale and delivery;

"seller" means a person who sells or agrees to sell goods;

"specific goods" means goods identified and agreed on at the time a contract of sale is made; and includes an undivided share, specified as a fraction or percentage, of goods identified and agreed on as aforesaid

"warranty" (as regards England and Wales and Northern Ireland) means an agreement with reference to goods which are the subject of a contract of sale, but collateral to the main purpose of such contract, the breach of which gives rise to a claim for damages, but not to a right to reject the goods and treat the contract as repudiated.

(3) A thing is deemed to be done in good faith within the meaning of this Act when it is in fact done honestly, whether it is done negligently or not.

(4) A person is deemed to be insolvent within the meaning of this Act if he has either ceased to pay his debts in the ordinary course of business or he cannot pay his debts as they become due, ...

(5) Goods are in a deliverable state within the meaning of this Act when they are in such a state that the buyer would under the contract be bound to take delivery of them.

(6) As regards the definition of "business" in subsection (1) above, paragraph 14 of Schedule 1 below applies in relation to a contract made on or after 18 May 1973 and before 1 February 1978, and paragraph 15 in relation to one made before 18 May 1973.

62 Savings: rule of law etc.

(1) The rules in bankruptcy relating to contracts of sale apply to those contracts, notwithstanding anything in this Act.

(2) The rules of the common law, including the law merchant, except in so far as they are inconsistent with the provisions of legislation including this Act and the Consumer Rights Act 2015, and in particular the rules relating to the law of principal and agent and the effect of fraud, misrepresentation, duress or coercion, mistake, or other invalidating cause, apply to contracts for the sale of goods.

(3) Nothing in this Act or the Sale of Goods Act 1893 affects the enactments relating to bills of sale, or any enactment relating to the sale of goods which is not expressly repealed or amended by this Act or that.

(4) The provisions of this Act about contracts of sale do not apply to a transaction in the form of a contract of sale which is intended to operate by way of mortgage, pledge, charge, or other security.

(5) Nothing in this Act prejudices or affects the landlord's right of hypothec ... in Scotland.

64 Short title and commencement

(1) This Act may be cited as the Sale of Goods Act 1979.

(2) This act comes into force on 1 January 1980.

VACCINE DAMAGE PAYMENTS ACT 1979
(1979, c. 17)

1   **Payments to persons severely disabled by vaccination**

(1)   If, on consideration of a claim, the Secretary of State is satisfied—

     (a)   that a person is, or was immediately before his death, severely disabled as a result of vaccination against any of the diseases to which this Act applies; and

     (b)   that the conditions of entitlement which are applicable in accordance with section 2 below are fulfilled,

   he shall in accordance with this Act make a payment of the relevant statutory sum to or for the benefit of that person or to his personal representatives.

(1A)   In subsection (1) above "statutory sum" means £30,000 or such other sum as is specified by the Secretary of State for the purposes of this Act by order made by statutory instrument with the consent of the Treasury; and the relevant statutory sum for the purposes of that subsection is the statutory sum at the time when a claim for payment is first made.

(2)   The diseases to which this Act applies are—

     (a)   diphtheria,

     (b)   tetanus,

     (c)   whooping cough,

     (d)   poliomyelitis,

     (e)   measles,

     (f)   rubella,

     (g)   tuberculosis,

     (h)   smallpox, and

     (i)   any other disease which is specified by the Secretary of State for the purposes of this Act by order made by statutory instrument.

(3)   Subject to section 2(3) below, this Act has effect with respect to a person who is severely disabled as a result of a vaccination given to his mother before he was born as if the vaccination had been given directly to him and, in such circumstances as may be prescribed by regulations under this Act, this Act has effect with respect to a person who is severely disabled as a result of contracting a disease through contact with a third person who was vaccinated against it as if the vaccination had been given to him and the disablement resulted from it.

2   **Conditions of entitlement**

(1)   Subject to the provisions of this section, the conditions of entitlement referred to in section 1(1)(b) above are—

     (a)   that the vaccination in question was carried out—

         (i)   in the United Kingdom or the Isle of Man, and

         (ii)   on or after 5 July 1948, and

         (iii)   in the case of vaccination against smallpox, before 1st August 1971;

     (b)   except in the case of vaccination against poliomyelitis or rubella, that the vaccination was carried out either at a time when the person to whom it was given was under the age of eighteen or at the time of an outbreak within the United Kingdom or the Isle of Man of the disease against which the vaccination was given; and

     (c)   that the disabled person was over the age of two on the date when the claim was made or, if he died before that date, that he died after 9th May 1978 and was over the age of two when he died.

3   **Determination of claims**

(1)   Any reference in this Act, other than section 7, to a claim is a reference to a claim for a payment under section 1(1) above which is made—

     (a)   by or on behalf of the disabled person concerned or, as the case may be, by his personal representatives; and

     (b)   in the manner prescribed by regulations under this Act; and

     (c)   on or before whichever is the later of—

    (i)   the date on which the disabled person attains the age of 21, or where he has died, the date on which he would have attained 21; and

    (ii)   the end of the period of six years beginning with the date of the vaccination to which the claim relates; ...

6 Payments to or for the benefit of disabled persons

(1) Where a payment under section 1(1) above falls to be made in respect of a disabled person who is over eighteen and capable of managing his own affairs, the payment shall be made to him.

(2) Where such a payment falls to be made in respect of a disabled person who has died, the payment shall be made to his personal representatives.

(3) Where such a payment falls to be made in respect of any other disabled person, the payment shall be made for his benefit by paying it to such trustees as the Secretary of State may appoint to be held by them upon such trusts or, in Scotland, for such purposes and upon such conditions as may be declared by the Secretary of State.

(4) The making of a claim for, or the receipt of, a payment under section 1(1) above does not prejudice the right of any person to institute or carry on proceedings in respect of disablement suffered as a result of vaccination against any disease to which this Act applies; but in any civil proceedings brought in respect of disablement resulting from vaccination against such a disease, the court shall treat a payment made to or in respect of the disabled person concerned under section 1(1) above as paid on account of any damages which the court awards in respect of such disablement.

HIGHWAYS ACT 1980
(1980, c. 66)

41 Duty to maintain highways maintainable at public expense

(1) The authority who are for the time being the highway authority for a highway maintainable at the public expense are under a duty, subject to subsections (2) and (4) below, to maintain the highway.

(1A) In particular, a highway authority are under a duty to ensure, so far as is reasonably practicable, that safe passage along a highway is not endangered by snow or ice.

58 Special defence in action against a highway authority for damages for nonrepair of highway

(1) In an action against a highway authority in respect of damage resulting from their failure to maintain a highway maintainable at the public expense it is a defence (without prejudice to any other defence or the application of the law relating to contributory negligence) to prove that the authority had taken such care as in all the circumstances was reasonably required to secure that the part of the highway to which the action relates was not dangerous for traffic.

102 Provision of works for protecting highways against hazards of nature

(1) The highway authority for a highway maintainable at the public expense may provide and maintain such barriers or other works as they consider necessary for the purpose of affording to the highway protection against snow, flood, landslide or other hazards of nature; and those works may be provided on the highway or on land which, or rights over which, has or have been acquired by the highway authority in the exercise of highway land acquisition powers for that purpose.

(3) A highway authority shall pay compensation to any person who suffers damage by reason of the execution by them under this section of any works on a highway.

165 Dangerous land adjoining street

(1) If, in or on any land adjoining a street, there is an unfenced or inadequately fenced source of danger to persons using the street, the local authority in whose area the street is situated may, by notice to the owner or occupier of that land, require him within such time as may be specified in the notice to execute such works of repair, protection, removal or enclosure as will obviate the danger.

(3)   Subject to any order made on appeal, if a person on whom a notice is served under this section fails to comply with the notice within the time specified in it, the authority by whom the notice was served may execute such works as are necessary to comply with the notice and may recover the expenses reasonably incurred by them in so doing from that person.

LIMITATION ACT 1980
(1980, c. 58)

PART I

1   Time limits under Part I subject to exclusion under Part II

(1)   This Part of this Act gives the ordinary time limits for bringing actions of the various classes mentioned in the following provisions of this Part.

(2)   The ordinary time limits given in this Part of this Act are subject to extension or exclusion in accordance with the provisions of Part II of this Act.

2   Time limit for actions founded on tort

An action founded on tort shall not be brought after the expiration of six years from the date on which the cause of action accrued.

3   Time limit in case of successive conversions and extinction of title of owner of converted goods

(1)   Where any cause of action in respect of the conversion of a chattel has accrued to any person and, before he recovers possession of the chattel, a further conversion takes place, no action shall be brought in respect of the further conversion after the expiration of six years from the accrual of the cause of action in respect of the original conversion.

(2)   Where any such cause of action has accrued to any person and the period prescribed for bringing that action has expired and he has not during that period recovered possession of the chattel, the title of that person to the chattel shall be extinguished.

4   Special time limit in case of theft

(1)   The right of any person from whom a chattel is stolen to bring an action in respect of the theft shall not be subject to the time limits under sections 2 and 3(1) of this Act, but if his title to the chattel is extinguished under section 3(2) of this Act he may not bring an action in respect of a theft preceding the loss of his title, unless the theft in question preceded the conversion from which time began to run for the purposes of section 3(2).

(2)   Subsection (1) above shall apply to any conversion related to the theft of a chattel as it applies to the theft of a chattel; and, except as provided below, every conversion following the theft of a chattel before the person from whom it is stolen recovers possession of it shall be regarded for the purposes of this section as related to the theft.

If anyone purchases the stolen chattel in good faith neither the purchase nor any conversion following it shall be regarded as related to the theft.

(3)   Any cause of action accruing in respect of the theft or any conversion related to the theft of a chattel to any person from whom the chattel is stolen shall be disregarded for the purpose of applying section 3(1) or (2) of this Act to his case.

(4)   Where in any action brought in respect of the conversion of a chattel it is proved that the chattel was stolen from the plaintiff or anyone through whom he claims it shall be presumed that any conversion following the theft is related to the theft unless the contrary is shown.

(5)   In this section "theft" includes—

(a)   any conduct outside England and Wales which would be theft if committed in England and Wales; and

(b)   obtaining any chattel (in England and Wales or elsewhere) by—
    (i)   blackmail (within the meaning of section 21 of the Theft Act 1968), or
    (ii)   fraud (within the meaning of the Fraud Act 2006);
and references in this section to a chattel being "stolen" shall be construed accordingly.

4A   Time limit for actions for defamation or malicious falsehood

The time limit under section 2 of this Act shall not apply to an action for—
(a)   libel or slander, or
(b)   slander of title, slander of goods or other malicious falsehood,
but no such action shall be brought after the expiration of one year from the date on which the cause of action accrued.

5   Time limit for actions founded on simple contract

An action founded on simple contract shall not be brought after the expiration of six years from the date on which the cause of action accrued.

5A   Additional time limit for actions for damages for late payment of insurance claims

(1)   An action in respect of breach of the term implied into a contract of insurance by section 13A of the Insurance Act 2015 (late payment of claims) may not be brought after the expiration of one year from the date on which the insurer has paid all the sums referred to in subsection (1) of that section.

(2)   Any payment which extinguishes an insurer's liability to pay a sum referred to in section 13A of the Insurance Act 2015 is to be treated for the purposes of this section as payment of that sum.

6   Special time limit for actions in respect of certain loans

(1)   Subject to subsection (3) below, section 5 of this Act shall not bar the right of action on a contract of loan to which this section applies.

(2)   This section applies to any contract of loan which—
(a)   does not provide for repayment of the debt on or before a fixed or determinable date; and
(b)   does not effectively (whether or not it purports to do so) make the obligation to repay the debt conditional on a demand for repayment made by or on behalf of the creditor or on any other matter;
except where in connection with taking the loan the debtor enters into any collateral obligation to pay the amount of the debt or any part of it (as, for example, by delivering a promissory note as security for the debt) on terms which would exclude the application of this section to the contract of loan if they applied directly to repayment of the debt.

(3)   Where a demand in writing for repayment of the debt under a contract of loan to which this section applies is made by or on behalf of the creditor (or, where there are joint creditors, by or on behalf of any one of them) section 5 of this Act shall thereupon apply as if the cause of action to recover the debt had accrued on the date on which the demand was made.

(4)   In this section "promissory note" has the same meaning as in the Bills of Exchange Act 1882.

8   Time limit for actions on a specialty

(1)   An action upon a specialty shall not be brought after the expiration of twelve years from the date on which the cause of action accrued.

(2)   Subsection (1) above shall not affect any action for which a shorter period of limitation is prescribed by any other provision of this Act.

9   Time limit for actions for sums recoverable by statute

(1)   An action to recover any sum recoverable by virtue of any enactment shall not be brought after the expiration of six years from the date on which the cause of action accrued.

(2)   Subsection (1) above shall not affect any action to which section 10 of this Act applies.

10   Special time limit for claiming contribution

(1)   Where under section 1 of the Civil Liability (Contribution) Act 1978 any person becomes entitled to a right to recover contribution in respect of any damage from any other person, no action to recover contribution by virtue of that right shall be brought after the expiration of two years from the date on which that right accrued.

(2)   For the purposes of this section the date on which a right to recover contribution in respect of any damage accrues to any person (referred to below in this section as "the relevant date") shall be ascertained as provided in subsections (3) and (4) below.

(3)   If the person in question is held liable in respect of that damage—

    (a)   by a judgment given in any civil proceedings; or

    (b)   by an award made on any arbitration;

the relevant date shall be the date on which the judgment is given, or the date of the award (as the case may be).

For the purposes of this subsection no account shall be taken of any judgment or award given or made on appeal in so far as it varies the amount of damages awarded against the person in question.

(4)   If, in any case not within subsection (3) above, the person in question makes or agrees to make any payment to one or more persons in compensation for that damage (whether he admits any liability in respect of the damage or not), the relevant date shall be the earliest date on which the amount to be paid by him is agreed between him (or his representative) and the person (or each of the persons, as the case may be) to whom the payment is to be made.

(5)   An action to recover contribution shall be one to which sections 28, 32, 33A and 35 of this Act apply, but otherwise Parts II and III of this Act (except sections 34, 37 and 38) shall not apply for the purposes of this section.

11   Special time limit for actions in respect of personal injuries

(1)   This section applies to any action for damages for negligence, nuisance or breach of duty (whether the duty exists by virtue of a contract or of provision made by or under a statute or independently of any contract or any such provision) where the damages claimed by the plaintiff for the negligence, nuisance or breach of duty consist of or include damages in respect of personal injuries to the plaintiff or any other person.

(1A) This section does not apply to any action brought for damages under section 3 of the Protection from Harassment Act 1997.

(3)   An action to which this section applies shall not be brought after the expiration of the period applicable in accordance with subsection (4) or (5) below.

(4)   Except where subsection (5) below applies, the period applicable is three years from—

    (a)   the date on which the cause of action accrued; or

    (b)   the date of knowledge (if later) of the person injured.

(5)   If the injured person dies before the expiration of the period mentioned in subsection (4) above, the period applicable as respects the cause of action surviving for the benefit of his estate by virtue of section 1 of the Law Reform (Miscellaneous Provisions) Act 1934 shall be three years from—

    (a)   the date of death; or

    (b)   the date of the personal representative's knowledge; whichever is the later.

11A   Actions in respect of defective products

(1)   This section shall apply to an action for damages by virtue of any provision of Part I of the Consumer Protection Act 1987.

(2)   None of the time limits given in the preceding provisions of this Act shall apply to an action to which this section applies.

(3)   An action to which this section applies shall not be brought after the expiration of the period of ten years from the relevant time, within the meaning of section 4 of the said Act of 1987; and this subsection shall operate to extinguish a right of action and shall do so whether or not that right of action had accrued, or time under the following provisions of this Act had begun to run, at the end of the said period of ten years.

(4)   Subject to subsection (5) below, an action to which this section applies in which the damages claimed by the plaintiff consist of or include damages in respect of personal injuries to the plaintiff or any other person or loss of or damage to any property, shall

not be brought after the expiration of the period of three years from whichever is the later of—

    (a)   the date on which the cause of action accrued; and

    (b)   the date of knowledge of the injured person or, in the case of loss of or damage to property, the date of knowledge of the plaintiff or (if earlier) of any person in whom his cause of action was previously vested.

(5)   If in a case where the damages claimed by the plaintiff consist of or include damages in respect of personal injuries to the plaintiff or any other person the injured person died before the expiration of the period mentioned in subsection (4) above, the subsection shall have effect as respects the cause of action surviving for the benefit of his estate by virtue of section I of the Law Reform (Miscellaneous Provisions) Act 1934 as if for the reference to that period there were substituted a reference to the period of three years from whichever is the later of—

    (a)   the date of death; and

    (b)   the date of the personal representative's knowledge.

(6)   For the purposes of this section "personal representative" includes any person who is or has been a personal representative of the deceased, including an executor who has not proved the will (whether or not he has renounced probate) but not anyone appointed only as a special personal representative in relation to settled land; and regard shall be had to any knowledge acquired by any such person while a personal representative or previously.

(7)   If there is more than one personal representative and their dates of knowledge are different, subsection (5)(b) above shall be read as referring to the earliest of those dates.

(8)   Expressions used in this section or section 14 of this Act and in Part I of the Consumer Protection Act 1987 have the same meanings in this section or that section as in that Part; and section 1(1) of that Act (Part I to be construed as enacted for the purpose of complying with the product liability Directive) shall apply for the purpose of construing this section and the following provisions of this Act so far as they relate to an action by virtue of any provision of that Part as it applies for the purpose of construing that Part.

12   Special time limit for actions under Fatal Accidents legislation

(1)   An action under the Fatal Accidents Act 1976 shall not be brought if the death occurred when the person injured could no longer maintain an action and recover damages in respect of the injury (whether because of a time limit in this Act or in any other Act, or for any other reason).

Where any such action by the injured person would have been barred by the time limit in section 11 or 11A of this Act, no account shall be taken of the possibility of that time limit being overridden under section 33 of this Act.

(2)   None of the time limits given in the preceding provisions of this Act shall apply to an action under the Fatal Accidents Act 1976, but no such action shall be brought after the expiration of three years from—

    (a)   the date of death; or

    (b)   the date of knowledge of the person for whose benefit the action is brought; whichever is the later.

(3)   An action under the Fatal Accidents Act 1976 shall be one to which sections 28, 33, 33A, 33B and 35 of this Act apply, and the application to any such action of the time limit under subsection (2) above shall be subject to section 39; but otherwise Parts II and III of this Act shall not apply to any such action.

13   Operation of time limit under section 12 in relation to different dependants

(1)   Where there is more than one person for whose benefit an action under the Fatal Accidents Act 1976 is brought, section 12(2)(b) of this Act shall be applied separately to each of them.

(2)   Subject to subsection (3) below, if by virtue of subsection (1) above the action would be outside the time limit given by section 12(2) as regards one or more, but not all, of the persons for whose benefit it is brought, the court shall direct that any person as regards whom the action would be outside that limit shall be excluded from those for whom the action is brought.

(3)   The court shall not give such a direction if it is shown that if the action were brought exclusively for the benefit of the person in question it would not be defeated by a defence of limitation (whether in consequence of section 28 of this Act or an agreement between the parties not to raise the defence, or otherwise).

14   Definition of date of knowledge for purposes of sections 11 and 12

(1)   Subject to subsection (1A) below, in sections 11 and 12 of this Act references to a person's date of knowledge are references to the date on which he first had knowledge of the following facts—
(a)   that the injury in question was significant; and
(b)   that the injury was attributable in whole or in part to the act or omission which is alleged to constitute negligence, nuisance or breach of duty; and
(c)   the identity of the defendant; and
(d)   if it is alleged that the act or omission was that of a person other than the defendant, the identity of that person and the additional facts supporting the bringing of an action against the defendant;
and knowledge that any acts or omissions did or did not, as a matter of law, involve negligence, nuisance or breach of duty is irrelevant.

(1A) In section 11A of this Act and in section 12 of this Act so far as that section applies to an action by virtue of section 6(1)(a) of the Consumer Protection Act 1987 (death caused by defective product) references to a person's date of knowledge are references to the date on which he first had knowledge of the following facts—
(a)   such facts about the damage caused by the defect as would lead a reasonable person who had suffered such damage to consider it sufficiently serious to justify his instituting proceedings for damages against a defendant who did not dispute liability and was able to satisfy a judgment; and
(b)   that the damage was wholly or partly attributable to the facts and circumstances alleged to constitute the defect; and (c) the identity of the defendant;
but, in determining the date on which a person first had such knowledge there shall be disregarded both the extent (if any) of that person's knowledge on any date of whether particular facts or circumstances would or would not, as a matter of law, constitute a defect and, in a case relating to loss of or damage to property, any knowledge which that person had on a date on which he had no right of action by virtue of Part of I of that Act in respect of the loss or damage.

(2)   For the purposes of this section an injury is significant if the person whose date of knowledge is in question would reasonably have considered it sufficiently serious to justify his instituting proceedings for damages against a defendant who did not dispute liability and was able to satisfy a judgment.

(3)   For the purposes of this section a person's knowledge includes knowledge which he might reasonably have been expected to acquire—
(a)   from facts observable or ascertainable by him; or
(b)   from facts ascertainable by him with the help of medical or other appropriate expert advice which it is reasonable for him to seek;
but a person shall not be fixed under this subsection with knowledge of a fact ascertainable only with the help of expert advice so long as he has taken all reasonable steps to obtain (and, where appropriate, to act on) that advice.

14A   Special time limit for negligence actions where facts relevant to cause of action are not known at date of accrual

(1)   This section applies to any action for damages for negligence, other than one to which section 11 of this Act applies, where the starting date for reckoning the period of limitation under subsection (4)(b) below falls after the date on which the cause of action accrued.
(2)   Section 2 of this Act shall not apply to an action to which this section applies.
(3)   An action to which this section applies shall not be brought after the expiration of the period applicable in accordance with subsection (4) below.
(4)   That period is either—
(a)   six years from the date on which the cause of action accrued; or
(b)   three years from the starting date as defined by subsection (5) below, if that period expires later than the period mentioned in paragraph (a) above.

(5)   For the purposes of this section, the starting date for reckoning the period of limitation under subsection (4)(b) above is the earliest date on which the plaintiff or any person in whom the cause of action was vested before him first had both the knowledge required for bringing an action for damages in respect of the relevant damage and a right to bring such an action.

(6)   In subsection (5) above "the knowledge required for bringing an action for damages in respect of the relevant damage" means knowledge both—

    (a)   of the material facts about the damage in respect of which damages are claimed; and

    (b)   of the other facts relevant to the current action mentioned in subsection (8) below.

(7)   For the purposes of subsection (6)(a) above, the material facts about the damage are such facts about the damage as would lead a reasonable person who had suffered such damage to consider it sufficiently serious to justify his instituting proceedings for damages against a defendant who did not dispute liability and was able to satisfy a judgment.

(8)   The other facts referred to in subsection (6)(b) above are—

    (a)   that the damage was attributable in whole or in part to the act or omission which is alleged to constitute negligence; and

    (b)   the identity of the defendant; and

    (c)   if it is alleged that the act or omission was that of a person other than the defendant, the identity of that person and the additional facts supporting the bringing of an action against the defendant.

(9)   Knowledge that any acts or omissions did or did not, as a matter of law, involve negligence is irrelevant for the purposes of subsection (5) above.

(10)   For the purposes of this section a person's knowledge includes knowledge which he might reasonably have been expected to acquire—

    (a)   from facts observable or ascertainable by him; or

    (b)   from facts ascertainable by him with the help of appropriate expert advice which it is reasonable for him to seek;

but a person shall not be taken by virtue of this subsection to have knowledge of a fact ascertainable only with the help of expert advice so long as he has taken all reasonable steps to obtain (and, where appropriate, to act on) that advice.

14B Overriding time limit for negligence actions not involving personal injuries

(1)   An action for damages for negligence, other than one to which section 11 of this Act applies, shall not be brought after the expiration of fifteen years from the date (or, if more than one, from the last of the dates) on which there occurred any act or omission—

    (a)   which is alleged to constitute negligence; and

    (b)   to which the damage in respect of which damages are claimed is alleged to be attributable (in whole or in part).

(2)   This section bars the right of action in a case to which subsection (1) above applies notwithstanding that—

    (a)   the cause of action has not yet accrued; or

    (b)   where section 14A of this Act applies to the action, the date which is for the purposes of that section the starting date for reckoning the period mentioned in subsection (4)(b) of that section has not yet occurred;

before the end of the period of limitation prescribed by this section.

15 Time limit for actions to recover land

(1)   No action shall be brought by any person to recover any land after the expiration of twelve years from the date on which the right of action accrued to him or, if it first accrued to some person through whom he claims, to that person.

(2)   Subject to the following provisions of this section, where—

    (a)   the estate or interest claimed was an estate or interest in reversion or remainder or any other future estate or interest and the right of action to recover the land accrued on the date on which the estate or interest fell into possession by the determination of the preceding estate or interest; and

(b)   the person entitled to the preceding estate or interest (not being a term of years absolute) was not in possession of the land on that date;

no action shall be brought by the person entitled to the succeeding estate or interest after the expiration of twelve years from the date on which the right of action accrued to the person entitled to the preceding estate or interest or six years from the date on which the right of action accrued to the person entitled to the succeeding estate or interest, whichever period last expires.

(3)   Subsection (2) above shall not apply to any estate or interest which falls into possession on the determination of an entailed interest and which might have been barred by the person entitled to the entailed interest.

(4)   No person shall bring an action to recover any estate or interest in land under an assurance taking effect after the right of action to recover the land had accrued to the person by whom the assurance was made or some person through whom he claimed or some person entitled to a preceding estate or interest, unless the action is brought within the period during which the person by whom the assurance was made could have brought such an action.

(5)   Where any person is entitled to any estate or interest in land in possession and, while so entitled, is also entitled to any future estate or interest in that land, and his right to recover the estate or interest in possession is barred under this Act, no action shall be brought by that person, or by any person claiming through him, in respect of the future estate or interest, unless in the meantime possession of the land has been recovered by a person entitled to an intermediate estate or interest.

(6)   Part I of Schedule 1 to this Act contains provisions for determining the date of accrual of rights of action to recover land in the cases there mentioned.

(7)   Part II of that Schedule contains provisions modifying the provisions of this section in their application to actions brought by, or by a person claiming through, the Crown or any spiritual or eleemosynary corporation sole.

Note: Section 96 of the Land Registration Act 2002 disapplies this section to registered land.

16   Time limit for redemption actions

When a mortgagee of land has been in possession of any of the mortgaged land for a period of twelve years, no action to redeem the land of which the mortgagee has been so in possession shall be brought after the end of that period by the mortgagor or any person claiming through him.

Note: Section 96 of the Land Registration Act 2002 disapplies this section to registered land.

17   Extinction of title to land after expiration of time limit

Subject to—
        (a)   section 18 of this Act;
at the expiration of the period prescribed by this Act for any person to bring an action to recover land (including a redemption action) the title of that person to the land shall be extinguished.

18   Settled land and land held on trust

(1)   Subject to section 21(1) and (2) of this Act, the provisions of this Act shall apply to equitable interests in land, ... as they apply to legal estates.

Accordingly a right of action to recover the land shall, for the purposes of this Act but not otherwise, be treated as accruing to a person entitled in possession to such an equitable interest in the like manner and circumstances, and on the same date, as it would accrue if his interest were a legal estate in the land (and any relevant provision of Part I of Schedule 1 to this Act shall apply in any such case accordingly).

(2)   Where the period prescribed by this Act has expired for the bringing of an action to recover land by a tenant for life or a statutory owner of settled land—
        (a)   his legal estate shall not be extinguished if and so long as the right of action to recover the land of any person entitled to a beneficial interest in the land either has not accrued or has not been barred by this Act; and
        (b)   the legal estate shall accordingly remain vested in the tenant for life or statutory owner and shall devolve in accordance with the Settled Land Act 1925;

but if and when every such right of action has been barred by this Act, his legal estate shall be extinguished.

(3) Where any land is held upon trust ... and the period prescribed by this Act has expired for the bringing of an action to recover the land by the trustees, the estate of the trustees shall not be extinguished if and so long as the right of action to recover the land of any person entitled to a beneficial interest in the land ... either has not accrued or has not been barred by this Act; but if and when every such right of action has been so barred the estate of the trustees shall be extinguished.

(4) Where—

    (a)   any settled land is vested in a statutory owner; or

    (b)   any land is held upon trust ...;

an action to recover the land may be brought by the statutory owner or trustees on behalf of any person entitled to a beneficial interest in possession in the land ... whose right of action has not been barred by this Act, notwithstanding that the right of action of the statutory owner or trustees would apart from this provision have been barred by this Act.

19   Time limit for actions to recover rent

No action shall be brought, and the power conferred by section 72(1) of the Tribunals, Courts and Enforcement Act 2007 shall not be exercisable, to recover arrears of rent, or damages in respect of arrears of rent, after the expiration of six years from the date on which the arrears became due.

19A   Actions for breach of commonhold duty

An action in respect of a right or duty of a kind referred to in section 37(1) of the Commonhold and Leasehold Reform Act 2002 (enforcement) shall not be brought after the expiration of six years from the date on which the cause of action accrued.

20   Time limit for actions to recover money secured by a mortgage or charge or to recover proceeds of the sale of land

(1) No action shall be brought to recover—

    (a)   any principal sum of money secured by a mortgage or other charge on property (whether real or personal); or

    (b)   proceeds of the sale of land; after the expiration of twelve years from the date on which the right to receive the money accrued.

(2) No foreclosure action in respect of mortgaged personal property shall be brought after the expiration of twelve years from the date on which the right to foreclose accrued. But if the mortgagee was in possession of the mortgaged property after that date, the right to foreclose on the property which was in his possession shall not be treated as having accrued for the purposes of this subsection until the date on which his possession discontinued.

(3) The right to receive any principal sum of money secured by a mortgage or other charge and the right to foreclose on the property subject to the mortgage or charge shall not be treated as accruing so long as that property comprises any future interest or any life insurance policy which has not matured or been determined.

(4) Nothing in this section shall apply to a foreclosure action in respect of mortgaged land, but the provisions of this Act relating to actions to recover land shall apply to such an action.

(5) Subject to subsections (6) and (7) below, no action to recover arrears of interest payable in respect of any sum of money secured by a mortgage or other charge or payable in respect of proceeds of the sale of land, or to recover damages in respect of such arrears shall be brought after the expiration of six years from the date on which the interest became due.

(6) Where—

    (a)   a prior mortgagee or other incumbrancer has been in possession of the property charged; and

    (b)   an action is brought within one year of the discontinuance of that possession by the subsequent incumbrancer;

the subsequent incumbrancer may recover by that action all the arrears of interest which fell due during the period of possession by the prior incumbrancer or damages in respect of those arrears, notwithstanding that the period exceeded six years.

(7) Where—
  (a) the property subject to the mortgage or charge comprises any future interest or life insurance policy; and
  (b) it is a term of the mortgage or charge that arrears of interest shall be treated as part of the principal sum of money secured by the mortgage or charge;

interest shall not be treated as becoming due before the right to recover the principal sum of money has accrued or is treated as having accrued.

21   Time limit for actions in respect of trust property

(1) No period of limitation prescribed by this Act shall apply to an action by a beneficiary under a trust, being an action—
  (a) in respect of any fraud or fraudulent breach of trust to which the trustee was a party or privy; or
  (b) to recover from the trustee trust property or the proceeds of trust property in the possession of the trustee, or previously received by the trustee and converted to his use.

(2) Where a trustee who is also a beneficiary under the trust receives or retains trust property or its proceeds as his share on a distribution of trust property under the trust, his liability in any action brought by virtue of subsection (1)(b) above to recover that property or its proceeds after the expiration of the period of limitation prescribed by this Act for bringing an action to recover trust property shall be limited to the excess over his proper share.

This subsection only applies if the trustee acted honestly and reasonably in making the distribution.

(3) Subject to the preceding provisions of this section, an action by a beneficiary to recover trust property or in respect of any breach of trust, not being an action for which a period of limitation is prescribed by any other provision of this Act, shall not be brought after the expiration of six years from the date on which the right of action accrued.

For the purposes of this subsection, the right of action shall not be treated as having accrued to any beneficiary entitled to a future interest in the trust property until the interest fell into possession.

(4) No beneficiary as against whom there would be a good defence under this Act shall derive any greater or other benefit from a judgment or order obtained by any other beneficiary than he could have obtained if he had brought the action and this Act had been pleaded in defence.

22   Time limit for actions claiming personal estate of a deceased person

Subject to section 21(1) and (2) of this Act—
  (a) no action in respect of any claim to the personal estate of a deceased person or to any share or interest in any such estate (whether under a will or on intestacy) shall be brought after the expiration of twelve years from the date on which the right to receive the share or interest accrued; and
  (b) no action to recover arrears of interest in respect of any legacy, or damages in respect of such arrears, shall be brought after the expiration of six years from the date on which the interest became due.

23   Time limit in respect of actions for an account

An action for an account shall not be brought after the expiration of any time limit under this Act which is applicable to the claim which is the basis of the duty to account.

24   Time limit for actions to enforce judgments

(1) An action shall not be brought upon any judgment after the expiration of six years from the date on which the judgment became enforceable.

(2) No arrears of interest in respect of any judgment debt shall be recovered after the expiration of six years from the date on which the interest became due.

26   Administration to date back to death

For the purposes of the provisions of this Act relating to actions for the recovery of land and advowsons an administrator of the estate of a deceased person shall be treated as claiming as if there had been no interval of time between the death of the deceased person and the grant of the letters of administration.

27A   Actions for recovery of property obtained through unlawful conduct etc.

(1)   None of the time limits given in the preceding provisions of this Act applies to any proceedings under Chapter 2 of Part 5 of the Proceeds of Crime Act 2002 (civil recovery of proceeds of unlawful conduct).

(2)   Proceedings under that Chapter for a recovery order in respect of any recoverable property shall not be brought after the expiration of the period of 20 years from the date on which the relevant person's cause of action accrued.

(3)   Proceedings under that Chapter are brought when—
  (a)   a claim form is issued,
  (aa)   an application is made for a property freezing order, or
  (b)   an application is made for an interim receiving order, whichever is the earliest.

(4)   The relevant person's cause of action accrues in respect of any recoverable property—
  (a)   in the case of proceedings for a recovery order in respect of property obtained through unlawful conduct, when the property is so obtained,
  (b)   in the case of proceedings for a recovery order in respect of any other recoverable property, when the property obtained through unlawful conduct which it represents is so obtained.

(5)   If—
  (a)   a person would (but for the preceding provisions of this Act) have a cause of action in respect of the conversion of a chattel, and
  (b)   proceedings are started under that Chapter for a recovery order in respect of the chattel,
  section 3(2) of this Act does not prevent his asserting on an application under section 281 of that Act that the property belongs to him, or the court making a declaration in his favour under that section.

(6)   If the court makes such a declaration, his title to the chattel is to be treated as not having been extinguished by section 3(2) of this Act.

(7)   Expressions used in this section and Part 5 of that Act have the same meaning in this section as in that Part.

(8)   In this section "relevant person" means—
  (a)   the National Crime Agency,
  (b)   the Director of Public Prosecutions,
  (c)   ..., or
  (d)   the Director of the Serious Fraud Office.

27AB   Actions to prohibit dealing with property subject to an external request—

(1)   None of the time limits given in the preceding provisions of this Act applies to any proceedings under Part 4A of the Proceeds of Crime Act 2002 (External Requests and Orders) Order 2005 (giving effect to external request by means of civil proceedings).

(2)   Proceedings under that Part for a prohibition order in respect of relevant property shall not be brought after the expiration of the period of 20 years from the date on which the relevant person's cause of action accrued.

(3)   Proceedings under that Part are brought when an application is made for a prohibition order.

(4)   The relevant person's cause of action accrues in respect of relevant property when the property is obtained (or when it is believed to have been obtained) as a result of or in connection with criminal conduct.

(5)   In this section—
  (a)   "criminal conduct" is to be construed in accordance with section 447(8) of the Act,
  (b)   expressions used in this section and Part 4A of the Proceeds of Crime Act 2002 (External Requests and Orders) Order 2005 have the same meaning in this section as in that Part.

(6) In this section "relevant person" means—
    (a)   the National Crime Agency,
    (b)   the Director of Public Prosecutions,
    (c)   ..., or
    (d)   the Director of the Serious Fraud Office.

27B Actions for recovery of property for purposes of an external order

(1) None of the time limits given in the preceding provisions of this Act applies to any proceedings under Chapter 2 of Part 5 of the Proceeds of Crime Act 2002 (External Requests and Orders) Order 2005 (civil proceedings for the realisation of property to give effect to an external order).

(2) Proceedings under that Chapter for a recovery order in respect of any recoverable property shall not be brought after the expiration of the period of 20 years from the date on which the relevant person's cause of action accrued.

(3) Proceedings under that Chapter are brought when—
    (a)   a claim form is issued, or
    (b)   an application is made for a property freezing order, or
    (c)   an application is made for an interim receiving order, whichever is earliest.

(3A) If, before an event mentioned in subsection (3) occurs, an application is made for a prohibition order under Part 4A of the Order, the proceedings under Chapter 2 of Part 5 of the Order are to be treated as having been brought when that application is made.

(4) The relevant person's cause of action accrues in respect of any recoverable property—
    (a)   in the case of proceedings for a recovery order in respect of property obtained, or believed to have been obtained, as a result of or in connection with criminal conduct, when the property is so obtained,
    (b)   in the case of proceedings for a recovery order in respect of any other recoverable property, when the property obtained, or believed to have been obtained, as a result of or in connection with criminal conduct which it represents is so obtained.

(5) If—
    (a)   a person would (but for the preceding provisions of this Act) have a cause of action in respect of the conversion of a chattel, and
    (b)   proceedings are started under that Chapter for a recovery order in respect of the chattel,
  section 3(2) of this Act does not prevent his asserting on an application under article 192 of that Order that the property belongs to him, or the court making a declaration in his favour under that article.

(6) If the court makes such a declaration, his title to the chattel is to be treated as not having been extinguished by section 3(2) of this Act.

(7) In this section—
    (a)   "criminal conduct" is to be construed in accordance with section 447(8) of the Proceeds of Crime Act 2002, and
    (b)   expressions used in this section which are also used in Part 5 of the Proceeds of Crime Act 2002 (External Requests and Orders) Order 2005 have the same meaning in this section as in that Part.

(8) In this section "relevant person" means—
    (a)   the National Crime Agency,
    (b)   the Director of Public Prosecutions,
    (c)   ..., or
    (d)   the Director of the Serious Fraud Office.

PART II

28 Extension of limitation period in case of disability

(1) Subject to the following provisions of this section, if on the date when any right of action accrued for which a period of limitation is prescribed by this Act, the person to whom it accrued was under a disability, the action may be brought at any time before

the expiration of six years from the date when he ceased to be under a disability or died (whichever first occurred) notwithstanding that the period of limitation has expired.

(2) This section shall not affect any case where the right of action first accrued to some person (not under a disability) through whom the person under a disability claims.

(3) When a right of action which has accrued to a person under a disability accrues, on the death of that person while still under a disability, to another person under a disability, no further extension of time shall be allowed by reason of the disability of the second person.

(4A) If the action is one to which section 4A of this Act applies, subsection (1) above shall have effect—

    (a) in the case of an action for libel or slander, as if for the words from "at any time" to "occurred)" there were substituted the words "by him at any time before the expiration of one year from the date on which he ceased to be under a disability"; and

    (b) in the case of an action for slander of title, slander of goods or other malicious falsehood, as if for the words "six years" there were substituted the words "one year".

(5) If the action is one to which section 10 of this Act applies, subsection (1) above shall have effect as if for the words "six years" there were substituted the words "two years".

(6) If the action is one to which section 11 or 12(2) of this Act applies, subsection (1) above shall have effect as if for the words "six years" there were substituted the words "three years".

(7) If the action is one to which section 11A of this Act applies or one by virtue of section 6(1)(a) of the Consumer Protection Act 1987 (death caused by defective product), subsection (1) above—

    (a) shall not apply to the time limit prescribed by subsection (3) of the said section 11A or to that time limit as applied by virtue of section 12(1) of this Act; and

    (b) in relation to any other time limit prescribed by this Act shall have effect as if for the words "six years" there were substituted the words "three years".

28A Extension for cases where the limitation period is the period under section 14A(4)(b)

(1) Subject to subsection (2) below, if in the case of any action for which a period of limitation is prescribed by section 14A of this Act—

    (a) the period applicable in accordance with subsection (4) of that section is the period mentioned in paragraph (b) of that subsection;

    (b) on the date which is for the purposes of that section the starting date for reckoning that period the person by reference to whose knowledge that date fell to be determined under subsection (5) of that section was under a disability; and

    (c) section 28 of this Act does not apply to the action;

the action may be brought at any time before the expiration of three years from the date when he ceased to be under a disability or died (whichever first occurred) notwithstanding that the period mentioned above has expired.

(2) An action may not be brought by virtue of subsection (1) above after the end of the period of limitation prescribed by section 14B of this Act.

29 Fresh accrual of action on acknowledgment or part payment

(5) Subject to subsection (6) below, where any right of action has accrued to recover—

    (a) any debt or other liquidated pecuniary claim; or

    (b) any claim to the personal estate of a deceased person or to any share or interest in any such estate;

and the person liable or accountable for the claim acknowledges the claim or makes any payment in respect of it the right shall be treated as having accrued on and not before the date of the acknowledgment or payment.

(6) A payment of a part of the rent or interest due at any time shall not extend the period for claiming the remainder then due, but any payment of interest shall be treated as a payment in respect of the principal debt.

(7) Subject to subsection (6) above, a current period of limitation may be repeatedly extended under this section by further acknowledgments or payments, but a right of action, once barred by this Act shall not be revived by any subsequent acknowledgment or payment.

30 Formal provisions as to acknowledgments and part payments

(1) To be effective for the purposes of section 29 of this Act, an acknowledgment must be in writing and signed by the person making it.

(2) For the purposes of section 29, any acknowledgment or payment—
    (a) may be made by the agent of the person by whom it is required to be made under that section; and
    (b) shall be made to the person, or to an agent of the person, whose title or claim is being acknowledged or, as the case may be, in respect of whose claim the payment is being made.

31 Effect of acknowledgment or part payment on persons other than the maker or recipient

(6) An acknowledgment of any debt or other liquidated pecuniary claim shall bind the acknowledgor and his successors but not any other person.

(7) A payment made in respect of any debt or other liquidated pecuniary claim shall bind all persons liable in respect of the debt or claim.

(8) An acknowledgment by one of several personal representatives of any claim to the personal estate of a deceased person or to any share or interest in any such estate, or a payment by one of several personal representatives in respect of any such claim, shall bind the estate of the deceased person.

(9) In this section "successor", in relation to any mortgagee or person liable in respect of any debt or claim, means his personal representatives and any other person on whom the rights under the mortgage or, as the case may be, the liability in respect of the debt or claim devolve (whether on death or bankruptcy or the disposition of property or the determination of a limited estate or interest in settled property or otherwise).

32 Postponement of limitation period in case of fraud, concealment or mistake

(1) Subject to subsections (3) and (4A) below, where in the case of any action for which a period of limitation is prescribed by this Act, either—
    (a) the action is based upon the fraud of the defendant; or
    (b) any fact relevant to the plaintiff's right of action has been deliberately concealed from him by the defendant; or
    (c) the action is for relief from the consequences of a mistake;
    the period of limitation shall not begin to run until the plaintiff has discovered the fraud, concealment or mistake (as the case may be) or could with reasonable diligence have discovered it.
    References in this subsection to the defendant include references to the defendant's agent and to any person through whom the defendant claims and his agent.

(2) For the purposes of subsection (1) above, deliberate commission of a breach of duty in circumstances in which it is unlikely to be discovered for some time amounts to deliberate concealment of the facts involved in that breach of duty.

(3) Nothing in this section shall enable any action—
    (a) to recover, or recover the value of, any property; or
    (b) to enforce any charge against, or set aside any transaction affecting, any property;
    to be brought against the purchaser of the property or any person claiming through him in any case where the property has been purchased for valuable consideration by an innocent third party since the fraud or concealment or (as the case may be) the transaction in which the mistake was made took place.

(4) A purchaser is an innocent third party for the purposes of this section—
    (a) in the case of fraud or concealment of any fact relevant to the plaintiff's right of action, if he was not a party to the fraud or (as the case may be) to the concealment of that fact and did not at the time of the purchase know or have reason to believe that the fraud or concealment had taken place; and

(b)　in the case of mistake, if he did not at the time of the purchase know or have reason to believe that the mistake had been made.

(4A)　Subsection (1) above shall not apply in relation to the time limit prescribed by section 11A(3) of this Act or in relation to that time limit as applied by virtue of section 12(1) of this Act.

(5)　Sections 14A and 14B of this Act shall not apply to any action to which subsection (1) (b) above applies (and accordingly the period of limitation referred to in that subsection, in any case to which either of those sections would otherwise apply, is the period applicable under section 23 of this Act).

32A　Discretionary exclusion of time limit for actions for defamation or malicious falsehood

(1)　If it appears to the court that it would be equitable to allow an action to proceed having regard to the degree to which—

(a)　the operation of section 4A of this Act prejudices the plaintiff or any person whom he represents, and

(b)　any decision of the court under this subsection would prejudice the defendant or any person whom he represents,

the court may direct that that section shall not apply to the action or shall not apply to any specified cause of action to which the action relates.

(2)　In acting under this section the court shall have regard to all the circumstances of the case and in particular to—

(a)　the length of, and the reasons for, the delay on the part of the plaintiff;

(b)　where the reason or one of the reasons for the delay was that all or any of the facts relevant to the cause of action did not become known to the plaintiff until after the end of the period mentioned in section 4A—

(i)　the date on which any such facts did become known to him, and

(ii)　the extent to which he acted promptly and reasonably once he knew whether or not the facts in question might be capable of giving rise to an action; and

(c)　the extent to which, having regard to the delay, relevant evidence is likely—

(i)　to be unavailable, or

(ii)　to be less cogent than if the action had been brought within the period mentioned in section 4A.

(3)　In the case of an action for slander of title, slander of goods or other malicious falsehood brought by a personal representative—

(a)　the references in subsection (2) above to the plaintiff shall be construed as including the deceased person to whom the cause of action accrued and any previous personal representative of that person; and

(b)　nothing in section 28(3) of this Act shall be construed as affecting the court's discretion under this section.

(4)　In this section "the court" means the court in which the action has been brought.

33　Discretionary exclusion of time limit for actions in respect of personal injuries or death

(1)　If it appears to the court that it would be equitable to allow an action to proceed having regard to the degree to which—

(a)　the provisions of section 11 or 11A or 12 of this Act prejudice the plaintiff or any person whom he represents; and

(b)　any decision of the court under this subsection would prejudice the defendant or any person whom he represents;

the court may direct that those provisions shall not apply to the action, or shall not apply to any specified cause of action to which the action relates.

(1A)　The court shall not under this section disapply—

(a)　subsection (3) of section 11A; or

(b)　where the damages claimed by the plaintiff are confined to damages for loss of or damage to any property, any other provision in its application to an action by virtue of Part I of the Consumer Protection Act 1987.

(2) The court shall not under this section disapply section 12(1) except where the reason why the person injured could no longer maintain an action was because of the time limit in section 11 or subsection (4) of section 11A.

If, for example, the person injured could at his death no longer maintain an action under the Fatal Accidents Act 1976 because of the time limit in Article 29 in Schedule 1 to the Carriage by Air Act 1961, the court has no power to direct that section 12(1) shall not apply.

(3) In acting under this section the court shall have regard to all the circumstances of the case and in particular to—

(a) the length of, and the reasons for, the delay on the part of the plaintiff;

(b) the extent to which, having regard to the delay, the evidence adduced or likely to be adduced by the plaintiff or the defendant is or is likely to be less cogent than if the action had been brought within the time allowed by section 11, by section 11A or (as the case may be) by section 12;

(c) the conduct of the defendant after the cause of action arose, including the extent (if any) to which he responded to requests reasonably made by the plaintiff for information or inspection for the purpose of ascertaining facts which were or might be relevant to the plaintiff's cause of action against the defendant;

(d) the duration of any disability of the plaintiff arising after the date of the accrual of the cause of action;

(e) the extent to which the plaintiff acted promptly and reasonably once he knew whether or not the act or omission of the defendant, to which the injury was attributable, might be capable at that time of giving rise to an action for damages;

(f) the steps, if any, taken by the plaintiff to obtain medical, legal or other expert advice and the nature of any such advice he may have received.

(4) In a case where the person injured died when, because of section 11 or subsection (4) of section 11A, he could no longer maintain an action and recover damages in respect of the injury, the court shall have regard in particular to the length of, and the reasons for, the delay on the part of the deceased.

(5) In a case under subsection (4) above, or any other case where the time limit, or one of the time limits, depends on the date of knowledge of a person other than the plaintiff, subsection (3) above shall have effect with appropriate modifications, and shall have effect in particular as if references to the plaintiff included references to any person whose date of knowledge is or was relevant in determining a time limit.

(6) A direction by the court disapplying the provisions of section 12(1) shall operate to disapply the provisions to the same effect in section 1(1) of the Fatal Accidents Act 1976.

(7) In this section "the court" means the court in which the action has been brought.

(8) References in this section to section 11 or 11A include references to that section as extended by any of the provisions of this Part other than this section or by any provision of Part III of this Act.

33A   Extension of time limits because of mediation in certain cross-border disputes

(1) In this section—

(a) "Mediation Directive" means Directive 2008/52/EC of the European Parliament and of the Council of 21 May 2008 on certain aspects of mediation in civil and commercial matters,

(b) "mediation" has the meaning given by article 3(a) of the Mediation Directive,

(c) "mediator" has the meaning given by article 3(b) of the Mediation Directive, and

(d) "relevant dispute" means a dispute to which article 8(1) of the Mediation Directive applies (certain cross-border disputes).

(2) Subsection (3) applies where—

(a) a time limit under this Act relates to the subject of the whole or part of a relevant dispute,

(b) a mediation in relation to the relevant dispute starts before the time limit expires, and

(c) if not extended by this section, the time limit would expire before the mediation ends or less than eight weeks after it ends.

(3)   For the purposes of initiating judicial proceedings or arbitration, the time limit expires instead at the end of eight weeks after the mediation ends (subject to subsection (4)).

(4)   If a time limit has been extended by this section, subsections (2) and (3) apply to the extended time limit as they apply to a time limit mentioned in subsection (2)(a).

(5)   Where more than one time limit applies in relation to a relevant dispute, the extension by subsection (3) of one of those time limits does not affect the others.

(6)   For the purposes of this section, a mediation starts on the date of the agreement to mediate that is entered into by the parties and the mediator.

(7)   For the purposes of this section, a mediation ends on the date of the first of these to occur—

(a)   the parties reach an agreement in resolution of the relevant dispute,

(b)   a party completes the notification of the other parties that it has withdrawn from the mediation,

(c)   a party to whom a qualifying request is made fails to give a response reaching the other parties within 14 days of the request,

(d)   after the parties are notified that the mediator's appointment has ended (by death, resignation or otherwise), they fail to agree within 14 days to seek to appoint a replacement mediator,

(e)   the mediation otherwise comes to an end pursuant to the terms of the agreement to mediate.

(8)   For the purpose of subsection (7), a qualifying request is a request by a party that another (A) confirm to all parties that A is continuing with the mediation.

(9)   In the case of any relevant dispute, references in this section to a mediation are references to the mediation so far as it relates to that dispute, and references to a party are to be read accordingly.

35   New claims in pending actions; rules of court

(1)   For the purposes of this Act, any new claim made in the course of any action shall be deemed to be a separate action and to have been commenced—

(a)   in the case of a new claim made in or by way of third party proceedings, on the date on which those proceedings were commenced; and

(b)   in the case of any other new claim, on the same date as the original action.

(2)   In this section a new claim means any claim by way of set-off or counterclaim, and any claim involving either—

(a)   the addition or substitution of a new cause of action; or

(b)   the addition or substitution of a new party;

and "third party proceedings" means any proceedings brought in the course of any action by any party to the action against a person not previously a party to the action, other than proceedings brought by joining any such person as defendant to any claim already made in the original action by the party bringing the proceedings.

(3)   Except as provided by section 33 of this Act or by rules of court, neither the High Court nor the county court shall allow a new claim within subsection (1)(b) above, other than an original set-off or counterclaim, to be made in the course of any action after the expiry of any time limit under this Act which would affect a new action to enforce that claim.

For the purposes of this subsection, a claim is an original set-off or an original counterclaim if it is a claim made by way of set-off or (as the case may be) by way of counterclaim by a party who has not previously made any claim in the action.

(4)   Rules of court may provide for allowing a new claim to which subsection (3) above applies to be made as there mentioned, but only if the conditions specified in subsection (5) below are satisfied, and subject to any further restrictions the rules may impose.

(5)   The conditions referred to in subsection (4) above are the following—

(a)   in the case of a claim involving a new cause of action, if the new cause of action arises out of the same facts or substantially the same facts as are already in issue on any claim previously made in the original action; and

(b)   in the case of a claim involving a new party, if the addition or substitution of the new party is necessary for the determination of the original action.

(6) The addition or substitution of a new party shall not be regarded for the purposes of subsection (5)(b) above as necessary for the determination of the original action unless either—

(a) the new party is substituted for a party whose name was given in any claim made in the original action in mistake for the new party's name; or

(b) any claim already made in the original action cannot be maintained by or against an existing party unless the new party is joined or substituted as plaintiff or defendant in that action.

(7) Subject to subsection (4) above, rules of court may provide for allowing a party to any action to claim relief in a new capacity in respect of a new cause of action notwithstanding that he had no title to make that claim at the date of the commencement of the action. This subsection shall not be taken as prejudicing the power of rules of court to provide for allowing a party to claim relief in a new capacity without adding or substituting a new cause of action.

(8) Subsections (3) to (7) above shall apply in relation to a new claim made in the course of third party proceedings as if those proceedings were the original action, and subject to such other modifications as may be prescribed by rules of court in any case or class of case.

PART III

36 Equitable jurisdiction and remedies

(1) The following time limits under this Act, that is to say—

(a) the time limit under section 2 for actions founded on tort;

(aa) the time limit under section 4A for actions for libel or slander;

(b) the time limit under section 5 for actions founded on simple contract;

(c) the time limit under section 7 for actions to enforce awards where the submission is not by an instrument under seal;

(d) the time limit under section 8 for actions on a specialty;

(e) the time limit under section 9 for actions to recover a sum recoverable by virtue of any enactment; and

(f) the time limit under section 24 for actions to enforce a judgment;

shall not apply to any claim for specific performance of a contract or for an injunction or for other equitable relief, except in so far as any such time limit may be applied by the court by analogy in like manner as the corresponding time limit under any enactment repealed by the Limitation Act 1939 was applied before 1st July 1940.

(2) Nothing in this Act shall affect any equitable jurisdiction to refuse relief on the ground of acquiescence or otherwise.

37 Application to the Crown and the Duke of Cornwall

(1) Except as otherwise expressly provided in this Act, and without prejudice to section 39, this Act shall apply to proceedings by or against the Crown in like manner as it applies to proceedings between subjects.

38 Interpretation

(1) In this Act, unless the context otherwise requires—

...

"personal injuries" includes any disease and any impairment of a person's physical or mental condition, and "injury" and cognate expressions shall be construed accordingly;

...

(2) For the purposes of this Act a person shall be treated as under a disability while he is an infant, or lacks capacity (within the meaning of the Mental Capacity Act 2005) to conduct legal proceedings.

39 Saving for other limitation enactments

This Act shall not apply to any action or arbitration for which a period of limitation is prescribed by or under any other enactment (whether passed before or after the passing of this Act) or to any action or arbitration to which the Crown is a party and for which, if it were between subjects, a period of limitation would be prescribed by or under any such other enactment.

SENIOR COURTS ACT 1981
(1981, c. 54)

32   Orders for interim payment

(1)   As regards proceedings pending in the High Court, provision may be made by rules of court for enabling the court, in such circumstances as may be prescribed, to make an order requiring a party to the proceedings to make an interim payment of such amount as may be specified in the order, with provision for the payment to be made to such other party to the proceedings as may be so specified or, if the order so provides, by paying it into court.

(2)   Any rules of court which make provision in accordance with subsection (1) may include provision for enabling a party to any proceedings who, in pursuance of such an order, has made an interim payment to recover the whole or part of the amount of the payment in such circumstances, and from such other party to the proceedings, as may be determined in accordance with the rules.

(3)   Any rules made by virtue of this section may include such incidental, supplementary and consequential provisions as the rule-making authority may consider necessary or expedient.

(4)   Nothing in this section shall be construed as affecting the exercise of any power relating to costs, including any power to make rules of court relating to costs.

(5)   In this section "interim payment", in relation to a party to any proceedings, means a payment on account of any damages, debt or other sum (excluding any costs) which that party may be held liable to pay to or for the benefit of another party to the proceedings if a final judgment or order of the court in the proceedings is given or made in favour of that other party.

32A   Orders for provisional damages for personal injuries

(1)   This section applies to an action for damages for personal injuries in which there is proved or admitted to be a chance that at some definite or indefinite time in the future the injured person will, as a result of the act or omission which gave rise to the cause of action, develop some serious disease or suffer some serious deterioration in his physical or mental condition.

(2)   Subject to subsection (4) below, as regards any action for damages to which this section applies in which a judgment is given in the High Court, provision may be made by rules of court for enabling the court, in such circumstances as may be prescribed, to award the injured person—

    (a)   damages assessed on the assumption that the injured person will not develop the disease or suffer the deterioration in his condition; and

    (b)   further damages at a future date if he develops the disease or suffers the deterioration.

(3)   Any rules made by virtue of this section may include such incidental, supplementary and consequential provisions as the rule-making authority may consider necessary or expedient.

(4)   Nothing in this section shall be construed—

    (a)   as affecting the exercise of any power relating to costs, including any power to make rules of court relating to costs; or

    (b)   as prejudicing any duty of the court under any enactment or rule of law to reduce or limit the total damages which would have been recoverable apart from any such duty.

35   Provisions supplementary to ss. 33 and 34

(5)   In sections 32A, 33 and 34 and this section—

    ...

    "personal injuries" includes any disease and any impairment of a person's physical or mental condition.

35A   Powers of High Court to award interest on debts and damages

(1)   Subject to rules of court, in proceedings (whenever instituted) before the High Court for the recovery of a debt or damages there may be included in any sum for which judgment is given simple interest, at such rate as the court thinks fit or as rules of court may provide, on all or any part of the debt or damages in respect of which judgment is given, or payment is made before judgment, for all or any part of the period between the date when the cause of action arose and—

     (a)   in the case of any sum paid before judgment, the date of the payment; and

     (b)   in the case of the sum for which judgment is given, the date of the judgment.

(2)   In relation to a judgment given for damages for personal injuries or death which exceed £200 subsection (1) shall have effect—

     (a)   with the substitution of "shall be included" for "may be included"; and

     (b)   with the addition of "unless the court is satisfied that there are special reasons to the contrary" after "given", where first occurring.

(3)   Subject to rules of court, where—

     (a)   there are proceedings (whenever instituted) before the High Court for the recovery of a debt; and

     (b)   the defendant pays the whole debt to the plaintiff (otherwise than in pursuance of a judgment in the proceedings),

   the defendant shall be liable to pay the plaintiff simple interest at such rate as the court thinks fit or as rules of court may provide on all or any part of the debt for all or any part of the period between the date when the cause of action arose and the date of the payment.

(4)   Interest in respect of a debt shall not be awarded under this section for a period during which, for whatever reason, interest on the debt already runs.

(5)   Without prejudice to the generality of section 84, rules of court may provide for a rate of interest by reference to the rate specified in section 17 of the Judgments Act 1838 as that section has effect from time to time or by reference to a rate for which any other enactment provides.

(6)   Interest under this section may be calculated at different rates in respect of different periods.

(7)   In this section "plaintiff" means the person seeking the debt or damages and "defendant" means the person from whom the plaintiff seeks the debt or damages and "personal injuries" includes any disease and any impairment of a person's physical or mental condition.

37   Powers of High Court with respect to injunctions and receivers

(1)   The High Court may by order (whether interlocutory or final) grant an injunction or appoint a receiver in all cases in which it appears to the court to be just and convenient to do so.

49   Concurrent administration of law and equity

(1)   Subject to the provisions of this or any other Act, every court exercising jurisdiction in England and Wales in any civil cause or matter shall continue to administer law and equity on the basis that, wherever there is any conflict or variance between the rules of equity and the rules of the common law with reference to the same matter, the rules of equity shall prevail.

50   Power to award damages as well as, or in substitution for, injunction or specific performance

Where the Court of Appeal or the High Court has jurisdiction to entertain an application for an injunction or specific performance, it may award damages in addition to, or in substitution for, an injunction or specific performance.

69   Trial by jury

(1)   Where, on the application of any party to an action to be tried in the Queen's Bench Division, the court is satisfied that there is in issue—

     (a)   a charge of fraud against that party; or

     (b)   a claim in respect of malicious prosecution or false imprisonment; or

(c)   any question or issue of a kind prescribed for the purposes of this paragraph,
the action shall be tried with a jury, unless the court is of opinion that the trial requires
any prolonged examination of documents or accounts or any scientific or local
investigation which cannot conveniently be made with a jury.

ADMINISTRATION OF JUSTICE ACT 1982
(1982, c. 53)

1   Abolition of right to damages for loss of expectation of life

(1)   In an action under the law of England and Wales or the law of Northern Ireland for
damages for personal injuries—

(a)   no damages shall be recoverable in respect of any loss of expectation of life
caused to the injured person by the injuries; but

(b)   if the injured person's expectation of life has been reduced by the injuries, the
court, in assessing damages in respect of pain and suffering caused by the
injuries, shall take account of any suffering caused or likely to be caused to him
by awareness that his expectation of life has been so reduced.

(2)   The reference in subsection (1)(a) above to damages in respect of loss of expectation
of life does not include damages in respect of loss of income.

2   Abolition of actions for loss of services, etc.

No person shall be liable in tort under the law of England and Wales or the law of Northern
Ireland—

(a)   to a husband on the ground only of having deprived him of the services or
society of his wife;

(b)   to a parent (or person standing in the place of a parent) on the ground only of his
having deprived him of the services of a child; or

(c)   on the ground only—

(i)   of having deprived another of the services of his menial servant;

(ii)   of having deprived another of the services of his female servant by raping
or seducing her; or

(iii)   of enticement of a servant or harbouring a servant.

**5   Maintenance at public expense to be taken into account in assessment
of damages**

In an action under the law of England and Wales or the law of Northern Ireland for damages
for personal injuries (including any such action arising out of a contract) any saving to the
injured person which is attributable to his maintenance wholly or partly at public expense
in a hospital, nursing home or other institution shall be set off against any income lost by
him as a result of his injuries.

CIVIL AVIATION ACT 1982
(1982, c. 16)

76   Liability of aircraft in respect of trespass, nuisance and surface damage

(1)   No action shall lie in respect of trespass or in respect of nuisance, by reason only of
the flight of an aircraft over any property at a height above the ground which, having
regard to wind, weather and all the circumstances of the case is reasonable, or the
ordinary incidents of such flight, so long as the provisions of any Air Navigation Order
and of any orders under section 62 above have been duly complied with ...

(2)   Subject to subsection (3) below, where material loss or damage is caused to any
person or property on land or water by, or by a person in, or an article, animal or
person falling from, an aircraft while in flight, taking off or landing, then unless the loss
or damage was caused or contributed to by the negligence of the person by whom it
was suffered, damages in respect of the loss or damage shall be recoverable without
proof of negligence or intention or other cause of action, as if the loss or damage had
been caused by the wilful act, neglect, or default of the owner of the aircraft.

(3)   Where material loss or damage is caused as aforesaid in circumstances in which—
(a)   damages are recoverable in respect of the said loss or damage by virtue only of subsection (2) above, and
(b)   a legal liability is created in some person other than the owner to pay damages in respect of the said loss or damage,
the owner shall be entitled to be indemnified by that other person against any claim in respect of the said loss or damage.

77   Nuisance caused by aircraft on aerodromes

(1)   An Air Navigation Order may provide for regulating the conditions under which noise and vibration may be caused by aircraft on aerodromes and may provide that subsection (2) below shall apply to any aerodrome as respects which provision as to noise and vibration caused by aircraft is so made.
(2)   No action shall lie in respect of nuisance by reason only of the noise and vibration caused by aircraft on an aerodrome to which this subsection applies by virtue of an Air Navigation Order, as long as the provisions of any such Order are duly complied with.

FORFEITURE ACT 1982
(1982, c. 34)

1   The "forfeiture rule"

(1)   In this Act, the "forfeiture rule" means the rule of public policy which in certain circumstances precludes a person who has unlawfully killed another from acquiring a benefit in consequence of the killing.

2   Power to modify the rule

(1)   Where a court determines that the forfeiture rule has precluded a person (in this section referred to as "the offender") who has unlawfully killed another from acquiring any interest in property mentioned in subsection (4) below, the court may make an order under this section modifying or excluding the effect of that rule.
(2)   The court shall not make an order under this section modifying or excluding the effect of the forfeiture rule in any case unless it is satisfied that, having regard to the conduct of the offender and of the deceased and to such other circumstances as appear to the court to be material, the justice of the case requires the effect of the rule to be so modified or excluded in that case.
(3)   In any case where a person stands convicted of an offence of which unlawful killing is an element, the court shall not make an order under this section modifying or excluding the effect of the forfeiture rule in that case unless proceedings for the purpose are brought before the expiry of the relevant period.
(3A) In subsection (3) above, the "relevant period" is the period of six months beginning with—
(a)   the end of the period allowed for bringing the appeal against the conviction, or
(b)   if such an appeal is brought, the conclusion of proceedings on the appeal.
(4)   The interests in property referred to in subsection (1) above are—
(a)   any beneficial interest in property which (apart from the forfeiture rule) the offender would have acquired—
(i)   under the deceased's will (including, as respects Scotland, any writing having testamentary effect) or the law relating to intestacy or by way of ius relicti, ius relictae or legitim;
(ii)   on the nomination of the deceased in accordance with the provisions of any enactment;
(iii) as a donatio mortis causa made by the deceased; or
(iv)   under a special destination (whether relating to heritable or moveable property); or
(b)   any beneficial interest in property which (apart from the forfeiture rule) the offender would have acquired in consequence of the death of the deceased, being property which, before the death, was held on trust for any person.

(5) An order under this section may modify or exclude the effect of the forfeiture rule in respect of any interest in property to which the determination referred to in subsection (1) above relates and may do so in either or both of the following ways, that is—

(a) where there is more than one such interest, by excluding the application of the rule in respect of any or all of those interests; and

(b) in the case of any such interest in property, by excluding the application of the rule in respect of all or any part of the property.

(6) On the making of an order under this section modifying the effect of the forfeiture rule, the forfeiture rule shall have effect for all purposes (including purposes relating to anything done before the order is made) subject to the modifications made by the order ...

5 Exclusion of murderers

Nothing in this Act or in any order made under section 2 or referred to in section 3(1) of this Act or in any decision made under section 4(1A) of this Act shall affect the application of the forfeiture rule in the case of a person who stands convicted of murder.

SUPPLY OF GOODS AND SERVICES ACT 1982
(1982, c. 29)

PART I
SUPPLY OF GOODS

Contracts for the transfer of property in goods

1 The contracts concerned

(1) In this Act in its application to England and Wales and Northern Ireland a "relevant contract for the transfer of goods" means a contract under which one person transfers or agrees to transfer to another the property in goods, other than an excepted contract, and other than a contract to which Chapter 2 of Part 1 of the Consumer Rights Act 2015 applies.

(2) For the purposes of this section an excepted contract means any of the following:—

(a) a contract of sale of goods;

(b) a hire-purchase agreement;

(c) ...

(d) a transfer or agreement to transfer which is made by deed and for which there is no consideration other than the presumed consideration imported by the deed;

(e) a contract intended to operate by way of mortgage, pledge, charge or other security.

(3) For the purposes of this Act in its application to England and Wales and Northern Ireland a contract is a relevant contract for the transfer of goods whether or not services are also provided or to be provided under the contract, and (subject to subsection (2) above) whatever is the nature of the consideration for the transfer or agreement to transfer.

2 Implied terms about title, etc.

(1) In a relevant contract for the transfer of goods, other than one to which subsection (3) below applies, there is an implied condition on the part of the transferor that in the case of a transfer of the property in the goods he has a right to transfer the property and in the case of an agreement to transfer the property in the goods he will have such a right at the time when the property is to be transferred.

(2) In a relevant contract for the transfer of goods, other than one to which subsection (3) below applies, there is also an implied warranty that—

(a) the goods are free, and will remain free until the time when the property is to be transferred, from any charge or encumbrance not disclosed or known to the transferee before the contract is made, and

(b)   the transferee will enjoy quiet possession of the goods except so far as it may be disturbed by the owner or other person entitled to the benefit of any charge or encumbrance so disclosed or known.

(3)   This subsection applies to a relevant contract for the transfer of goods in the case of which there appears from the contract or is to be inferred from its circumstances an intention that the transferor should transfer only such title as he or a third person may have.

(4)   In a contract to which subsection (3) above applies there is an implied warranty that all charges or encumbrances known to the transferor and not known to the transferee have been disclosed to the transferee before the contract is made.

(5)   In a contract to which subsection (3) above applies there is also an implied warranty that none of the following will disturb the transferee's quiet possession of the goods, namely—

(a)   the transferor;

(b)   in a case where the parties to the contract intend that the transferor should transfer only such title as a third person may have, that person;

(c)   anyone claiming through or under the transferor or that third person otherwise than under a charge or encumbrance disclosed or known to the transferee before the contract is made.

3   Implied terms where transfer is by description

(1)   This section applies where, under a relevant contract for the transfer of goods, the transferor transfers or agrees to transfer the property in the goods by description.

(2)   In such case there is an implied condition that the goods will correspond with the description.

(3)   If the transferor transfers or agrees to transfer the property in the goods by sample as well as by description it is not sufficient that the bulk of the goods corresponds with the sample if the goods do not also correspond with the description.

(4)   A contract is not prevented from falling within subsection (1) above by reason only that, being exposed for supply, the goods are selected by the transferee.

4   Implied terms about quality or fitness

(1)   Except as provided by this section and section 5 below and subject to the provision of any other enactment, there is no implied condition or warranty about the quality or fitness for any particular purpose of goods supplied under a relevant contract for the transfer of goods.

(2)   Where, under such a contract, the transferor transfers the property in goods in the course of a business, there is an implied condition that the goods supplied under the contract are of satisfactory quality.

(2A)   For the purposes of this section and section 5 below, goods are of satisfactory quality if they meet the standard that a reasonable person would regard as satisfactory, taking account of any description of the goods, the price (if relevant) and all the other relevant circumstances.

(3)   The condition implied by subsection (2) above does not extend to any matter making the quality of goods unsatisfactory—

(a)   which is specifically drawn to the transferee's attention before the contract is made,

(b)   where the transferee examines the goods before the contract is made, which that examination ought to reveal, or

(c)   where the property in the goods is transferred by reference to a sample, which would have been apparent on a reasonable examination of the sample.

(4)   Subsection (5) below applies where, under a relevant contract for the transfer of goods, the transferor transfers the property in goods in the course of a business and the transferee, expressly or by implication, makes known—

(a)   to the transferor, or

(b)   where the consideration or part of the consideration for the transfer is a sum payable by instalments and the goods were previously sold by a credit-broker to the transferor, to that credit-broker,

any particular purpose for which the goods are being acquired.

(5)   In that case there is (subject to subsection (6) below) an implied condition that the goods supplied under the contract are reasonably fit for that purpose, whether or not that is a purpose for which such goods are commonly supplied.

(6)   Subsection (5) above does not apply where the circumstances show that the transferee does not rely, or that it is unreasonable for him to rely, on the skill or judgment of the transferor or credit-broker.

(7)   An implied condition or warranty about quality or fitness for a particular purpose may be annexed by usage to a relevant contract for the transfer of goods.

(8)   The preceding provisions of this section apply to a transfer by a person who in the course of a business is acting as agent for another as they apply to a transfer by a principal in the course of a business, except where that other is not transferring in the course of a business and either the transferee knows that fact or reasonable steps are taken to bring it to the transferee's notice before the contract concerned is made.

5   Implied terms where transfer is by sample

(1)   This section applies where, under a relevant contract for the transfer of goods, the transferor transfers or agrees to transfer the property in the goods by reference to a sample.

(2)   In such a case there is an implied condition—
   (a)   that the bulk will correspond with the sample in quality; and
   (b)   that the transferee will have a reasonable opportunity of comparing the bulk with the sample; and
   (c)   that the goods will be free from any defect, making their quality unsatisfactory, which would not be apparent on reasonable examination of the sample.

(4)   For the purposes of this section a transferor transfers or agrees to transfer the property in goods by reference to a sample where there is an express or implied term to that effect in the contract concerned.

5A   Modification of remedies for breach of statutory condition in non-consumer cases

(1)   Where in the case of a relevant contract for the transfer of goods—
   (a)   the transferee would, apart from this subsection, have the right to treat the contract as repudiated by reason of a breach on the part of the transferor of a term implied by section 3, 4 or 5(2)(a) or (c) above, but
   (b)   the breach is so slight that it would be unreasonable for him to do so,
   the breach is not to be treated as a breach of condition but may be treated as a breach of warranty.

(2)   This section applies unless a contrary intention appears in, or is to be implied from, the contract.

(3)   It is for the transferor to show that a breach fell within subsection (1)(b) above.

Contracts for the hire of goods

6   The contracts concerned

(1)   In this Act in its application to England and Wales and Northern Ireland a "relevant contract for the hire of goods" means a contract under which one person bails or agrees to bail goods to another by way of hire, other than an excepted contract, and other than a contract to which Chapter 2 of Part 1 of the Consumer Rights Act 2015 applies.

(2)   For the purposes of this section an excepted contract means any of the following:—
   (a)   a hire-purchase agreement;
   (b)   ...

(3)   For the purposes of this Act in its application to England and Wales and Northern Ireland a contract is a relevant contract for the hire of goods whether or not services are also provided or to be provided under the contract, and (subject to subsection (2) above) whatever is the nature of the consideration for the bailment or agreement to bail by way of hire.

7   Implied terms about right to transfer possession, etc.

(1)   In a relevant contract for the hire of goods there is an implied condition on the part of the bailor that in the case of a bailment he has a right to transfer possession of the goods by way of hire for the period of the bailment and in the case of an agreement to bail he will have such a right at the time of the bailment.

(2)   In a relevant contract for the hire of goods there is also an implied warranty that the bailee will enjoy quiet possession of the goods for the period of the bailment except so far as the possession may be disturbed by the owner or other person entitled to the benefit of any charge or encumbrance disclosed or known to the bailee before the contract is made.

(3)   The preceding provisions of this section do not affect the right of the bailor to repossess the goods under an express or implied term of the contract.

8   Implied terms where hire is by description

(1)   This section applies where, under a relevant contract for the hire of goods, the bailor bails or agrees to bail the goods by description.

(2)   In such a case there is an implied condition that the goods will correspond with the description.

(3)   If under the contract the bailor bails or agrees to bail the goods by reference to a sample as well as a description it is not sufficient that the bulk of the goods corresponds with the sample if the goods do not also correspond with the description.

(4)   A contract is not prevented from falling within subsection (1) above by reason only that, being exposed for supply, the goods are selected by the bailee.

9   Implied terms about quality or fitness

(1)   Except as provided by this section and section 10 below and subject to the provisions of any other enactment, there is no implied condition or warranty about the quality or fitness for any particular purpose of goods bailed under a relevant contract for the hire of goods.

(2)   Where, under such a contract, the bailor bails goods in the course of a business, there is an implied condition that the goods supplied under the contract are of satisfactory quality.

(2A) For the purposes of this section and section 10 below, goods are of satisfactory quality if they meet the standard that a reasonable person would regard as satisfactory, taking account of any description of the goods, the consideration for the bailment (if relevant) and all the other relevant circumstances.

(3)   The condition implied by subsection (2) above does not extend to any matter making the quality of goods unsatisfactory—
(a)   which is specifically drawn to the bailee's attention before the contract is made,
(b)   where the bailee examines the goods before the contract is made, which that examination ought to reveal, or
(c)   where the goods are bailed by reference to a sample, which would have been apparent on a reasonable examination of the sample.

(4)   Subsection (5) below applies where, under a relevant contract for the hire of goods, the bailor bails goods in the course of a business and the bailee, expressly or by implication, makes known—
(a)   to the bailor in the course of negotiations conducted by him in relation to the making of the contract, or
(b)   to a credit-broker in the course of negotiations conducted by that broker in relation to goods sold by him to the bailor before forming the subject matter of the contract,
any particular purpose for which the goods are being bailed.

(5)   In that case there is (subject to subsection (6) below) an implied condition that the goods supplied under the contract are reasonably fit for that purpose, whether or not that is a purpose for which such goods are commonly supplied.

(6)   Subsection (5) above does not apply where the circumstances show that the bailee does not rely, or that it is unreasonable for him to rely, on the skill or judgment of the bailor or credit-broker.

(7)   An implied condition or warranty about quality or fitness for a particular purpose may be annexed by usage to a relevant contract for the hire of goods.

(8)   The preceding provisions of this section apply to a bailment by a person who in the course of a business is acting as agent for another as they apply to a bailment by a principal in the course of a business, except where that other is not bailing in the course of a business and either the bailee knows that fact or reasonable steps are taken to bring it to the bailee's notice before the contract concerned is made.

10   Implied terms where hire is by sample

(1)   This section applies where, under a relevant contract for the hire of goods, the bailor bails or agrees to bail the goods by reference to a sample.

(2)   In such a case there is an implied condition—

    (a)   that the bulk will correspond with the sample in quality; and

    (b)   that the bailee will have a reasonable opportunity of comparing the bulk with the sample; and

    (c)   that the goods will be free from any defect, making their quality unsatisfactory, which would not be apparent on reasonable examination of the sample.

(4)   For the purposes of this section a bailor bails or agrees to bail goods by reference to a sample where there is an express or implied term to that effect in the contract concerned.

10A   Modification of remedies for breach of statutory condition in non-consumer cases

(1)   Where in the case of a relevant contract for the hire of goods—

    (a)   the bailee would, apart from this subsection, have the right to treat the contract as repudiated by reason of a breach on the part of the bailor of a term implied by section 8, 9 or 10(2)(a) or (c) above, but

    (b)   the breach is so slight that it would be unreasonable for him to do so,

the breach is not to be treated as a breach of condition but may be treated as a breach of warranty.

(2)   This section applies unless a contrary intention appears in, or is to be implied from, the contract.

(3)   It is for the bailor to show that a breach fell within subsection (1)(b) above.

Exclusion of implied terms, etc.

11   Exclusion of implied terms, etc.

(1)   Where a right, duty or liability would arise under a relevant contract for the transfer of goods or a relevant contract for the hire of goods by implication of law, it may (subject to subsection (2) below and the 1977 Act) be negatived or varied by express agreement, or by the course of dealing between the parties, or by such usage as binds both parties to the contract.

(2)   An express condition or warranty does not negative a condition or warranty implied by the preceding provisions of this Act unless inconsistent with it.

(3)   Nothing in the preceding provisions of this Act prejudices the operation of any other enactment or any rule of law whereby any condition or warranty (other than one relating to quality or fitness) is to be implied in a relevant contract for the transfer of goods or a relevant contract for the hire of goods.

PART II
SUPPLY OF SERVICES

12   The contracts concerned

(1)   In this Act a "relevant contract for the supply of a service" means, subject to subsection (1) below, a contract under which a person ("the supplier") agrees to carry out a service, other than a contract to which Chapter 4 of Part 1 of the Consumer Rights Act 2015 applies.

(2) For the purposes of this Act, a contract of service or apprenticeship is not a relevant contract for the supply of a service.

(3) Subject to subsection (2) above, a contract is a relevant contract for the supply of a service for the purposes of this Act whether or not goods are also—
    (a)   transferred or to be transferred, or
    (b)   bailed or to be bailed by way of hire,
    under the contract, and whatever is the nature of the consideration for which the service is to be carried out.

(4) The Secretary of State may by order provide that one or more of sections 13 to 15 below shall not apply to services of a description specified in the order, and such an order may make different provision for different circumstances.

(5) The power to make an order under subsection (4) above shall be exercisable by statutory instrument subject to annulment in pursuance of a resolution of either House of Parliament.

13   Implied term about care and skill

In a relevant contract for the supply of a service where the supplier is acting in the course of a business, there is an implied term that the supplier will carry out the service with reasonable care and skill.

14   Implied term about time of performance

(1) Where, under a relevant contract for the supply of a service by a supplier acting in the course of a business, the time for the service to be carried out is not fixed by the contract, left to be fixed in a manner agreed by the contract or determined by the course of dealing between the parties, there is an implied term that the supplier will carry out the service within a reasonable time.

(2) What is a reasonable time is a question of fact.

15   Implied term about consideration

(1) Where, under a relevant contract for the supply of a service, the consideration for the service is not determined by the contract, left to be determined in a manner agreed by the contract or determined by the course of dealing between the parties, there is an implied term that the party contracting with the supplier will pay a reasonable charge.

(2) What is a reasonable charge is a question of fact.

16   Exclusion of implied terms, etc.

(1) Where a right, duty or liability would arise under a relevant contract for the supply of a service by virtue of this Part of this Act, it may (subject to subsection (2) below and the 1977 Act) be negatived or varied by express agreement, or by the course of dealing between the parties, or by such usage as binds both parties to the contract.

(2) An express term does not negative a term implied by this Part of this Act unless inconsistent with it.

(3) Nothing in this Part of this Act prejudices—
    (a)   any rule of law which imposes on the supplier a duty stricter than that imposed by section 13 or 14 above; or
    (b)   subject to paragraph (a) above, any rule of law whereby any term not inconsistent with this Part of this Act is to be implied in a contract for the supply of a service.

(4) This Part of this Act has effect subject to any other enactment which defines or restricts the rights, duties or liabilities arising in connection with a service of any description.

PART III
SUPPLEMENTARY

18   Interpretation: general

(1) In the preceding provisions of this Act and this section—
    "bailee", in relation to a relevant contract for the hire of goods means (depending on the context) a person to whom the goods are bailed under the contract, or a person to

whom they are to be so bailed, or a person to whom the rights under the contract of either of those persons have passed;

"bailor", in relation to a relevant contract for the hire of goods, means (depending on the context) a person who bails the goods under the contract, or a person who agrees to do so, or a person to whom the duties under the contract of either of those persons have passed; "business" includes a profession and the activities of any government department or local or public authority;

"credit-broker" means a person acting in the course of a business of credit brokerage carried on by him;

"credit brokerage" means the effecting of introductions—

(a) of individuals desiring to obtain credit to persons carrying on any business so far as it relates to the provision of credit; or

(b) of individuals desiring to obtain goods on hire to persons carrying on a business which comprises or relates to the bailment or as regards Scotland the hire of goods under a contract for the hire of goods; or

(c) of individuals desiring to obtain credit, or to obtain goods on hire, to other creditbrokers;

"enactment" means any legislation (including subordinate legislation) of the United Kingdom or Northern Ireland;

"goods" includes all personal chattels ... and as regards Scotland all corporeal moveables; and in particular "goods" includes emblements, industrial growing crops, and things attached to or forming part of the land which are agreed to be severed before the transfer bailment or hire concerned or under the contract concerned;

"hire-purchase agreement" has the same meaning as in the 1974 Act;

"property", in relation to goods, means the general property in them and not merely a special property;

"transferee", in relation to a relevant contract for the transfer of goods, means (depending on the context) a person to whom the property in the goods is transferred under the contract, or a person to whom the property is to be so transferred, or a person to whom the rights under the contract of either of those persons have passed;

"transferor", in relation to a relevant contract for the transfer of goods, means (depending on the context) a person who transfers the property in the goods under the contract, or a person who agrees to do so, or a person to whom the duties under the contract of either of those persons have passed.

(2) In subsection (1) above, in the definitions of bailee, bailor, transferee and transferor, a reference to rights or duties passing is to their passing by assignment, assignation operation of law or otherwise.

(3) For the purposes of this Act, the quality of goods includes their state and condition and the following (among others) are in appropriate cases aspects of the quality of goods—

(a) fitness for all the purposes for which goods of the kind in question are commonly supplied,

(b) appearance and finish,

(c) freedom from minor defects,

(d) safety, and

(e) durability.

19 Interpretation: references to Acts

In this Act—

"the 1973 Act" means the Supply of Goods (Implied Terms) Act 1973;

"the 1974 Act" means the Consumer Credit Act 1974;

"the 1977 Act" means the Unfair Contract Terms Act 1977; and

"the 1979 Act" means the Sale of Goods Act 1979.

20 Citation, transitional provisions, commencement and extent

(1) This Act may be cited as the Supply of Goods and Services Act 1982.

OCCUPIERS' LIABILITY ACT 1984
(1984, c. 3)

1   Duty of occupier to persons other than his visitors

(1)   The rules enacted by this section shall have effect, in place of the rules of the common law, to determine—

    (a)   whether any duty is owed by a person as occupier of premises to persons other than his visitors in respect of any risk of their suffering injury on the premises by reason of any danger due to the state of the premises or to things done or omitted to be done on them; and

    (b)   if so, what that duty is.

(2)   For the purposes of this section, the persons who are to be treated respectively as an occupier of any premises (which, for those purposes, include any fixed or movable structure) and as his visitors are—

    (a)   any person who owes in relation to the premises the duty referred to in section 2 of the Occupiers' Liability Act 1957 (the common duty of care), and (b) those who are his visitors for the purposes of that duty.

(3)   An occupier of premises owes a duty to another (not being his visitor) in respect of any such risk as is referred to in subsection (1) above if—

    (a)   he is aware of the danger or has reasonable grounds to believe that it exists;

    (b)   he knows or has reasonable grounds to believe that the other is in the vicinity of the danger concerned or that he may come into the vicinity of the danger (in either case, whether the other has lawful authority for being in that vicinity or not); and

    (c)   the risk is one against which, in all the circumstances of the case, he may reasonably be expected to offer the other some protection.

(4)   Where, by virtue of this section, an occupier of premises owes a duty to another in respect of such a risk, the duty is to take such care as is reasonable in all the circumstances of the case to see that he does not suffer injury on the premises by reason of the danger concerned.

(5)   Any duty owed by virtue of this section in respect of a risk may, in an appropriate case, be discharged by taking such steps as are reasonable in all the circumstances of the case to give warning of the danger concerned or to discourage persons from incurring the risk.

(6)   No duty is owed by virtue of this section to any person in respect of risks willingly accepted as his by that person (the question whether a risk was so accepted to be decided on the same principles as in other cases in which one person owes a duty of care to another).

(6A) At any time when the right conferred by section 2(1) of the Countryside and Rights of Way Act 2000 is exercisable in relation to land which is access land for the purposes of Part I of that Act, an occupier of the land owes (subject to subsection (6C) below) no duty by virtue of this section to any person in respect of—

    (a)   a risk resulting from the existence of any natural feature of the landscape, or any river, stream, ditch or pond whether or not a natural feature, or

    (b)   a risk of that person suffering injury when passing over, under or through any wall, fence or gate, except by proper use of the gate or of a stile.

(6AA) Where the land is coastal margin for the purposes of Part 1 of that Act (including any land treated as coastal margin by virtue of section 16 of that Act), subsection (6A) has effect as if for paragraphs (a) and (b) of that subsection there were substituted "a risk resulting from the existence of any physical feature (whether of the landscape or otherwise)".

(6B) For the purposes of subsection (6A) above, any plant, shrub or tree, of whatever origin, is to be regarded as a natural feature of the landscape.

(6C) Subsection (6A) does not prevent an occupier from owing a duty by virtue of this section in respect of any risk where the danger concerned is due to anything done by the occupier—

    (a)   with the intention of creating that risk, or

    (b)   being reckless as to whether that risk is created.

(7) No duty is owed by virtue of this section to persons using the highway, and this section does not affect any duty owed to such persons.

(8) Where a person owes a duty by virtue of this section, he does not, by reason of any breach of the duty, incur any liability in respect of any loss of or damage to property.

(9) In this section—

"highway" means any part of a highway other than a ferry or waterway;

"injury" means anything resulting in death or personal injury, including any disease and any impairment of physical or mental condition; and

"movable structure" includes any vessel, vehicle or aircraft.

1A   Special considerations relating to access land

In determining whether any, and if so what, duty is owed by virtue of section 1 by an occupier of land at any time when the right conferred by section 2(1) of the Countryside and Rights of Way Act 2000 is exercisable in relation to the land, regard is to be had, in particular, to—

(a) the fact that the existence of that right ought not to place an undue burden (whether financial or otherwise) on the occupier,

(b) the importance of maintaining the character of the countryside, including features of historic, traditional or archaeological interest, and

(c) any relevant guidance given under section 20 of that Act.

3   Application to Crown

Section 1 of this Act shall bind the Crown, but as regards the Crown's liability in tort shall not bind the Crown further than the Crown is made liable in tort by the Crown Proceedings Act 1947.

POLICE AND CRIMINAL EVIDENCE ACT 1984
(1984, c. 60)

17   Entry for purpose of arrest etc.

(1) Subject to the following provisions of this section, and without prejudice to any other enactment, a constable may enter and search any premises for the purpose—

(a) of executing—

(i) a warrant of arrest issued in connection with or arising out of criminal proceedings; or

(ii) a warrant of commitment issued under section 76 of the Magistrates' Courts Act 1980;

(b) of arresting a person for an indictable offence;

...

(e) of saving life or limb or preventing serious damage to property.

(4) The power of search conferred by this section is only a power to search to the extent that is reasonably required for the purpose for which the power of entry is exercised.

(5) Subject to subsection (6) below, all the rules of common law under which a constable has power to enter premises without a warrant are hereby abolished.

(6) Nothing in subsection (5) above affects any power of entry to deal with or prevent a breach of the peace.

19   General power of seizure etc.

(1) The powers conferred by subsections (2), (3) and (4) below are exercisable by a constable who is lawfully on any premises.

(2) The constable may seize anything which is on the premises if he has reasonable grounds for believing—

(a) that it has been obtained in consequence of the commission of an offence; and

(b) that it is necessary to seize it in order to prevent it being concealed, lost, damaged, altered or destroyed.

22   Retention

(1) Subject to subsection (4) below, anything which has been seized by a constable or taken away by a constable following a requirement made by virtue of section 19 or 20 above may be retained so long as is necessary in all the circumstances.

(3) Nothing seized on the ground that it may be used—
  (a) to cause physical injury to any person;
  (b) to damage property;
  (c) to interfere with evidence; or
  (d) to assist in escape from police detention or lawful custody,
  may be retained when the person from whom it was seized is no longer in police detention or the custody of a court or is in the custody of a court but has been released on bail.

24   Arrest without warrant: constables

(1) A constable may arrest without a warrant—
  (a) anyone who is about to commit an offence;
  (b) anyone who is in the act of committing an offence;
  (c) anyone whom he has reasonable grounds for suspecting to be about to commit an offence.
  (d) anyone whom he has reasonable grounds for suspecting to be committing an offence.
(2) If a constable has reasonable grounds for suspecting that an offence has been committed, he may arrest without a warrant anyone whom he has reasonable grounds to suspect of being guilty of it.
(3) If an offence has been committed, a constable may arrest without a warrant—
  (a) anyone who is guilty of the offence;
  (b) anyone whom he has reasonable grounds for suspecting to be guilty of it.
(4) But the power of summary arrest conferred by subsection (1), (2) or (3) is exercisable only if the constable has reasonable grounds for believing that for any of the reasons mentioned in subsection (5) it is necessary to arrest the person in question.
(5) The reasons are—
  (a) to enable the name of the person in question to be ascertained (in the case where the constable does not know, and cannot readily ascertain, the person's name, or has reasonable grounds for doubting whether a name given by the person as his name is his real name);
  (b) correspondingly as regards the person's address;
  (c) to prevent the person in question—
    (i) causing physical injury to himself or any other person;
    (ii) suffering physical injury;
    (iii) causing loss of or damage to property;
    (iv) committing an offence against public decency (subject to subsection (6)); or
    (v) causing an unlawful obstruction of the highway;
  (d) to protect a child or other vulnerable person from the person in question;
  (e) to allow the prompt and effective investigation of the offence or of the conduct of the person in question;
  (f) to prevent any prosecution for the offence from being hindered by the disappearance of the person in question.
(6) Subsection (5)(c)(iv) applies only where members of the public going about their normal business cannot reasonably be expected to avoid the person in question.

24A   Arrest without warrant: other persons

(1) A person other than a constable may arrest without a warrant—
  (a) anyone who is in the act of committing an indictable offence;
  (b) anyone whom he has reasonable grounds for suspecting to be committing an indictable offence.
(2) Where an indictable offence has been committed, a person other than a constable may arrest without a warrant—
  (a) anyone who is guilty of the offence;
  (b) anyone whom he has reasonable grounds for suspecting to be guilty of it.

(3)   But the power of summary arrest conferred by subsection (1) or (2) is exercisable only if—

    (a)   the person making the arrest has reasonable grounds for believing that for any of the reasons mentioned in subsection (4) it is necessary to arrest the person in question; and

    (b)   it appears to the person making the arrest that it is not reasonably practicable for a constable to make it instead.

(4)   The reasons are to prevent the person in question—

    (a)   causing physical injury to himself or any other person;

    (b)   suffering physical injury;

    (c)   causing loss of or damage to property; or

    (d)   making off before a constable can assume responsibility for him.

(5)   This section does not apply in relation to an offence under Part 3 of 3A of the Public Order Act 1986.

32   Search upon arrest

(1)   A constable may search an arrested person, in any case where the person to be searched has been arrested at a place other than a police station, if the constable has reasonable grounds for believing that the arrested person may present a danger to himself or others.

34   Limitations on police detention

(1)   A person arrested for an offence shall not be kept in police detention except in accordance with the provisions of this Part of this Act.

(2)   Subject to subsection (3) below, if at any time a custody officer—

    (a)   becomes aware, in relation to any person in police detention, that the grounds for the detention of that person have ceased to apply; and

    (b)   is not aware of any other grounds on which the continued detention of that person could be justified under the provisions of this Part of this Act,

it shall be the duty of the custody officer, subject to subsection (4) below, to order his immediate release from custody.

55   Intimate searches

(2)   An officer may not authorise an intimate search of a person for anything unless he has reasonable grounds for believing that it cannot be found without his being intimately searched.

62   Intimate samples

(1)   Subject to section 63B below An intimate sample may be taken from a person in police detention only—

    (a)   if a police officer of at least the rank of inspector authorises it to be taken; and

    (b)   if the appropriate consent is given.

(1A) An intimate sample may be taken from a person who is not in police detention but from whom, in the course of the investigation of an offence, two or more intimate samples suitable for the same means of analysis have been taken which have proved insufficient—

    (a)   if a police officer of at least the rank of inspector authorises it to be taken; and

    (b)   if the appropriate consent is given.

65   Part V — supplementary

In this Part of this Act—

...

"intimate sample" means—

(a)   a sample of blood, semen or any other tissue fluid, urine or pubic hair;

(b)   a dental impression;

(c)   a swab taken from any part of a person's genitals (including pubic hair) or from a person's body orifice other than the mouth;

...

INSOLVENCY ACT 1986
(1986, c. 45)

238 Transactions at an undervalue (England and Wales)

(1) This section applies in the case of a company where—
   (a) the company enters administration; or
   (b) the company goes into liquidation; and "the office-holder" means the administrator or the liquidator, as the case may be.

(2) Where the company has at a relevant time (defined in section 240) entered into a transaction with any person at an undervalue, the office-holder may apply to the court for an order under this section.

(3) Subject as follows, the court shall, on such an application, make such order as it thinks fit for restoring the position to what it would have been if the company had not entered into that transaction.

(4) For the purposes of this section and section 241, a company enters into a transaction with a person at an undervalue if—
   (a) the company makes a gift to that person or otherwise enters into a transaction with that person on terms that provide for the company to receive no consideration, or
   (b) the company enters into a transaction with that person for a consideration the value of which, in money or money's worth, is significantly less than the value, in money or money's worth, of the consideration provided by the company.

(5) The court shall not make an order under this section in respect of a transaction at an undervalue if it is satisfied—
   (a) that the company which entered into the transaction did so in good faith and for the purpose of carrying on its business, and
   (b) that at the time it did so there were reasonable grounds for believing that the transaction would benefit the company.

LATENT DAMAGE ACT 1986
(1986, c. 37)

1 Time limits for negligence actions in respect of latent damage not involving personal injuries

The following sections shall be inserted in the Limitation Act 1980 (referred to below in this Act as the 1980 Act) ...

3 Accrual of cause of action to successive owners in respect of latent damage to property

(1) Subject to the following provisions of this section, where—
   (a) a cause of action ("the original cause of action") has accrued to any person in respect of any negligence to which damage to any property in which he has an interest is attributable (in whole or in part); and
   (b) another person acquires an interest in that property after the date on which the original cause of action accrued but before the material facts about the damage have become known to any person who, at the time when he first has knowledge of those facts, has any interest in the property;

a fresh cause of action in respect of that negligence shall accrue to that other person on the date on which he acquires his interest in the property.

(2) A cause of action accruing to any person by virtue of subsection (1) above—
   (a) shall be treated as if based on breach of a duty of care at common law owed to the person to whom it accrues; and
   (b) shall be treated for the purposes of section 14A of the 1980 Act (special time limit for negligence actions where facts relevant to cause of action are not known at date of accrual) as having accrued on the date on which the original cause of action accrued.

(3) Section 28 of the 1980 Act (extension of limitation period in case of disability) shall not apply in relation to any such cause of action.

(4) Subsection (1) above shall not apply in any case where the person acquiring an interest in the damaged property is either—

(a) a person in whom the original cause of action vests by operation of law; or

(b) a person in whom the interest in that property vests by virtue of any order made by a court under section 538 of the Companies Act 1985 (vesting of company property in liquidator).

(5) For the purposes of subsection (1)(b) above, the material facts about the damage are such facts about the damage as would lead a reasonable person who has an interest in the damaged property at the time when those facts become known to him to consider it sufficiently serious to justify his instituting proceedings for damages against a defendant who did not dispute liability and was able to satisfy a judgment.

(6) For the purposes of this section a person's knowledge includes knowledge which he might reasonably have been expected to acquire—

(a) from facts observable or ascertainable by him; or

(b) from facts ascertained by him with the help of appropriate expert advice which it is reasonable for him to seek;

but a person shall not be taken by virtue of this subsection to have knowledge of a fact ascertainable by him only with the help of expert advice so long as he has taken all reasonable steps to obtain (and, where appropriate, to act on) that advice.

(7) This section shall bind the Crown, but as regards the Crown's liability in tort shall not bind the Crown further than the Crown is made liable in tort by the Crown Proceedings Act 1947.

4 Transitional provisions

(1) Nothing in section 1 or 2 of this Act shall—

(a) enable any action to be brought which was barred by the 1980 Act or (as the case may be) by the Limitation Act 1939 before this Act comes into force; or

(b) affect any action commenced before this Act comes into force.

(2) Subject to subsection (1) above, sections 1 and 2 of this Act shall have effect in relation to causes of action accruing before, as well as in relation to causes of action accruing after, this Act comes into force.

(3) Section 3 of this Act shall only apply in cases where an interest in damaged property is acquired after this Act comes into force but shall so apply, subject to subsection (4) below, irrespective of whether the original cause of action accrued before or after this Act comes into force.

(4) Where—

(a) a person acquires an interest in damaged property in circumstances to which section 3 would apart from this subsection apply; but

(b) the original cause of action accrued more than six years before this Act comes into force;

a cause of action shall not accrue to that person by virtue of subsection (1) of that section unless section 32(1)(b) of the 1980 Act (postponement of limitation period in case of deliberate concealment of relevant facts) would apply to any action founded on the original cause of action.

CONSUMER PROTECTION ACT 1987
(1987, c. 43)

PART I
PRODUCT LIABILITY

1 Purpose and construction of Part I

(1) This Part shall have effect for the purpose of making such provision as is necessary in order to comply with the product liability Directive and shall be construed accordingly.

(2) In this Part, except in so far as the context otherwise requires—

...

"dependant" and "relative" have the same meaning as they have in, respectively, the Fatal Accidents Act 1976 and the Damages (Scotland) Act 2011;

"producer", in relation to a product, means—

(a) the person who manufactured it;

(b) in the case of a substance which has not been manufactured but has been won or abstracted, the person who won or abstracted it;

(c) in the case of a product which has not been manufactured, won or abstracted but essential characteristics of which are attributable to an industrial or other process having been carried out (for example, in relation to agricultural produce), the person who carried out that process;

"product" means any goods or electricity and (subject to subsection (3) below) includes a product which is comprised in another product, whether by virtue of being a component part or raw material or otherwise; and

"the product liability Directive" means the Directive of the Council of the European Union, dated 25th July 1985, (No. 85/374/EEC) on the approximation of the laws, regulations and administrative provisions of the member States concerning liability for defective products.

(3) For the purposes of this Part a person who supplies any product in which products are comprised, whether by virtue of being component parts or raw materials or otherwise, shall not be treated by reason only of his supply of that product as supplying any of the products so comprised.

2 Liability for defective products

(1) Subject to the following provisions of this Part, where any damage is caused wholly or partly by a defect in a product, every person to whom subsection (2) below applies shall be liable for the damage.

(2) This subsection applies to—

(a) the producer of the product;

(b) any person who, by putting his name on the product or using a trade mark or other distinguishing mark in relation to the product, has held himself out to be the producer of the product;

(c) any person who has imported the product into a member State from a place outside the member States in order, in the course of any business of his, to supply it to another.

(3) Subject as aforesaid, where any damage is caused wholly or partly by a defect in a product, any person who supplied the product (whether to the person who suffered the damage, to the producer of any product in which the product in question is comprised or to any other person) shall be liable for the damage if—

(a) the person who suffered the damage requests the supplier to identify one or more of the persons (whether still in existence or not) to whom subsection (2) above applies in relation to the product;

(b) that request is made within a reasonable period after the damage occurs and at a time when it is not reasonably practicable for the person making the request to identify all those persons; and

(c) the supplier fails, within a reasonable period after receiving the request, either to comply with the request or to identify the person who supplied the product to him.

(5) Where two or more persons are liable by virtue of this Part for the same damage, their liability shall be joint and several.

(6) This section shall be without prejudice to any liability arising otherwise than by virtue of this Part.

3 Meaning of "defect"

(1) Subject to the following provisions of this section, there is a defect in a product for the purposes of this Part if the safety of the product is not such as persons generally are entitled to expect; and for those purposes "safety", in relation to a product, shall

include safety with respect to products comprised in that product and safety in the context of risks of damage to property, as well as in the context of risks of death or personal injury.

(2) In determining for the purposes of subsection (1) above what persons generally are entitled to expect in relation to a product all the circumstances shall be taken into account, including—

   (a) the manner in which, and purposes for which, the product has been marketed, its get-up, the use of any mark in relation to the product and any instructions for, or warnings with respect to, doing or refraining from doing anything with or in relation to the product;

   (b) what might reasonably be expected to be done with or in relation to the product; and

   (c) the time when the product was supplied by its producer to another;

   and nothing in this section shall require a defect to be inferred from the fact alone that the safety of a product which is supplied after that time is greater than the safety of the product in question.

4 Defences

(1) In any civil proceedings by virtue of this Part against any person ("the person proceeded against") in respect of a defect in a product it shall be a defence for him to show—

   (a) that the defect is attributable to compliance with any requirement imposed by or under any enactment or with any EU obligation; or

   (b) that the person proceeded against did not at any time supply the product to another; or

   (c) that the following conditions are satisfied, that is to say—

      (i) that the only supply of the product to another by the person proceeded against was otherwise than in the course of a business of that person's; and

      (ii) that section 2(2) above does not apply to that person or applies to him by virtue only of things done otherwise than with a view to profit; or

   (d) that the defect did not exist in the product at the relevant time; or

   (e) that the state of scientific and technical knowledge at the relevant time was not such that a producer of products of the same description as the product in question might be expected to have discovered the defect if it had existed in his products while they were under his control; or

   (f) that the defect—

      (i) constituted a defect in a product ("the subsequent product") in which the product in question had been comprised; and

      (ii) was wholly attributable to the design of the subsequent product or to compliance by the producer of the product in question with instructions given by the producer of the subsequent product.

(2) In this section "the relevant time", in relation to electricity, means the time at which it was generated, being a time before it was transmitted or distributed, and in relation to any other product, means—

   (a) if the person proceeded against is a person to whom subsection (2) of section 2 above applies in relation to the product, the time when he supplied the product to another;

   (b) if that subsection does not apply to that person in relation to the product, the time when the product was last supplied by a person to whom that subsection does apply in relation to the product.

5 Damage giving rise to liability

(1) Subject to the following provisions of this section, in this Part "damage" means death or personal injury or any loss of or damage to any property (including land).

(2) A person shall not be liable under section 2 above in respect of any defect in a product for the loss of or any damage to the product itself or for the loss of or any damage to the whole or any part of any product which has been supplied with the product in question comprised in it.

(3)　A person shall not be liable under section 2 above for any loss of or damage to any property which, at the time it is lost or damaged, is not—

(a)　of a description of property ordinarily intended for private use, occupation or consumption; and

(b)　intended by the person suffering the loss or damage mainly for his own private use, occupation or consumption.

(4)　No damages shall be awarded to any person by virtue of this Part in respect of any loss of or damage to any property if the amount which would fall to be so awarded to that person, apart from this subsection and any liability for interest, does not exceed £275.

(5)　In determining for the purposes of this Part who has suffered any loss of or damage to property and when any such loss or damage occurred, the loss or damage shall be regarded as having occurred at the earliest time at which a person with an interest in the property had knowledge of the material facts about the loss or damage.

(6)　For the purposes of subsection (5) above the material facts about any loss of or damage to any property are such facts about the loss or damage as would lead a reasonable person with an interest in the property to consider the loss or damage sufficiently serious to justify his instituting proceedings for damages against a defendant who did not dispute liability and was able to satisfy a judgment.

(7)　For the purposes of subsection (5) above a person's knowledge includes knowledge which he might reasonably have been expected to acquire—

(a)　from facts observable or ascertainable by him; or

(b)　from facts ascertainable by him with the help of appropriate expert advice which it is reasonable for him to seek;

but a person shall not be taken by virtue of this subsection to have knowledge of a fact ascertainable by him only with the help of expert advice unless he has failed to take all reasonable steps to obtain (and, where appropriate, to act on) that advice.

6　Application of certain enactments

(1)　Any damage for which a person is liable under section 2 above shall be deemed to have been caused—

(a)　for the purposes of the Fatal Accidents Act 1976, by that person's wrongful act, neglect or default;

　…

(2)　Where—

(a)　a person's death is caused wholly or partly by a defect in a product, or a person dies after suffering damage which has been so caused;

(b)　a request such as mentioned in paragraph (a) of subsection (3) of section 2 above is made to a supplier of the product by that person's personal representatives or, in the case of a person whose death is caused wholly or partly by the defect, by any dependant or relative of that person; and

(c)　the conditions specified in paragraphs (b) and (c) of that subsection are satisfied in relation to that request,

this Part shall have effect for the purposes of the Law Reform (Miscellaneous Provisions) Act 1934, the Fatal Accidents Act 1976 and the Damages (Scotland) Act 2011 as if liability of the supplier to that person under that subsection did not depend on that person having requested the supplier to identify certain persons or on the said conditions having been satisfied in relation to a request made by that person.

(3)　Section 1 of the Congenital Disabilities (Civil Liability) Act 1976 shall have effect for the purposes of this Part as if—

(a)　a person were answerable to a child in respect of an occurrence caused wholly or partly by a defect in a product if he is or has been liable under section 2 above in respect of any effect of the occurrence on a parent of the child, or would be so liable if the occurrence caused a parent of the child to suffer damage;

(b)　the provisions of this Part relating to liability under section 2 above applied in relation to liability by virtue of paragraph (a) above under the said section 1; and

(c)　subsection (6) of the said section 1 (exclusion of liability) were omitted.

(4)   Where any damage is caused partly by a defect in a product and partly by the fault of the person suffering the damage, the Law Reform (Contributory Negligence) Act 1945 and section 5 of the Fatal Accidents Act 1976 (contributory negligence) shall have effect as if the defect were the fault of every person liable by virtue of this Part for the damage caused by the defect.

(5)   In subsection (4) above "fault" has the same meaning as in the said Act of 1945.

(6)   Schedule 1 to this Act shall have effect for the purpose of amending the Limitation Act 1980 and the Prescription and Limitation (Scotland) Act 1973 in their application in relation to the bringing of actions by virtue of this Part.

(7)   It is hereby declared that liability by virtue of this Part is to be treated as liability in tort for the purposes of any enactment conferring jurisdiction on any court with respect to any matter.

(8)   Nothing in this Part shall prejudice the operation of section 12 of the Nuclear Installations Act 1965 (rights to compensation for certain breaches of duties confined to rights under that Act).

7   Prohibition on exclusions from liability

The liability of a person by virtue of this Part to a person who has suffered damage caused wholly or partly by a defect in a product, or to a dependant or relative of such a person, shall not be limited or excluded by any contract term, by any notice or by any other provision.

8   Power to modify Part I

(1)   Her Majesty may by Order in Council make such modifications of this Part and of any other enactment (including an enactment contained in the following Parts of this Act, or in an Act passed after this Act) as appear to Her Majesty in Council to be necessary or expedient in consequence of any modification of the product liability Directive which is made at any time after the passing of this Act.

9   Application of Part I to Crown

(1)   Subject to subsection (2) below, this Part shall bind the Crown.

(2)   The Crown shall not, as regards the Crown's liability by virtue of this Part, be bound by this Part further than the Crown is made liable in tort or in reparation under the Crown Proceedings Act 1947, as that Act has effect from time to time.

MINORS' CONTRACTS ACT 1987
(1987, c. 13)

2   Guarantees

Where—

(a)   a guarantee is given in respect of an obligation of a party to a contract made after the commencement of this Act, and

(b)   the obligation is unenforceable against him (or he repudiates the contract) because he was a minor when the contract was made,

the guarantee shall not for that reason alone be unenforceable against the guarantor.

3   Restitution

(1)   Where—

(a)   a person ("the plaintiff") has after the commencement of this Act entered into a contract with another ("the defendant"), and

(b)   the contract is unenforceable against the defendant (or he repudiates it) because he was a minor when the contract was made,

the court may, if it is just and equitable to do so, require the defendant to transfer to the plaintiff any property acquired by the defendant under the contract, or any property representing it.

(2)   Nothing in this section shall be taken to prejudice any other remedy available to the plaintiff.

COPYRIGHT, DESIGNS AND PATENTS ACT 1988
(1988, c. 48)

Rights and remedies of copyright owner

96   Infringement actionable by copyright owner

(1)   An infringement of copyright is actionable by the copyright owner.

(2)   In an action for infringement of copyright all such relief by way of damages, injunctions, accounts or otherwise is available to the plaintiff as is available in respect of the infringement of any other property right.

(3)   This section has effect subject to the following provisions of this Chapter.

97   Provisions as to damages in infringement action

(1)   Where in an action for infringement of copyright it is shown that at the time of the infringement the defendant did not know, and had no reason to believe, that copyright subsisted in the work to which the action relates, the plaintiff is not entitled to damages against him, but without prejudice to any other remedy.

(2)   The court may in an action for infringement of copyright having regard to all the circumstances, and in particular to—

(a)   the flagrancy of the infringement, and

(b)   any benefit accruing to the defendant by reason of the infringement, award such additional damages as the justice of the case may require.

Remedies for infringement

229   Rights and remedies of design right owner

(1)   An infringement of design right is actionable by the design right owner.

(2)   In an action for infringement of design right all such relief by way of damages, injunctions, accounts or otherwise is available to the plaintiff as is available in respect of the infringement of any other property right.

(3)   The court may in an action for infringement of design right, having regard to all the circumstances and in particular to—

(a)   the flagrancy of the infringement, and

(b)   any benefit accruing to the defendant by reason of the infringement, award such additional damages as the justice of the case may require.

(4)   This section has effect subject to section 233 (innocent infringement).

253   Remedy for groundless threats of infringement proceedings

(1)   Where a person threatens another person with proceedings for infringement of design right, a person aggrieved by the threats may bring an action against him claiming—

(a)   a declaration to the effect that the threats are unjustifiable;

(b)   an injunction against the continuance of the threats;

(c)   damages in respect of any loss which he has sustained by the threats.

(2)   If the plaintiff proves that the threats were made and that he is a person aggrieved by them, he is entitled to the relief claimed unless the defendant shows that the acts in respect of which proceedings were threatened did constitute, or if done would have constituted, an infringement of the design right concerned.

(3)   Proceedings may not be brought under this section in respect of a threat to bring proceedings for an infringement alleged to consist of making or importing anything.

(4)   Mere notification that a design is protected by design right does not constitute a threat of proceedings for the purposes of this section.

HOUSING ACT 1988
(1988, c. 50)

27   Damages for unlawful eviction

(1)   This section applies if, at any time after 9th June 1988, a landlord (in this section referred to as "the landlord in default") or any person acting on behalf of the landlord in default unlawfully deprives the residential occupier of any premises of his occupation of the whole or part of the premises.

(2)   This section also applies if, at any time after 9th June 1988, a landlord (in this section referred to as "the landlord in default") or any person acting on behalf of the landlord in default—

  (a)   attempts unlawfully to deprive the residential occupier of any premises of his occupation of the whole or part of the premises, or

  (b)   knowing or having reasonable cause to believe that the conduct is likely to cause the residential occupier of any premises—

    (i)   to give up his occupation of the premises or any part thereof, or

    (ii)   to refrain from exercising any right or pursuing any remedy in respect of the premises or any part thereof, does acts likely to interfere with the peace or comfort of the residential occupier or members of his household, or persistently withdraws or withholds services reasonably required for the occupation of the premises as a residence, and, as a result, the residential occupier gives up his occupation of the premises as a residence.

(3)   Subject to the following provisions of this section, where this section applies, the landlord in default shall, by virtue of this section, be liable to pay to the former residential occupier, in respect of his loss of the right to occupy the premises in question as his residence, damages assessed on the basis set out in section 28 below.

(4)   Any liability arising by virtue of subsection (3) above—

  (a)   shall be in the nature of a liability in tort; and

  (b)   subject to subsection (5) below, shall be in addition to any liability arising apart from this section (whether in tort, contract or otherwise).

(5)   Nothing in this section affects the right of a residential occupier to enforce any liability which arises apart from this section in respect of his loss of the right to occupy premises as his residence; but damages shall not be awarded both in respect of such a liability and in respect of a liability arising by virtue of this section on account of the same loss.

(6)   No liability shall arise by virtue of subsection (3) above if—

  (a)   before the date on which proceedings to enforce the liability are finally disposed of, the former residential occupier is reinstated in the premises in question in such circumstances that he becomes again the residential occupier of them; or

  (b)   at the request of the former residential occupier, a court makes an order (whether in the nature of an injunction or otherwise) as a result of which he is reinstated as mentioned in paragraph (a) above; and, for the purposes of paragraph (a) above, proceedings to enforce a liability are finally disposed of on the earliest date by which the proceedings (including any proceedings on or in consequence of an appeal) have been determined and any time for appealing or further appealing has expired, except that if any appeal is abandoned, the proceedings shall be taken to be disposed of on the date of the abandonment.

(7)   If, in proceedings to enforce a liability arising by virtue of subsection (3) above, it appears to the court—

  (a)   that, prior to the event which gave rise to the liability, the conduct of the former residential occupier or any person living with him in the premises concerned was such that it is reasonable to mitigate the damages for which the landlord in default would otherwise be liable, or

  (b)   that, before the proceedings were begun, the landlord in default offered to reinstate the former residential occupier in the premises in question and either it was unreasonable of the former residential occupier to refuse that offer or, if he had obtained alternative accommodation before the offer was made, it would have been unreasonable of him to refuse that offer if he had not obtained that accommodation, the court may reduce the amount of damages which would otherwise be payable to such amount as it thinks appropriate.

(8) In proceedings to enforce a liability arising by virtue of subsection (3) above, it shall be a defence for the defendant to prove that he believed, and had reasonable cause to believe—

(a) that the residential occupier had ceased to reside in the premises in question at the time when he was deprived of occupation as mentioned in subsection (1) above or, as the case may be, when the attempt was made or the acts were done as a result of which he gave up his occupation of those premises; or

(b) that, where the liability would otherwise arise by virtue only of the doing of acts or the withdrawal or withholding of services, he had reasonable grounds for doing the acts or withdrawing or withholding the services in question.

28   The measure of damages

(1) The basis for the assessment of damages referred to in section 27(3) above is the difference in value, determined as at the time immediately before the residential occupier ceased to occupy the premises in question as his residence, between—

(a) the value of the interest of the landlord in default determined on the assumption that the residential occupier continues to have the same right to occupy the premises as before that time; and

(b) the value of that interest determined on the assumption that the residential occupier has ceased to have that right.

(2) In relation to any premises, any reference in this section to the interest of the landlord in default is a reference to his interest in the building in which the premises in question are comprised (whether or not that building contains any other premises) together with its curtilage.

(3) For the purposes of the valuations referred to in subsection (1) above, it shall be assumed—

(a) that the landlord in default is selling his interest on the open market to a willing buyer;

(b) that neither the residential occupier nor any member of his family wishes to buy; and

(c) that it is unlawful to carry out any substantial development of any of the land in which the landlord's interest subsists or to demolish the whole or part of any building on that land.

ROAD TRAFFIC ACT 1988
(1988, c. 52)

38   The Highway Code

(7) A failure on the part of a person to observe a provision of the Highway Code shall not of itself render that person liable to criminal proceedings of any kind but any such failure may in any proceedings (whether civil or criminal, and including proceedings for an offence under the Traffic Acts, the Public Passenger Vehicles Act 1981 or sections 18 to 23 of the Transport Act 1985) be relied upon by any party to the proceedings as tending to establish or negative any liability which is in question in those proceedings.

143   Users of motor vehicles to be insured or secured against third-party risks

(1) Subject to the provisions of this Part of this Act—

(a) a person must not use a motor vehicle on a road or other public place unless there is in force in relation to the use of the vehicle by that person such a policy of insurance or such a security in respect of third party risks as complies with the requirements of this Part of this Act, and

(b) a person must not cause or permit any other person to use a motor vehicle on a road or other public place unless there is in force in relation to the use of the vehicle by that other person such a policy of insurance or such a security in respect of third party risks as complies with the requirements of this Part of this Act.

(2)   If a person acts in contravention of subsection (1) above he is guilty of an offence.

(3)   A person charged with using a motor vehicle in contravention of this section shall not be convicted if he proves—

(a)   that the vehicle did not belong to him and was not in his possession under a contract of hiring or of loan,

(b)   that he was using the vehicle in the course of his employment, and

(c)   that he neither knew nor had reason to believe that there was not in force in relation to the vehicle such a policy of insurance or security as is mentioned in subsection (1) above.

(4)   This Part of this Act does not apply to invalid carriages.

144   Exceptions from requirement of third-party insurance or security

(1)   Section 143 of this Act does not apply to a vehicle owned by a person who has deposited and keeps deposited with the Accountant General of the Senior Courts the sum of £500,000, at a time when the vehicle is being driven under the owner's control.

(1A)   The Secretary of State may by order made by statutory instrument substitute a greater sum for the sum for the time being specified in subsection (1) above.

(1B)   No order shall be made under subsection (1A) above unless a draft of it has been laid before and approved by resolution of each House of Parliament.

(2)   Section 143 does not apply—

(a)   to a vehicle owned—

(i)   by the council of a county or county district in England and Wales, the Broads Authority, the Common Council of the City of London, the council of a London borough, a National Park authority, the Inner London Education Authority, the London Fire and Emergency Planning Authority, an authority established for an area in England by an order under section 207 of the Local Government and Public Involvement in Health Act 2007 (joint waste authorities), a joint authority established by Part 4 of the Local Government Act 1985, an economic prosperity board established under section 88 of the Local Democracy, Economic Development and Construction Act 2009 or a combined authority established under section 103 of that Act,

(ii)   by a council constituted under section 2 of the Local Government etc. (Scotland) Act 1994 in Scotland, or

(iii)   by a joint board or committee in England or Wales, or joint committee in Scotland, which is so constituted as to include among its members representatives of any such council,

at a time when the vehicle is being driven under the owner's control,

(b)   to a vehicle owned by a local policing body or police authority at a time when it is being driven under the owner's control, or to a vehicle at a time when it is being driven for police purposes by or under the direction of a constable, by a member of a police and crime commissioner's staff (within the meaning of Part 1 of the Police Reform and Social Responsibility Act 2011), by a member of the staff of the Mayor's Office for Policing and Crime (within the meaning of that Part of that Act), by a member of the civilian staff of a police force (within the meaning of that Part of that Act), by a member of the civilian staff of the metropolitan police force (within the meaning of that Part of that Act), by a person employed by the Common Council of the City of London in its capacity as a police authority, or by a person employed by a police authority,

(ba)   ...

(c)   to a vehicle at a time when it is being driven on a journey to or from any place undertaken for salvage purposes pursuant to Part IX of the Merchant Shipping Act 1995,

(d)   ...

(da)   to a vehicle owned by a health service body, as defined in section 60(7) of the National Health Service and Community Care Act 1990, by a Primary Care Trust established under section 18 of the National Health Service Act 2006, or by a local Health Board established under section 11 of the National Health Service (Wales) Act 2006 at a time when the vehicle is being driven under the owner's control, (db)   to an ambulance owned by a National Health Service trust established under section 25 of the National Health Service Act 2006, section 18 of the National Health Service (Wales) Act 2006 or the National Health Service (Scotland) Act 1978, at a time when a vehicle is being driven under the owner's control,

(dc)   to an ambulance owned by an NHS foundation trust, at a time when the vehicle is being driven under the owner's control,

(e)   to a vehicle which is made available by the Secretary of State or the Welsh Ministers to any person, body or local authority in pursuance of section 12 or 80 of the National Health Service Act 2006 or section 38 of the National Health Service (Wales) Act 2006, at a time when it is being used in accordance with the terms on which it is so made available,

(f)   to a vehicle which is made available by the Secretary of State to any local authority, education authority or voluntary organisation in Scotland in pursuance of section 15 or 16 of the National Health Service (Scotland) Act 1978 at a time when it is being used in accordance with the terms on which it is so made available,

(g)   to a vehicle owned by the Care Quality Commission, at a time when the vehicle is being driven under the owner's control.

145   Requirements in respect of policies of insurance

(1)   In order to comply with the requirements of this Part of this Act, a policy of insurance must satisfy the following conditions.

(2)   The policy must be issued by an authorised insurer.

(3)   Subject to subsection (4) below, the policy—

(a)   must insure such person, persons or classes of persons as may be specified in the policy in respect of any liability which may be incurred by him or them in respect of the death of or bodily injury to any person or damage to property caused by, or arising out of, the use of the vehicle on a road or other public place in Great Britain, and

(aa)   must, in the case of a vehicle normally based in the territory of another member State, insure him or them in respect of any civil liability which may be incurred by him or them as a result of an event related to the use of the vehicle in Great Britain if,—

(i)   according to the law of that territory, he or they would be required to be insured in respect of a civil liability which would arise under that law as a result of that event if the place where the vehicle was used when the event occurred were in that territory, and

(ii)   the cover required by that law would be higher than that required by paragraph (a) above, and

(b)   must, in the case of a vehicle normally based in Great Britain, insure him or them in respect of any liability which may be incurred by him or them in respect of the use of the vehicle and of any trailer, whether or not coupled, in the territory other than Great Britain and Gibraltar of each of the member States of the Communities according to

(i)   the law on compulsory insurance against civil liability in respect of the use of vehicles of the State in whose territory the event giving rise to the liability occurred; or

(ii)   if it would give higher cover, the law which would be applicable under this Part of this Act if the place where the vehicle was used when that event occurred were in Great Britain; and

(c)   must also insure him or them in respect of any liability which may be incurred by him or them under the provisions of this Part of this Act relating to payment for emergency treatment.

(4)   The policy shall not, by virtue of subsection (3)(a) above, be required—

(a)   to cover liability in respect of the death, arising out of and in the course of his employment, of a person in the employment of a person insured by the policy or of bodily injury sustained by such a person arising out of and in the course of his employment, or

(b)   to provide insurance of more than £1,000,000 in respect of all such liabilities as may be incurred in respect of damage to property caused by, or arising out of, any one accident involving the vehicle, or

(c)   to cover liability in respect of damage to the vehicle, or

(d)   to cover liability in respect of damage to goods carried for hire or reward in or on the vehicle or in or on any trailer (whether or not coupled) drawn by the vehicle, or

(e)   to cover any liability of a person in respect of damage to property in his custody or under his control, or

(f)   to cover any contractual liability.

(4A) In the case of a person—

(a)   carried in or upon a vehicle, or

(b)   entering or getting on to, or alighting from, a vehicle,

the provisions of paragraph (a) of subsection (4) above do not apply unless cover in respect of the liability referred to in that paragraph is in fact provided pursuant to a requirement of the Employers' Liability (Compulsory Insurance) Act 1969.

148   Avoidance of certain exceptions to policies or securities

(1)   Where a policy or security is issued or given for the purposes of this Part of this Act, so much of the policy or security as purports to restrict—

(a)   the insurance of the persons insured by the policy, or

(b)   the operation of the security,

(as the case may be) by reference to any of the matters mentioned in subsection (2) below shall, as respects such liabilities as are required to be covered by a policy under section 145 of this Act, be of no effect.

(2)   Those matters are—

(a)   the age or physical or mental condition of persons driving the vehicle,

(b)   the condition of the vehicle,

(c)   the number of persons that the vehicle carries,

(d)   the weight or physical characteristics of the goods that the vehicle carries,

(e)   the time at which or the areas within which the vehicle is used,

(f)   the horsepower or cylinder capacity or value of the vehicle,

(g)   the carrying on the vehicle of any particular apparatus, or

(h)   the carrying on the vehicle of any particular means of identification other than any means of identification required to be carried by or under the Vehicles Excise and Registration Act 1994.

(3)   Nothing in subsection (1) above requires an insurer or the giver of a security to pay any sum in respect of the liability of any person otherwise than in or towards the discharge of that liability.

(4)   Any sum paid by an insurer or the giver of a security in or towards the discharge of any liability of any person which is covered by the policy or security by virtue only of subsection (1) above is recoverable by the insurer or giver of the security from that person.

(5)   A condition in a policy or security issued or given for the purposes of this Part of this Act providing—

(a)   that no liability shall arise under the policy or security, or

(b)   that any liability so arising shall cease,

in the event of some specified thing being done or omitted to be done after the happening of the event giving rise to a claim under the policy or security, shall be of no effect in connection with such liabilities as are required to be covered by a policy under section 145 of this Act.

(6)   Nothing in subsection (5) above shall be taken to render void any provision in a policy or security requiring the person insured or secured to pay to the insurer or the giver of the security any sums which the latter may have become liable to pay under the policy or security and which have been applied to the satisfaction of the claims of third parties.

(7)   Notwithstanding anything in any enactment, a person issuing a policy of insurance under section 145 of this Act shall be liable to indemnify the persons or classes of persons specified in the policy in respect of any liability which the policy purports to cover in the case of those persons or classes of persons.

149   Avoidance of certain agreements as to liability towards passengers

(1)   This section applies where a person uses a motor vehicle in circumstances such that under section 143 of this Act there is required to be in force in relation to his use of it such a policy of insurance or such a security in respect of third-party risks as complies with the requirements of this Part of this Act.

(2)   If any other person is carried in or upon the vehicle when the user is so using it, any antecedent agreement or understanding between them (whether intended to be legally binding or not) shall be of no effect so far as it purports or might be held —

(a)   to negative or restrict any such liability of the user in respect of persons carried in or upon the vehicle as is required by section 145 of this Act to be covered by a policy of insurance, or

(b)   to impose any conditions with respect to the enforcement of any such liability of the user.

(3)   The fact that a person so carried has willingly accepted as his the risk of negligence on the part of the user shall not be treated as negativing any such liability of the user.

(4)   For the purposes of this section —

(a)   references to a person being carried in or upon a vehicle include references to a person entering or getting on to, or alighting from, the vehicle, and

(b)   the reference to an antecedent agreement is to one made at any time before the liability arose.

151   Duty of insurers of persons giving security to satisfy judgment against persons insured or secured against third-party risks

(1)   This section applies where, after a policy or security is issued or given for the purposes of this Part of this Act, a judgment to which this subsection applies is obtained.

(2)   Subsection (1) above applies to judgments relating to a liability with respect to any matter where liability with respect to that matter is required to be covered by a policy of insurance under section 145 of this Act and either —

(a)   it is a liability covered by the terms of the policy or security, and the judgment is obtained against any person who is insured by the policy or whose liability is covered by the security, as the case may be, or

(b)   it is a liability, other than an excluded liability, which would be so covered if the policy insured all persons or, as the case may be, the security covered the liability of all persons, and the judgment is obtained against any person other than one who is insured by the policy or, as the case may be, whose liability is covered by the security.

(3)   In deciding for the purposes of subsection (2) above whether a liability is or would be covered by the terms of a policy or security, so much of the policy or security as purports to restrict, as the case may be, the insurance of the persons insured by the policy or the operation of the security by reference to the holding by the driver of the vehicle of a licence authorising him to drive it shall be treated as of no effect.

(4)   In subsection (2)(b) above "excluded liability" means a liability in respect of the death of, or bodily injury to, or damage to the property of any person who, at the time of the use which gave rise to the liability, was allowing himself to be carried in or upon the vehicle and knew or had reason to believe that the vehicle had been stolen or unlawfully taken, not being a person who —

(a)   did not know and had no reason to believe that the vehicle had been stolen or unlawfully taken until after the commencement of his journey, and

(b)   could not reasonably have been expected to have alighted from the vehicle. In this subsection the reference to a person being carried in or upon a vehicle includes a reference to a person entering or getting on to, or alighting from, the vehicle.

(5)   Notwithstanding that the insurer may be entitled to avoid or cancel, or may have avoided or cancelled, the policy or security, he must, subject to the provisions of this section, pay to the persons entitled to the benefit of the judgment —

(a)   as regards liability in respect of death or bodily injury, any sum payable under the judgment in respect of the liability, together with any sum which, by virtue of any enactment relating to interest on judgments, is payable in respect of interest on that sum,

(b)   as regards liability in respect of damage to property, any sum required to be paid under subsection (6) below, and

(c)   any amount payable in respect of costs.

(6)   This subsection requires—

    (a)   where the total of any amounts paid, payable or likely to be payable under the policy or security in respect of damage to property caused by, or arising out of, the accident in question does not exceed £1,000,000, the payment of any sum payable under the judgment in respect of the liability, together with any sum which, by virtue of any enactment relating to interest on judgments, is payable in respect of interest on that sum,

    (b)   where that total exceeds £1,000,000, the payment of either—

        (i)   such proportion of any sum payable under the judgment in respect of the liability as £1,000,000 bears to that total, together with the same proportion of any sum which, by virtue of any enactment relating to interest on judgments, is payable in respect of interest on that sum, or

        (ii)   the difference between the total of any amounts already paid under the policy or security in respect of such damage and £1,000,000, together with such proportion of any sum which, by virtue of any enactment relating to interest on judgments, is payable in respect of interest on any sum payable under the judgment in respect of the liability as the difference bears to that sum,

    whichever is the less, unless not less than £1,000,000 has already been paid under the policy or security in respect of such damage (in which case nothing is payable).

(7)   Where an insurer becomes liable under this section to pay an amount in respect of a liability of a person who is insured by a policy or whose liability is covered by a security, he is entitled to recover from that person—

    (a)   that amount, in a case where he became liable to pay it by virtue only of subsection (3) above, or

    (b)   in a case where that amount exceeds the amount for which he would, apart from the provisions of this section, be liable under the policy or security in respect of that liability, the excess.

(8)   Where an insurer becomes liable under this section to pay an amount in respect of a liability of a person who is not insured by a policy or whose liability is not covered by a security, he is entitled to recover the amount from that person or from any person who—

    (a)   is insured by the policy, or whose liability is covered by the security, by the terms of which the liability would be covered if the policy insured all persons or, as the case may be, the security covered the liability of all persons, and

    (b)   caused or permitted the use of the vehicle which gave rise to the liability.

(9)   In this section—

    (a)   "insurer" includes a person giving a security,

    (c)   "liability covered by the terms of the policy or security" means a liability which is covered by the policy or security or which would be so covered but for the fact that the insurer is entitled to avoid or cancel, or has avoided or cancelled, the policy or security.

153   Bankruptcy, etc., of insured or secured persons not to affect claims by third parties

(1)   Where, after a person has effected a policy of insurance or been given a security for the purposes of this Part of this Act, an event which results in that person being a relevant person for the purposes of the Third Parties (Rights against Insurers) Act 2010 happens, the happening of that event shall, notwithstanding anything in that Act, not affect any such liability of that person as is required to be covered by a policy of insurance under section 145 of this Act.

(3)   Nothing in subsection (1) above affects any rights conferred by the Third Parties (Rights against Insurers) Act 2010 on the person to whom the liability was incurred, being rights so conferred against the person by whom the policy was issued or the security was given.

157   Payment for hospital treatment of traffic casualties

(1)   Subject to subsection (2) below, where—

     (a)   a payment, other than a payment under section 158 of this Act, is made (whether or not with an admission of liability) in respect of the death of, or bodily injury to, any person arising out of the use of a motor vehicle on a road or in a place to which the public have a right of access, and

     (b)   the payment is made—

         (i)   by an authorised insurer, the payment being made under or in consequence of a policy issued under section 145 of this Act, or

         (ii)   by the owner of a vehicle in relation to the use of which a security under this Part of this Act is in force, or

         (iii)   by the owner of a vehicle who has made a deposit under this Part of this Act, and

     (c)   the person who has so died or been bodily injured has to the knowledge of the insurer or owner, as the case may be, received treatment at a hospital, whether as an in-patient or as an out-patient, in respect of the injury so arising,

the insurer or owner must pay the expenses reasonably incurred by the hospital in affording the treatment, after deducting from the expenses any moneys actually received in payment of a specific charge for the treatment, not being moneys received under any contributory scheme.

(2)   The amount to be paid shall not exceed £2,949.00 for each person treated as an in-patient or £295.00 for each person treated as an out-patient.

(3)   For the purposes of this section "expenses reasonably incurred" means—

     (a)   in relation to a person who receives treatment at a hospital as an in-patient, an amount for each day he is maintained in the hospital representing the average daily cost, for each in-patient, of the maintenance of the hospital and the staff of the hospital and the maintenance and treatment of the in-patients in the hospital, and

     (b)   in relation to a person who receives treatment at a hospital as an out-patient, reasonable expenses actually incurred.

158   Payment for emergency treatment of traffic casualties

(1)   Subsection (2) below applies where—

     (a)   medical or surgical treatment or examination is immediately required as a result of bodily injury (including fatal injury) to a person caused by, or arising out of, the use of a motor vehicle on a road, and

     (b)   the treatment or examination so required (in this Part of this Act referred to as "emergency treatment") is effected by a legally qualified medical practitioner.

(2)   The person who was using the vehicle at the time of the event out of which the bodily injury arose must, on a claim being made in accordance with the provisions of section 159 of this Act, pay to the practitioner (or, where emergency treatment is effected by more than one practitioner, to the practitioner by whom it is first effected)—

     (a)   a fee of £21.30 in respect of each person in whose case the emergency treatment is effected by him, and

     (b)   a sum, in respect of any distance in excess of two miles which he must cover in order—

         (i)   to proceed from the place from which he is summoned to the place where the emergency treatment is carried out by him, and

         (ii)   to return to the first mentioned place,

equal to 41 pence for every complete mile and additional part of a mile of that distance.

(3)   Where emergency treatment is first effected in a hospital, the provisions of subsections (1) and (2) above with respect to payment of a fee shall, so far as applicable, but subject (as regards the recipient of a payment) to the provisions of section 159 of this Act, have effect with the substitution of references to the hospital for references to a legally qualified medical practitioner.

(4)   Liability incurred under this section by the person using a vehicle shall, where the event out of which it arose was caused by the wrongful act of another person, be treated for the purposes of any claim to recover damage by reason of that wrongful act as damage sustained by the person using the vehicle.

159   Supplementary provisions as to payments for treatment

(2)   A claim for a payment under section 158 of this Act may be made at the time when the emergency treatment is effected, by oral request to the person who was using the vehicle, and if not so made must be made by request in writing served on him within seven days from the day on which the emergency treatment was effected.

(4)   A payment made under section 158 of this Act shall operate as a discharge, to the extent of the amount paid, of any liability of the person who was using the vehicle, or of any other person, to pay any sum in respect of the expenses of remuneration of the practitioner or hospital concerned of or for effecting the emergency treatment.

ROAD TRAFFIC (CONSEQUENTIAL PROVISIONS) ACT 1988
(1988, c. 54)

7   Saving for law of nuisance

Nothing in the Road Traffic Acts authorises a person to use on a road a vehicle so constructed or used as to cause a public or private nuisance ... or affects the liability, whether under statute or common law, of the driver or owner so using a vehicle.

EMPLOYMENT ACT 1989
(1989, c. 38)

11   Exemption of Sikhs from requirements as to wearing of safety helmets at workplaces

(1)   Any requirement to wear a safety helmet which (apart from this section) would, by virtue of any statutory provision or rule of law, be imposed on a Sikh who is at a workplace shall not apply to him at any time when he is wearing a turban.

(2)   Accordingly, where—

(a)   a Sikh who is at a workplace is for the time being wearing a turban, and

(b)   (apart from this section) any associated requirement would, by virtue of any statutory provision or rule of law, be imposed—

(i)   on the Sikh, or

(ii)   on the other person,

in connection with the wearing by the Sikh of a safety helmet,

that requirement shall not apply to the Sikh or (as the case may be) to that other person.

(4)   It is hereby declared that, where a person does not comply with any requirement, being a requirement which for the time being does not apply to him by virtue of subsection (1) or (2)—

(a)   he shall not be liable in tort to any person in respect of any injury, loss or damage caused by his failure to comply with that requirement ...

(5)   If a Sikh who is at a workplace—

(a)   does not comply with any requirement to wear a safety helmet, being a requirement which for the time being does not apply to him by virtue of subsection (1), and

(b)   in consequence of any act or omission of some other person sustains any injury, loss or damage which is to any extent attributable to the fact that he is not wearing a safety helmet in compliance with the requirement, that other person shall, if liable to the Sikh in tort (or, in Scotland, in an action for reparation), be so liable only to the extent that injury, loss or damage would have been sustained by the Sikh even if he had been wearing a safety helmet in compliance with the requirement.

(6)   Where—

(a)   the act or omission referred to in subsection (5) causes the death of the Sikh, and

(b)   the Sikh would have sustained some injury (other than loss of life) in consequence of the act or omission even if he had been wearing a safety helmet in compliance with the requirement in question, the amount of any damages which, by virtue of that subsection, are recoverable in tort (or, in Scotland, in an action for reparation) in respect of that injury shall not exceed the amount of any damages which would (apart from that subsection) be so recoverable in respect of the Sikh's death.

(6A) This section does not apply to a Sikh who—
    (a)   works, or is training to work, in an occupation that involves (to any extent) providing an urgent response to fire, riot or other hazardous situations, and
    (b)   is at the workplace—
        (i)   to provide such a response in circumstances where the wearing of a safety helmet is necessary to protect the Sikh from a risk of injury, or
        (ii)   to receive training in how to provide such a response in circumstances of that kind.

(6B) This section also does not apply to a Sikh who—
    (a)   is a member of Her Majesty's forces or a person providing support to Her Majesty's forces, and
    (b)   is at the workplace—
        (i)   to take part in a military operation in circumstances where the wearing of a safety helmet is necessary to protect the Sikh from a risk of injury, or
        (ii)   to receive training in how to take part in such an operation in circumstances of that kind.

(7)   In this section—
"injury" includes loss of life, any impairment of a person's physical or mental condition and any disease;
…

LAW OF PROPERTY (MISCELLANEOUS PROVISIONS) ACT 1989
(1989, c. 34)

1   Deeds and their execution

(1)   Any rule of law which—
    (a)   restricts the substances on which a deed may be written;
    (b)   requires a seal for the valid execution of an instrument as a deed by an individual; or
    (c)   requires authority by one person to another to deliver an instrument as a deed on his behalf to be given by deed, is abolished.

(2)   An instrument shall not be a deed unless—
    (a)   it makes it clear on its face that it is intended to be a deed by the person making it or, as the case may be, by the parties to it (whether by describing itself as a deed or expressing itself to be executed or signed as a deed or otherwise); and
    (b)   it is validly executed as a deed—
        (i)   by that person or a person authorised to execute it in the name or on behalf of that person, or
        (ii)   by one or more of those parties or a person authorised to execute it in the name or on behalf of one or more of those parties.

(2A) For the purposes of subsection (2)(a) above, an instrument shall not be taken to make it clear on its face that it is intended to be a deed merely because it is executed under seal.

(3)   An instrument is validly executed as a deed by an individual if, and only if—
    (a)   it is signed—
        (i)   by him in the presence of a witness who attests the signature; or
        (ii)   at his direction and in his presence and the presence of two witnesses who each attest the signature; and
    (b)   it is delivered as a deed.

(4)   In subsections (2) and (3) above "sign", in relation to an instrument, includes—
    (a)   an individual signing the name of the person or party on whose behalf he executes the instrument; and
    (b)   making one's mark on the instrument, and "signature" is to be construed accordingly.

(4A) Subsection (3) above applies in the case of an instrument executed by an individual in the name or on behalf of another person whether or not that person is an individual

(5) Where a relevant lawyer, or an agent or employee of a relevant lawyer, in the course of or in connection with a transaction, purports to deliver an instrument as a deed on behalf of a party to the instrument, it shall be conclusively presumed in favour of a purchaser that he is authorised so to deliver the instrument.

(6) In subsection (5) above—

"purchaser" has the same meaning as in the Law of Property Act 1925; and

"relevant lawyer" means a person who, for the purposes of the Legal Services Act 2007, is an authorised person in relation to an activity which constitutes a reserved instrument activity (within the meaning of that Act).

(7) Where an instrument under seal that constitutes a deed is required for the purposes of an Act passed before this section comes into force, this section shall have effect as to signing, sealing or delivery of an instrument by an individual in place of any provision of that Act as to signing, sealing or delivery.

(10) The references in this section to the execution of a deed by an individual do not include execution by a corporation sole and the reference in subsection (7) above to signing, sealing or delivery by an individual does not include signing, sealing or delivery by such a corporation.

(11) Nothing in this section applies in relation to instruments delivered as deeds before this section comes into force.

2   Contracts for sale etc. of land to be made by signed writing

(1) A contract for the sale or other disposition of an interest in land can only be made in writing and only by incorporating all the terms which the parties have expressly agreed in one document or, where contracts are exchanged, in each.

(2) The terms may be incorporated in a document either by being set out in it or by reference to some other document.

(3) The document incorporating the terms or, where contracts are exchanged, one of the documents incorporating them (but not necessarily the same one) must be signed by or on behalf of each party to the contract.

(4) Where a contract for the sale or other disposition of an interest in land satisfies the conditions of this section by reason only of the rectification of one or more documents in pursuance of an order of a court, the contract shall come into being, or be deemed to have come into being, at such time as may be specified in the order.

(5) This section does not apply in relation to—

(a) a contract to grant such a lease as is mentioned in section 54(2) of the Law of Property Act 1925 (short leases);

(b) a contract made in the course of a public auction; or

(c) a contract regulated under the Financial Services and Markets Act 2000, other than a regulated mortgage contract, a regulated home reversion plan, a regulated home purchase plan or a regulated sale and rent back agreement;

and nothing in this section affects the creation or operation of resulting, implied or constructive trusts.

(6) In this section—

"disposition" has the same meaning as in the Law of Property Act 1925;

"interest in land" means any estate, interest or charge in or over land ...

"regulated mortgage contract" must be read with—

(a) section 22 of the Financial Services and Markets Act 2000,

(b) any relevant order under that section, and

(c) Schedule 2 to that Act.

(7) Nothing in this section shall apply in relation to contracts made before this section comes into force.

(8) Section 40 of the Law of Property Act 1925 (which is superseded by this section) shall cease to have effect.

3   Abolition of rule in *Brian v Fothergill*

The rule of law known as the rule in *Brian v Fothergill* is abolished in relation to contracts made after this section comes into force.

BROADCASTING ACT 1990
(1990, c. 42)

166   Defamatory material

(1)   For the purposes of the law of libel and slander the publication of words in the course of any programme included in a programme service shall be treated as publication in permanent form.

(2)   Subsection (1) above shall apply for the purposes of section 3 of each of the Defamation Acts (slander of title etc.) as it applies for the purposes of the law of libel and slander.

(4)   In this section "the Defamation Acts" means the Defamation Act 1952 and the Defamation Act (Northern Ireland) 1955.

Section 203(1)   SCHEDULE 20
              MINOR AND CONSEQUENTIAL AMENDMENTS

PARLIAMENTARY PAPERS ACT 1840 (c. 9)

1.   Section 3 (protection in respect of proceedings for printing extracts from or abstracts of parliamentary papers) shall have effect as if the reference to printing included a reference to including in a programmed service.

CONTRACTS (APPLICABLE LAW) ACT 1990
(1990, c. 36)

1   Meaning of "the Conventions"
In this Act—

(a)   "the Rome Convention" means the Convention on the law applicable to contractual obligations opened for signature in Rome on 19th June 1980 and signed by the United Kingdom on December 7, 1981;

...

2   Conventions to have force of law

(1)   Subject to subsections (2) and (3) below, the Conventions shall have the force of law in the United Kingdom.

4A   Disapplication where the rules in the Rome I Regulations apply: England and Wales and Northern Ireland

(1)   Nothing in this Act applies to affect the determination of issues relating to contractual obligations which fall to be determined under the Rome I Regulation.

Section 2   SCHEDULE 1
              TITLE I. SCOPE OF THE CONVENTION

Article 1   Scope of the Covention
1.   The rules of the Convention shall apply to contractual obligations in any situation involving a choice between the laws of different countries.

TITLE II. UNIFORM RULES

Article 3   Freedom of choice
1.   A contract shall be governed by the law chosen by the parties. The choice must be express or demonstrated with reasonable certainty by the terms of the contract or the circumstances

of the case. By their choice the parties can select the law applicable to the whole or a part only of the contract.

3. The fact that the parties have chosen a foreign law, whether or not accompanied by the choice of a foreign tribunal, shall not, where all the other elements relevant to the situation at the time of the choice are connected with one country only, prejudice the application of rules of the law of that country which cannot be derogated from by contract, hereinafter called "mandatory rules".

Article 5   Certain consumer contracts

1. This Article applies to a contract the object of which is the supply of goods or services to a person ("the consumer") for a purpose which can be regarded as being outside his trade or profession, or a contract for the provision of credit for that object.
2. Notwithstanding the provisions of Article 3, a choice of law made by the parties shall not have the result of depriving the consumer of the protection afforded to him by the mandatory rules of the law of the country in which he has his habitual residence:
    —if in that country the conclusion of the contract was preceded by a specific invitation addressed to him or by advertising, and he had taken in that country all the steps necessary on his part for the conclusion of the contract, or
    —if the other party or his agent received the consumer's order in that country, or
    —if the contract is for the sale of goods and the consumer travelled from that country to another country and there gave his order, provided that the consumer's journey was arranged by the seller for the purpose of inducing the consumer to buy.
3. Notwithstanding the provisions of Article 4, a contract to which this Article applies shall, in the absence of choice in accordance with Article 3, be governed by the law of the country in which the consumer has his habitual residence if it is entered into in the circumstances described in paragraph 2 of this Article.
4. This Article shall not apply to:
    (a) a contract of carriage;
    (b) a contract for the supply of services where the services are to be supplied to the consumer exclusively in a country other than that in which he has his habitual residence.
5. Notwithstanding the provisions of paragraph 4, this Article shall apply to a contract which, for an inclusive price, provides for a combination of travel and accommodation.

Article 11   Incapacity

In a contract concluded between persons who are in the same country, a natural person who would have capacity under the law of that country may invoke his incapacity resulting from another law only if the other party to the contract was aware of this incapacity at the time of the conclusion of the contract or was not aware thereof as a result of negligence.

COURTS AND LEGAL SERVICES ACT 1990
(1990, c. 41)

61   Right of barrister to enter into contract for the provision of his services

(1) Any rule of law which prevents a barrister from entering into a contract for the provision of his services as a barrister is hereby abolished.

(2) Nothing in subsection (1) prevents the General Council of the Bar from making rules (however described) which prohibit barristers from entering into contracts or restrict their right to do so.

WATER INDUSTRY ACT 1991
(1991, c. 56)

209   Civil liability of undertakers for escapes of water etc.

(1) Where an escape of water, however caused, from a pipe vested in a water undertaker causes loss or damage, the undertaker shall be liable, except as otherwise provided in this section, for the loss or damage.

(2)   A water undertaker shall not incur any liability under subsection (1) above if the escape was due wholly to the fault of the person who sustained the loss or damage or of any servant, agent or contractor of his.

(3)   A water undertaker shall not incur any liability under subsection (1) above in respect of any loss or damage for which the undertaker would not be liable apart from that subsection and which is sustained—

    (a)   by the Environment Agency, the NRBW, a relevant undertaker or any statutory undertakers, within the meaning of section 336(1) of the Town and Country Planning Act 1990;

    (b)   by any public gas supplier within the meaning of Part I of the Gas Act 1986 or the holder of a licence under section 6(1) of the Electricity Act 1989;

    (c)   by any highway authority; or

    (d)   by any person on whom a right to compensation is conferred by section 82 of the New Roads and Street Works Act 1991.

(4)   The Law Reform (Contributory Negligence) Act 1945, the Fatal Accidents Act 1976 and the Limitation Act 1980 shall apply in relation to any loss or damage for which a water undertaker is liable under this section, but which is not due to the undertaker's fault, as if it were due to its fault.

(5)   Nothing in subsection (1) above affects any entitlement which a water undertaker may have to recover contribution under the Civil Liability (Contribution) Act 1978; and for the purposes of that Act, any loss for which a water undertaker is liable under that subsection shall be treated as if it were damage.

(6)   Where a water undertaker is liable under any enactment or agreement passed or made before April 1, 1982, to make any payment in respect of any loss or damage the undertaker shall not incur liability under subsection (1) above in respect of the same loss or damage.

(7)   In this section "fault" has the same meaning as in the Law Reform (Contributory Negligence) Act 1945.

WATER RESOURCES ACT 1991
(1991, c. 57)

208   Civil liability of the Agency for escapes of water etc.

(1)   Where an escape of water, however caused, from a pipe vested in the Agency or the NRBW causes loss or damage, the Agency or the NRBW shall be liable, except as otherwise provided in this section, for the loss or damage.

(2)   The Agency or the NRBW shall not incur any liability under subsection (1) above if the escape was due wholly to the fault of the person who sustained the loss or damage or of any servant, agent or contractor of his.

(3)   The Agency or the NRBW shall not incur any liability under subsection (1) above in respect of any loss or damage for which the Agency or the NRBW would not be liable apart from that subsection and which is sustained—

    (a)   by any water undertaker or sewerage undertaker or by any statutory undertakers, within the meaning of section 336(1) of the Town and Country Planning Act 1990;

    (b)   by any public gas supplier within the meaning of Part I of the Gas Act 1986 or the holder of a licence under section 6(1) of the Electricity Act 1989;

    (c)   by any highway authority; or

    (d)   by any person on whom a right to compensation is conferred by section 82 of the New Roads and Street Works Act 1991.

(4)   The Law Reform (Contributory Negligence) Act 1945, the Fatal Accidents Act 1976 and the Limitation Act 1980 shall apply in relation to any loss or damage for which the Agency or the NRBW is liable under this section, but which is not due to the Agency's or the NRBW's fault, as if it were due to its fault.

(5)   Nothing in subsection (1) above affects any entitlement which the Agency or the NRBW may have to recover contribution under the Civil Liability (Contribution) Act 1978; and for the purposes of that Act, any loss for which the Agency or the NRBW is liable under that subsection shall be treated as if it were damage.

(6)   Where the Agency or the NRBW is liable under any enactment or agreement passed or made before April 1, 1982, to make any payment in respect of any loss or damage the Agency or the NRBW shall not incur liability under subsection (1) above in respect of the same loss or damage.

(7)   In this section "fault" has the same meaning as in the Law Reform (Contributory Negligence) Act 1945.

ACCESS TO NEIGHBOURING LAND ACT 1992
(1992, c. 23)

1   Access orders

(1)   A person—

    (a)   who, for the purpose of carrying out works to any land (the "dominant land"), desires to enter upon any adjoining or adjacent land (the "servient land"), and

    (b)   who needs, but does not have, the consent of some other person to that entry,

    may make an application to the court for an order under this section ("an access order") against that other person.

(2)   On an application under this section, the court shall make an access order if, and only if, it is satisfied—

    (a)   that the works are reasonably necessary for the preservation of the whole or any part of the dominant land; and

    (b)   that they cannot be carried out, or would be substantially more difficult to carry out, without entry upon the servient land;

    but this subsection is subject to subsection (3) below.

(3)   The court shall not make an access order in any case where it is satisfied that, were it to make such an order—

    (a)   the respondent or any other person would suffer interference with, or disturbance of, his use or enjoyment of the servient land, or

    (b)   the respondent, or any other person (whether of full age or capacity or not) in occupation of the whole or any part of the servient land, would suffer hardship,

    to such a degree by reason of the entry (notwithstanding any requirement of this Act or any term or condition that may be imposed under it) that it would be unreasonable to make the order.

(4)   Where the court is satisfied on an application under this section that it is reasonably necessary to carry out any basic preservation works to the dominant land, those works shall be taken for the purposes of this Act to be reasonably necessary for the preservation of the land; and in this subsection "basic preservation works" means any of the following, that is to say—

    (a)   the maintenance, repair or renewal of any part of a building or other structure comprised in, or situate on, the dominant land;

    (b)   the clearance, repair or renewal of any drain, sewer, pipe or cable so comprised or situate;

    (c)   the treatment, cutting back, felling, removal or replacement of any hedge, tree, shrub or other growing thing which is so comprised and which is, or is in danger of becoming, damaged, diseased, dangerous, insecurely rooted or dead;

    (d)   the filling in, or clearance, of any ditch so comprised;

    but this subsection is without prejudice to the generality of the works which may, apart from it, be regarded by the court as reasonably necessary for the preservation of any land.

(5)   If the court considers it fair and reasonable in all the circumstances of the case, works may be regarded for the purposes of this Act as being reasonably necessary for the preservation of any land (or, for the purposes of subsection (4) above, as being basic preservation works which it is reasonably necessary to carry out to any land) notwithstanding that the works incidentally involve—

    (a)   the making of some alteration, adjustment or improvement to the land, or

    (b)   the demolition of the whole or any part of a building or structure comprised in or situate upon the land.

(6)   Where any works are reasonably necessary for the preservation of the whole or any part of the dominant land, the doing to the dominant land of anything which is requisite for, incidental to, or consequential on, the carrying out of those works shall be treated for the purposes of this Act as the carrying out of works which are reasonably necessary for the preservation of that land; and references in this Act to works, or to the carrying out of works, shall be construed accordingly.

(7)   Without prejudice to the generality of subsection (6) above, if it is reasonably necessary for a person to inspect the dominant land—

(a)   for the purpose of ascertaining whether any works may be reasonably necessary for the preservation of the whole or any part of that land,

(b)   for the purpose of making any map or plan, or ascertaining the course of any drain, sewer, pipe or cable, in preparation for, or otherwise in connection with, the carrying out of works which are so reasonably necessary, or

(c)   otherwise in connection with the carrying out of any such works,

the making of such an inspection shall be taken for the purposes of this Act to be the carrying out to the dominant land of works which are reasonably necessary for the preservation of that land; and references in this Act to works, or to the carrying out of works, shall be construed accordingly.

2   Terms and conditions of access orders

(1)   An access order shall specify—

(a)   the works to the dominant land that may be carried out by entering upon the servient land in pursuance of the order;

(b)   the particular area of servient land that may be entered upon by virtue of the order for the purpose of carrying out those works to the dominant land; and

(c)   the date on which, or the period during which, the land may be so entered upon;

and in the following provisions of this Act any reference to the servient land is a reference to the area specified in the order in pursuance of paragraph (b) above.

(2)   An access order may impose upon the applicant or the respondent such terms and conditions as appear to the court to be reasonably necessary for the purpose of avoiding or restricting—

(a)   any loss, damage, or injury which might otherwise be caused to the respondent or any other person by reason of the entry authorised by the order; or

(b)   any inconvenience or loss of privacy that might otherwise be so caused to the respondent or any other person.

(3)   Without prejudice to the generality of subsection (2) above, the terms and conditions which may be imposed under that subsection include provisions with respect to—

(a)   the manner in which the specified works are to be carried out;

(b)   the days on which, and the hours between which, the work involved may be executed;

(c)   the persons who may undertake the carrying out of the specified works or enter upon the servient land under or by virtue of the order;

(d)   the taking of any such precautions by the applicant as may be specified in the order.

(4)   An access order may also impose terms and conditions—

(a)   requiring the applicant to pay, or to secure that such person connected with him as may be specified in the order pays, compensation for—

(i)   any loss, damage or injury, or

(ii)   any substantial loss of privacy or other substantial inconvenience,

which will, or might, be caused to the respondent or any other person by reason of the entry authorised by the order;

(b)   requiring the applicant to secure that he, or such person connected with him as may be specified in the order, is insured against any such risks as may be so specified;

(c)   requiring such a record to be made of the condition of the servient land, or of such part of it as may be so specified, as the court may consider expedient with a view to facilitating the determination of any question that may arise concerning damage to that land.

(5) An access order may include provision requiring the applicant to pay the respondent such sum by way of consideration for the privilege of entering the servient land in pursuance of the order as appears to the court to be fair and reasonable having regard to all the circumstances of the case, including in particular—

(a) the likely financial advantage of the order to the applicant and any persons connected with him; and

(b) the degree of inconvenience likely to be caused to the respondent or any other person by the entry;

but no payment shall be ordered under this subsection if and to the extent that the works which the applicant desires to carry out by means of the entry are works to residential land.

(6) For the purposes of subsection (5)(a) above, the likely financial advantage of an access order to the applicant and any persons connected with him shall in all cases be taken to be a sum of money equal to the greater of the following amounts, that is to say—

(a) the amount (if any) by which so much of any likely increase in the value of any land—

(i) which consists of or includes the dominant land, and

(ii) which is owned or occupied by the same person as the dominant land, as may reasonably be regarded as attributable to the carrying out of the specified works exceeds the likely cost of carrying out those works with the benefit of the access order; and

(b) the difference (if it would have been possible to carry out the specified works without entering upon the servient land) between—

(i) the likely cost of carrying out those works without entering upon the servient land; and

(ii) the likely cost of carrying them out with the benefit of the access order.

(7) For the purposes of subsection (5) above, "residential land" means so much of any land as consists of—

(a) a dwelling or part of a dwelling;

(b) a garden, yard, private garage or outbuilding which is used and enjoyed wholly or mainly with a dwelling; or

(c) in the case of a building which includes one or more dwellings, any part of the building which is used and enjoyed wholly or mainly with those dwellings or any of them.

(8) The persons who are to be regarded for the purposes of this section as "connected with" the applicant are—

(a) the owner of any estate or interest in, or right over, the whole or any part of the dominant land;

(b) the occupier of the whole or any part of the dominant land; and

(c) any person whom the applicant may authorise under section 3(7) below to exercise the power of entry conferred by the access order.

(9) The court may make provision—

(a) for the reimbursement by the applicant of any expenses reasonably incurred by the respondent in connection with the application which are not otherwise recoverable as costs;

(b) for the giving of security by the applicant for any sum that might become payable to the respondent or any other person by virtue of this section or section 3 below.

3   Effect of access order

(1) An access order requires the respondent, so far as he has power to do so, to permit the applicant or any of his associates to do anything which the applicant or associate is authorised or required to do under or by virtue of the order or this section.

(2) Except as otherwise provided by or under this Act, an access order authorises the applicant or any of his associates, without the consent of the respondent,—

(a) to enter upon the servient land for the purpose of carrying out the specified works;

(b) to bring on to that land, leave there during the period permitted by the order and, before the end of that period, remove, such materials, plant and equipment as are reasonably necessary for the carrying out of those works; and

(c)   to bring on to that land any waste arising from the carrying out of those works, if it is reasonably necessary to do so in the course of removing it from the dominant land;

but nothing in this Act or in any access order shall authorise the applicant or any of his associates to leave anything in, on or over the servient land (otherwise than in discharge of their duty to make good that land) after their entry for the purpose of carrying out works to the dominant land ceases to be authorised under or by virtue of the order.

(3)   An access order requires the applicant—
(a)   to secure that any waste arising from the carrying out of the specified works is removed from the servient land forthwith;
(b)   to secure that, before the entry ceases to be authorised under or by virtue of the order, the servient land is, so far as reasonably practicable, made good; and
(c)   to indemnify the respondent against any damage which may be caused to the servient land or any goods by the applicant or any of his associates which would not have been so caused had the order not been made; but this subsection is subject to subsections (4) and (5) below.

(4)   In making an access order, the court may vary or exclude, in whole or in part,—
(a)   any authorisation that would otherwise be conferred by subsection 2(b) or (c) above; or
(b)   any requirement that would otherwise be imposed by subsection (3) above.

(5)   Without prejudice to the generality of subsection (4) above, if the court is satisfied that it is reasonably necessary for any such waste as may arise from the carrying out of the specified works to be left on the servient land for some period before removal, the access order may, in place of subsection (3)(a) above, include provision—
(a)   authorising the waste to be left on that land for such period as may be permitted by the order; and
(b)   requiring the applicant to secure that the waste is removed before the end of that period.

(6)   Where the applicant or any of his associates is authorised or required under or by virtue of an access order or this section to enter, or do any other thing, upon the servient land, he shall not (as respects that access order) be taken to be a trespasser from the beginning on account of his, or any other person's, subsequent conduct.

(7)   For the purposes of this section, the applicant's "associates" are such number of persons (whether or not servants or agents of his) whom he may reasonably authorise under this subsection to exercise the power of entry conferred by the access order as may be reasonably necessary for carrying out the specified works.

4   **Persons bound by access order, unidentified persons and bar on contracting out**

(1)   In addition to the respondent, an access order shall, subject to the provisions of the Land Charges Act 1972 and the Land Registration Act 2002, be binding on—
(a)   any of his successors in title to the servient land; and
(b)   any person who has an estate or interest in, or right over, the whole or any part of the servient land which was created after the making of the order and who derives his title to that estate, interest or right under the respondent; and references to the respondent shall be construed accordingly.

(2)   If and to the extent that the court considers it just and equitable to allow him to do so, a person on whom an access order becomes binding by virtue of subsection (1)(a) or (b) above shall be entitled, as respects anything falling to be done after the order becomes binding on him, to enforce the order or any of its terms or conditions as if he were the respondent, and references to the respondent shall be construed accordingly.

(3)   Rules of court may—
(a)   provide a procedure which may be followed where the applicant does not know, and cannot reasonably ascertain, the name of any person whom he desires to make respondent to the application; and

(b)   make provision enabling such an applicant to make such a person respondent by description instead of by name;

and in this subsection "applicant" includes a person who proposes to make an application for an access order.

(4)   Any agreement, whenever made, shall be void if and to the extent that it would, apart from this subsection, prevent a person from applying for an access order or restrict his right to do so.

6   Variation of orders and damages for breach

(1)   Where an access order or an order under this subsection has been made, the court may, on the application of any party to the proceedings in which the order was made or of any other person on whom the order is binding—

(a)   discharge or vary the order or any of its terms or conditions;

(b)   suspend any of its terms or conditions; or

(c)   revive any term or condition suspended under paragraph (b) above; and in the application of subsections (1) and (2) of section 4 above in relation to an access order, any order under this subsection which relates to the access order shall be treated for the purposes of those subsections as included in the access order.

(2)   If any person contravenes or fails to comply with any requirement, term or condition imposed upon him by or under this Act, the court may, without prejudice to any other remedy available, make an order for the payment of damages by him to any other person affected by the contravention or failure who makes an application for relief under this subsection.

TRADE UNION AND LABOUR RELATIONS (CONSOLIDATION) ACT 1992 (1992, c. 52)

20   Liability of trade union in certain proceedings in tort

(1)   Where proceedings in tort are brought against a trade union—

(a)   on the ground that an act—

(i)   induces another person to break a contract or interferes or induces another person to interfere with its performance, or

(ii)   consists in threatening that a contract (whether one to which the union is a party or not) will be broken or its performance interfered with, or that the union will induce another person to break a contract or interfere with its performance, or

(b)   in respect of an agreement or combination by two or more persons to do or to procure the doing of an act which, if it were done without any such agreement or combination, would be actionable in tort on such a ground,

then, for the purpose of determining in those proceedings whether the union is liable in respect of the act in question, that act shall be taken to have been done by the union if, but only if, it is to be taken to have been authorised or endorsed by the trade union in accordance with the following provisions.

(5)   Where for the purposes of any proceedings an act is by virtue of this section taken to have been done by a trade union, nothing in this section shall affect the liability of any other person, in those or any other proceedings, in respect of that act.

(6)   In proceedings arising out of an act which is by virtue of this section taken to have been done by a trade union, the power of the court to grant an injunction or interdict includes power to require the union to take such steps as the court considers appropriate for ensuring—

(a)   that there is no, or no further, inducement of persons to take part or to continue to take part in industrial action, and

(b)   that no person engages in any conduct after the granting of the injunction or interdict by virtue of having been induced before it was granted to take part or to continue to take part in industrial action.

The provisions of subsections (2) to (4) above apply in relation to proceedings for failure to comply with any such injunction or interdict as they apply in relation to the original proceedings.

22   Limit on damages awarded against trade unions in actions in tort

(1)   This section applies to any proceedings in tort brought against a trade union, except —

    (a)   proceedings for personal injury as a result of negligence, nuisance or breach of duty;

    (b)   proceedings for breach of duty in connection with the ownership, occupation, possession, control or use of property;

    (c)   proceedings brought by virtue of Part I of the Consumer Protection Act 1987 (product liability).

In any proceedings in tort to which this section applies the amount which may be awarded against the union by way of damages shall not exceed the following limit —

Number of members of union	Maximum award of damages
Less than 5,000	£10,000
5,000 or more but less than 25,000	£50,000
25,000 or more but less than 100,000	£125,000
100,000 or more	£250,000

(3)   The Secretary of State may by order amend subsection (2) so as to vary any of the sums specified ...

178   Collective agreements and collective bargaining

(1)   In this Act "collective agreement" means any agreement or arrangement made by or on behalf of one or more trade unions and one or more employers or employers' associations and relating to one or more of the matters specified below; and "collective bargaining" means negotiations relating to or connected with one or more of those matters.

(2)   The matters referred to above are —

    (a)   terms and conditions of employment, or the physical conditions in which any workers are required to work;

    (b)   engagement or non-engagement, or termination or suspension of employment or the duties of employment, of one or more workers;

    (c)   allocation of work or the duties of employment between workers or groups of workers;

    (d)   matters of discipline;

    (e)   a worker's membership or non-membership of a trade union;

    (f)   facilities for officials of trade unions; and

    (g)   machinery for negotiation or consultation, and other procedures, relating to any of the above matters, including the recognition by employers or employers' associations of the right of a trade union to represent workers in such negotiation or consultation or in the carrying out of such procedures.

179   Whether agreement intended to be a legally enforceable contract

(1)   A collective agreement shall be conclusively presumed not to have been intended by the parties to be a legally enforceable contract unless the agreement —

    (a)   is in writing, and

    (b)   contains a provision which (however expressed) states that the parties intend that the agreement shall be a legally enforceable contract.

(2)   A collective agreement which does satisfy those conditions shall be conclusively presumed to have been intended by the parties to be a legally enforceable contract.

(3)   If a collective agreement is in writing and contains a provision which (however expressed) states that the parties intend that one or more parts of the agreement specified in that provision, but not the whole of the agreement, shall be a legally enforceable contract, then —

    (a)   the specified part or parts shall be conclusively presumed to have been intended by the parties to be a legally enforceable contract, and

    (b)   the remainder of the agreement shall be conclusively presumed not to have been intended by the parties to be such a contract.

(4)   A part of a collective agreement which by virtue of subsection (3)(b) is not a legally enforceable contract may be referred to for the purpose of interpreting a part of the agreement which is such a contract.

180   Effect of provisions restricting right to take industrial action

(1)   Any terms of a collective agreement which prohibit or restrict the right of workers to engage in a strike or other industrial action, or have the effect of prohibiting or restricting that right, shall not form part of any contract between a worker and the person for whom he works unless the following conditions are met.

(2)   The conditions are that the collective agreement—

(a)   is in writing,

(b)   contains a provision expressly stating that those terms shall or may be incorporated in such a contract,

(c)   is reasonably accessible at his place of work to the worker to whom it applies and is available for him to consult during working hours, and

(d)   is one where each trade union which is a party to the agreement is an independent trade union;

and that the contract with the worker expressly or impliedly incorporates those terms in the contract.

(3)   The above provisions have effect notwithstanding anything in section 179 and notwithstanding any provision to the contrary in any agreement (including a collective agreement or a contract with any worker).

219   Protection from certain tort liabilities

(1)   An act done by a person in contemplation or furtherance of a trade dispute is not actionable in tort on the ground only—

(a)   that it induces another person to break a contract or interferes or induces another person to interfere with its performance, or

(b)   that it consists in his threatening that a contract (whether one to which he is a party or not) will be broken or its performance interfered with, or that he will induce another person to break a contract or interfere with its performance.

(2)   An agreement or combination by two or more persons to do or procure the doing of an act in contemplation or furtherance of a trade dispute is not actionable in tort if the act is one which if done without any such agreement or combination would not be actionable in tort.

(3)   Nothing in subsections (1) and (2) prevents an act done in the course of picketing from being actionable in tort unless—

(a)   it is done in the course of attendance declared lawful by section 220 (peaceful picketing), and

(b)   in the case of picketing to which section 220A applies, the requirements in that section (union suspension of picketing) are complied with.

(4)   Subsections (1) and (2) have effect subject to sections 222 to 225 (action excluded from protection) and to sections 226 (requirement of ballot before action by trade union) and 234A (requirement of notice to employer of industrial action); and in those sections "not protected" means excluded from the protection afforded by this section or, where the expression is used with reference to a particular person, excluded from that protection as respects that person.

220   Peaceful picketing

(1)   It is lawful for a person in contemplation or furtherance of a trade dispute to attend—

(a)   at or near his own place of work, or

(b)   if he is an official of a trade union, at or near the place of work of a member of the union whom he is accompanying and whom he represents,

for the purpose only of peacefully obtaining or communicating information, or peacefully persuading any person to work or abstain from working.

220A Union supervision of picketing

(1)   Section 220 does not make lawful any picketing that a trade union organises, or encourages its members to take part in, unless the requirements in subsections (2) to (8) are complied with.

(2)   The union must appoint a person to supervise the picketing.
(3)   That person ("the picket supervisor") must be an official or other member of the union who is familiar with any provisions of a Code of Practice issued under section 203 that deal with picketing.
(4)   The union or picket supervisor must take reasonable steps to tell the police—
       (a)   the picket supervisor's name;
       (b)   where the picketing will take place;
       (c)   how to contact the picket supervisor.
(5)   The union must provide the picket supervisor with a letter stating that the picketing is approved by the union.
(6)   If an individual who is, or is acting on behalf of, the employer asks the picket supervisor for sight of the approval letter, the picket supervisor must show it to that individual as soon as is reasonably practicable.
(7)   While the picketing is taking place, the picket supervisor must—
       (a)   be present where it is taking place, or
       (b)   be readily contactable by the union and the police, and be able to attend at short notice.
(8)   While present where the picketing is taking place, the picket supervisor must wear something that readily identifies the picket supervisor as such.
(9)   In this section—
       "approval letter" means the letter referred to in subsection (5);
       "employer" means the employer to which the trade dispute relates;
       "picketing" means attendance at or near a place of work, in contemplation or furtherance of a trade dispute, for the purpose of—
       (a)   obtaining or communicating information, or
       (b)   persuading any person to work or abstain from working.
(10)   In relation to picketing that two or more unions organise or encourage members to take part in—
       (a)   In subsection (2) "the union" means any one of those unions, and
       (b)   other references in this section to "the union" are to that union.

222   Action to enforce trade union membership

(1)   An act is not protected if the reason, or one of the reasons, for which it is done is the fact or belief that a particular employer—
       (a)   is employing, has employed or might employ a person who is not a member of a trade union, or
       (b)   is failing, has failed or might fail to discriminate against such a person.
(2)   For the purposes of subsection (1)(b) an employer discriminates against a person if, but only if, he ensures that his conduct in relation to—
       (a)   persons, or persons of any description, employed by him, or who apply to be, or are, considered by him for employment, or
       (b)   that provision of employment for such persons, is different, in some or all cases, according to whether or not they are members of a trade union, and is more favourable to those who are.
(3)   An act is not protected if it constitutes, or is one of a number of acts which together constitute, an inducement or attempted inducement of a person—
       (a)   to incorporate in a contract to which that person is a party, or a proposed contract to which he intends to be a party, a term or condition which is or would be void by virtue of section 144 (union membership requirement in contract for goods or services), or
       (b)   to contravene section 145 (refusal to deal with person on grounds relating to union membership).

224   Secondary action

(1)   An Act is not protected if one of the facts relied on for the purpose of establishing liability is that there has been secondary action which is not lawful picketing.
(2)   There is secondary action in relation to a trade dispute when, and only when, a person—
       (a)   induces another to break a contract of employment or interferes or induces another to interfere with its performance, or

(b)   threatens that a contract of employment under which he or another is employed will be broken or its performance interfered with, or that he will induce another to break a contract of employment or to interfere with its performance,

and the employer under the contract of employment is not the employer party to the dispute.

(3)   Lawful picketing means acts done in the course of such attendance as is declared lawful by section 220 (peaceful picketing)—

(a)   by a worker employed (or, in the case of a worker not in employment, last employed) by the employer party to the dispute, or

(b)   by a trade union official whose attendance is lawful by virtue of subsection (1)(b) of that section.

(4)   For the purposes of this section an employer shall not be treated as party to a dispute between another employer and workers of that employer; and where more than one employer is in dispute with his workers, the dispute between each employer and his workers shall be treated as a separate dispute.

In this subsection "worker" has the same meaning as in section 244 (meaning of "trade dispute").

(5)   An act in contemplation or furtherance of a trade dispute which is primary action in relation to that dispute may not be relied on as secondary action in relation to another trade dispute. Primary action means such action as is mentioned in paragraph (a) or (b) of subsection (2) where the employer under the contract of employment is the employer party to the dispute.

(6)   In this section "contract of employment" includes any contract under which one person personally does work or performs services for another, and related expressions shall be construed accordingly.

225   Pressure to impose union recognition requirement

(1)   An act is not protected if it constitutes, or is one of a number of acts which together constitute, an inducement or attempted inducement of a person—

(a)   to incorporate in a contract to which that person is a party, or a proposed contract to which he intends to be a party, a term or condition which is or would be void by virtue of section 186 (recognition requirement in contract for goods or services), or

(b)   to contravene section 187 (refusal to deal with person on grounds of union exclusion).

(2)   An act is not protected if—

(a)   it interferes with the supply (whether or not under a contract) of goods or services, or can reasonably be expected to have that effect, and

(b)   one of the facts relied upon for the purpose of establishing liability is that a person has—

(i)   induced another to break a contract of employment or interfered or induced another to interfere with its performance, or

(ii)   threatened that a contract of employment under which he or another is employed will be broken or its performance interfered with, or that he will induce another to break a contract of employment or to interfere with its performance, and

(c)   the reason, or one of the reasons, for doing the act is the fact or belief that the supplier (not being the employer under the contract of employment mentioned in paragraph (b)) does not, or might not—

(i)   recognise one or more trade unions for the purpose of negotiating on behalf of workers, or any class of worker, employed by him, or

(ii)   negotiate or consult with, or with an official of, one or more trade unions.

226   Requirement of ballot before action by trade union

(1)   An act done by a trade union to induce a person to take part, or continue to take part, in industrial action—

(a)   is not protected unless the industrial action has the support of a ballot, and

(b)   where section 226A falls to be complied with in relation to the person's employer, is not protected as respects the employer unless the trade union has complied with section 226A in relation to him.

236 No compulsion to work

No court shall, whether by way of—

(a) an order for specific performance or specific implement of a contract of employment, or

(b) an injunction or interdict restraining a breach or threatened breach of such a contract,

compel an employee to do any work or attend at any place for the doing of any work.

244 Meaning of "trade dispute" in Part V

(1) In this Part a "trade dispute" means a dispute between workers and their employer which relates wholly or mainly to one or more of the following—

(a) terms and conditions of employment, or the physical conditions in which any workers are required to work;

(b) engagement or non-engagement, or termination or suspension of employment or the duties of employment, of one or more workers;

(c) allocation of work or the duties of employment between workers or groups of workers;

(d) matters of discipline;

(e) a worker's membership or non-membership of a trade union;

(f) facilities for officials of trade unions; and

(g) machinery for negotiation or consultation, and other procedures, relating to any of the above matters, including the recognition by employers or employers' associations of the right of a trade union to represent workers in such negotiation or consultation or in the carrying out of such procedures.

245 Crown employees and contracts

Where a person holds any office or employment under the Crown on terms which do not constitute a contract of employment between that person and the Crown, those terms shall nevertheless be deemed to constitute such a contract for the purposes of—

(a) the law relating to liability in tort of a person who commits an act which—

(i) induces another person to break a contract, interferes with the performance of a contract or induces another person to interfere with its performance, or

(ii) consists in a threat that a contract will be broken or its performance interfered with, or that any person will be induced to break a contract or interfere with its performance, and

(b) the provisions of this or any other Act which refer (whether in relation to contracts generally or only in relation to contracts of employment) to such an act.

RAILWAYS ACT 1993
(1993, c. 43)

122 Statutory authority as a defence to actions in nuisance etc.

(1) Subject to the following provisions of this section—

(a) any person shall have authority—

(i) to use, or to cause or permit any agent or independent contractor of his to use, rolling stock on any track, or

(ii) to use, or to cause or permit any agent or independent contractor of his to use, any land comprised in a network, station or light maintenance depot for or in connection with the provision of network services, station services in light maintenance services, and

(b) any person who is the owner or occupier of any land shall have authority to authorise, consent to or acquiesce in—

(i) the use by another of rolling stock on any track comprised in that land, or

(ii) the use by another of that land for or in connection with the provision of network services, station services or light maintenance services,

if and so long as the qualifying conditions are satisfied in the particular case.

(3) The authority conferred by this section is conferred only for the purpose of providing a defence of statutory authority—
    (a) in England and Wales—
        (i) in any proceedings, whether civil or criminal, in nuisance; or
        (ii) in any civil proceedings, other than proceedings for breach of statutory duty, in respect of the escape of things from land;
    ...
(4) Nothing in this section shall be construed as excluding a defence of statutory authority otherwise available under or by virtue of any enactment.

CRIMINAL JUSTICE AND PUBLIC ORDER ACT 1994
(1994, c. 33)

60   Powers to stop and search in anticipation of or after violence

(1) If a police officer of or above the rank of inspector reasonably believes—
    (a) that incidents involving serious violence may take place in any locality in his police area, and that it is expedient to give an authorisation under this section to prevent their occurrence;
    (aa) that—
        (i) an incident involving serious violence has taken place in England and Wales in his police area;
        (ii) a dangerous instrument or offensive weapon used in the incident is being carried in any locality in his police area by a person; and
        (iii) it is expedient to give an authorisation under this section to find the instrument or weapon; or
    (b) that persons are carrying dangerous instruments or offensive weapons in any locality in his police area without good reason,
he may give an authorisation that the powers conferred by this section are to be exercisable at any place within that locality for a specified period not exceeding twenty four hours.
(4A) This section also confers on any constable in uniform power—
    (a) to require any person to remove any item which the constable reasonably believes that person is wearing wholly or mainly for the purpose of concealing his identity;
    (b) to seize any item which the constable reasonably believes any person intends to wear wholly or mainly for that purpose.
(5) A constable may, in the exercise of the powers conferred by subsection (4) above, stop any person or vehicle and make any search he thinks fit whether or not he has any grounds for suspecting that the person or vehicle is carrying weapons or articles of that kind.
(6) If in the course of a search under this section a constable discovers a dangerous instrument or an article which he has reasonable grounds for suspecting to be an offensive weapon, he may seize it.

61   Power to remove trespassers on land

(1) If the senior police officer present at the scene reasonably believes that two or more persons are trespassing on land and are present there with the common purpose of residing there for any period, that reasonable steps have been taken by or on behalf of the occupier to ask them to leave and—
    (a) that any of those persons has caused damage to the land or to property on the land or used threatening, abusive or insulting words or behaviour towards the occupier, a member of his family or an employee or agent of his, or
    (b) that those persons have between them six or more vehicles on the land, he may direct those persons, or any of them, to leave the land and to remove any vehicles or other property they have with them on the land.
(2) Where the persons in question are reasonably believed by the senior police officer to be persons who were not originally trespassers but have become trespassers on

the land, the officer must reasonably believe that the other conditions specified in subsection (1) are satisfied after those persons became trespassers before he can exercise the power conferred by that subsection.

(4) If a person knowing that a direction under subsection (1) above has been given which applies to him—

(a) fails to leave the land as soon as reasonably practicable, or

(b) having left again enters the land as a trespasser within the period of three months beginning with the day on which the direction was given,

he commits an offence ...

62   Supplementary powers of seizure

(1) If a direction has been given under section 61 and a constable reasonably suspects that any person to whom the direction applies has, without reasonable excuse—

(a) failed to remove any vehicle on the land which appears to the constable to belong to him or to be in his possession or under his control; or

(b) entered the land as a trespasser with a vehicle within the period of three months beginning with the day on which the direction was given,

the constable may seize and remove that vehicle.

62A   Power to remove trespassers: alternative site available

(1) If the senior police officer present at a scene reasonably believes that the conditions in subsection (2) are satisfied in relation to a person and land, he may direct the person—

(a) to leave the land;

(b) to remove any vehicle and other property he has with him on the land.

(2) The conditions are—

(a) that the person and one or more others ("the trespassers") are trespassing on the land;

(b) that the trespassers have between them at least one vehicle on the land;

(c) that the trespassers are present on the land with the common purpose of residing there for any period;

(d) if it appears to the officer that the person has one or more caravans in his possession or under his control on the land, that there is a suitable pitch on a relevant caravan site for that caravan or each of those caravans;

(e) that the occupier of the land or a person acting on his behalf has asked the police to remove the trespassers from the land.

(3) A direction under subsection (1) may be communicated to the person to whom it applies by any constable at the scene.

(4) Subsection (5) applies if—

(a) a police officer proposes to give a direction under subsection (1) in relation to a person and land, and

(b) it appears to him that the person has one or more caravans in his possession or under his control on the land.

(5) The officer must consult every local authority within whose area the land is situated as to whether there is a suitable pitch for the caravan or each of the caravans on a relevant caravan site which is situated in the local authority's area.

(6) In this section—

"caravan" and "caravan site" have the same meanings as in Part 1 of the Caravan Sites and Control of Development Act 1960;

"relevant caravan site" means a caravan site which is—

(a) situated in the area of a local authority within whose area the land is situated, and

(b) managed by a relevant site manager;

"relevant site manager" means—

(a) a local authority within whose area the land is situated;

(aa) a private registered provider of social housing;

(b) a registered social landlord;

"registered social landlord" means a body registered as a social landlord under Chapter 1 of Part 1 of the Housing Act 1996.

(7) The Secretary of State may by order amend the definition of "relevant site manager" in subsection (6) by adding a person or description of person.

(8) An order under subsection (7) must be made by statutory instrument and is subject to annulment in pursuance of a resolution of either House of Parliament.

62B Failure to comply with direction under section 62A: offences

(1) A person commits an offence if he knows that a direction under section 62A(1) has been given which applies to him and—

  (a) he fails to leave the relevant land as soon as reasonably practicable, or

  (b) he enters any land in the area of the relevant local authority as a trespasser before the end of the relevant period with the intention of residing there.

(2) The relevant period is the period of 3 months starting with the day on which the direction is given.

(3) A person guilty of an offence under this section is liable on summary conviction to imprisonment for a term not exceeding 3 months or a fine not exceeding level 4 on the standard scale or both.

(5) In proceedings for an offence under this section it is a defence for the accused to show—

  (a) that he was not trespassing on the land in respect of which he is alleged to have committed the offence, or

  (b) that he had a reasonable excuse—

    (i) for failing to leave the relevant land as soon as reasonably practicable, or

    (ii) for entering land in the area of the relevant local authority as a trespasser with the intention of residing there, or

  (c) that, at the time the direction was given, he was under the age of 18 years and was residing with his parent or guardian.

62C Failure to comply with direction under section 62A: seizure

(1) This section applies if a direction has been given under section 62A(1) and a constable reasonably suspects that a person to whom the direction applies has, without reasonable excuse—

  (a) failed to remove any vehicle on the relevant land which appears to the constable to belong to him or to be in his possession or under his control; or

  (b) entered any land in the area of the relevant local authority as a trespasser with a vehicle before the end of the relevant period with the intention of residing there.

(2) The relevant period is the period of 3 months starting with the day on which the direction is given.

(3) The constable may seize and remove the vehicle.

63 Powers to remove persons attending or preparing for a rave

(1) This section applies to a gathering on land in the open air of 20 or more persons (whether or not trespassers) at which amplified music is played during the night (with or without intermissions) and is such as, by reason of its loudness and duration and the time at which it is played, is likely to cause serious distress to the inhabitants of the locality; and for this purpose

  (a) such a gathering continues during intermissions in the music and where the gathering extends over several days, throughout the period during which amplified music is played at night (with or without intermissions); and

  (b) "music" includes sounds wholly or predominantly characterised by the emission of a succession of repetitive beats.

(1A) This section also applies to a gathering if—

  (a) it is a gathering on land of 20 persons or more who are trespassing on the land; and

  (b) it would be a gathering of a kind mentioned in subsection (1) above if it took place on land in the open air.

(2) If, as respects any land, a police officer of at least the rank of superintendent reasonably believes that—

  (a) two or more persons are making preparations for the holding there of a gathering to which this section applies,

(b)   ten or more persons are waiting for such a gathering to begin there, or (c) ten or more persons are attending such a gathering which is in progress, he may give a direction that those persons and any other persons who come to prepare or wait for or to attend the gathering are to leave the land and remove any vehicles or other property which they have with them on the land.

(6)   If a person knowing that a direction has been given which applies to him—

     (a)   fails to leave the land as soon as reasonably practicable, or

     (b)   having left again enters the land within the period of 7 days beginning with the day on which the direction was given,

     he commits an offence …

64   Supplementary powers of entry and seizure

(4)   If a direction has been given under section 63 and a constable reasonably suspects that any person to whom the direction applies has, without reasonable excuse—

     (a)   failed to remove any vehicle or sound equipment on the land which appears to the constable to belong to him or to be in his possession or under his control; or

     (b)   entered the land as a trespasser with a vehicle or sound equipment within the period of 7 days beginning with the day on which the direction was given,

     the constable may seize and remove that vehicle or sound equipment.

65   Raves: power to stop persons from proceeding

(1)   If a constable in uniform reasonably believes that a person is on his way to a gathering to which section 63 applies in relation to which a direction under section 63(2) is in force, he may, subject to subsections (2) and (3) below—

     (a)   stop that person, and

     (b)   direct him not to proceed in the direction of the gathering.

(2)   The power conferred by subsection (1) above may only be exercised at a place within 5 miles of the boundary of the site of the gathering.

66   Power of court to forfeit sound equipment

(1)   Where a person is convicted of an offence under section 63 in relation to a gathering to which that section applies and the court is satisfied that any sound equipment which has been seized from him under section 64(4), or which was in his possession or under his control at the relevant time, has been used at the gathering the court may make an order for forfeiture under this subsection in respect of that property.

(2)   The court may make an order under subsection (1) above whether or not it also deals with the offender in respect of the offence in any other way and without regard to any restrictions on forfeiture in any enactment.

(3)   In considering whether to make an order under subsection (1) above in respect of any property a court shall have regard—

     (a)   to the value of the property; and

     (b)   to the likely financial and other effects on the offender of the making of the order (taken together with any other order that the court contemplates making).

(4)   An order under subsection (1) above shall operate to deprive the offender of his rights, if any, in the property to which it relates, and the property shall (if not already in their possession) be taken into the possession of the police.

(5)   Except in a case to which subsection (6) below applies, where any property has been forfeited under subsection (1) above, a magistrates' court may, on application by a claimant of the property, other than the offender from whom it was forfeited under subsection (1) above, make an order for delivery of the property to the applicant if it appears to the court that he is the owner of the property.

(7)   No application shall be made under subsection (5), or by virtue of subsection (6), above by any claimant of the property after the expiration of 6 months from the date on which an order under subsection (1) above was made in respect of the property.

(8)   No such application shall succeed unless the claimant satisfies the court either that he had not consented to the offender having possession of the property or that he did not know, and had no reason to suspect, that the property was likely to be used at a gathering to which section 63 applies.

68   Offence of aggravated trespass

(1)   A person commits the offence of aggravated trespass if he trespasses on land ... and, in relation to any lawful activity which persons are engaging in or are about to engage in on that or adjoining land ..., does there anything which is intended by him to have the effect—

(a)   of intimidating those persons or any of them so as to deter them or any of them from engaging in that activity,

(b)   of obstructing that activity, or

(c)   of disrupting that activity.

(2)   Activity on any occasion on the part of a person or persons on land is "lawful" for the purposes of this section if he or they may engage in the activity on the land on that occasion without committing an offence or trespassing on the land.

69   Powers to remove persons committing or participating in aggravated trespass

(1)   If the senior police officer present at the scene reasonably believes—

(a)   that a person is committing, has committed or intends to commit the offence of aggravated trespass on land ...; or

(b)   that two or more persons are trespassing on land ... and are present there with the common purpose of intimidating persons so as to deter them from engaging in a lawful activity or of obstructing or disrupting a lawful activity, he may direct that person or (as the case may be) those persons (or any of them) to leave the land.

(2)   A direction under subsection (1) above, if not communicated to the persons referred to in subsection (1) by the police officer giving the direction, may be communicated to them by any constable at the scene.

(3)   If a person knowing that a direction under subsection (1) above has been given which applies to him—

(a)   fails to leave the land as soon as practicable, or

(b)   having left again enters the land as a trespasser within the period of three months beginning with the day on which the direction was given,

he commits an offence.

CRIMINAL INJURIES COMPENSATION ACT 1995
(1995, c. 53)

1   The Criminal Injuries Compensation Scheme

(1)   The Secretary of State shall make arrangements for the payment of compensation to, or in respect of, persons who have sustained one or more criminal injuries.

(2)   Any such arrangements shall include the making of a scheme providing, in particular, for—

(a)   the circumstances in which awards may be made; and

(b)   the categories of person to whom awards may be made.

(3)   The scheme shall be known as the Criminal Injuries Compensation Scheme.

(4)   In this Act—

...

"award" means an award of compensation made in accordance with the provisions of the Scheme;

"claims officer" means a person appointed by the Secretary of State under section 3(4)(b);

"compensation" means compensation payable under an award;

"criminal injury", "loss of earnings" and "special expenses" have such meaning as may be specified;

"the Scheme" means the Criminal Injuries Compensation Scheme;

"Scheme manager" means a person appointed by the Secretary of State to have overall responsibility for managing the provisions of the Scheme (other than those to which section 5(2) applies); and

"specified" means specified by the Scheme.

2   Basis on which compensation is to be calculated

(1)   The amount of compensation payable under an award shall be determined in accordance with the provisions of the Scheme.

(2)   Provision shall be made for—

(a)   a standard amount of compensation, determined by reference to the nature of theinjury;

(b)   in such cases as may be specified, an additional amount of compensation calculated with respect to loss of earnings;

(c)   in such cases as may be specified, an additional amount of compensation calculated with respect to special expenses; and

(d)   in cases of fatal injury, such additional amounts as may be specified or otherwise determined in accordance with the Scheme.

(3)   Provision shall be made for the standard amount to be determined—

(a)   in accordance with a table ("the Tariff") prepared by the Secretary of State as part of the Scheme and such other provisions of the Scheme as may be relevant; or

(b)   where no provision is made in the Tariff with respect to the injury in question, in accordance with such provisions of the Scheme as may be relevant.

(4)   The Tariff shall show, in respect of each description of injury mentioned in the Tariff, the standard amount of compensation payable in respect of that description of injury.

(5)   An injury may be described in the Tariff in such a way, including by reference to the nature of the injury, its severity or the circumstances in which it was sustained, as the Secretary of State considers appropriate.

(6)   The Secretary of State may at any time alter the Tariff—

(a)   by adding to the descriptions of injury mentioned there;

(b)   by removing a description of injury;

(c)   by increasing or reducing the amount shown as the standard amount of compensation payable in respect of a particular description of injury; or

(d)   in such other way as he considers appropriate.

(7)   The Scheme may—

(a)   provide for amounts of compensation not to exceed such maximum amounts as may be specified;

(b)   include such transitional provision with respect to any alteration of its provisions relating to compensation as the Secretary of State considers appropriate.

3   Claims and awards

(1)   The Scheme may, in particular, include provision—

(a)   as to the circumstances in which an award may be withheld or the amount of compensation reduced;

(b)   for an award to be made subject to conditions;

(c)   for the whole or any part of any compensation to be repayable in specified circumstances;

(d)   for compensation to be held subject to trusts, in such cases as may be determined in accordance with the Scheme;

(e)   requiring claims under the Scheme to be made within such periods as may be specified by the Scheme; and (f) imposing other time limits.

(2)   Where, in accordance with any provision of the Scheme, it falls to one person to satisfy another as to any matter, the standard of proof required shall be that applicable in civil proceedings.

(3)   Where, in accordance with any provision of the Scheme made by virtue of subsection(1) (c), any amount falls to be repaid it shall be recoverable as a debt due to the Crown.

(4)   The Scheme shall include provision for claims for compensation to be determined and awards and payments of compensation to be made—

(a)   if a Scheme manager has been appointed, by persons appointed for the purpose by the Scheme manager; but

(b)   otherwise by persons ("claims officers") appointed for the purpose by the Secretary of State.

(5) A claims officer—
- (a) shall be appointed on such terms and conditions as the Secretary of State considers appropriate; but
- (b) shall not be regarded as having been appointed to exercise functions of the Secretary of State or to act on his behalf.

(6) No decision taken by a claims officer shall be regarded as having been taken by, or on behalf of, the Secretary of State.

(7) If a Scheme manager has been appointed—
- (a) he shall not be regarded as exercising functions of the Secretary of State or as acting on his behalf; and
- (b) no decision taken by him or by any person appointed by him shall be regarded as having been taken by, or on behalf of, the Secretary of State.

7 Inalienability of awards

(1) Every assignment (or, in Scotland, assignation) of, or charge on, an award and every agreement to assign or charge an award shall be void.

(2) On the bankruptcy of a person in whose favour an award is made (or, in Scotland, on the sequestration of such a person's estate), the award shall not pass to any trustee or other person acting on behalf of his creditors.

REQUIREMENTS OF WRITING (SCOTLAND) ACT 1995
(1995, c. 7)

PART 1

1 Writing required for certain contracts, obligations, trusts, conveyances and wills

(1) Subject to subsection (2) below and any other enactment, writing shall not be required for the constitution of a contract, unilateral obligation or trust.

(2) Subject to subsection (3) below, a written document which is a traditional document complying with section 2 or an electronic document complying with section 9B of this Act shall be required for—
- (a) the constitution of—
  - (i) a contract or unilateral obligation for the creation, transfer, variation or extinction of a real right in land;
  - (ii) a gratuitous unilateral obligation except an obligation undertaken in the course of business; and
  - (iii) a trust whereby a person declares himself to be sole trustee of his own property or any property which he may acquire;
- (b) the creation, transfer, variation or extinction of a real right in land otherwise than by the operation of a court decree, enactment or rule of law;
- (ba) the constitution of an agreement under section 66(1) of the Land Registration etc. (Scotland) Act 2012; and
- (c) the making of any will, testamentary trust disposition and settlement or codicil.

(3) Where a contract, obligation or trust mentioned in subsection (2)(a) above is not constituted in a document complying with section 2 or, as the case may be, 9B of this Act, but one of the parties to the contract, a creditor in the obligation or a beneficiary under the trust ("the first person") has acted or refrained from acting in reliance on the contract, obligation or trust with the knowledge and acquiescence of the other party to the contract, the debtor in the obligation or the truster ("the second person")—
- (a) the second person shall not be entitled to withdraw from the contract, obligation or trust; and
- (b) the contract, obligation or trust shall not be regarded as invalid, on the ground that it is not so constituted, if the condition set out in subsection (4) below is satisfied.

(4) The condition referred to in subsection (3) above is that the position of the first person—
 (a) as a result of acting or refraining from acting as mentioned in that subsection has been affected to a material extent; and
 (b) as a result of such a withdrawal as is mentioned in that subsection would be adversely affected to a material extent.

(5) In relation to the constitution of any contract, obligation or trust mentioned in subsection (2)(a) above, subsections (3) and (4) above replace the rules of law known as *rei interventus* and homologation.

(6) This section shall apply to the variation of a contract, obligation or trust as it applies to the constitution thereof but as if in subsections (3) and (4) for the references to acting or refraining from acting in reliance on the contract, obligation or trust and withdrawing therefrom there were substituted respectively references to acting or refraining from acting in reliance on the variation of the contract, obligation or trust and withdrawing from the variation.

(7) In this section "real right" means any real right in or over land, including any right to occupy or to use land or to restrict the occupation or use of land, but does not include—
 (a) a tenancy;
 (b) a right to occupy or use land; or
 (c) a right to restrict the occupation or use of land,
 if the tenancy or right is not granted for more than one year, unless the tenancy or right is not granted for more than one year, unless the tenancy or right is for a recurring period or recurring periods and there is a gap of more than one year between the beginning of the first, and the end of the last, such period.

(8) For the purposes of subsection (7) above "land" does not include—
 (a) growing crops; or
 (b) a moveable building or other moveable structure.

PART 2

1A   Application of Part 2

This Part of this Act applies to documents written on paper, parchment or some other tangible surface (traditional documents).

2   Type of writing required for formal validity of certain traditional documents

(1) No traditional document required by section 1(2) of this Act shall be valid in respect of the formalities of execution unless it is subscribed by the granter of it or, if there is more than one granter, by each granter, but nothing apart from such subscription shall be required for the document to be valid as aforesaid.

(2) A contract mentioned in section 1(2)(a)(i) of this Act may be regarded as constituted or varied (as the case may be) if the offer is contained in one or more traditional documents and the acceptance is contained in another traditional document or other documents, and each traditional document is subscribed by the granter or granters thereof.

(3) Nothing in this section shall prevent a traditional document which has not been subscribed by the granter or granters of it from being used as evidence in relation to any right or obligation to which the document relates.

(4) This section is without prejudice to any other enactment which makes different provision in respect of the formalities of execution of a document to which this section applies.

BROADCASTING ACT 1996
(1996, c. 55)

121   Certain statements etc. protected by qualified privilege for purposes of defamation

(1) For the purposes of the law relating to defamation—
 (a) publication of any statement in the course of the consideration by OFCOM of, and their adjudication on, a fairness complaint,

    (b)   publication by OFCOM of directions under section 119(1) relating to a fairness complaint, or

    (c)   publication of a report of OFCOM, so far as the report relates to fairness complaints, is privileged unless the publication is shown to be made with malice.

(2)   Nothing in subsection (1) shall be construed as limiting any privilege subsisting apart from that subsection.

DAMAGES ACT 1996
(1996, c. 48)

1   Assumed rate of return on investment of damages

(1)   In determining the return to be expected from the investment of a sum awarded as general damages for future pecuniary loss in an action for personal injury the court shall, subject to and in accordance with rules of court made for the purposes of this section, take into account such rate of return as may from time to time be prescribed by an order made by the Lord Chancellor.

(2)   Subsection (1) above shall not however prevent the court taking a different rate of return into account if any party to the proceedings shows that it is more appropriate in the case in question.

(3)   An order under subsection (1) above may prescribe different rates of return for different classes of case.

(4)   Before making an order under subsection (1) above the Lord Chancellor shall consult the Government Actuary and the Treasury; and any order under that subsection shall be made by statutory instrument subject to annulment in pursuance of a resolution of either House of Parliament.

(5)   In the application of this section to Scotland—

    (a)   for the reference to the Lord Chancellor in subsections (1) and (4) there is substituted a reference to the Scottish Ministers; and

    (b)   in subsection (4)—

        (i)   "and the Treasury" is omitted; and

        (ii)   for "either House of Parliament" there is substituted "the Scottish Parliament".

2   Consent orders for periodical payments

(A1)   In cases where Regulation (EC) No. 1371/2007 of the European Parliament and of the Council of 23rd October 2007 on rail passengers' rights and obligations applies, this section needs to be read in the light of Article 30 of the Uniform Rules concerning the contract for the international carriage of passengers and luggage by rail (damages to be awarded as annuity on request), as set out in Annex I to that Regulation.

(1)   A court awarding damages for future pecuniary loss in respect of personal injury—

    (a)   may order that the damages are wholly or partly to take the form of periodical payments, and

    (b)   shall consider whether to make that order.

(2)   A court awarding other damages in respect of personal injury may, if the parties consent, order that the damages are wholly or partly to take the form of periodical payments.

(3)   A court may not make an order for periodical payments unless satisfied that the continuity of payment under the order is reasonably secure.

(4)   For the purpose of subsection (3) the continuity of payment under an order is reasonably secure if—

    (a)   it is protected by a guarantee given under section 6 of or the Schedule to this Act,

    (b)   it is protected by a scheme under section 213 of the Financial Services and Markets Act 2000 (compensation) (whether or not as modified by section 4 of this Act), or

    (c)   the source of payment is a government or health service body.

(5)   An order for periodical payments may include provision—
    (a)   requiring the party responsible for the payments to use a method (selected or to be selected by him) under which the continuity of payment is reasonably secure by virtue of subsection (4);
    (b)   about how the payments are to be made, if not by a method under which the continuity of payment is reasonably secure by virtue of subsection (4);
    (c)   requiring the party responsible for the payments to take specified action to secure continuity of payment, where continuity is not reasonably secure by virtue of subsection (4);
    (d)   enabling a party to apply for a variation of provision included under paragraph (a), (b) or (c).
(6)   Where a person has a right to receive payments under an order for periodical payments, or where an arrangement is entered into in satisfaction of an order which gives a person a right to receive periodical payments, that person's right under the order or arrangement may not be assigned or charged without the approval of the court which made the order; and—
    (a)   a court shall not approve an assignment or charge unless satisfied that special circumstances make it necessary, and
    (b)   a purported assignment or charge, or agreement to assign or charge, is void unless approved by the court.
(7)   Where an order is made for periodical payments, an alteration of the method by which the payments are made shall be treated as a breach of the order (whether or not the method was specified under subsection (5)(b)) unless—
    (a)   the court which made the order declares its satisfaction that the continuity of payment under the new method is reasonably secure,
    (b)   the new method is protected by a guarantee given under section 6 of or the Schedule to this Act,
    (c)   the new method is protected by a scheme under section 213 of the Financial Services and Markets Act 2000 (compensation) (whether or not as modified by section 4 of this Act), or
    (d)   the source of payment under the new method is a government or health service body.
(8)   An order for periodical payments shall be treated as providing for the amount of payments to vary by reference to the retail prices index (within the meaning of section 833(2) of the Income and Corporation Taxes Act 1988) at such times, and in such a manner, as may be determined by or in accordance with Civil Procedure Rules.
(9)   But an order for periodical payments may include provision—
    (a)   disapplying subsection (8), or
    (b)   modifying the effect of subsection (8).

2A   Periodical payments: supplementary

(1)   Civil Procedure Rules may require a court to take specified matters into account in considering—
    (a)   whether to order periodical payments;
    (b)   the security of the continuity of payment;
    (c)   whether to approve an assignment or charge.
(2)   For the purposes of section 2(4)(c) and (7)(d) "government or health service body" means a body designated as a government body or a health service body by order made by the Lord Chancellor.
(3)   An order under subsection (2)—
    (a)   shall be made by statutory instrument, and
    (b)   shall be subject to annulment in pursuance of a resolution of either House of Parliament.
(4)   Section 2(6) is without prejudice to a person's power to assign a right to the scheme manager established under section 212 of the Financial Services and Markets Act 2000.
(5)   In section 2 "damages" includes an interim payment which a court orders a defendant to make to a claimant.
(6)   …
(7)   Section 2 is without prejudice to any power exercisable apart from that section.

2B Variation of orders and settlements

(1) The Lord Chancellor may by order enable a court which has made an order for periodical payments to vary the order in specified circumstances (otherwise than in accordance with section 2(5)(d)).

(2) The Lord Chancellor may by order enable a court in specified circumstances to vary the terms on which a claim or action for damages for personal injury is settled by agreement between the parties if the agreement—
   (a) provides for periodical payments, and
   (b) expressly permits a party to apply to a court for variation in those circumstances.

(3) An order under this section may make provision—
   (a) which operates wholly or partly by reference to a condition or other term of the court's order or of the agreement;
   (b) about the nature of an order which may be made by a court on a variation;
   (c) about the matters to be taken into account on considering variation;
   (d) of a kind that could be made by Civil Procedure Rules or, in relation to Northern Ireland, rules of court (and which may be expressed to be with or without prejudice to the power to make those rules).

(4) An order under this section may apply (with or without modification) or amend an enactment about provisional or further damages.

(5) An order under this section shall be subject to any order under section 1 of the Courts and Legal Services Act 1990 (allocation between High Court and county courts).

(6) An order under this section—
   (a) shall be made by statutory instrument,
   (b) may not be made unless the Lord Chancellor has consulted such persons as he thinks appropriate,
   (c) may not be made unless a draft has been laid before and approved by resolution of each House of Parliament, and
   (d) may include transitional, consequential or incidental provision.

(7) In subsection (4)—
   "provisional damages" means damages awarded by virtue of subsection (2)(a) of section 32A of the Senior Courts Act 1981 or section 51 of the County Courts Act 1984 (or, in relation to Northern Ireland, paragraph 10(2)(a) of Schedule 6 to the Administration of Justice Act 1982), and
   "further damages" means damages awarded by virtue of subsection (2)(b) of either of those sections (or, in relation to Northern Ireland, paragraph 10(2)(b) of Schedule 6 to the Administration of Justice Act 1982).

3 Provisional damages and fatal accident claims

(1) This section applies where a person—
   (a) is awarded provisional damages; and
   (b) subsequently dies as a result of the act or omission which gave rise to the cause of action for which the damages were awarded.

(2) The award of the provisional damages shall not operate as a bar to an action in respect of that person's death under the Fatal Accidents Act 1976.

(3) Such part (if any) of—
   (a) the provisional damages; and
   (b) any further damages awarded to the person in question before his death,
   as was intended to compensate him for pecuniary loss in a period which in the event falls after his death, shall be taken into account in assessing the amount of any loss of support suffered by the person or persons for whose benefit the action under the Fatal Accidents Act 1976 is brought.

(4) No award of further damages made in respect of that person after his death shall include any amount for loss of income in respect of any period after his death.

(5) In this section "provisional damages" means damages awarded by virtue of subsection (2)(a) of section 32A of the Senior Courts Act 1981 or section 51 of the County Courts Act 1984 and "further damages" means damages awarded by virtue of subsection (2) (b) of either of those sections.

(6)   Subsection (2) above applies whether the award of provisional damages was before or after the coming into force of that subsection; and subsections (3) and (4) apply to any award of damages under the 1976 Act or, as the case may be, further damages after the coming into force of those subsections.

(7)   In the application of this section to Northern Ireland—

    (a)   for references to the Fatal Accidents Act 1976 there shall be substituted references to the Fatal Accidents (Northern Ireland) Order 1977;

    (b)   for the reference to subsection (2)(a) and (b) of section 32A of the Senior Courts Act 1981 and section 51 of the County Courts Act 1984 there shall be substituted a reference to paragraph 10(2)(a) and (b) of Schedule 6 to the Administration of Justice Act 1982.

4   Enhanced protection for structured settlement annuitants

(1)   In relation to an annuity purchased for a person pursuant to a structured settlement from an authorised insurance company within the meaning of the Policyholders Protection Act 1975 (and in respect of which that person as annuitant is accordingly the policyholder for the purposes of that Act) sections 10 and 11 of that Act (protection in the event of liquidation of the insurer) as applied by any transitional provisions made by order under section 426 of the 2000 Act shall have effect as if any reference to ninety per cent. of the liability, of any future benefit or of the value attributed to the policy were a reference to the full amount of liability, benefit or value.

(2)   Those sections as applied by any transitional provisions made by order under section 426 of the 2000 Act shall also have effect as mentioned in subsection (1) above in relation to an annuity purchased from an authorised insurance company within the meaning of the 1975 Act pursuant to any order incorporating terms corresponding to those of a structured settlement which a court makes when awarding damages for personal injury.

(3)   Those sections as applied by any transitional provisions made by order under section 426 of the 2000 Act shall also have effect a mentioned in subsection (1) above in relation to an annuity purchased from or otherwise provided by an authorised insurance company within the meaning of the 1975 Act pursuant to terms corresponding to those of a structured settlement contained in an agreement made by—

    (a)   the Motor Insurers' Bureau; or

    (b)   a Domestic Regulations Insurer,

in respect of damages for personal injury which the Bureau or Insurer undertakes to pay in satisfaction of a claim or action against an uninsured driver.

(3A)   In relation to an annuity—

    (a)   purchased for a person pursuant to a structured settlement from an authorised insurer;

    (b)   purchased from such an insurer pursuant to an order of the kind referred to in subsection (2); or

    (c)   purchased from or otherwise provided by such an insurer pursuant to terms corresponding to those of a structured settlement contained in an agreement of the kind referred to in subsection (3),

any long term insurance provision in the Financial Services Compensation Scheme has effect in accordance with subsection (3B).

(3B)   To the extent that any long term insurance provision limits the obligation of the scheme manager to make payments or secure continuity of insurance by reference to any amount less than the full amount of any liability, benefit or value due under a contract of long term insurance, the provision has the effect as if the reference to that amount were a reference to the full amount of the liability, benefit or value.

(3C)   In this section—

"the 2000 Act" means the Financial Services and Markets Act 2000;

"authorised insurer" means an authorised person within the meaning of the 2000 Act with permission under that Act to effect or carry out contracts of insurance as principal;

"Financial Services Compensation Scheme" means the Financial Services Compensation Scheme referred to in section 213(2) of the Financial Services and Markets Act 2000;

"long term insurance provision" means any provision in the Financial Services Compensation Scheme requiring the scheme manager to—

(a)   pay compensation in respect of a liability of an authorised insurer in liquidation under a contract of long term insurance;

(b)   secure continuity of insurance for parties to contracts of long term insurance in the event that an authorised insurer goes into liquidation; or

(c)   secure that payments are made in respect of benefits falling due under contracts of long term insurance during any period while the scheme manager is seeking to make arrangements to secure continuity of insurance as mentioned in (b) above;

"scheme manager" means a body corporate established in accordance with section 212(1) of the 2000 Act.

(3D) In subsections (3B) and (3C) above—

(a)   a reference to a contract of long term insurance must be read with—

(i)   section 22 of the 2000 Act;

(ii)   any relevant order under that section; and

(iii)   Schedule 2 to that Act;

(b)   an authorised insurer is in liquidation when—

(i)   a resolution has been passed in accordance with the provisions of the Insolvency Act 1986 or (as the case may be) of the Insolvency (Northern Ireland) Order 1989 for the voluntary winding up of the insurer, otherwise than merely for the purpose of reconstruction of the insurer or of amalgamation with another insurer; or

(ii)   without any such resolution having been passed beforehand, an order has been made for the winding up of the insurer by the court under that Act or that Order.

(4)   In subsection (3) above "the Motor Insurers' Bureau" means the company of that name incorporated on the 14th of June 1946 under the Companies Act 1929 and "a Domestic Regulations Insurer" has the meaning given in the Bureau's Domestic Regulations.

(5)   Subsections (1) to (3) of this section apply if the liquidation of the authorised insurance company begins (within the meaning of the 1975 Act) after the coming into force of this section irrespective of when the annuity was purchased or provided.

(6)   Subsections (3A) to (3D) of this section apply if the liquidation of the authorised insurer begins (within the meaning of subsection (3D)) after the coming into force of section 19 of the 2000 Act, irrespective of when the annuity was purchased or provided.

6   Guarantees for public sector settlements

(1)   This section applies where—

(a)   a claim or action for damages for personal injury is settled on terms whereby the damages are to consist wholly or partly of periodical payments; or

(b)   a court awarding damages for personal injury makes an order incorporating such terms.

(2)   If it appears to a Minister of the Crown that the payments are to be made by a body in relation to which he has, by virtue of this section, power to do so, he may guarantee the payments to be made under the agreement or order.

(3)   The bodies in relation to which a Minister may give such a guarantee shall, subject to subsection (4) below, be such bodies as are designated in relation to the relevant government department by guidelines agreed upon between that department and the Treasury.

(4)   A guarantee purporting to be given by a Minister under this section shall not be invalidated by any failure on his part to act in accordance with such guidelines as are mentioned in subsection (3) above.

(5)   A guarantee under this section shall be given on such terms as the Minister concerned may determine but those terms shall in every case require the body in question to reimburse the Minister, with interest, for any sums paid by him in fulfilment of the guarantee.

(6)   Any sums required by a Minister for fulfilling a guarantee under this section shall be defrayed out of money provided by Parliament and any sums received by him by way of reimbursement or interest shall be paid into the Consolidated Fund.

(7)   A Minister who has given one or more guarantees under this section shall, as soon as possible after the end of each financial year, lay before each House of Parliament a statement showing what liabilities are outstanding in respect of the guarantees in that year, what sums have been paid in that year in fulfilment of the guarantees and what sums (including interest) have been recovered in that year in respect of the guarantees or are still owing.

(8)   In this section "government department" means any department of Her Majesty's government in the United Kingdom and for the purposes of this section a government department is a relevant department in relation to a Minister if he has responsibilities in respect of that department.

(8A) In the application of subsection (3) above to Scotland, for the words from "guidelines" to the end there shall be substituted "the Minister".

(8B) In the application of this section to Scotland, "relevant government department" shall be read as if it was a reference to any part of the Scottish Administration and subsection (8) shall cease to have effect.

(9)   The Schedule to this act has effect for conferring corresponding powers on Northern Ireland departments.

7   Interpretation

(1)   Subject to subsection (2) below, in this Act "personal injury" includes any disease and any impairment of a person's physical or mental condition and references to a claim or action for personal injury include references to such a claim or action brought by virtue of the Law Reform (Miscellaneous Provisions) Act 1934 and to a claim or action brought by virtue of the Fatal Accidents Act 1976.

(2)   In the application of this Act to Scotland "personal injury" has the same meaning as in the Damages (Scotland) Act 2011.

(3)   In the application of subsection (1) above to Northern Ireland for the references to the Law Reform (Miscellaneous Provisions) Act 1934 and to the Fatal Accidents Act 1976 there shall be substituted respectively references to the Law Reform (Miscellaneous Provisions) Act (Northern Ireland) 1937 and the Fatal Accidents (Northern Ireland) Order 1977.

8   Short title, extent and commencement

(2)   Section 3 does not extend to Scotland but, subject to that, this Act extends to the whole of the United Kingdom.

DEFAMATION ACT 1996
(1996, c. 31)

Responsibility for publication

1   Responsibility for publication

(1)   In defamation proceedings a person has a defence if he shows that—
    (a)   he was not the author, editor or publisher of the statement complained of,
    (b)   he took reasonable care in relation to its publication, and
    (c)   he did not know, and had no reason to believe, that what he did caused or contributed to the publication of a defamatory statement.

(2)   For this purpose "author", "editor" and "publisher" have the following meanings, which are further explained in subsection (3)—
    "author" means the originator of the statement, but does not include a person who did not intend that his statement be published at all;
    "editor" means a person having editorial or equivalent responsibility for the content of the statement or the decision to publish it; and
    "publisher" means a commercial publisher, that is, a person whose business is issuing material to the public, or a section of the public, who issues material containing the statement in the course of that business.

(3)   A person shall not be considered the author, editor or publisher of a statement if he is only involved—
    (a)   in printing, producing, distributing or selling printed material containing the statement;
    (b)   in processing, making copies of, distributing, exhibiting or selling a film or sound recording (as defined in Part I of the Copyright, Designs and Patents Act 1988) containing the statement;
    (c)   in processing, making copies of, distributing or selling any electronic medium in or on which the statement is recorded, or in operating or providing any equipment, system or service by means of which the statement is retrieved, copied, distributed or made available in electronic form;
    (d)   as the broadcaster of a live programme containing the statement in circumstances in which he has no effective control over the maker of the statement;
    (e)   as the operator of or provider of access to a communications system by means of which the statement is transmitted, or made available, by a person over whom he has no effective control.
In a case not within paragraphs (a) to (e) the court may have regard to those provisions by way of analogy in deciding whether a person is to be considered the author, editor or publisher of a statement.

(4)   Employees or agents of an author, editor or publisher are in the same position as their employer or principal to the extent that they are responsible for the content of the statement or the decision to publish it.

(5)   In determining for the purposes of this section whether a person took reasonable care, or had reason to believe that what he did caused or contributed to the publication of a defamatory statement, regard shall be had to—
    (a)   the extent of his responsibility for the content of the statement or the decision to publish it,
    (b)   the nature or circumstances of the publication, and
    (c)   the previous conduct or character of the author, editor or publisher.

(6)   This section does not apply to any cause of action which arose before the section came into force.

Offer to make amends

2   Offer to make amends

(1)   A person who has published a statement alleged to be defamatory of another may offer to make amends under this section.

(2)   The offer may be in relation to the statement generally or in relation to a specific defamatory meaning which the person making the offer accepts that the statement conveys ("a qualified offer").

(3)   An offer to make amends—
    (a)   must be in writing,
    (b)   must be expressed to be an offer to make amends under section 2 of the Defamation Act 1996, and
    (c)   must state whether it is a qualified offer and, if so, set out the defamatory meaning in relation to which it is made.

(4)   An offer to make amends under this section is an offer—
    (a)   to make a suitable correction of the statement complained of and a sufficient apology to the aggrieved party,
    (b)   to publish the correction and apology in a manner that is reasonable and practicable in the circumstances, and
    (c)   to pay the aggrieved party such compensation (if any), and such costs, as may be agreed or determined to be payable.
The fact that the offer is accompanied by an offer to take specific steps does not affect the fact that an offer to make amends under this section is an offer to do all the things mentioned in paragraphs (a) to (c).

(5)   An offer to make amends under this section may not be made by a person after serving a defence in defamation proceedings brought against him by the aggrieved party in respect of the publication in question.

(6)   An offer to make amends under this section may be withdrawn before it is accepted; and a renewal of an offer which has been withdrawn shall be treated as a new offer.

3   Accepting an offer to make amends

(1)   If an offer to make amends under section 2 is accepted by the aggrieved party, the following provisions apply.

(2)   The party accepting the offer may not bring or continue defamation proceedings in respect of the publication concerned against the person making the offer, but he is entitled to enforce the offer to make amends, as follows.

(3)   If the parties agree on the steps to be taken in fulfilment of the offer, the aggrieved party may apply to the court for an order that the other party fulfil his offer by taking the steps agreed.

(4)   If the parties do not agree on the steps to be taken by way of correction, apology and publication, the party who made the offer may take such steps as he thinks appropriate, and may in particular—

(a)   make the correction and apology by a statement in open court in terms approved by the court, and

(b)   give an undertaking to the court as to the manner of their publication.

(5)   If the parties do not agree on the amount to be paid by way of compensation, it shall be determined by the court on the same principles as damages in defamation proceedings.

The court shall take account of any steps taken in fulfilment of the offer and (so far as not agreed between the parties) of the suitability of the correction, the sufficiency of the apology and whether the manner of their publication was reasonable in the circumstances, and may reduce or increase the amount of compensation accordingly.

(6)   If the parties do not agree on the amount to be paid by way of costs, it shall be determined by the court on the same principles as costs awarded in court proceedings.

(7)   The acceptance of an offer by one person to make amends does not affect any cause of action against another person in respect of the same publication, subject as follows.

(8)   In England and Wales or Northern Ireland, for the purposes of the Civil Liability (Contribution) Act 1978—

(a)   the amount of compensation paid under the offer shall be treated as paid in bona fide settlement or compromise of the claim; and

(b)   where another person is liable in respect of the same damage (whether jointly or otherwise), the person whose offer to make amends was accepted is not required to pay by virtue of any contribution under section 1 of that Act a greater amount than the amount of the compensation payable in pursuance of the offer.

(9)   In Scotland—

(a)   subsection (2) of section 3 of the Law Reform (Miscellaneous Provisions) (Scotland) Act 1940 (right of one joint wrongdoer as respects another to recover contribution towards damages) applies in relation to compensation paid under an offer to make amends as it applies in relation to damages in an action to which that section applies; and

(b)   where another person is liable in respect of the same damage (whether jointly or otherwise), the person whose offer to make amends was accepted is not required to pay by virtue of any contribution under section 3(2) of that Act a greater amount than the amount of compensation payable in pursuance of the offer.

(10)   Proceedings under this section shall be heard and determined without a jury.

4   Failure to accept offer to make amends

(1)   If an offer to make amends under section 2, duly made and not withdrawn, is not accepted by the aggrieved party, the following provisions apply.

(2)   The fact that the offer was made is a defence (subject to subsection (3)) to defamation proceedings in respect of the publication in question by that party against the person making the offer.

A qualified offer is only a defence in respect of the meaning to which the offer related.

(3)   There is no such defence if the person by whom the offer was made knew or had reason to believe that the statement complained of—

    (a)   referred to the aggrieved party or was likely to be understood as referring to him, and

    (b)   was both false and defamatory of that party; but it shall be presumed until the contrary is shown that he did not know and had no reason to believe that was the case.

(4)   The person who made the offer need not rely on it by way of defence, but if he does he may not rely on any other defence.

If the offer was a qualified offer, this applies only in respect of the meaning to which the offer related.

(5)   The offer may be relied on in mitigation of damages whether or not it was relied on as a defence.

The meaning of a statement

7   Ruling on the meaning of a statement

In defamation proceedings the court shall not be asked to rule whether a statement is arguably capable, as opposed to capable, of bearing a particular meaning or meanings attributed to it.

Summary disposal of claim

8   Summary disposal of claim

(1)   In defamation proceedings the court may dispose summarily of the plaintiff's claim in accordance with the following provisions.

(2)   The court may dismiss the plaintiff's claim if it appears to the court that it has no realistic prospect of success and there is no reason why it should be tried.

(3)   The court may give judgment for the plaintiff and grant him summary relief (see section 9) if it appears to the court that there is no defence to the claim which has a realistic prospect of success, and that there is no other reason why the claim should be tried.

Unless the plaintiff asks for summary relief, the court shall not act under this subsection unless it is satisfied that summary relief will adequately compensate him for the wrong he has suffered.

(4)   In considering whether a claim should be tried the court shall have regard to—

    (a)   whether all the persons who are or might be defendants in respect of the publication complained of are before the court;

    (b)   whether summary disposal of the claim against another defendant would be inappropriate;

    (c)   the extent to which there is a conflict of evidence;

    (d)   the seriousness of the alleged wrong (as regards the content of the statement and the extent of publication); and

    (e)   whether it is justifiable in the circumstances to proceed to a full trial.

(5)   Proceedings under this section shall be heard and determined without a jury.

9   Meaning of summary relief

(1)   For the purposes of section 8 (summary disposal of claim) "summary relief" means such of the following as may be appropriate—

    (a)   a declaration that the statement was false and defamatory of the plaintiff;

    (b)   an order that the defendant publish or cause to be published a suitable correction and apology;

    (c)   damages not exceeding £10,000 or such other amount as may be prescribed by order of the Lord Chancellor;

    (d)   an order restraining the defendant from publishing or further publishing the matter complained of.

(2)   The content of any correction and apology, and the time, manner, form and place of publication, shall be for the parties to agree.

If they cannot agree on the content, the court may direct the defendant to publish or cause to be published a summary of the court's judgment agreed by the parties or settled by the court in accordance with rules of court.

If they cannot agree on the time, manner, form or place of publication, the court may direct the defendant to take such reasonable and practicable steps as the court considers appropriate.

(2A) The Lord Chancellor must consult the Lord Chief Justice of England and Wales before making any order under subsection (1)(c) in relation to England and Wales.

(3)   Any order under subsection (1)(c) shall be made by statutory instrument which shall be subject to annulment in pursuance of a resolution of either House of Parliament.

10   Summary disposal: rules of court

(1)   Provision may be made by rules of court as to the summary disposal of the plaintiff's claim in defamation proceedings.

(2)   Without prejudice to the generality of that power, provision may be made—

(a)   authorising a party to apply for summary disposal at any stage of the proceedings;

(b)   authorising the court at any stage of the proceedings—

(i)   to treat any application, pleading or other step in the proceedings as an application for summary disposal, or

(ii)   to make an order for summary disposal without any such application;

(c)   as to the time for serving pleadings or taking any other step in the proceedings in a case where there are proceedings for summary disposal;

(d)   requiring the parties to identify any question of law or construction which the court is to be asked to determine in the proceedings;

(e)   as to the nature of any hearing on the question of summary disposal, and in particular—

(i)   authorising the court to order affidavits or witness statements to be prepared for use as evidence at the hearing, and

(ii)   requiring the leave of the court for the calling of oral evidence, or the introduction of new evidence, at the hearing;

(f)   authorising the court to require a defendant to elect, at or before the hearing, whether or not to make an offer to make amends under section 2.

Statutory privilege

14   Reports of court proceedings absolutely privileged

(1)   A fair and accurate report of proceedings in public before a court to which this section applies, if published contemporaneously with the proceedings, is absolutely privileged.

(2)   A report of proceedings which by an order of the court, or as a consequence of any statutory provision, is required to be postponed shall be treated as published contemporaneously if it is published as soon as practicable after publication is permitted.

(3)   This section applies to—

(a)   any court in the United Kingdom;

(b)   any court established under the law of a country or territory outside the United Kingdom;

(c)   any international court or tribunal established by the Security Council of the United Nations or by an international agreement;

and in paragraphs (a) and (b) "court" includes any tribunal or body exercising the judicial powers of the State.

15   Reports, &c. protected by qualified privilege

(1)   The publication of any report or other statement mentioned in Schedule 1 to this Act is privileged unless the publication is shown to be made with malice, subject as follows.

(2)   In defamation proceedings in respect of the publication of a report or other statement mentioned in Part II of that Schedule, there is no defence under this section if the plaintiff shows that the defendant—

(a)   was requested by him to publish in a suitable manner a reasonable letter or statement by way of explanation or contradiction, and

(b)   refused or neglected to do so.

For this purpose "in a suitable manner" means in the same manner as the publication complained of or in a manner that is adequate and reasonable in the circumstances.

(3)   This section does not apply to the publication to the public, or a section of the public, of matter which is not of public interest and the publication of which is not for the public benefit.

(4)   Nothing in this section shall be construed—

(a)   as protecting the publication of matter the publication of which is prohibited by law, or

(b)   as limiting or abridging any privilege subsisting apart from this section.

Supplementary provisions

17   Interpretation

(1)   In this Act—

"publication" and "publish", in relation to a statement, have the meaning they have for the purposes of the law of defamation generally, but "publisher" is specially defined for the purposes of section 1;

"statement" means words, pictures, visual images, gestures or any other method of signifying meaning; and

"statutory provision" means—

(a)   a provision contained in an Act or in subordinate legislation within the meaning of the Interpretation Act 1978,

(aa)   a provision contained in an Act of the Scottish Parliament or in an instrument made under such an Act, or

(b)   a statutory provision within the meaning given by section 1(f) of the Interpretation Act (Northern Ireland) 1954.

20   Short title and saving

(2)   Nothing in this Act affects the law relating to criminal libel.

SCHEDULES

Section 15   SCHEDULE 1
                                           QUALIFIED PRIVILEGE

PART I
STATEMENTS HAVING QUALIFIED PRIVILEGE WITHOUT
EXPLANATION OR CONTRADICTION

1.   A fair and accurate report of proceedings in public of a legislature anywhere in the world.

2.   A fair and accurate report of proceedings in public before a court anywhere in the world.

3.   A fair and accurate report of proceedings in public of a person appointed to hold a public inquiry by a government or legislature anywhere in the world.

4.   A fair and accurate report of proceedings in public anywhere in the world of an international organisation or an international conference.

5.   A fair and accurate copy of or extract from any register or other document required by law to be open to public inspection.

6.   A notice or advertisement published by or on the authority of a court, or of a judge or officer of a court, anywhere in the world.

7.   A fair and accurate copy of or extract from matter published by or on the authority of a government or legislature anywhere in the world.

8.   A fair and accurate copy of or extract from matter published anywhere in the world by an international organisation or an international conference.

PART II
STATEMENTS PRIVILEGED SUBJECT TO EXPLANATION OR CONTRADICTION

9.   (1)   A fair and accurate copy of, or extract from or summary of a notice issued for the information of the public by or on behalf of—

           (a)   a legislature or government anywhere in the world;

           (b)   an authority anywhere in the world performing governmental functions;

           (c)   an international organisation or international conference.

     (2)   In this paragraph "governmental functions" includes police functions.

10.   A fair and accurate copy of, or extract from or summary of a document made available by a court anywhere in the world, or by a judge or officer of such court.

11.   (1)   A fair and accurate report of proceedings at any public meeting or sitting in the United Kingdom of—

           (a)   a local authority or local authority committee;

           (aa)   or in the case of a local authority which are operating executive arrangements, the executive of that authority or a committee of that executive;

           (b)   a justice or justices of the peace acting otherwise than as a court exercising judicial authority;

           (c)   a commission, tribunal, committee or person appointed for the purposes of any inquiry by any statutory provision, by Her Majesty or by a Minister of the Crown a member of the Scottish Executive, the Welsh Ministers or the Counsel General to the Welsh Assembly Government or a Northern Ireland Department;

           (d)   a person appointed by a local authority to hold a local inquiry in pursuance of any statutory provision;

           (e)   any other tribunal, board, committee or body constituted by or under, and exercising functions under, any statutory provision.

     (1A)   In the case of a local authority which are operating executive arrangements, a fair and accurate record of any decision made by any member of the executive where that record is required to be made and available for public inspection by virtue of section 22 of the Local Government Act 2000 or of any provision in regulations made under that section.

     (2)   In sub-paragraphs (1)(a) and (1A)—

"executive" and "executive arrangements" have the same meaning as in Part II of the Local Government Act 2000;

"local authority" means—

           (a)   in relation to England and Wales, a principal council within the meaning of the Local Government Act 1972, any body falling within any paragraph of section 100J(1) of that Act or an authority or body to which the Public Bodies (Admission to Meetings) Act 1960 applies,

           (b)   in relation to Scotland, a council constituted under section 2 of the Local Government etc. (Scotland) Act 1994 or an authority or body to which the Public Bodies (Admission to Meetings) Act 1960 applies,

           (c)   in relation to Northern Ireland, any authority or body to which sections 23 to 27 of the Local Government Act (Northern Ireland) 1972 apply; and

"local authority committee" means any committee of a local authority or of local authorities, and includes—

           (a)   any committee or sub-committee in relation to which sections 100A to 100D of the Local Government Act 1972 apply by virtue of section 100E of that Act (whether or not also by virtue of section 100J of that Act), and

           (b)   any committee or sub-committee in relation to which sections 50A to 50D of the Local Government (Scotland) Act 1973 apply by virtue of section 50E of that Act.

(3) A fair and accurate report of any corresponding proceedings in any of the Channel Islands or the Isle of Man or in another member State.

11A. A fair and accurate report of proceedings at a press conference held anywhere in the world for the discussion of a matter of public interest.

12. (1) A fair and accurate report of proceedings at any public meeting held in anywhere in the world.

(2) In this paragraph a "public meeting" means a meeting bona fide and lawfully held for a lawful purpose and for the furtherance or discussion of a matter of public interest, whether admission to the meeting is general or restricted.

13. (1) A fair and accurate report of proceedings at a general meeting of a listed company.

(2) A fair and accurate copy of, extract from or summary of any document circulated to members of a listed company—

(a) by or with the authority of the board of directors of the company,

(b) by the auditors of the company,

(c) by any member of the company in pursuance of a right conferred by any statutory provision.

(3) A fair and accurate copy of, extract from or summary of any document circulated to members of a listed company which relates to the appointment, resignation, retirement or dismissal of the directors of the company or its auditors.

(4) In this paragraph "listed company" has the same meaning as in Part 12 of the Corporation Tax Act 2009 (see section 1005 of that Act).

14. A fair and accurate report of any finding or decision of any of the following descriptions of association, formed anywhere in the world, or of any committee or governing body of such an association—

(a) an association formed for the purpose of promoting or encouraging the exercise of or interest in any art, science, religion or learning, and empowered by its constitution to exercise control over or adjudicate on matters of interest or concern to the association, or the actions or conduct of any person subject to such control or adjudication;

(b) an association formed for the purpose of promoting or safeguarding the interests of any trade, business, industry or profession, or of the persons carrying on or engaged in any trade, business, industry or profession, and empowered by its constitution to exercise control over or adjudicate upon matters connected with that trade, business, industry or profession, or the actions or conduct of those persons;

(c) an association formed for the purpose of promoting or safeguarding the interests of a game, sport or pastime to the playing or exercise of which members of the public are invited or admitted, and empowered by its constitution to exercise control over or adjudicate upon persons connected with or taking part in the game, sport or pastime;

(d) an association formed for the purpose of promoting charitable objects or other objects beneficial to the community and empowered by its constitution to exercise control over or to adjudicate on matters of interest or concern to the association, or the actions or conduct of any person subject to such control or adjudication.

14A. A fair and accurate—

(a) report of proceedings of a scientific or academic conference held anywhere in the world, or

(b) copy of, extract from or summary of matter published by such a conference.

15. (1) A fair and accurate report of or summary of, copy of or extract from, any adjudication, report, statement or notice issued by a body, officer or other designated person for the purposes of this paragraph by order of the Lord Chancellor.

(2) An order under this paragraph shall be made by statutory instrument which shall be subject to annulment in pursuance of a resolution of either House of Parliament.

PART III
SUPPLEMENTARY PROVISIONS

16.   (1)   In this Schedule—
                "court" includes—
                (a)   any tribunal or body established under the law of any country or territory exercising the judicial power of the state;
                (b)   any international tribunal established by the Security Council of the United Nations or by an international agreement;
                (c)   any international tribunal deciding matters in dispute between states;
                "international conference" means a conference attended by two or more governments;
                "international organisation" means an organisation of which two or more governments are members, and includes any committee or other subordinate body of such an organisation;
                "legislature" includes a local legislature; and
                "member state" includes any European dependent territory of a member state.

EDUCATION ACT 1996
(1996, c. 56)

521   Examination of pupils for cleanliness

(1)   A local authority may by directions in writing authorise a medical officer of theirs to have the persons and clothing of pupils in attendance at relevant schools examined whenever in his opinion such examinations are necessary in the interests of cleanliness.

(3)   An examination under this section shall be made by a person authorised by the authority to make such examinations; and, if the examination is of a girl, it shall not be made by a man unless he is a registered medical practitioner.

522   Compulsory cleansing of a pupil

(1)   If, on an examination under section 521, the person or clothing of a pupil is found to be infested with vermin or in a foul condition, any officer of the local authority may serve a notice on the pupil's parent requiring him to cause the pupil's person and clothing to be cleansed.

(2)   The notice shall inform the parent that, unless within the period specified in the notice the pupil's person and clothing are cleansed to the satisfaction of such person as is specified in the notice, the cleansing will be carried out under arrangements made by the authority.

(3)   The period so specified shall not be less than 24 hours from the service of the notice.

(4)   If, on a report being made to him by the specified person at the end of the specified period, a medical officer of the authority is not satisfied that the pupil's person and clothing have been properly cleansed, he may by order direct that they shall be cleansed under arrangements made by the authority under section 523.

(5)   An order made under subsection (4) shall be sufficient to authorise any officer of the authority—
        (a)   to cause the pupil's person and clothing to be cleansed in accordance with arrangements made by the authority under section 523, and
        (b)   for that purpose to convey the pupil to, and detain him at, any premises provided in accordance with such arrangements.

523   Arrangements for cleansing of pupils

(1)   A local authority shall make arrangements for securing that the person or clothing of any pupil required to be cleansed under section 522 may be cleansed (whether at the request of a parent or in pursuance of an order under section 522(4)) at suitable premises, by suitable persons and with suitable appliances.

(2)   Where the council of a district in the area of the authority are entitled to the use of any premises or appliances for cleansing the person or clothing of persons infested with vermin, the authority may require the council to permit the authority to use those premises or appliances for such purposes upon such terms as may be determined—

(a)   by agreement between the authority and the council, or

(b)   in default of such agreement, by the Secretary of State.

(3)   Subsection (2) does not apply in relation to Wales.

(4)   A girl may be cleansed under arrangements under this section only by a registered medical practitioner or by a woman authorised for the purpose by the authority.

548   No right to give corporal punishment

(1)   Corporal punishment given by, or on the authority of, a member of staff to a child—

(a)   for whom education is provided at any school, or

(b)   for whom education is provided, otherwise than at school, under any arrangements made by a local authority, or

(c)   for whom specified nursery education is provided otherwise than at school, cannot be justified in any proceedings on the ground that it was given in pursuance of a right exercisable by the member of staff by virtue of his position as such.

(2)   Subsection (1) applies to corporal punishment so given to a child at any time, whether at the school or other place at which education is provided for the child, or elsewhere.

(3)   The following provisions have effect for the purposes of this section.

(4)   Any reference to giving corporal punishment to a child is to doing anything for the purpose of punishing that child (whether or not there are other reasons for doing it) which, apart from any justification, would constitute battery.

(5)   However, corporal punishment shall not be taken to be given to a child by virtue of anything done for reasons that include averting—

(a)   an immediate danger of personal injury to, or

(b)   an immediate danger to the property of,

any person (including the child himself).

(6)   "Member of staff", in relation to the child concerned, means—

(a)   any person who works as a teacher at the school or other place at which education is provided for the child, or

(b)   any other person who (whether in connection with the provision of education for the child or otherwise)—

(i)   works at that school or place, or—

(ii)   otherwise provides his services there (whether or not for payment), and has lawful control or charge of the child.

(7)   "Child" (except in subsection (8)) means a person under the age of 18.

(8)   "Specified nursery education" means full-time or part-time education suitable for children who have not attained compulsory school age which is provided—

(a)   by a local authority; or

(b)   by any other person—

(i)   who is (or is to be) in receipt of financial assistance given by such an authority and whose provision of nursery education is taken into account by the authority in formulating proposals for the purposes of section 120(2)(a) of the School Standards and Framework Act 1998.

POLICE ACT 1996
(1996, c. 16)

88   Liability for wrongful acts of constables

(1)   The chief officer of police for a police area shall be liable in respect of any unlawful conduct of constables under his direction and control in the performance or purported performance of their functions in like manner as a master is liable in respect of any unlawful conduct of his servants in the course of their employment, and accordingly shall, in the case of a tort, be treated for all purposes as a joint tortfeasor.

(2)   There shall be paid out of the police fund—

(a)   any damages or costs awarded against the chief officer of police in any proceedings brought against him by virtue of this section and any costs incurred by him in any such proceedings so far as not recovered by him in the proceedings; and

     (b)   any sum required in connection with the settlement of any claim made against the chief officer of police by virtue of this section, if the settlement is approved by the local policing body.

(3)   Any proceedings in respect of a claim made by virtue of this section shall be brought against the chief officer of police for the time being or, in the case of a vacancy in that office, against the person for the time being performing the functions of the chief officer of police; and references in subsections (1) and (2) to the chief officer of police shall be construed accordingly.

(4)   A local policing body may, in such cases and to such extent as appear to it to be appropriate, pay out of the police fund—

     (a)   any damages or costs awarded against a person to whom this subsection applies in proceedings for any unlawful conduct of that person,

     (b)   any costs incurred and not recovered by such a person in such proceedings, and

     (c)   any sum required in connection with the settlement of a claim that has or might have given rise to such proceedings.

CONTRACT (SCOTLAND) ACT 1997
(1997, c. 34)

1   Extrinsic evidence of additional contract term etc.

(1)   Where a document appears (or two or more documents appear) to comprise all the express terms of a contract or unilateral voluntary obligation, it shall be presumed, unless the contrary is proved, that the document does (or the documents do) comprise all the express terms of the contract or unilateral voluntary obligation.

(2)   Extrinsic oral or documentary evidence shall be admissible to prove, for the purposes of subsection (1) above, that the contract or unilateral voluntary obligation includes additional express terms (whether or not written terms).

(3)   Notwithstanding the foregoing provisions of this section, where one of the terms in the document (or in the documents) is to the effect that the document does (or the documents do) comprise all the express terms of the contract or unilateral voluntary obligation, that term shall be conclusive in the matter.

(4)   This section is without prejudice to any enactment which makes provision as respects the constitution, or formalities of execution, of a contract or unilateral voluntary obligation.

2   Supersession

(1)   Where a deed is executed in implement, or purportedly in implement, of a contract, an unimplemented, or otherwise unfulfilled, term of the contract shall not be taken to be superseded by virtue only of that execution or of the delivery and acceptance of the deed.

(2)   Subsection (1) above is without prejudice to any agreement which the parties to a contract may reach (whether or not an agreement incorporated into the contract) as to supersession of the contract.

3   Damages for breach of contract of sale

Any rule of law which precludes the buyer in a contract of sale of property from obtaining damages for breach of that contract by the seller unless the buyer rejects the property and rescinds the contract shall cease to have effect.

4   Short title, extent etc.

(4)   This Act extends to Scotland only.

PROTECTION FROM HARASSMENT ACT 1997
(1997, c. 40)

1   Prohibition of harassment

(1)   A person must not pursue a course of conduct—

     (a)   which amounts to harassment of another, and

     (b)   which he knows or ought to know amounts to harassment of the other.

(1A) A person must not pursue a course of conduct—
- (a) which involves harassment of two or more persons, and
- (b) which he knows or ought to know involves harassment of those persons, and
- (c) by which he intends to persuade any person (whether or not one of those mentioned above)—
  - (i) not to do something that he is entitled or required to do, or
  - (ii) to do something that he is not under any obligation to do.

(2) For the purposes of this section or section 2A(2)(c), the person whose course of conduct is in question ought to know that it amounts to or involves harassment of another if a reasonable person in possession of the same information would think the course of conduct amounted to or involved harassment of the other.

(3) Subsection (1) or (1A) does not apply to a course of conduct if the person who pursued it shows—
- (a) that it was pursued for the purpose of presenting or detecting crime,
- (b) that it was pursued under any enactment or rule of law or to comply with any condition or requirement imposed by any person under any enactment, or
- (c) that in the particular circumstances the pursuit of the course of conduct was reasonable.

2 Offence of harassment

(1) A person who pursues a course of conduct in breach of section 1(1) or (1A) is guilty of an offence.

...

2A Offence of stalking

(1) A person is guilty of an offence if—
- (a) the person pursues a course of conduct in breach of section 1(1), and
- (b) the course of conduct amounts to stalking.

(2) For the purposes of subsection (1)(b) (and section 4A(1)(a)) a person's course of conduct amounts to stalking of another person if—
- (a) it amounts to harassment of that person,
- (b) the acts or omissions involved are ones associated with stalking, and
- (c) the person whose course of conduct it is knows or ought to know that the course of conduct amounts to harassment of the other person.

(3) The following are examples of acts or omissions which, in particular circumstances, are ones associated with stalking—
- (a) following a person,
- (b) contacting, or attempting to contact, a person by any means,
- (c) publishing any statement or other material—
  - (i) relating or purporting to relate to a person, or
  - (ii) purporting to originate from a person,
- (d) monitoring the use by a person of the internet, email or any other form of electronic communication,
- (e) loitering in any place (whether public or private),
- (f) interfering with any property in the possession of a person,
- (g) watching or spying on a person.

(4) A person guilty of an offence under this section is liable on summary conviction to imprisonment for a term not exceeding 51 weeks, or a fine not exceeding level 5 on the standard scale, or both.

(5) In relation to an offence committed before the commencement of section 281(5) of the Criminal Justice Act 2003, the reference in subsection (4) to 51 weeks is to be read as a reference to six months.

(6) This section is without prejudice to the generality of section 2.

3 Civil remedy

(1) An actual or apprehended breach of section 1(1) may be the subject of a claim in civil proceedings by the person who is or may be the victim of the course of conduct in question.

(2) On such a claim, damages may be awarded for (among other things) any anxiety caused by the harassment and any financial loss resulting from the harassment.

(3)   Where—
   (a)   in such proceedings the High Court or the county court grants an injunction for the purpose of restraining the defendant from pursuing any conduct which amounts to harassment, and
   (b)   the plaintiff considers that the defendant has done anything which he is prohibited from doing by the injunction,
   the plaintiff may apply for the issue of a warrant for the arrest of the defendant.
(5)   The judge to whom an application under subsection (3) is made may only issue a warrant if—
   (a)   the application is substantiated on oath, and
   (b)   the judge has reasonable grounds for believing that the defendant has done anything which he is prohibited from doing by the injunction.
(6)   Where—
   (a)   the High Court or the county court grants an injunction for the purpose mentioned in subsection (3)(a), and
   (b)   without reasonable excuse the defendant does anything which he is prohibited from doing by the injunction,
   he is guilty of an offence.

3A   Injunctions to protect persons from harassment within section 1(1A)

(1)   This section applies where there is an actual or apprehended breach of section 1(1A) by any person ("the relevant person").
(2)   In such a case—
   (a)   any person who is or may be a victim of the course of conduct in question, or
   (b)   any person who is or may be a person falling within section 1(1A)(c),
   may apply to the High Court or the county court for an injunction restraining the relevant person from pursuing any conduct which amounts to harassment in relation to any person or persons mentioned or described in the injunction.
(3)   Section 3(3) to (9) apply in relation to an injunction granted under subsection (2) above as they apply in relation to an injunction granted as mentioned in section 3(3)(a).

4   Putting people in fear of violence

(1)   A person whose course of conduct causes another to fear, on at least two occasions, that violence will be used against him is guilty of an offence if he knows or ought to know that his course of conduct will cause the other so to fear on each of those occasions.
(2)   For the purposes of this section, the person whose course of conduct is in question ought to know that it will cause another to fear that violence will be used against him on any occasion if a reasonable person in possession of the same information would think the course of conduct would cause the other so to fear on that occasion.
(3)   It is a defence for a person charged with an offence under this section to show that—
   (a)   his course of conduct was pursued for the purpose of preventing or detecting crime,
   (b)   his course of conduct was pursued under any enactment or rule of law or to comply with any condition or requirement imposed by any person under any enactment, or
   (c)   the pursuit of his course of conduct was reasonable for the protection of himself or another or for the protection of his or another's property.

4A   Stalking involving fear of violence or serious alarm or distress

(1)   A person ("A") whose course of conduct—
   (a)   amounts to stalking, and
   (b)   either—
      (i)   causes another ("B") to fear, on at least two occasions, that violence will be used against B, or
      (ii)   causes B serious alarm or distress which has a substantial adverse effect on B's usual day-to-day activities,
   is guilty of an offence if A knows or ought to know that A's course of conduct will cause B so to fear on each of those occasions or (as the case may be) will cause such alarm or distress.

(2) For the purposes of this section A ought to know that A's course of conduct will cause B to fear that violence will be used against B on any occasion if a reasonable person in possession of the same information would think the course of conduct would cause B so to fear on that occasion.

(3) For the purposes of this section A ought to know that A's course of conduct will cause B serious alarm or distress which has a substantial adverse effect on B's usual day-to-day activities if a reasonable person in possession of the same information would think the course of conduct would cause B such alarm or distress.

(4) It is a defence for A to show that—
   (a) A's course of conduct was pursued for the purpose of preventing or detecting crime,
   (b) A's course of conduct was pursued under any enactment or rule of law or to comply with any condition or requirement imposed by any person under any enactment, or
   (c) the pursuit of A's course of conduct was reasonable for the protection of A or another or for the protection of A's or another's property.

(5) A person guilty of an offence under this section is liable—
   (a) on conviction on indictment, to imprisonment for a term not exceeding five years, or a fine, or both, or
   (b) on summary conviction, to imprisonment for a term not exceeding twelve months, or a fine not exceeding the statutory maximum, or both.

(6) In relation to an offence committed before the commencement of section 154(1) of the Criminal Justice Act 2003, the reference in subsection (5)(b) to twelve months is to be read as a reference to six months.

(7) If on the trial on indictment of a person charged with an offence under this section the jury find the person not guilty of the offence charged, they may find the person guilty of an offence under section 2 or 2A.

(8) The Crown Court has the same powers and duties in relation to a person who is by virtue of subsection (7) convicted before it of an offence under section 2 or 2A as a magistrates' court would have on convicting the person of the offence.

(9) This section is without prejudice to the generality of section 4.

5 Restraining orders on conviction

(1) A court sentencing or otherwise dealing with a person ("the defendant") convicted of an offence ... may (as well as sentencing him or dealing with him in any other way) make an order under this section.

(2) The order may, for the purpose of protecting the victim or victims of the offence, or any other person mentioned in the order, from ... conduct which—
   (a) amounts to harassment, or
   (b) will cause a fear of violence,
   prohibit the defendant from doing anything described in the order.

(5) ...

7 Interpretation of this group of sections

(1) This section applies for the interpretation of sections 1 to 5A.

(2) References to harassing a person include alarming the person or causing the person distress.

(3) A "course of conduct" must involve—
   (a) in the case of conduct in relation to a single person (see section 1(1)), conduct on at least two occasions in relation to that person, or
   (b) in the case of conduct in relation to two or more persons (see section 1(1A)), conduct on at least one occasion in relation to each of those persons.

(3A) A person's conduct on any occasion shall be taken, if aided, abetted, counselled or procured by another—
   (a) to be conduct on that occasion of the other (as well as conduct of the person whose conduct it is); and
   (b) to be conduct in relation to which the other's knowledge and purpose, and what he ought to have known, are the same as they were in relation to what was contemplated or reasonably foreseeable at the time of the aiding, abetting, counselling or procuring.

(4) "Conduct" includes speech.

12   National security, etc.

(1)   If the Secretary of State certifies that in his opinion anything done by a specified person on a specified occasion related to—

(a)   national security,

(b)   the economic well-being of the United Kingdom, or

(c)   the prevention or detection of serious crime,

and was done on behalf of the Crown, the certificate is conclusive evidence that this Act does not apply to any conduct of that person on that occasion.

SOCIAL SECURITY (RECOVERY OF BENEFITS) ACT 1997
(1997, c. 27)

1   Cases in which this Act applies

(1)   This Act applies in cases where—

(a)   a person makes a payment (whether on his own behalf or not) to or in respect of any other person in consequence of any accident, injury or disease suffered by the other, and

(b)   any listed benefits have been, or are likely to be, paid to or for the other during the relevant period in respect of the accident, injury or disease.

(2)   The reference above to a payment in consequence of any accident, injury or disease is to a payment made—

(a)   by or on behalf of a person who is, or is alleged to be, liable to any extent in respect of the accident, injury or disease,

(b)   in pursuance of a compensation scheme for motor accidents; or

(c)   under the Diffuse Mesothelioma Payment Scheme (established under the Mesothelioma Act 2014);

but does not include a payment mentioned in Part I of Schedule 1.

(3)   Subsection (1)(a) applies to a payment made—

(a)   voluntarily, or in pursuance of a court order or an agreement, or otherwise, and

(b)   in the United Kingdom or elsewhere.

(4)   In a case where this Act applies—

(a)   the "injured person" is the person who suffered the accident, injury or disease,

(b)   the "compensation payment" is the payment within subsection (1)(a), and

(c)   "recoverable benefit" is any listed benefit which has been or is likely to be paid as mentioned in subsection (1)(b).

2   Compensation payments to which this Act applies

This Act applies in relation to compensation payments made on or after the day on which this section comes into force, unless they are made in pursuance of a court order or agreement made before that day.

3   "The relevant period"

(1)   In relation to a person ("the claimant") who has suffered any accident, injury or disease, "the relevant period" has the meaning given by the following subsections.

(2)   Subject to subsection (4), if it is a case of accident or injury, the relevant period is the period of five years immediately following the day on which the accident or injury in question occurred.

(3)   Subject to subsection (4), if it is a case of disease, the relevant period is the period of five years beginning with the date on which the claimant first claims a listed benefit in consequence of the disease.

(4)   If at any time before the end of the period referred to in subsection (2) or (3)—

(a)   a person makes a compensation payment in final discharge of any claim made by or in respect of the claimant and arising out of the accident, injury or disease, or

(b)   an agreement is made under which an earlier compensation payment is treated as having been made in final discharge of any such claim,

the relevant period ends at that time.

4   Applications for certificates of recoverable benefits

(1)   Before a person ("the compensator") makes a compensation payment he must apply to the Secretary of State for a certificate of recoverable benefits.

5   Information contained in certificates

(1)   A certificate of recoverable benefits must specify, for each recoverable benefit—

(a)   the amount which has been or is likely to have been paid on or before a specified date, and

(b)   if the benefit is paid or likely to be paid after the specified date, the rate and period for which, and the intervals at which, it is or is likely to be so paid.

(2)   In a case where the relevant period has ended before the day on which the Secretary of State receives the application for the certificate, the date specified in the certificate for the purposes of subsection (1) must be the day on which the relevant period ended.

(3)   In any other case, the date specified for those purposes must not be earlier than the day on which the Secretary of State received the application.

(4)   The Secretary of State may estimate, in such manner as he thinks fit, any of the amounts, rates or periods specified in the certificate.

(5)   Where the Secretary of State issues a certificate of recoverable benefits, he must provide the information contained in the certificate to—

(a)   the person who appears to him to be the injured person, or

(b)   any person who he thinks will receive a compensation payment in respect of the injured person.

(6)   A person to whom a certificate of recoverable benefits is issued or who is provided with information under subsection (5) is entitled to particulars of the manner in which any amount, rate or period specified in the certificate has been determined, if he applies to the Secretary of State for those particulars.

6   Liability to pay Secretary of State amount of benefits

(1)   A person who makes a compensation payment in any case is liable to pay to the Secretary of State an amount equal to the total amount of the recoverable benefits.

(2)   The liability referred to in subsection (1) arises immediately before the compensation payment or, if there is more than one, the first of them is made.

(3)   No amount becomes payable under this section before the end of the period of 14 days following the day on which the liability arises.

(4)   Subject to subsection (3), an amount becomes payable under this section at the end of the period of 14 days beginning with the day on which a certificate of recoverable benefits is first issued showing that the amount of recoverable benefit to which it relates has been or is likely to have been paid before a specified date.

7   Recovery of payments due under section 6

(1)   This section applies where a person has made a compensation payment but—

(a)   has not applied for a certificate of recoverable benefits, or

(b)   has not made a payment to the Secretary of State under section 6 before the end of the period allowed under that section.

(2)   The Secretary of State may—

(a)   issue the person who made the compensation payment with a certificate of recoverable benefits, if none has been issued, or

(b)   issue him with a copy of the certificate of recoverable benefits or (if more than one has been issued) the most recent one,

and (in either case) issue him with a demand that payment of any amount due under section 6 be made immediately.

(3)   The Secretary of State may, in accordance with subsections (4) and (5), recover the amount for which a demand for payment is made under subsection (2) from the person who made the compensation payment.

(4)   If the person who made the compensation payment resides or carries on business in England and Wales and the county court so orders, any amount recoverable under subsection (3) is recoverable by execution issued from the county court or otherwise as if it were payable under an order of that court.

(5) If the person who made the payment resides or carries on business in Scotland, any amount recoverable under subsection (3) may be enforced in like manner as an extract registered decree arbitral bearing a warrant for execution issued by the sheriff court of any sheriffdom in Scotland.

(6) A document bearing a certificate which—
    (a) is signed by a person authorised to do so by the Secretary of State, and
    (b) states that the document, apart from the certificate, is a record of the amount recoverable under subsection (3),
is conclusive evidence that that amount is so recoverable.

(7) A certificate under subsection (6) purporting to be signed by a person authorised to do so by the Secretary of State is to be treated as so signed unless the contrary is proved.

8   Reduction of compensation payment

(1) This section applies in a case where, in relation to any head of compensation listed in column 1 of Schedule 2—
    (a) any of the compensation payment is attributable to the head, and
    (b) any recoverable benefit is shown against that head in column 2 of the Schedule.

(2) In such a case, any claim of a person to receive the compensation payment is to be treated for all purposes as discharged if—
    (a) he is paid the amount (if any) of the compensation payment calculated in accordance with this section, and
    (b) if the amount of the compensation payment so calculated is nil, he is given a statement saying so by the person who (apart from this section) would have paid the gross amount of the compensation payment.

(3) For each head of compensation listed in column 1 of the Schedule for which paragraphs (a) and (b) of subsection (1) are met, so much of the gross amount of the compensation payment as is attributable to that head is to be reduced (to nil, if necessary) by deducting the amount of the recoverable benefit or, as the case may be, the aggregate amount of the recoverable benefits shown against it.

(4) Subsection (3) is to have effect as if a requirement to reduce a payment by deducting an amount which exceeds the payment were a requirement to reduce that payment to nil.

(5) The amount of the compensation payment calculated in accordance with this section is—
    (a) the gross amount of the compensation payment, less
    (b) the sum of the reductions made under subsection (3),
(and, accordingly, the amount may be nil).

8A   Reduction of payment under Diffuse Mesothelioma Payment Scheme

(1) This section applies instead of section 8 in a case where the compensation payment is a payment under the Diffuse Mesothelioma Payment Scheme.

(2) The gross amount of the compensation payment—
    (a) is to be reduced by the amount of the recoverable benefit, and
    (b) accordingly, is to be reduced to nil in any case where the amount of the recoverable benefit is equal to or greater than the gross amount of the compensation payment.

(3) Any claim of a person to receive the compensation payment is to be treated for all purposes as discharged if—
    (a) the person is paid the gross amount of the compensation payment less the amount of the recoverable benefit, or
    (b) the amount of the recoverable benefit is equal to or greater than the gross amount of the compensation payment and the person is given a statement b the scheme administrator saying that the compensation payment has been reduced to nil.

9   Section 8: supplementary

(1) A person who makes a compensation payment calculated in accordance with section 8 or 8A must inform the person to whom the payment is made—
    (a) that the payment has been so calculated, and
    (b) of the date for payment by reference to which the calculation has been made.

(2) If the amount of a compensation payment calculated in accordance with section 8 or 8A is nil, a person giving a statement saying so is to be treated for the purposes of this Act as making a payment within section 1(1)(a) on the day on which he gives the statement.

(3) Where a person—
 (a) makes a compensation payment calculated in accordance with section 8 or 8A, and
 (b) if the amount of the compensation payment so calculated is nil, gives a statement saying so,

 he is to be treated, for the purpose of determining any rights and liabilities in respect of contribution or indemnity, as having paid the gross amount of the compensation payment.

(4) For the purposes of this Act—
 (a) the gross amount of the compensation payment is the amount of the compensation payment apart from section 8 or 8A, and
 (b) the amount of any recoverable benefit is the amount determined in accordance with the certificate of recoverable benefits.

10 Review of certificates of recoverable benefits

(1) Any certificate of recoverable benefits may be reviewed by the Secretary of State—
 (a) either within the prescribed period or in prescribed cases or circumstances; and
 (b) either on an application made for the purpose or on his own initiative.

(2) On a review under this section the Secretary of State may either—
 (a) confirm the certificate, or
 (b) (subject to subsection (3)) issue a fresh certificate containing such variations as he considers appropriate, or
 (c) revoke the certificate.

(3) The Secretary of State may not vary the certificate so as to increase the total amount of the recoverable benefits unless it appears to him that the variation is required as a result of the person who applied for the certificate supplying him with incorrect or insufficient information.

(4) The scheme administrator of the Diffuse Mesothelioma Payment Scheme may not apply for a review under this section.

11 Appeals against certificates of recoverable benefits

(1) An appeal against a certificate of recoverable benefits may be made on the ground—
 (a) that any amount, rate or period specified in the certificate is incorrect, or
 (b) that listed benefits which have been, or are likely to be, paid otherwise than in respect of the accident, injury or disease in question have been brought into account or
 (c) that listed benefits which have not been, and are not likely to be, paid to the injured person during the relevant period have been brought into account, or
 (d) that the payment on the basis of which the certificate was issued is not a payment within section 1(1)(a).

(2) An appeal under this section may be made by—
 (a) the person who applied for the certificate of recoverable benefits, or
 (aa) (in a case where that certificate was issued under section 7(2)(a)) the person to whom it was so issued, or
 (b) (in a case where the amount of the compensation payment has been calculated under section 8 or 8A) the injured person or other person to whom the payment is made; but the scheme administrator of the Diffuse Mesothelioma Payment Scheme may not appeal under this section.

(2A) Regulations may provide that, in such cases or circumstances as may be prescribed, an appeal may be made under this section only if the Secretary of State has reviewed the certificate under section 10.

(2B) The regulations may in particular provide that the condition is met only where—
 (a) the review by the Secretary of State was on an application,
 (b) the Secretary of State considered issues of a specified description, or
 (c) the review by the Secretary of State satisfied any other condition specified in the regulations.

(3)   No appeal may be made under this section until—
    (a)   the claim giving rise to the compensation payment has been finally disposed of, and
    (b)   the liability under section 6 has been discharged.
(4)   For the purposes of subsection (3)(a), if an award of damages in respect of a claim has been made under or by virtue of—
    (a)   section 32A(2)(a) of the Supreme Court Act 1981,
    (b)   section 12(2)(a) of the Administration of Justice Act 1982, or
    (c)   section 51(2)(a) of the County Courts Act 1984,
(orders for provisional damages in personal injury cases), the claim is to be treated as having been finally disposed of.
(5)   Regulations may make provision—
    (a)   as to the manner in which, and the time within which, appeals under this section may be made, and
    (b)   ...
    (c)   for the purpose of enabling any such appeal (or, where in accordance with regulations under subsection (2A) there is no right of appeal, any purported appeal) to be treated as an application for review under section 10.

12   Reference of questions to the First-tier Tribunal

(1)   The Secretary of State must refer an appeal under section 11 to the First-tier Tribunal.
(3)   In determining any appeal under section 11, the tribunal must take into account any decision of a court relating to the same, or any similar, issue arising in connection with the accident, injury or disease in question.
(4)   On an appeal under section 11 to the First-tier Tribunal may either—
    (a)   confirm the amounts, rates and periods specified in the certificate of recoverable benefits, or
    (b)   specify any variations which are to be made on the issue of a fresh certificate under subsection (5) or
    (c)   declare that the certificate of recoverable benefits is to be revoked.
(5)   When the Secretary of State has received the decision of the tribunal on the appeal under section 11, he must in accordance with that decision either—
    (a)   confirm the certificate against which the appeal was brought, or
    (b)   issue a fresh certificate or
    (c)   revoke the certificate..
(7)   Regulations ... may (among other things) provide for the non-disclosure of medical advice or medical evidence given or submitted following a reference under subsection (1).

13   Appeal to the Upper Tribunal

(1)   ...
(2)   An appeal to the Upper Tribunal under section 11 of the Tribunals, Courts and Enforcement Act 2007 which arises from any decision of the First-tier Tribunal made under section 12 of this Act may be made by—
    (a)   the Secretary of State,
    (b)   the person who applied for the certificate of recoverable benefits,
    ...
    (bb)   (in a case where that certificate was issued under section 7(2)(a)) the person to whom it was so issued, or
    (c)   (in a case where the amount of the compensation payment has been calculated in accordance with section 8) the injured person or other person to whom the payment is made; but the scheme administrator of the Diffuse Mesothelioma Payment Scheme may not appeal under this section.

14   Reviews and appeals: supplementary

(1)   This section applies in cases where a fresh certificate of recoverable benefits is issued as a result of a review under section 10 or an appeal under section 11.
(2)   If—
    (a)   a person has made one or more payments to the Secretary of State under section 6, and
    (b)   in consequence of the review or appeal, it appears that the total amount paid is more than the amount that ought to have been paid,

regulations may provide for the Secretary of State to pay the difference to that person, or to the person to whom the compensation payment is made, or partly to one and partly to the other.

(3) If—

(a) a person has made one or more payments to the Secretary of State under section 6, and

(b) in consequence of the review or appeal, it appears that the total amount paid is less than the amount that ought to have been paid,

regulations may provide for that person to pay the difference to the Secretary of State.

(4) Regulations under this section may provide—

(a) for the re-calculation in accordance with section 8 or 8A of the amount of any compensation payment,

(b) for giving credit for amounts already paid, and

(c) for the payment by any person of any balance or the recovery from any person of any excess,

and may provide for any matter by modifying this Act.

15 Court orders

(1) This section applies where a court makes an order for a compensation payment to be made in any case, unless the order is made with the consent of the injured person and the person by whom the payment is to be made.

(2) The court must, in the case of each head of compensation listed in column 1 of Schedule 2 to which any of the compensation payment is attributable, specify in the order the amount of the compensation payment which is attributable to that head.

16 Payments into court

(1) Regulations may make provision (including provision modifying this Act) for any case in which a payment into court is made.

(2) The regulations may (among other things) provide—

(a) for the making of a payment into court to be treated in prescribed circumstances as the making of a compensation payment,

(b) for application for, and issue of, certificates of recoverable benefits, and

(c) for the relevant period to be treated as ending on a date determined in accordance with the regulations.

(3) Rules of court may make provision governing practice and procedure in such cases.

(4) This section does not extend to Scotland.

17 Benefits irrelevant to assessment of damages

In assessing damages in respect of any accident, injury or disease, the amount of any listed benefits paid or likely to be paid is to be disregarded.

18 Lump sum and periodical payments

(1) Regulations may make provision (including provision modifying this Act) for any case in which two or more compensation payments in the form of lump sums are made by the same person to or in respect of the injured person in consequence of the same accident, injury or disease.

(2) The regulations may (among other things) provide—

(a) for the re-calculation in accordance with section 8 of the amount of any compensation payment,

(b) for giving credit for amounts already paid, and

(c) for the payment by any person of any balance or the recovery from any person of any excess.

(3) For the purposes of subsection (2), the regulations may provide for the gross amounts of the compensation payments to be aggregated and for—

(a) the aggregate amount to be taken to be the gross amount of the compensation payment for the purposes of section 8,

(b) so much of the aggregate amount as is attributable to a head of compensation listed in column 1 of Schedule 2 to be taken to be the part of the gross amount which is attributable to that head;

and for the amount of any recoverable benefit shown against any head in column 2 of that Schedule to be taken to be the amount determined in accordance with the most recent certificate of recoverable benefits.

(4) Regulations may make provision (including provision modifying this Act) for any case in which, in final settlement of the injured person's claim, an agreement is entered into for the making of—
  (a) periodical compensation payments (whether of an income or capital nature), or
  (b) periodical compensation payments and lump sum compensation payments.
(5) Regulations made by virtue of subsection (4) may (among other things) provide—
  (a) for the relevant period to be treated as ending at a prescribed time,
  (b) for the person who is to make the payments under the agreement to be treated for the purposes of this Act as if he had made a single compensation payment on a prescribed date.
(6) A periodical payment may be a compensation payment for the purposes of this section even though it is a small payment (as defined in Part II of Schedule 1).

19   Payments by more than one person

(1) Regulations may make provision (including provision modifying this Act) for any case in which two or more persons ("the compensators") make compensation payments to or in respect of the same injured person in consequence of the same accident, injury or disease.
(2) In such a case, the sum of the liabilities of the compensators under section 6 is not to exceed the total amount of the recoverable benefits, and the regulations may provide for determining the respective liabilities under that section of each of the compensators.
(3) The regulations may (among other things) provide in the case of each compensator—
  (a) for determining or re-determining the part of the recoverable benefits which may be taken into account in his case,
  (b) for calculating or re-calculating in accordance with section 8 or 8A the amount of any compensation payment,
  (c) for giving credit for amounts already paid, and
  (d) for the payment by any person of any balance or the recovery from any person of any excess.

20   Amounts overpaid under section 6

(1) Regulations may make provision (including provision modifying this Act) for cases where a person has paid to the Secretary of State under section 6 any amount ("the amount of the overpayment") which he was not liable to pay.
(2) The regulations may provide—
  (a) for the Secretary of State to pay the amount of the overpayment to that person, or to the person to whom the compensation payment is made, or partly to one and partly to the other, or
  (b) for the receipt by the Secretary of State of the amount of the overpayment to be treated as the recovery of that amount.
(3) Regulations made by virtue of subsection (2)(b) are to have effect in spite of anything in section 71 of the Social Security Administration Act 1992 (overpayments—general).
(4) The regulations may also (among other things) provide—
  (a) for the re-calculation in accordance with section 8 or 8A of the amount of any compensation payment,
  (b) for giving credit for amounts already paid, and
  (c) for the payment by any person of any balance or the recovery from any person of any excess.
(5) This section does not apply in a case where section 14 applies.

21   Compensation payments to be disregarded

(1) If, when a compensation payment is made, the first and second conditions are met, the payment is to be disregarded for the purposes of sections 6 and 8 or 8A.
(2) The first condition is that the person making the payment—
  (a) has made an application for a certificate of recoverable benefits which complies with subsection (3), and
  (b) has in his possession a written acknowledgement of the receipt of his application.
(3) An application complies with this subsection if it—
  (a) accurately states the prescribed particulars relating to the injured person and the accident, injury or disease in question, and
  (b) specifies the name and address of the person to whom the certificate is to be sent.

(4) The second condition is that the Secretary of State has not sent the certificate to the person, at the address, specified in the application, before the end of the period allowed under section 4.

(5) In any case where—
   (a) by virtue of subsection (1), a compensation payment is disregarded for the purposes of sections 6 and 8 or 8A, but
   (b) the person who made the compensation payment nevertheless makes a payment to the Secretary of State for which (but for subsection (1)) he would be liable under section 6,
   subsection (1) is to cease to apply in relation to the compensation payment.

(6) If, in the opinion of the Secretary of State, circumstances have arisen which adversely affect normal methods of communication—
   (a) he may by order provide that subsection (1) is not to apply during a specified period not exceeding three months, and
   (b) he may continue any such order in force for further periods not exceeding three months at a time.

22 Liability of insurers

(1) If a compensation payment is made in a case where—
   (a) a person is liable to any extent in respect of the accident, injury or disease, and
   (b) the liability is covered to any extent by a policy of insurance, the policy is also to be treated as covering any liability of that person under section 6.

(2) Liability imposed on the insurer by subsection (1) cannot be excluded or restricted.

(3) For that purpose excluding or restricting liability includes—
   (a) making the liability or its enforcement subject to restrictive or onerous conditions,
   (b) excluding or restricting any right or remedy in respect of the liability, or subjecting a person to any prejudice in consequence of his pursuing any such right or remedy, or
   (c) excluding or restricting rules of evidence or procedure.

(4) Regulations may in prescribed cases limit the amount of the liability imposed on the insurer by subsection (1).

(5) This section applies to policies of insurance issued before (as well as those issued after) its coming into force.

(6) References in this section to policies of insurance and their issue include references to contracts of insurance and their making.

23 Provision of information

(1) Where compensation is sought in respect of any accident, injury or disease suffered by any person ("the injured person"), the following persons must give the Secretary of State the prescribed information about the injured person—
   (a) anyone who is, or is alleged to be, liable in respect of the accident, injury or disease, and
   (b) anyone acting on behalf of such a person.

(2) A person who receives or claims a listed benefit which is or is likely to be paid in respect of an accident, injury or disease suffered by him, must give the Secretary of State the prescribed information about the accident, injury or disease.

(3) Where a person who has received a listed benefit dies, the duty in subsection (2) is imposed on his personal representative.

(4) Any person who makes a payment (whether on his own behalf or not)—
   (a) in consequence of, or
   (b) which is referable to any costs (in Scotland, expenses) incurred by reason of,
   any accident, injury or disease, or any damage to property, must, if the Secretary of State requests him in writing to do so, give the Secretary of State such particulars relating to the size and composition of the payment as are specified in the request.

(5) The employer of a person who suffers or has suffered an accident, injury or disease, and anyone who has been the employer of such a person at any time during the relevant period, must give the Secretary of State the prescribed information about the payment of statutory sick pay in respect of that person.

(6) In subsection (5) "employer" has the same meaning as it has in Part XI of the Social Security Contributions and Benefits Act 1992.

(6A) The following persons must give the Secretary of State the prescribed information for the purposes of this Act—

(a)   the scheme administrator of the Diffuse Mesothelioma Payment Scheme, and

(b)   any person providing services to the scheme administrator.

(7)   A person who is required to give information under this section must do so in the prescribed manner, at the prescribed place and within the prescribed time.

(8)   Section 1 does not apply in relation to this section.

28   The Crown

This Act applies to the Crown.

29   General interpretation

In this Act—

"appeal tribunal" means an appeal tribunal constituted under Chapter I of Part I of the Social Security Act 1998;

"benefit" means any benefit under the Social Security Contributions and Benefits Act 1992, a jobseeker's allowance, an employment or support allowance or mobility allowance,

"Commissioner" has the same meaning as in Chapter II of Part I of the Social Security Act 1998 (see section 39);

"compensation scheme for motor accidents" means any scheme or arrangement under which funds are available for the payment of compensation in respect of motor accidents caused, or alleged to have been caused, by uninsured or unidentified persons,

"listed benefit" means a benefit listed in column 2 of Schedule 2,

"payment" means payment in money or money's worth, and related expressions are to be interpreted accordingly,

"prescribed" means prescribed by regulations, and

"regulations" means regulations made by the Secretary of State.

"scheme administrator" in relation to the Diffuse Mesothelioma Payment Scheme has the meaning given by section 18 of the Mesothelioma Act 2014.

SCHEDULES

Section 1   SCHEDULE 1

COMPENSATION PAYMENTS

PART I
EXEMPTED PAYMENTS

1.   Any small payment (defined in Part II of this Schedule)

2.   Any payment made to or for the injured person under section 130 of the Powers of Criminal Courts (Sentencing) Act 2000, section 8 of the Modern Slavery Act 2015 or section 175 of the Armed Forces Act 2006 or section 249 of the Criminal Procedure (Scotland) Act 1995 (compensation orders against convicted persons).

3.   Any payment made in the exercise of a discretion out of property held subject to a trust in a case where no more than 50 per cent. by value of the capital contributed to the trust was directly or indirectly provided by persons who are, or are alleged to be, liable in respect of—

(a)   the accident, injury or disease suffered by the injured person, or

(b)   the same or any connected accident, injury or disease suffered by another.

4.   Any payment made out of property held for the purposes of any prescribed trust (whether the payment also falls within paragraph 3 or not).

5.   (1)   Any payment made to the injured person by an insurer under the terms of any contract of insurance entered into between the injured person and the insurer before—

(a)   the date on which the injured person first claims a listed benefit in consequence of the disease in question, or

(b)   the occurrence of the accident or injury in question.

(2)   "Insurer" means—

(a)   a person who has permission under Part 4A of the Financial Services and Markets Act 2000 to effect or carry out contracts of insurance; or

      (b)   an EEA firm of the kind mentioned in paragraph 5(d) of Schedule 3 to that Act which has permission under paragraph 15 of that Schedule (as a result of qualifying for authorisation under paragraph 12 of that Schedule) to effect or carry out contracts of insurance.

    (3)   Sub-paragraph (2) must be read with—
      (a)   section 22 of the Financial Services and Markets Act 2000;
      (b)   any relevant order under that section; and
      (c)   Schedule 2 to that Act.

6.   Any redundancy payment falling to be taken into account in the assessment of damages in respect of an accident, injury or disease.

7.   So much of any payment as is referable to costs.

8.   Any prescribed payment.

PART II
POWER TO DISREGARD SMALL PAYMENTS

9.   (1)   Regulations may make provision for compensation payments to be disregarded for the purposes of sections 6 and 8 in prescribed cases where the amount of the compensation payment, or the aggregate amount of two or more connected compensation payments, does not exceed the prescribed sum.

    (2)   A compensation payment disregarded by virtue of this paragraph is referred to in paragraph 1 as a "small payment".

    (3)   For the purposes of this paragraph—
      (a)   two or more compensation payments are "connected" if each is made to or in respect of the same injured person and in respect of the same accident, injury or disease, and
      (b)   any reference to a compensation payment is a reference to a payment which would be such a payment apart from paragraph 1.

Section 8   SCHEDULE 2

CALCULATION OF COMPENSATION PAYMENT

(1) *Head of compensation*	(2) *Benefit*
1. Compensation for earnings lost during the the relevant period	… Universal Credit Disablement pension payable under section 103 of the 1992 Act Employment and support allowance Incapacity benefit Invalidity pension and allowance Jobseeker's allowance Reduced earnings allowance Severe disablement allowance Sickness benefit Statutory sick pay Unemployability supplement Unemployment benefit
2. Compensation for cost of care incurred during the relevant period	Attendance allowance Daily living component of personal independence payment Disablement pension increase payable under section 104 or 105 of the 1992 Act
3. Compensation for loss of mobility during the during the relevant period	Mobility allowance Mobility component of personal independence payment

Notes

1. (1) References to incapacity benefit, invalidity pension and allowance, severe disablement allowance, sickness benefit and unemployment benefit also include any income support paid with each of those benefits on the same instrument of payment or paid concurrently with each of those benefits by means of an instrument for benefit payment.

   (2) For the purpose of this Note, income support includes personal expenses addition, special transitional additions and transitional addition as defined in the Income Support (Transitional) Regulations 1987.

2. Any reference to statutory sick pay—

   (a) includes only 80 per cent. of payments made between 6 April 1991 and 5 April 1994, and

   (b) does not include payments made on or after 6 April 1994.

3. In this Schedule "the 1992 Act" means the Social Security Contributions and Benefits Act 1992.

HUMAN RIGHTS ACT 1998
(1998, c. 42)

1 The Convention Rights

(1) In this Act "the Convention rights" means the rights and fundamental freedoms set out in—

(a) Articles 2 to 12 and 14 of the Convention,

(b) Articles 1 to 3 of the First Protocol, and

(c) Articles 1 of the Thirteenth Protocol, as

read with Articles 16 to 18 of the Convention.

(2) Those Articles are to have effect for the purposes of this Act subject to any designated derogation or reservation (as to which see sections 14 and 15).

(3) The Articles are set out in Schedule 1.

(4) The Secretary of State may by order make such amendments to this Act as he considers appropriate to reflect the effect, in relation to the United Kingdom, of a protocol.

2 Interpretation of Convention rights

(1) A court or tribunal determining a question which has arisen in connection with a Convention right must take into account any—

(a) judgment, decision, declaration or advisory opinion of the European Court of Human Rights,

(b) opinion of the Commission given in a report adopted under Article 31 of the Convention,

(c) decision of the Commission in connection with Article 26 or 27(2) of the Convention, or

(d) decision of the Committee of Ministers taken under Article 46 of the Convention,

whenever made or given, so far as, in the opinion of the court or tribunal, it is relevant to the proceedings in which that question has arisen.

3 Interpretation of legislation

(1) So far as it is possible to do so, primary legislation and subordinate legislation must be read and given effect in a way which is compatible with the Convention rights.

(2) This section—

(a) applies to primary legislation and subordinate legislation whenever enacted;

(b) does not affect the validity, continuing operation or enforcement of any incompatible primary legislation; and

(c) does not affect the validity, continuing operation or enforcement of any incompatible subordinate legislation if (disregarding any possibility of revocation) primary legislation prevents removal of the incompatibility.

6 Acts of public authorities

(1) It is unlawful for a public authority to act in a way which is incompatible with a Convention right.

(2) Subsection (1) does not apply to an act if—
  (a) as the result of one or more provisions of primary legislation, the authority could not have acted differently; or
  (b) in the case of one or more provisions of, or made under, primary legislation which cannot be read or given effect in a way which is compatible with the Convention rights, the authority was acting so as to give effect to or enforce those provisions.

7 Proceedings

(1) A person who claims that a public authority has acted (or proposes to act) in a way which is made unlawful by section 6(1) may—
  (a) bring proceedings against the authority under this Act in the appropriate court or tribunal, or
  (b) rely on the Convention right or rights concerned in any legal proceedings, but only if he is (or would be) a victim of the unlawful act.

(8) Nothing in this Act creates a criminal offence.

8 Judicial remedies

(1) In relation to any act (or proposed act) of a public authority which the court finds is (or would be) unlawful, it may grant such relief or remedy, or make such order, within its powers as it considers just and appropriate.

(2) But damages may be awarded only by a court which has power to award damages, or to order the payment of compensation, in civil proceedings.

(3) No award of damages is to be made unless, taking account of all the circumstances of the case, including—
  (a) any other relief or remedy granted, or order made, in relation to the act in question (by that or any other court), and
  (b) the consequences of any decision (of that or any other court) in respect of that act,

  the court is satisfied that the award is necessary to afford just satisfaction to the person in whose favour it is made.

(4) In determining—
  (a) whether to award damages, or
  (b) the amount of an award,

  the court must take into account the principles applied by the European Court of Human Rights in relation to the award of compensation under Article 41 of the Convention.

(5) A public authority against which damages are awarded is to be treated—
  (a) in Scotland, for the purposes of section 3 of the Law Reform (Miscellaneous Provisions) (Scotland) Act 1940 as if the award were made in an action of damages in which the authority has been found liable in respect of loss or damage to the person to whom the award is made;
  (b) for the purposes of the Civil Liability (Contribution) Act 1978 as liable in respect of damage suffered by the person to whom the award is made.

(6) In this section—
  "court" includes a tribunal;
  "damages" means damages for an unlawful act of a public authority; and "unlawful" means unlawful under section 6(1).

9 Judicial acts

(1) Proceedings under section 7(1)(a) in respect of a judicial act may be brought only—
  (a) by exercising a right of appeal;
  (b) on an application (in Scotland a petition) for judicial review; or
  (c) in such other forum as may be prescribed by rules.

(3) In proceedings under this Act in respect of a judicial act done in good faith, damages may not be awarded otherwise than to compensate a person to the extent required by Article 5(5) of the Convention.

(4) An award of damages permitted by subsection (3) is to be made against the Crown; but no award may be made unless the appropriate person, if not a party to the proceedings, is joined.

11   Safeguard for existing human rights

A person's reliance on a Convention right does not restrict—

(a)   any other right or freedom conferred on him by or under any law having effect in any part of the United Kingdom; or

(b)   his right to make any claim or bring any proceedings which he could make or bring apart from sections 7 to 9.

12   Freedom of expression

(1)   This section applies if a court is considering whether to grant any relief which, if granted, might affect the exercise of the Convention right to freedom of expression.

(2)   If the person against whom the application for relief is made ("the respondent") is neither present nor represented, no such relief is to be granted unless the court is satisfied—

(a)   that the applicant has taken all practicable steps to notify the respondent; or

(b)   that there are compelling reasons why the respondent should not be notified.

(3)   No such relief is to be granted so as to restrain publication before trial unless the court is satisfied that the applicant is likely to establish that publication should not be allowed.

(4)   The court must have particular regard to the importance of the Convention right to freedom of expression and, where the proceedings relate to material which the respondent claims, or which appears to the court, to be journalistic, literary or artistic material (or to conduct connected with such material), to—

(a)   the extent to which—

(i)   the material has, or is about to, become available to the public; or

(ii)   it is, or would be, in the public interest for the material to be published;

(b)   any relevant privacy code.

(5)   In this section—

"court" includes a tribunal; and

"relief" includes any remedy or order (other than in criminal proceedings)

13   Freedom of thought, conscience and religion

(1)   If a court's determination of any question arising under this Act might affect the exercise by a religious organisation (itself or its members collectively) of the Convention right to freedom of thought, conscience and religion, it must have particular regard to the importance of that right.

(2)   In this section "court" includes a tribunal.

21   Interpretation, etc.

(1)   In this Act—

"the Commission" means the European Commission of Human Rights;

"the Convention" means the Convention for the Protection of Human Rights and Fundamental Freedoms, agreed by the Council of Europe at Rome on 4th November 1950 as it has effect for the time being in relation to the United Kingdom;

...

22   Short title, commencement, application and extent

(5)   This Act binds the Crown.

(6)   This Act extends to Northern Ireland.

SCHEDULE 1
THE ARTICLES

PART I
THE CONVENTION

RIGHTS AND FREEDOMS

Article 2   Right to life

1.   Everyone's right to life shall be protected by law. No one shall be deprived of his life intentionally save in the execution of a sentence of a court following his conviction of a crime for which this penalty is provided by law.

2.   Deprivation of life shall not be regarded as inflicted in contravention of this Article when it results from the use of force which is no more than absolutely necessary:
    (a)   in defence of any person from unlawful violence;
    (b)   in order to effect a lawful arrest or to prevent the escape of a person lawfully detained;
    (c)   in action lawfully taken for the purpose of quelling a riot or insurrection.

Article 3   Prohibition of torture
No one shall be subjected to torture or to inhuman or degrading treatment or punishment.

Article 4   Prohibition of slavery and forced labour
1.   No one shall be held in slavery or servitude.
2.   No one shall be required to perform forced or compulsory labour.
3.   For the purpose of this Article the term "forced or compulsory labour" shall not include:
    (a)   any work required to be done in the ordinary course of detention imposed according to the provisions of Article 5 of this Convention or during conditional release from such detention;
    (b)   any service of a military character or, in case of conscientious objectors in countries where they are recognised, service exacted instead of compulsory military service;
    (c)   any service exacted in case of an emergency or calamity threatening the life or well-being of the community;
    (d)   any work or service which forms part of normal civic obligations.

Article 5   Right to liberty and security
1.   Everyone has the right to liberty and security of person. No one shall be deprived of his liberty save in the following cases and in accordance with a procedure prescribed by law:
    (a)   the lawful detention of a person after conviction by a competent court;
    (b)   the lawful arrest or detention of a person for non-compliance with the lawful order of a court or in order to secure the fulfilment of any obligation prescribed by law;
    (c)   the lawful arrest or detention of a person effected for the purpose of bringing him before the competent legal authority on reasonable suspicion of having committed an offence or when it is reasonably considered necessary to prevent his committing an offence or fleeing after having done so;
    (d)   the detention of a minor by lawful order for the purpose of educational supervision or his lawful detention for the purpose of bringing him before the competent legal authority.
    (e)   the lawful detention of persons for the prevention of the spreading of infectious diseases, of persons of unsound mind, alcoholics or drug addicts or vagrants;
    (f)   the lawful arrest or detention of a person to prevent his effecting an unauthorised entry into the country or of a person against whom action is being taken with a view to deportation or extradition.
2.   Everyone who is arrested shall be informed promptly, in a language which he understands, of the reasons for his arrest and of any charge against him.
3.   Everyone arrested or detained in accordance with the provisions of paragraph 1(c) of this Article shall be brought promptly before a judge or other officer authorised by law to exercise judicial power and shall be entitled to trial within a reasonable time or to release pending trial. Release may be conditioned by guarantees to appear for trial.
4.   Everyone who is deprived of his liberty by arrest or detention shall be entitled to take proceedings by which the lawfulness of his detention shall be decided speedily by a court and his release ordered if the detention is not lawful.
5.   Everyone who has been the victim of arrest or detention in contravention of the provisions of this Article shall have an enforceable right to compensation.

Article 6   Right to a fair trial
1.   In the determination of his civil rights and obligations or of any criminal charge against him, everyone is entitled to a fair and public hearing within a reasonable time by an independent and impartial tribunal established by law. Judgment shall be pronounced

publicly but the press and public may be excluded from all or part of the trial in the interest of morals, public order or national security in a democratic society, where the interests of juveniles or the protection of the private life of the parties so require, or to the extent strictly necessary in the opinion of the court in special circumstances where publicity would prejudice the interests of justice.

2.   Everyone charged with a criminal offence shall be presumed innocent until proved guilty according to law.

3.   Everyone charged with a criminal offence has the following minimum rights:

(a)   to be informed promptly, in a language which he understands and in detail, of the nature and cause of the accusation against him;

(b)   to have adequate time and facilities for the preparation of his defence;

(c)   to defend himself in person or through legal assistance of his own choosing or, if he has not sufficient means to pay for legal assistance, to be given it free when the interests of justice so require;

(d)   to examine or have examined witnesses against him and to obtain the attendance and examination of witnesses on his behalf under the same conditions as witnesses against him;

(e)   to have the free assistance of an interpreter if he cannot understand or speak the language used in court.

Article 8   Right to respect for private and family life

1.   Everyone has the right to respect for his private and family life, his home and his correspondence.

2.   There shall be no interference by a public authority with the exercise of this right except such as is in accordance with the law and is necessary in a democratic society in the interests of national security, public safety or the economic well-being of the country, for the prevention of disorder or crime, for the protection of health or morals, or for the protection of the rights and freedoms of others.

Article 9   Freedom of thought, conscience and religion

1.   Everyone has the right to freedom of thought, conscience and religion; this right includes freedom to change his religion or belief and freedom, either alone or in community with others and in public or private, to manifest his religion or belief, in worship, teaching, practice and observance.

2.   Freedom to manifest one's religion or beliefs shall be subject only to such limitations as are prescribed by law and are necessary in a democratic society in the interests of public safety, for the protection of public order, health or morals, or for the protection of the rights and -freedoms of others.

Article 10   Freedom of expression

1.   Everyone has the right to freedom of expression. This right shall include freedom to hold opinions and to receive and impart information and ideas without interference by public authority and regardless of frontiers. This Article shall not prevent States from requiring the licensing of broadcasting, television or cinema enterprises.

2.   The exercise of these freedoms, since it carries with it duties and responsibilities, may be subject to such formalities, conditions, restrictions or penalties as are prescribed by law and are necessary in a democratic society, in the interests of national security, territorial integrity or public safety, for the prevention of disorder or crime, for the protection of health or morals, for the protection of the reputation or rights of others, for preventing the disclosure of information received in confidence, or for maintaining the authority and impartiality of the judiciary.

Article 11   Freedom of assembly and association

1.   Everyone has the right to freedom of peaceful assembly and to freedom of association with others, including the right to form and to join trade unions for the protection of his interests.

2.   No restrictions shall be placed on the exercise of these rights other than such as are prescribed by law and are necessary in a democratic society in the interests of national security or public safety, for the prevention of disorder or crime, for the protection of health or morals or for the protection of the rights and freedoms of others.

This Article shall not prevent the imposition of lawful restrictions on the exercise of these rights by members of the armed forces, of the police or of the administration of the State.

Article 12   Right to marry

Men and women of marriageable age have the right to marry and to found a family, according to the national laws governing the exercise of this right.

Article 14   Prohibition of discrimination

The enjoyment of the rights and freedoms set forth in this Convention shall be secured without discrimination on any ground such as sex, race, colour, language, religion, political or other opinion, national or social origin, association with a national minority, property, birth or other status.

Article 16   Restrictions on political activity of aliens

Nothing in Articles 10, 11 and 14 shall be regarded as preventing the High Contracting Parties from imposing restrictions on the political activity of aliens.

Article 17   Prohibition of abuse of rights

Nothing in this Convention may be interpreted as implying for any State, group or person any right to engage in any activity or perform any act aimed at the destruction of any of the rights and freedoms set forth herein or at their limitation to a greater extent than is provided for in the Convention.

PART II
THE FIRST PROTOCOL

Article 1   Protection of property

Every natural or legal person is entitled to the peaceful enjoyment of his possessions. No one shall be deprived of his possessions except in the public interest and subject to the conditions provided for by law and by the general principles of international law. The preceding provisions shall not, however, in any way impair the right of a State to enforce such laws as it deems necessary to control the use of property in accordance with the general interest or to secure the payment of taxes or other contributions or penalties.

LATE PAYMENT OF COMMERCIAL DEBTS (INTEREST) ACT 1998
(1998, c. 20)

PART I
STATUTORY INTEREST ON QUALIFYING DEBTS

1   Statutory interest

(1) It is an implied term in a contract to which this Act applies that any qualifying debt created by the contract carries simple interest subject to and in accordance with this Part.

(2) Interest carried under that implied term (in this Act referred to as "statutory interest") shall be treated, for the purposes of any rule of law or enactment (other than this Act) relating to interest on debts, in the same way as interest carried under an express contract term.

(3) This Part has effect subject to Part II (which in certain circumstances permits contract terms to oust or vary the right to statutory interest that would otherwise be conferred by virtue of the term implied by subsection (1)).

2   Contracts to which Act applies

(1) This Act applies to a contract for the supply of goods or services where the purchaser and the supplier are each acting in the course of a business, other than an excepted contract.

(2)   In this Act "contract for the supply of goods or services" means—
    (a)   a contract of sale of goods; or
    (b)   a contract (other than a contract of sale of goods) by which a person does any, or any combination, of the things mentioned in subsection (3) for a consideration that is (or includes) a money consideration.

(3)   Those things are—
    (a)   transferring or agreeing to transfer to another the property in goods;
    (b)   bailing or agreeing to bail goods to another by way of hire or, in Scotland, hiring or agreeing to hire goods to another; and (c) agreeing to carry out a service.

(4)   For the avoidance of doubt a contract of service or apprenticeship is not a contract for the supply of goods or services.

(5)   The following are excepted contracts—
    (a)   a consumer credit agreement;
    (b)   a contract intended to operate by way of mortgage, pledge, charge or other security; and

    ...

(7)   In this section—
"business" includes a profession and the activities of any government department or local or public authority;
"consumer credit agreement" has the same meaning as in the Consumer Credit Act 1974; "contract of sale of goods" and "goods" have the same meaning as in the Sale of Goods Act 1979;
"government department" incudes any part of the Scottish Administration;
"property in goods" means the general property in them and not merely a special property.

3   Qualifying debts

(1)   A debt created by virtue of an obligation under a contract to which this Act applies to pay the whole or any part of the contract price is a "qualifying debt" for the purposes of this Act, unless (when created) the whole of the debt is prevented from carrying statutory interest by this section.

(2)   A debt does not carry statutory interest if or to the extent that it consists of a sum to which a right to interest or to charge interest applies by virtue of any enactment (other than section 1 of this Act).
This subsection does not prevent a sum from carrying statutory interest by reason of the fact that a court, arbitrator or arbiter would, apart from this Act, have power to award interest on it.

(3)   A debt does not carry (and shall be treated as never having carried) statutory interest if or to the extent that a right to demand interest on it, which exists by virtue of any rule of law, is exercised.

4   Period for which statutory interest runs

(1)   Statutory interest runs in relation to a qualifying debt in accordance with this section (unless section 5 applies).

(2)   Statutory interest starts to run on the day after the relevant day for the debt, at the rate prevailing under section 6 at the end of the relevant day.

(2A) The relevant day for a debt is—
    (a)   where there is an agreed payment day, that day, unless a different day is given by subsection (2D), (2E) or (2G);
    (b)   where there is not an agreed payment day, the last day of the relevant 30-day period.

(2B) An "agreed payment day" is a date agreed between the supplier and purchaser for the payment of the debt (that is, the day on which the debt is to be created by the contract).

(2C) A date agreed for payment of a debt may be a fixed date or may depend on the happening of an event or the failure of an event to happen.

(2D) Where—
    (a)   the purchaser is a public authority, and
    (b)   the last day of the relevant 30-day period falls earlier than the agreed payment day,
the relevant day is the last day of the relevant 30-day period, unless subsection (2G) applies.

(2E) Where—
    (a)   the purchaser is not a public authority, and
    (b)   the last day of the relevant 60-day period falls earlier tan the agreed payment day,
    the relevant day is the last day of the relevant 60-day period, unless subsection (2G) applies.

(2F) But subsection (2E) does not apply (and so the relevant day is the agreed payment day, unless subsection (2G) applies) if the agreed payment day is not grossly unfair to the supplier (see subsection (7A)).

(2G) Where the debt relates to an obligation to make an advance payment, the relevant day is the day on which the debt is treated by section 11 as having been created (instead of the agreed payment day or the day given by subsection (2D) or (2E)).

(2H) "The relevant 30-day period" is the period of 30 days beginning with the later or latest of—
    (a)   the day on which the obligation of the supplier to which the debt relates is performed;
    (b)   the day on which the purchaser has notice of the amount of the debt or (where that amount is unascertained) the sum which the supplier claims is the amount of the debt;
    (c)   where subsection (5A) applies, the day determined under subsection (5B).

(2I) "The relevant 60-day period" is the period of 60 days beginning with the later or latest of—
    (a)   the day on which the obligation of the supplier to which the debt relates is performed;
    (b)   the day on which the purchaser has notice of the amount of the debt or (where the amount is unascertained) the sum which the supplier claims is the amount of the debt;
    (c)   where subsection (5A) applies, the day determined under subsection (5B).

(3)   ...
(4)   ...
(5)   ...

(5A) This subsection applies where—
    (a)   there is a procedure of acceptance or verification (whether provided for by an enactment or by contract), under which the conforming of goods or services with the contract is to be ascertained, and
    (b)   the purchaser has notice of the amount of the debt on or before the day on which the procedure is completed.

(5B) For the purposes of subsections (2H)(c) and (2I)(c), the day in question is the day which is 30 days after the day on which the procedure is completed.

(5C) Where, in a case where subsection (5A) applies, the procedure in question is completed after the end of the period of 30 days beginning with the day on which the obligation of the supplier to which the debt relates is performed, the procedure is to be treated for the purposes of subsection (5B) as being completed immediately after the end of that period.

(5D) Subsection (5C) does not apply if—
    (a)   the supplier and the purchaser expressly agree in the contract a period for completing the procedure in question that is longer than the period mentioned in that subsection, and
    (b)   that longer period is not grossly unfair to the supplier (see subsection (7A)).

(6)   Where the debt is created by virtue of an obligation to pay a sum due in respect of a period of hire of goods, subsections (2H)(a) and (2I)(a) have effect as if they referred to the last day of that period.

(7)   Statutory interest ceases to run when the interest would cease to run if it were carried under an express contract term.

(7A) In determining for the purposes of subsection (2F) or (5D) whether something is grossly unfair, all circumstances of the case shall be considered; and, for that purpose, the circumstances of the case include in particular—
    (a)   anything that is a gross deviation from good commercial practice and contrary to good faith and fair dealing,
    (b)   the nature of the goods or services in question,
    (c)   whether the purchaser has any objective reason to deviate from the result which is provided for by subsection (2E) or (5C).

(8)   In this section—
"advance payment" has the same meaning as in section 11;
"enactment" included an enactment contained in subordinate legislation (within the meaning of the Interpretation Act 1978);
"public authority" means a contracting authority (within the meaning of regulation 2(1) of the Public Contracts Regulations 2015).

5   Remission of statutory interest

(1)   This section applies where, by reason of any conduct of the supplier, the interests of justice require that statutory interest should be remitted in whole or part in respect of a period for which it would otherwise run in relation to a qualifying debt.

(2)   If the interests of justice require that the supplier should receive no statutory interest for a period, statutory interest shall not run for that period.

(3)   If the interests of justice require that the supplier should receive statutory interest at a reduced rate for a period, statutory interest shall run at such rate as meets the justice of the case for that period.

(4)   Remission of statutory interest under this section may be required—
(a)   by reason of conduct at any time (whether before or after the time at which the debt is created); and
(b)   for the whole period for which statutory interest would otherwise run or for one or more parts of that period.

(5)   In this section "conduct" includes any act or omission.

5A   Compensation arising out of late payment

(1)   Once statutory interest begins to run in relation to a qualifying debt, the supplier shall be entitled to a fixed sum (in addition to the statutory interest on the debt).

(2)   That sum shall be—
(a)   for a debt less than £1,000, the sum of £40;
(b)   for a debt of £1,000 or more, but less than £10,000, the sum of £70;
(c)   for a debt of £10,000 or more, the sum of £100.

(2A) If the reasonable costs of the supplier in recovering the debt are not met by the fixed sum, the supplier shall also be entitled to a sum equivalent to the difference between the fixed sum and those costs.

(3)   The obligation to pay a sum under this section in respect of a qualifying debt shall be treated as part of the term implied by section 1(1) in the contract creating the debt.

(4)   Section 3(2)(b) of the Unfair Contract Terms Act 1977 (no reliance to be placed on certain contract terms) shall apply in cases where a contract term is not contained in written standard terms of the purchaser as well as in cases where the term is contained in such standard terms.

(5)   In this section "contract term" means a term of the contract relating to a sum due to the supplier under this section.

6   Rate of statutory interest

(1)   The Secretary of State shall by order made with the consent of the Treasury set the rate of statutory interest by prescribing—
(a)   a formula for calculating the rate of statutory interest; or
(b)   the rate of statutory interest.

(2)   Before making such an order the Secretary of State shall, among other things, consider the extent to which it may be desirable to set the rate so as to—
(a)   protect suppliers whose financial position makes them particularly vulnerable if their qualifying debts are paid late; and
(b)   deter generally the late payment of qualifying debts.

PART II
CONTRACT TERMS RELATING TO LATE PAYMENT OFQUALIFYING DEBTS

7   Purpose of Part II

(1)   This Part deals with the extent to which the parties to a contract to which this Act applies may by reference to contract terms oust or vary the right to statutory interest

that would otherwise apply when a qualifying debt created by the contract (in this Part referred to as "the debt") is not paid.

(2) This Part applies to contract terms agreed before the debt is created; after that time the parties are free to agree terms dealing with the debt.

(3) This Part has effect without prejudice to any other ground which may affect the validity of a contract term.

8 Circumstances where statutory interest may be ousted or varied

(1) Any contract terms are void to the extent that they purport to exclude the right to statutory interest in relation to the debt, unless there is a substantial contractual remedy for late payment of the debt.

(2) Where the parties agree a contractual remedy for late payment of the debt that is a substantial remedy, statutory interest is not carried by the debt (unless they agree otherwise).

(3) The parties may not agree to vary the right to statutory interest in relation to the debt unless either the right to statutory interest as varied or the overall remedy for late payment of the debt is a substantial remedy.

(4) Any contract terms are void to the extent that they purport to—
  (a) confer a contractual right to interest that is not a substantial remedy for late payment of the debt, or
  (b) vary the right to statutory interest so as to provide for a right to statutory interest that is not a substantial remedy for late payment of the debt,
  unless the overall remedy for late payment of the debt is a substantial remedy.

(5) Subject to this section, the parties are free to agree contract terms which deal with the consequences of late payment of the debt.

9 Meaning of "substantial remedy"

(1) A remedy for the late payment of the debt shall be regarded as a substantial remedy unless—
  (a) the remedy is insufficient either for the purpose of compensating the supplier for late payment or for deterring late payment; and
  (b) it would not be fair or reasonable to allow the remedy to be relied on to oust or (as the case may be) to vary the right to statutory interest that would otherwise apply in relation to the debt.

(2) In determining whether a remedy is not a substantial remedy, regard shall be had to all the relevant circumstances at the time the terms in question are agreed.

(3) In determining whether subsection (1)(b) applies, regard shall be had (without prejudice to the generality of subsection (2)) to the following matters—
  (a) the benefits of commercial certainty;
  (b) the strength of the bargaining positions of the parties relative to each other;
  (c) whether the term was imposed by one party to the detriment of the other (whether by the use of standard terms or otherwise); and
  (d) whether the supplier received an inducement to agree to the term.

10 Interpretation of Part II

(1) In this Part—
  "contract term" means a term of the contract creating the debt or any other contract term binding the parties (or either of them);
  "contractual remedy" means a contractual right to interest or any contractual remedy other than interest;
  "contractual right to interest" includes a reference to a contractual right to charge interest; "overall remedy", in relation to the late payment of the debt, means any combination of a contractual right to interest, a varied right to statutory interest or a contractual remedy other than interest;
  "substantial remedy" shall be construed in accordance with section 9.

(2)   In this Part a reference (however worded) to contract terms which vary the right to statutory interest is a reference to terms altering in any way the effect of Part I in relation to the debt (for example by postponing the time at which interest starts to run or by imposing conditions on the right to interest).

(3)   In this Part a reference to late payment of the debt is a reference to late payment of the sum due when the debt is created (excluding any part of that sum which is prevented from carrying statutory interest by section 3).

PART III

GENERAL AND SUPPLEMENTARY

11   Treatment of advance payments of the contract price

(1)   A qualifying debt created by virtue of an obligation to make an advance payment shall be treated for the purposes of this Act as if it was created on the day mentioned in subsection (3), (4) or (5) (as the case may be).

(2)   In this section "advance payment" means a payment falling due before the obligation of the supplier to which the whole contract price relates ("the supplier's obligation") is performed, other than a payment of a part of the contract price that is due in respect of any part performance of that obligation and payable on or after the day on which that part performance is completed.

(3)   Where the advance payment is the whole contract price, the debt shall be treated as created on the day on which the supplier's obligation is performed.

(4)   Where the advance payment is a part of the contract price, but the sum is not due in respect of any part performance of the supplier's obligation, the debt shall be treated as created on the day on which the supplier's obligation is performed.

(5)   Where the advance payment is a part of the contract price due in respect of any part performance of the supplier's obligation, but is payable before that part performance is completed, the debt shall be treated as created on the day on which the relevant part performance is completed.

(6)   Where the debt is created by virtue of an obligation to pay a sum due in respect of a period of hire of goods, this section has effect as if—

    (a)   references to the day on which the supplier's obligation is performed were references to the last day of that period; and

    (b)   references to part performance of that obligation were references to part of that period.

(7)   For the purposes of this section an obligation to pay the whole outstanding balance of the contract price shall be regarded as an obligation to pay the whole contract price and not as an obligation to pay a part of the contract price.

13   Assignments, etc.

(1)   The operation of this Act in relation to a qualifying debt is not affected by—

    (a)   any change in the identity of the parties to the contract creating the debt; or

    (b)   the passing of the right to be paid the debt, or the duty to pay it (in whole or in part) to a person other than the person who is the original creditor or the original debtor when the debt is created.

(2)   Any reference in this Act to the supplier or the purchaser is a reference to the person who is for the time being the supplier or the purchaser or, in relation to a time after the debt in question has been created, the person who is for the time being the creditor or the debtor, as the case may be.

(3)   Where the right to be paid part of a debt passes to a person other than the person who is the original creditor when the debt is created, any reference in this Act to a debt shall be construed as (or, if the context so requires, as including) a reference to part of a debt.

(4)   A reference in this section to the identity of the parties to a contract changing, or to a right or duty passing, is a reference to it changing or passing by assignment or assignation, by operation of law or otherwise.

14   Contract terms relating to the date for payment of the contract price

(1)   This section applies to any contract term which purports to have the effect of postponing the time at which a qualifying debt would otherwise be created by a contract to which this Act applies.

(2)   Sections 3(2)(b) and 17(1)(b) of the Unfair Contract Terms Act 1977 (no reliance to be placed on certain contract terms) shall apply in cases where such a contract term is not contained in written standard terms of the purchaser as well as in cases where the term is contained in such standard terms.

(3)   In this section "contract term" has the same meaning as in section 10(1).

15   Orders and regulations

(1)   Any power to make an order or regulations under this Act is exercisable by statutory instrument.

(2)   Any statutory instrument containing an order or regulations under this Act, other than an order under section 17(2), shall be subject to annulment in pursuance of a resolution of either House of Parliament.

16   Interpretation

(1)   In this Act—

"contract for the supply of goods or services" has the meaning given in section 2(2); "contract price" means the price in a contract of sale of goods or the money consideration referred to in section 2(2)(b) in any other contract for the supply of goods or services; "purchaser" means (subject to section 13(2)) the buyer in a contract of sale or the person who contracts with the supplier in any other contract for the supply of goods or services;

"qualifying debt" means a debt falling within section 3(1);

"statutory interest" means interest carried by virtue of the term implied by section 1(1); and "supplier" means (subject to section 13(2)) the seller in a contract of sale of goods or the person who does one or more of the things mentioned in section 2(3) in any other contract for the supply of goods or services.

(2)   In this Act any reference (however worded) to an agreement or to contract terms includes a reference to both express and implied terms (including terms established by a course of dealing or by such usage as binds the parties).

17   Short title, commencement and extent

(2)   This Act (apart from this section) shall come into force on such day as the Secretary of State may by order appoint; and different days may be appointed for different descriptions of contract or for other different purposes.

An order under this subsection may specify a description of contract by reference to any feature of the contract (including the parties).

(3)   The Secretary of State may by regulations make such transitional, supplemental or incidental provision (including provision modifying any provision of this Act) as the Secretary of State may consider necessary or expedient in connection with the operation of this Act while it is not fully in force.

(5)   This Act extends to Northern Ireland.

CONTRACTS (RIGHTS OF THIRD PARTIES) ACT 1999
(1999, c. 31)

1   Right of third party to enforce contractual term

(1)   Subject to the provisions of this Act, a person who is not a party to a contract (a "third party") may in his own right enforce a term of the contract if—

(a)   the contract expressly provides that he may, or

(b)   subject to subsection (2), the term purports to confer a benefit on him.

(2)   Subsection (1)(b) does not apply if on a proper construction of the contract it appears that the parties did not intend the term to be enforceable by the third party.

(3)   The third party must be expressly identified in the contract by name, as a member of a class or as answering a particular description but need not be in existence when the contract is entered into.

(4)   This section does not confer a right on a third party to enforce a term of a contract otherwise than subject to and in accordance with any other relevant terms of the contract.

(5)   For the purpose of exercising his right to enforce a term of the contract, there shall be available to the third party any remedy that would have been available to him in an action for breach of contract if he had been a party to the contract (and the rules relating to damages, injunctions, specific performance and other relief shall apply accordingly).

(6)   Where a term of a contract excludes or limits liability in relation to any matter references in this Act to the third party enforcing the term shall be construed as references to his availing himself of the exclusion or limitation.

(7)   In this Act, in relation to a term of a contract which is enforceable by a third party—
"the promisor" means the party to the contract against whom the term is enforceable by the third party, and
"the promisee" means the party to the contract by whom the term is enforceable against the promisor.

2   Variation and rescission of contract

(1)   Subject to the provisions of this section, where a third party has a right under section 1 to enforce a term of the contract, the parties to the contract may not, by agreement, rescind the contract, or vary it in such a way as to extinguish or alter his entitlement under that right, without his consent if—
(a)   the third party has communicated his assent to the term to the promisor,
(b)   the promisor is aware that the third party has relied on the term, or
(c)   the promisor can reasonably be expected to have foreseen that the third party would rely on the term and the third party has in fact relied on it.

(2)   The assent referred to in subsection (1)(a)—
(a)   may be by words or conduct, and
(b)   if sent to the promisor by post or other means, shall not be regarded as communicated to the promisor until received by him.

(3)   Subsection (1) is subject to any express term of the contract under which—
(a)   the parties to the contract may by agreement rescind or vary the contract without the consent of the third party, or
(b)   the consent of the third party is required in circumstances specified in the contract instead of those set out in subsection (1)(a) to (c).

(4)   Where the consent of a third party is required under subsection (1) or (3), the court or arbitral tribunal may, on the application of the parties to the contract, dispense with his consent if satisfied—
(a)   that his consent cannot be obtained because his whereabouts cannot reasonably be ascertained, or
(b)   that he is mentally incapable of giving his consent.

(5)   The court or arbitral tribunal may, on the application of the parties to a contract, dispense with any consent that may be required under subsection (1)(c) if satisfied that it cannot reasonably be ascertained whether or not the third party has in fact relied on the term.

(6)   If the court or arbitral tribunal dispenses with a third party's consent, it may impose such conditions as it thinks fit, including a condition requiring the payment of compensation to the third party.

(7)   The jurisdiction conferred on the court by subsections (4) to (6) is exercisable in England and Wales by both the High Court and the County Court and In Northern Ireland by both the High Court and a county court.

3   Defences etc. available to promisor

(1)   Subsections (2) to (5) apply where, in reliance on section 1, proceedings for the enforcement of a term of a contract are brought by a third party.

(2)   The promisor shall have available to him by way of defence or set-off any matter that—
     (a)   arises from or in connection with the contract and is relevant to the term, and
     (b)   would have been available to him by way of defence or set-off if the proceedings had been brought by the promisee.
(3)   The promisor shall also have available to him by way of defence or set-off any matter if—
     (a)   an express term of the contract provides for it to be available to him in proceedings brought by the third party, and
     (b)   it would have been available to him by way of defence or set-off if the proceedings had been brought by the promisee.
(4)   The promisor shall also have available to him—
     (a)   by way of defence or set-off any matter, and
     (b)   by way of counterclaim any matter not arising from the contract,
     that would have been available to him by way of defence or set-off or, as the case may be, by way of counterclaim against the third party if the third party had been a party to the contract.
(5)   Subsections (2) and (4) are subject to any express term of the contract as to the matters that are not to be available to the promisor by way of defence, set-off or counterclaim.
(6)   Where in any proceedings brought against him a third party seeks in reliance on section 1 to enforce a term of a contract (including, in particular, a term purporting to exclude or limit liability), he may not do so if he could not have done so (whether by reason of any particular circumstances relating to him or otherwise) had he been a party to the contract.

4   Enforcement of contract by promisee

Section 1 does not affect any right of the promisee to enforce any term of the contract.

5   Protection of promisor from double liability

Where under section 1 a term of a contract is enforceable by a third party, and the promisee has recovered from the promisor a sum in respect of—
     (a)   the third party's loss in respect of the term, or
     (b)   the expense to the promisee of making good to the third party the default of the promisor,
then, in any proceedings brought in reliance on that section by the third party, the court or arbitral tribunal shall reduce any award to the third party to such extent as it thinks appropriate to take account of the sum recovered by the promisee.

6   Exceptions

(1)   Section 1 confers no rights on a third party in the case of a contract on a bill of exchange, promissory note or other negotiable instrument.
(2)   Section 1 confers no rights on a third party in the case of any contract binding on a company and its members under section 33 of the Companies Act 2006 (effect of a company's constitution).
(2A) Section 1 confers no rights on a third party in the case of any incorporation document of a limited liability partnership or any agreement (express or implied) between the members of a limited liability partnership, or between a limited liability partnership and its members, that determines the mutual rights of the members and their rights and duties in relation to the limited liability partnership.
(3)   Section 1 confers no right on a third party to enforce—
     (a)   any term of a contract of employment against an employee,
     (b)   any term of a worker's contract against a worker (including a home worker), or
     (c)   any term of a relevant contract against an agency worker.
(4)   In subsection (3)—
     (a)   "contract of employment", "employee", "worker's contract", and "worker" have the meaning given by section 54 of the National Minimum Wage Act 1998,
     (b)   "home worker" has the meaning given by section 35(2) of that Act,
     (c)   "agency worker" has the same meaning as in section 34(1) of that Act, and
     (d)   "relevant contract" means a contract entered into, in a case where section 34 of that Act applies, by the agency worker as respects work falling within subsection (1)(a) of that section.

(5) Section 1 confers no rights on a third party in the case of—
   (a) a contract for the carriage of goods by sea, or
   (b) a contract for the carriage of goods by rail or road, or for the carriage of cargo by air, which is subject to the rules of the appropriate international transport convention,

except that a third party may in reliance on that section avail himself of an exclusion or limitation of liability in such a contract.

(6) In subsection (5) "contract for the carriage of goods by sea" means a contract of carriage—
   (a) contained in or evidenced by a bill of lading, sea waybill or a corresponding electronic transaction, or
   (b) under or for the purposes of which there is given an undertaking which is contained in a ship's delivery order or a corresponding electronic transaction.

(7) For the purposes of subsection (6)—
   (a) "bill of lading", "sea waybill" and "ship's delivery order" have the same meaning as in the Carriage of Goods by Sea Act 1992, and
   (b) a corresponding electronic transaction is a transaction within section 1(5) of that Act which corresponds to the issue, indorsement, delivery or transfer of a bill of lading, sea waybill or ship's delivery order.

(8) In subsection (5) "the appropriate international transport convention" means—
   (a) in relation to a contract for the carriage of goods by rail, the Convention which has the force of law in the United Kingdom under regulation 3 of the Railways (Convention on International Carriage by Rail) Regulations 2005,
   (b) in relation to a contract for the carriage of goods by road, the Convention which has the force of law in the United Kingdom under section 1 of the Carriage of Goods by Road Act 1965, and
   (c) in relation to a contract for the carriage of cargo by air—
      (i) the Convention which has the force of law in the United Kingdom under section 1 of the Carriage by Air Act 1961, or
      (ii) the Convention which has the force of law under section 1 of the Carriage by Air (Supplementary Provisions) Act 1962, or
      (iii) either of the amended Conventions set out in Part B of Schedule 2 or 3 to the Carriage by Air Acts (Application of Provisions) Order 1967.

7   Supplementary provisions relating to third party

(1) Section 1 does not affect any right or remedy of a third party that exists or is available apart from this Act.
(2) Section 2(2) of the Unfair Contract Terms Act 1977 (restriction on exclusion etc. of liability for negligence) shall not apply where the negligence consists of the breach of an obligation arising from a term of a contract and the person seeking to enforce it is a third party acting in reliance on section 1.
(3) In sections 5 and 8 of the Limitation Act 1980 the references to an action founded on a simple contract and an action upon a specialty shall respectively include references to an action brought in reliance on section 1 relating to a simple contract and an action brought in reliance on that section relating to a specialty.
(4) A third party shall not, by virtue of section 1(5) or 3(4) or (6), be treated as a party to the contract for the purposes of any other Act (or any instrument made under any other Act).

8   Arbitration provisions

(1) Where—
   (a) a right under section 1 to enforce a term ("the substantive term") is subject to a term providing for the submission of disputes to arbitration ("the arbitration agreement"), and
   (b) the arbitration agreement is an agreement in writing for the purposes of Part I of the Arbitration Act 1996,

the third party shall be treated for the purposes of that Act as a party to the arbitration agreement as regards disputes between himself and the promisor relating to the enforcement of the substantive term by the third party.

(2)   Where—

    (a)   a third party has a right under section 1 to enforce a term providing for one or more descriptions of dispute between the third party and the promisor to be submitted to arbitration ("the arbitration agreement"),

    (b)   the arbitration agreement is an agreement in writing for the purposes of Part I of the Arbitration Act 1996, and

    (c)   the third party does not fall to be treated under subsection (1) as a party to the arbitration agreement,

the third party shall, if he exercises the right, be treated for the purposes of that Act as a party to the arbitration agreement in relation to the matter with respect to which the right is exercised, and be treated as having been so immediately before the exercise of the right.

9   Northern Ireland

(1)   In its application to Northern Ireland, this Act has effect with the modifications specified in subsections (2) and (3).

(3)   In section 7, for subsection (3) there is substituted—

"(3) In Articles 4(a) and 15 of the Limitation (Northern Ireland) Order 1989, the references to an action founded on a simple contract and an action upon an instrument under seal shall respectively include references to an action brought in reliance on section 1 relating to a simple contract and an action brought in reliance on that section relating to a contract under seal.".

10   Short title, commencement and extent

(1)   This Act may be cited as the Contracts (Rights of Third Parties) Act 1999.

(2)   This Act comes into force on the day on which it is passed but, subject to subsection (3), does not apply in relation to a contract entered into before the end of the period of six months beginning with that day.

(3)   The restriction in subsection (2) does not apply in relation to a contract which—

    (a)   is entered into on or after the day on which this Act is passed, and

    (b)   expressly provides for the application of this Act.

(4)   This Act extends as follows—

    (a)   section 9 extends to Northern Ireland only;

    (b)   the remaining provisions extend to England and Wales and Northern Ireland only.

COUNTRYSIDE AND RIGHTS OF WAY ACT 2000
(2000, c. 37)

1   Principal definitions for Part I

(1)   In this Part "access land" means any land which—

    (a)   is shown as open country on a map in conclusive form issued by the appropriate countryside body for the purposes of this Part,

    (b)   is shown on such a map as registered common land,

    (c)   is registered common land in any area outside Inner London for which no such map relating to registered common land has been issued,

    (d)   is situated more than 600 metres above sea level in any area for which no such map relating to open country has been issued,

    (da)   is coastal margin, or

    (e)   is dedicated for the purposes of this Part under section 16,

but does not (in any of those cases) include excepted land or land which is treated by section 15(1) as being accessible to the public apart from this Act.

2   Rights of public in relation to access land

(1)   Any person is entitled by virtue of this subsection to enter and remain on any access land for the purposes of open-air recreation, if and so long as—

    (a)   he does so without breaking or damaging any wall, fence, hedge, stile or gate, and

      (b)   he observes the general restrictions in Schedule 2 and any other restrictions imposed in relation to the land under Chapter II.

(2)   Subsection (1) has effect subject to subsections (3) and (4) and to the provisions of Chapter II.

(3)   Subsection (1) does not entitle a person to enter or be on any land, or do anything on any land, in contravention of any relevant statutory prohibition.

(3A) In subsection (3) "relevant statutory prohibition" means—

      (a)   in the case of land which is coastal margin, a prohibition contained in or having effect under any enactment, and

      (b)   in any other case, a prohibition contained in or having effect under any enactment other than an enactment contained in a local or private Act.

(4)   If a person becomes a trespasser on any access land by failing to comply with—

      (a)   subsection (1)(a),

      (b)   the general restrictions in Schedule 2, or

      (c)   any other restrictions imposed in relation to the land under Chapter II,

he may not, within 72 hours after leaving that land, exercise his right under subsection (1) to enter that land again or to enter other land in the same ownership.

12   Effect of right of access on rights and liabilities of owners

(1)   The operation of section 2(1) in relation to any access land does not increase the liability, under any enactment not contained in this Act or under any rule of law, of a person interested in the access land or any adjoining land in respect of the state of the land or of things done or omitted to be done on the land.

(2)   Any restriction arising under a covenant or otherwise as to the use of any access land shall have effect subject to the provisions of this Part, and any liability of a person interested in any access land in respect of such a restriction is limited accordingly.

(3)   For the purposes of any enactment or rule of law as to the circumstances in which the dedication of a highway or the grant of an easement may be presumed, or may be established by prescription, the use by the public or by any person of a way across land in the exercise of the right conferred by section 2(1) is to be disregarded.

(4)   The use of any land by the inhabitants of any locality for the purposes of open-air recreation in the exercise of the right conferred by section 2(1) is to be disregarded in determining whether the land has become a town or village green.

POSTAL SERVICES ACT 2000
(2000, c. 26)

PART 6
POSTAL SERVICES: SUPPLEMENTARY

Schemes and limitation of liability

89   Schemes as to terms and conditions for provision of postal services

(1)   A postal operator may make a scheme under this section in relation to any or all of the postal services provided by the operator.

(2)   A scheme under this section is a scheme for determining any or all of the following (so far as not otherwise agreed)—

      (a)   the charges which are to be imposed in respect of the services concerned, and

      (b)   the other terms and conditions which are to be applicable to the services concerned,

      (c)   ...

(3)   A scheme under this section may, in particular—

      (a)   adopt such system for the determination of the charges and other terms and conditions as the postal operator concerned considers appropriate (including determining them himself subject to any conditions and limitations provided for in the scheme),

     (b)   specify the manner in which, time and place at which and person by whom the charges are to be paid.

(4)   Subject to section 92(5) and (6), no provision may be made in any scheme under this section—

    (a)   for limiting the liability of the postal operator concerned for loss or damage, or

    (b)   for amending the rules of law relating to evidence.

(5)   A scheme under this section shall come into force on such day as is specified in the scheme; but no day earlier than the day after that on which the scheme has been published in the London, Edinburgh and Belfast Gazettes shall be so specified.

(6)   A scheme under this section may—

    (a)   make different provision for different cases or classes of case determined by, or in accordance with, the provisions of the scheme,

    (b)   modify any previous scheme made under this section.

(7)   Any charge payable by virtue of this section may be recovered by the postal operator concerned and in England and Wales and Northern Ireland may be so recovered as a civil debt due to him.

(8)   The production of a copy of any of the Gazettes mentioned in subsection (5) which purports to contain a scheme under this section shall be conclusive evidence in all legal proceedings of that scheme.

89A   Powers of OFCOM in relation to schemes

(1)   A postal operator may not make a scheme under section 89 unless—

    (a)   the operator has notified OFCOM of the scheme that the operator is proposing to make, and

    (b)   the operator has carried out a consultation exercise in relation to the proposed scheme in accordance with requirements contained in a notification published by OFCOM.

(2)   OFCOM may give a direction to a postal operator who has notified a scheme to them under subsection (1)(a) requiring the operator to make such modifications of the scheme as are specified in the direction.

(3)   Before giving a direction under subsection (2), OFCOM must publish a notification—

    (a)   setting out the terms of the scheme that the operator proposes to make,

    (b)   stating that OFCOM are proposing to give a direction under subsection (2) modifying the scheme,

    (c)   setting out the effect of the proposed modification,

    (d)   giving reasons for making the proposed modification, and

    (e)   specifying the period within which representations may be made to them about the proposed modification.

(4)   The specified period must be at least one month beginning with the day after the day the notification under subsection (3) is published.

(5)   OFCOM may not give a direction under subsection (2) unless they have considered every representation and proposal made to them during the period specified in that notification.

(6)   If the scheme is not in force at the time at which that notification is published, the operator may not bring the scheme into force until such time as OFCOM may direct.

(7)   OFCOM must publish a notification of any direction that they make under subsection (2).

(8)   The publication of a notification under this section must be in such manner as OFCOM consider appropriate for bringing its contents to the attention of such persons as they consider appropriate.

(9)   An obligation imposed on a postal operator by a direction under subsection (2) is enforceable by OFCOM under Schedule 7 to the Postal Services Act 2011 (enforcement of regulatory requirements).

90   Exclusion of liability

(A1) This section applies in relation to—

    (a)   the provision by a universal service provider of a universal postal service, and

    (b)   the provision by a postal operator of a service in relation to which a scheme under section 89 (made by the operator) applies.

(A2) In this section—
    (a)   "the operator" means the universal service provider or the postal operator concerned, and
    (b)   "the service" means the service mentioned in subsection (A1)(a) or (b) (as the case may be).

(1)   No proceedings in tort shall lie or, in Scotland, be competent against the operator in respect of loss or damage suffered by any person in connection with the provision of the service because of—
    (a)   anything done or omitted to be done in relation to any postal packet in the course of transmission by post, or
    (b)   any omission to carry out arrangements for the collection of anything to be conveyed by post.

(2)   No officer, servant, employee, agent or sub-contractor of the operator shall be subject, except at the suit or instance of the operator, to any civil liability for—
    (a)   any loss or damage in the case of which liability of the operator is excluded by subsection (1), or
    (b)   any loss of, or damage to, a postal packet to which section 91 applies.

(3)   No person engaged in or about the conveyance of postal packets and no officer, servant, employee, agent or sub-contractor of any such person shall be subject, except at the suit or instance of the operator, to any civil liability for—
    (a)   any loss or damage in the case of which liability of the operator is excluded by subsection (1), or
    (b)   any loss of, or damage to, a postal packet to which section 91 applies.

(4)   In the application of subsection (1) to Scotland, the reference to proceedings in tort shall be construed in the same way as in section 43(b) of the Crown Proceedings Act 1947.

(5)   This section is subject to section 91.

91   Limited liability for postal packets

(1)   Proceedings shall lie or, in Scotland, be competent against a postal operator under this section, but not otherwise, in respect of relevant loss of, or relevant damage to, a postal packet in respect of which the operator accepts liability under this section in pursuance of a scheme made under section 89.

(2)   The references in subsection (1) to relevant loss or damage are to loss or damage so far as it is due to any wrongful act of, or any neglect or default by, an officer, servant, employee, agent or sub-contractor of the postal operator while performing or purporting to perform in that capacity his functions in relation to the receipt, conveyance, delivery or other dealing with the packet.

(3)   No proceedings shall lie or, in Scotland, be competent under this section in relation to a packet unless they are begun within the period of twelve months starting with the day on which the packet was posted.

(4)   A postal operator shall not be liable under this section in respect of a packet of any description unless such conditions (if any) as are required by a scheme under section 89 to be complied with in relation to packets of that description at the time when they are posted have been complied with in the case of the packet.

(5)   For the purposes of this section and section 92 a scheme under section 89 may define a description of packet by reference to any circumstances whatever (including, in particular, the amount of any fee paid in respect of the packet in pursuance of the scheme).

(6)   ...

POWERS OF CRIMINAL COURTS (SENTENCING) ACT 2000
(2000, c. 6)

130   Compensation orders against convicted persons

(1)   A court by or before which a person is convicted of an offence, instead of or in addition to dealing with him in any other way, may, on application or otherwise, make an order (in this Act referred to as a "compensation order") requiring him—
    (a)   to pay compensation for any personal injury, loss or damage resulting from that offence or any other offence which is taken into consideration by the court in determining sentence; or

(b)   to make payments for funeral expenses or bereavement in respect of a death resulting from any such offence, other than a death due to an accident arising out of the presence of a motor vehicle on a road; but this is subject to the following provisions of this section and to section 131 below.

(2)   Where the person is convicted of an offence the sentence for which is fixed by law or falls to be imposed under a provision mentioned in subsection (2ZA), subsection (1) above shall have effect as if the words "instead of or" were omitted.

(2ZA)The provisions referred to in subsection (2) are—

    (a)   Section 1(2B) or 1A(5) of the Prevention of Crime Act 1953;

    (b)   Section 51A(2) of the Firearms Act 1968;

    (c)   Section 139(6B), 139A(5B) or 139AA(7) of the Criminal Justice Act 1988;

    (d)   Section 110(2) or 111(2) of this Act;

    (e)   Section 224A, 225(2) or 226(2) of the Criminal Justice Act 2003;

    (f)   Section 29(4) or (6) of the Violent Crime Reduction Act 2006.

(2A) A court must consider making a compensation order in any case where this section empowers it to do so.

(3)   A court shall give reasons, on passing sentence, if it does not make a compensation order in a case where this section empowers it to do so.

(4)   Compensation under subsection (1) above shall be of such amount as the court considers appropriate, having regard to any evidence and to any representations that are made by or on behalf of the accused or the prosecutor.

(5)   In the case of an offence under the Theft Act 1968 or the Fraud Act 2006, where the property in question is recovered, any damage to the property occurring while it was out of the owner's possession shall be treated for the purposes of subsection (1) above as having resulted from the offence, however and by whomever the damage was caused.

(6)   A compensation order may only be made in respect of injury, loss or damage (other than loss suffered by a person's dependants in consequence of his death) which was due to an accident arising out of the presence of a motor vehicle on a road, if

    (a)   it is in respect of damage which is treated by subsection (5) above as resulting from an offence under the Theft Act 1968 or the Fraud Act 2006; or

    (b)   it is in respect of injury, loss or damage as respects which—

        (i)   the offender is uninsured in relation to the use of the vehicle; and

        (ii)   compensation is not payable under any arrangements to which the Secretary of State is a party.

(7)   Where a compensation order is made in respect of injury, loss or damage due to an accident arising out of the presence of a motor vehicle on a road, the amount to be paid may include an amount representing the whole or part of any loss of or reduction in preferential rates of insurance attributable to the accident.

(8)   A vehicle the use of which is exempted from insurance by section 144 of the Road Traffic Act 1988 is not uninsured for the purposes of subsection (6) above.

(9)   A compensation order in respect of funeral expenses may be made for the benefit of anyone who incurred the expenses.

(10) A compensation order in respect of bereavement may be made only for the benefit of a person for whose benefit a claim for damages for bereavement could be made under section 1A of the Fatal Accidents Act 1976; and the amount of compensation in respect of bereavement shall not exceed the amount for the time being specified in section 1A(3) of that Act.

(11) In determining whether to make a compensation order against any person, and in determining the amount to be paid by any person under such an order, the court shall have regard to his means so far as they appear or are known to the court.

(12) Where the court considers—

    (a)   that it would be appropriate both to impose a fine and to make a compensation order, but

    (b)   that the offender has insufficient means to pay both an appropriate fine and appropriate compensation, the court shall give preference to compensation (though it may impose a fine as well).

134   Effect of compensation order on subsequent award of damages in civil proceedings

(1)   This section shall have effect where a compensation order, or a service compensation order, has been made in favour of any person in respect of any injury, loss or damage and a claim by him in civil proceedings for damages in respect of the injury, loss or damage subsequently falls to be determined.

(2)   The damages in the civil proceedings shall be assessed without regard to the order, but the plaintiff may only recover an amount equal to the aggregate of the following—

(a)   any amount by which they exceed the compensation; and

(b)   a sum equal to any portion of the compensation which he fails to recover,

and may not enforce the judgment, so far as it relates to a sum such as is mentioned in paragraph (b) above, without the leave of the court.

(3)   In this section a "service compensation order or award" means a service compensation order under the Armed Forces Act 2006.

POLICE REFORM ACT 2002
(2002, c. 29)

PART 4
POLICE POWERS ETC.

CHAPTER 1
EXERCISE OF POLICE POWERS ETC. BY CIVILIANS

38   Police powers for civilian staff

(1)   The chief officer of police of any police force may designate a relevant employee as an officer of one or more of the descriptions specified in subsection (2).

(2)   The description of officers are as follows—

(a)   community support officer;

(b)   investigating officer;

(c)   detention officer;

(d)   escort officer.

(3)   ...

(4)   A chief officer of police ... shall not designate a person under this section unless he is satisfied that that person—

(a)   is a suitable person to carry out the functions for the purposes of which he is designated;

(b)   is capable of effectively carrying out those functions; and

(c)   has received adequate training in the carrying out of those functions and in the exercise and performance of the powers and duties to be conferred or imposed on him by virtue of the designation.

(5)   A person designated under this section shall have the powers and duties conferred or imposed on him by the designation.

(5A)   A person designated under this section as a community support officer shall also have the standard powers and duties of a community support officer (see section 38A(2)).

(5B)   The reference in subsection (4)(c) to the powers and duties to be conferred or imposed on a person by virtue of his designation, so far as it is a reference to the standard powers and duties of a community support officer, is a reference to the powers and duties that at the time of the person's designation are the standard powers and duties of a community support officer.

(6)   Powers and duties may be conferred or imposed on a designated person by means only of the application to him by his designation of provisions of the applicable Part of Schedule 4 that are to apply to the designated person; and for this purpose the applicable part of that Schedule is—

(a)   in the case of a person designated as a community support officer, Part 1;

(b)   in the case of a person designated as an investigating officer, Part 2;

(c)   in the case of a person designated as a detention officer, Part 3; and

(d)   in the case of a person designated as an escort officer, Part 4.

(6A) Subsection (6) has effect subject to subsections (5A) and (8).

(7)   A relevant employee ... authorised or required to do anything by virtue of a designation under this section—

(a)   shall not be authorised or required by virtue of that designation to engage in any conduct otherwise than in the course of that employment; and

(b)   shall be so authorised or required subject to such restrictions and conditions (if any) as may be specified in his designation.

(8)   Where any power exercisable by any person in reliance on his designation under this section is a power which, in the case of its exercise by a constable, includes or is supplemented by a power to use reasonable force, any person exercising that power in reliance on that designation shall have the same entitlement as a constable to use reasonable force.

(9)   Where any power exercisable by any person in reliance on his designation under this section includes power to use force to enter any premises, that power shall not be exercisable by that person except—

(a)   in the company, and under the supervision, of a constable; or

(b)   for the purpose of saving life or limb or preventing serious damage to property.

(11) In this section "relevant employee" means—

(a)   in the case of—

(i)   a police force maintained for a police area in accordance with section 2 of the Police Act 1996.or

(ii)   the police force maintained for the metropolitan district in accordance with section 5A of that Act,

a member of the civilian staff of that police force (within the meaning of Part 1 of the Police Reform and Social Responsibility Act 2011);

(b)   in the case of any other police force, a person who—

(i)   is employed by the police authority maintaining that force, and

(ii)   is under the direction and control of the chief officer making a designation under subsection (1).

CRIMINAL JUSTICE ACT 2003
(2003, c. 39)

Civil proceedings brought by offenders

329   Civil proceedings for trespass to the person brought by offender

(1)   This section applies where—

(a)   a person ("the claimant") claims that another person ("the defendant") did an act amounting to trespass to the claimant's person, and

(b)   the claimant has been convicted in the United Kingdom of an imprisonable offence committed on the same occasion as that on which the act is alleged to have been done.

(2)   Civil proceedings relating to the claim may be brought only with the permission of the court.

(3)   The court may give permission for the proceedings to be brought only if there is evidence that either—

(a)   the condition in subsection (5) is not met, or

(b)   in all the circumstances, the defendant's act was grossly disproportionate.

(4)   If the court gives permission and the proceedings are brought, it is a defence for the defendant to prove both—

(a)   that the condition in subsection (5) is met, and

(b)   that, in all the circumstances, his act was not grossly disproportionate.

(5) The condition referred to in subsection (3)(a) and (4)(a) is that the defendant did the act only because—

    (a) he believed that the claimant—

        (i) was about to commit an offence,

        (ii) was in the course of committing an offence, or

        (iii) had committed an offence immediately beforehand; and

    (b) he believed that the act was necessary to—

        (i) defend himself or another person,

        (ii) protect or recover property,

        (iii) prevent the commission or continuation of an offence, or

        (iv) apprehend, or secure the conviction, of the claimant after he had committed an offence;

    or was necessary to assist in achieving any of those things.

(6) Subsection (4) is without prejudice to any other defence.

(7) Where—

    (a) a person is convicted of an offence under section 42 of the Armed Forces Act 2006 (criminal conduct), and

    (b) the corresponding civil offence (within the meaning of that Act) was an imprisonable offence,

he is to be treated for the purposes of this section as having been convicted in the United Kingdom of the corresponding civil offence; and in paragraph (a) the reference to conviction includes anything that under section 376(1) and (2) of that Act is to be treated as a conviction.

(8) In this section—

    (a) the reference to trespass to the person is a reference to—

        (i) assault,

        (ii) battery, or

        (iii) false imprisonment;

    (b) references to a defendant's belief are to his honest belief, whether or not the belief was also reasonable;

    (c) "court" means the High Court or the county court; and

    (d) "imprisonable offence" means an offence which, in the case of a person aged 18 or over, is punishable by imprisonment.

HEALTH AND SOCIAL CARE (COMMUNITY HEALTH AND STANDARDS) ACT 2003
(2003, c. 43)

PART 3
RECOVERY OF NHS CHARGES

NHS charges

150 Liability to pay NHS charges

(1) This section applies if—

    (a) a person makes a compensation payment to or in respect of any other person (the "injured person") in consequence of any injury, whether physical or psychological, suffered by the injured person, and

    (b) the injured person has—

        (i) received NHS treatment at a health service hospital as a result of the injury,

        (ii) been provided with NHS ambulance services as a result of the injury for the purpose of taking him to a health service hospital for NHS treatment (unless he was dead on arrival at that hospital), or

        (iii) received treatment as mentioned in sub-paragraph (i) and been provided with ambulance services as mentioned in sub-paragraph (ii).

(2) The person making the compensation payment is liable to pay the relevant NHS charges—

    (a) in respect of—

        (i)   the treatment, in so far as received at a hospital in England or Wales,

        (ii) the ambulance services, in so far as provided to take the injured person to such a hospital,

    to the Secretary of State,

    (b) in respect of—

        (i)   the treatment, in so far as received at a hospital in Scotland,

        (ii) the ambulance services, in so far as provided to take the injured person to such a hospital,

    to the Scottish Ministers.

(3) "Compensation payment" means a payment, including a payment in money's worth, made—

    (a) by or on behalf of a person who is, or is alleged to be, liable to any extent in respect of the injury, or

    (b) in pursuance of a compensation scheme for motor accidents, but does not include a payment mentioned in Schedule 10.

(4) Subsection (1)(a) applies—

    (a) to a payment made—

        (i)   voluntarily, or in pursuance of a court order or an agreement, or otherwise, and

        (ii) in the United Kingdom or elsewhere, and

    (b) if more than one payment is made, to each payment.

(5) "Injury" does not include any disease.

(6) Nothing in subsection (5) prevents this Part from applying to—

    (a) treatment received as a result of any disease suffered by the injured person, or

    (b) ambulance services provided as a result of any disease suffered by him,

if the disease in question is attributable to the injury suffered by the injured person (and accordingly that treatment is received or those services are provided as a result of the injury).

(7) "NHS treatment" means any treatment (including any examination of the injured person) other than—

    (a) treatment provided by virtue of—

        (i)   section 21(4) or 44(6) of the 2006 Act,

        (ii)   paragraph 15 of Schedule 2 to, or paragraph 11 of Schedule 6 to, the 2006 Act,

        (iii) paragraph 15 of Schedule 2 to, or paragraph 11 of Schedule 5 to, the National Health Service (Wales) Act 2006, or

        (iv)   section 57 of, or paragraph 14 of Schedule 7A to, the 1978 Act, (accommodation and services for private patients)

    (b) other treatment provided by an NHS foundation trust in pursuance of an undertaking to pay in respect of the treatment given by or on behalf of the injured person,

    (c) treatment provided at a health service hospital by virtue of section 267 of the 2006 Act or section 198 of the National Health Service (Wales) Act 2006 or section 64 of the 1978 Act (permission for use of national health service accommodation or facilities in private practice), or

    (d) treatment provided by virtue of—

        (i)   section 83, 84, 92, 99, 100 or 107 of the 2006 Act, or section 41, 42, 50, 56, 57 or 64 of the National Health Service (Wales) Act 2006 (primary medical and dental services), or

        (ii) section 17C, 19 or 25 of the 1978 Act (personal or general medical or dental services).

(8) In relation to any time before sections 170 and 172 come into force, the references in subsection (7)(d)(i) to sections 16CA and 28K of the 1977 Act are to be taken as a reference to section 35 of that Act (arrangements for general dental services).

(9) In relation to any time before sections 174 and 175 come into force, the references in subsection (7)(d)(i) to sections 16CC and 28Q of the 1977 Act are to be taken as a reference to section 29 of that Act (arrangements for general medical services).

(10) "Relevant NHS charges" means the amount (or amounts) specified in a certificate of NHS charges—
   (a)   issued under this Part, in respect of the injured person, to the person making the compensation payment, and
   (b)   in force.

(11) "Compensation scheme for motor accidents" means any scheme or arrangement under which funds are available for the payment of compensation in respect of motor accidents caused, or alleged to have been caused, by uninsured or unidentified persons.

(12) Regulations may amend Schedule 10 by omitting or modifying any payment for the time being specified in that Schedule.

(13) This section applies in relation to any injury which occurs after the date on which this section comes into force.

(14) For the purposes of this Part, it is irrelevant whether a compensation payment is made with or without an admission of liability.

Certificates of NHS charges

151   Applications for certificates of NHS charges

(1)   Before a person makes a compensation payment in consequence of any injury suffered by an injured person, he may apply for a certificate to the Secretary of State, the Scottish Ministers or both, according to whether he believes the relevant NHS charges payable by him (if any) would be due to the Secretary of State, the Scottish Ministers or both.

(2)   If the Secretary of State receives or the Scottish Ministers receive an application under subsection (1), he or they must arrange for a certificate to be issued as soon as is reasonably practicable (subject to section 152).

(3)   A certificate may provide that it is to remain in force—
   (a)   until a specified date,
   (b)   until the occurrence of a specified event, or
   (c)   indefinitely.

(4)   A person may apply under subsection (1) for a fresh certificate from time to time.

(5)   Subsection (2) does not require the Secretary of State or the Scottish Ministers to arrange for a fresh certificate to be issued to a person applying under subsection (4) if, when the application is received, a certificate issued to the applicant in respect of the injured person is still in force; but the Secretary of State or the Scottish Ministers (as the case may be) may arrange for a fresh certificate to be issued so as to have effect on the expiry of the current certificate.

(6)   If a certificate expires, the Secretary of State or the Scottish Ministers (as the case may be) may arrange for a fresh certificate to be issued without an application having to be made.

(7)   In the circumstances mentioned in subsection (8), a person who has made a compensation payment in consequence of an injury suffered by an injured person must apply for a certificate to the Secretary of State, the Scottish Ministers or both, according to whether he believes the relevant NHS charges payable by him (if any) would be due to the Secretary of State, the Scottish Ministers or both.

(8)   The circumstances are that—
   (a)   at the time the payment is made by the person—
      (i)   no certificate has been issued to him in respect of the injured person, or
      (ii)   if such a certificate has been issued to him, it is no longer in force, and
   (b)   no application for a certificate has been made by him during the prescribed period ending immediately before the day on which the compensation payment is made.

(9)   An application for a certificate must be made in the prescribed manner and, in the case of an application under subsection (7), within the prescribed period.

(10) On receiving an application under subsection (7), the Secretary of State or the Scottish Ministers must arrange for a certificate to be issued as soon as is reasonably practicable (subject to section 152).

(11) In this section and section 152, "relevant NHS charges" has the meaning given in section 150(10).

153   Information contained in certificates

(1)   A certificate must specify the amount (or amounts) for which the person to whom it is issued is liable under section 150(2).

(2)   The amount (or amounts) to be specified is (or are) to be that (or those) set out in, or determined in accordance with, regulations, reduced if applicable in accordance with subsection (3) or regulations under subsection (10).

(3)   If a certificate relates to a claim made by or on behalf of an injured person—

(a)   in respect of which a court in England and Wales or Scotland has ordered a reduction of damages in accordance with section 1 of the Law Reform (Contributory Negligence) Act 1945,

(b)   in respect of which a court in Northern Ireland has ordered a reduction of damages in accordance with section 2 of the Law Reform (Miscellaneous Provisions) Act (Northern Ireland) 1948,

(c)   in respect of which a court in a country other than England and Wales, Scotland or Northern Ireland has ordered a reduction of damages under any provision of the law of that country which appears to the Secretary of State or the Scottish Ministers (as the case may be) to correspond to section 1 of the Law Reform (Contributory Negligence) Act 1945,

(d)   in respect of which an officer of a court in England and Wales or Northern Ireland has entered or sealed an agreed judgement or order which specifies—

(i)   that the damages are to be reduced to reflect the injured person's share in the responsibility for the injury in question, and

(ii)   the amount or proportion by which they are to be so reduced,

(e)   in the case of which the parties to any resulting action before a court in Scotland have executed a joint minute which specifies—

(i)   that the action has been settled extra-judicially, and

(ii)   the matters mentioned in paragraph (d)(i) and (ii),

(f)   in respect of which a document has been made under any provision of the law of a country other than England and Wales, Scotland or Northern Ireland—

(i)   which appears to the Secretary of State to correspond to an agreed judgement or order entered or sealed by an officer of a court in England and Wales, and

(ii)   which specifies the matters mentioned in paragraph (d)(i) and (ii), or

(g)   in the case of which a document has been made under any provision of the law of a country other than England and Wales, Scotland or Northern Ireland—

(i)   which appears to the Scottish Ministers to correspond to a joint minute executed by the parties to a resulting action before a court in Scotland specifying that the action has been settled extra-judicially, and

(ii)   which specifies the matters mentioned in paragraph (d) (i) and (ii),

the amount (or amounts) specified in the certificate is (or are) to be that (or those) which would be so specified apart from this subsection, reduced by the same proportion as the reduction of damages.

(4)   If a certificate relates to an injured person who has not received NHS treatment at a health service hospital or been provided with NHS ambulance services as a result of the injury, it must indicate that no amount is payable to the Secretary of State or the Scottish Ministers (as the case may be) by reference to that certificate.

Recovery of NHS charges

154   Payment of NHS charges

(1)   If the certificate by reference to which an amount payable under section 150(2) is determined is issued before the settlement date, that amount must be paid before the end of the period of 14 days beginning with the settlement date.

(2)   If the certificate by reference to which an amount payable under section 150(2) is determined is issued on or after the settlement date, that amount must be paid before the end of the period of 14 days beginning with the day on which the certificate is issued.

(3)   "Settlement date" means the date on which the compensation payment is made.

(4)   This section is subject to section 155(2).

155   Recovery of NHS charges

(1)   This section applies if a person has made a compensation payment and either—

   (a)   subsection (7) of section 151 applies but he has not applied for a certificate as required by that subsection, or

   (b)   he has not made payment, in full, of any amount due under section 150(2) by the end of the period allowed under section 154.

(2)   The Secretary of State, the Scottish Ministers or both, according to the circumstances of the case, may—

   (a)   in a case within subsection (1)(a), issue the person who made the compensation payment with a certificate, and

   (b)   in a case within subsection (1)(b), issue him with a copy of the certificate or (if more than one has been issued) the most recent one,

   and, in either case, issue him with a demand that payment of any amount due under section 150(2) be made immediately.

(3)   Subsections (5) and (6) of section 152 apply to certificates issued under subsection (2) above as they apply to certificates issued under section 151.

(4)   A demand issued under subsection (2) may be issued jointly by the Secretary of State and the Scottish Ministers specifying—

   (a)   an amount due under subsection (2) of section 150 to the Secretary of State, and

   (b)   an amount due under that subsection to the Scottish Ministers, in respect of the same injured person in consequence of the same injury.

(5)   In the case of a demand specifying amounts as mentioned in subsection (4)(a) and (b), references in the following provisions of this section to a demand are to be taken as being (as the case may require) to—

   (a)   the demand in so far as it relates to any amount due to the Secretary of State, or

   (b)   the demand in so far as it relates to any amount due to the Scottish Ministers, and related expressions are to be read accordingly.

(6)   The Secretary of State or the Scottish Ministers may recover the amount for which a demand for payment is made under subsection (2) from the person who made the compensation payment.

(7)   If the person who made the compensation payment resides or carries on business in England or Wales and the county court so orders, the amount demanded is recoverable under section 85 of the County Courts Act 1984 or otherwise as if it were payable under an order of that court.

(8)   If the person who made the compensation payment resides or carries on business in Scotland, the demand may be enforced as if it were an extract registered decree arbitral bearing a warrant for execution issued by the sheriff court of any sheriffdom in Scotland.

(9)   A document which states that it is a record of the amount recoverable under subsection (6) is conclusive evidence that the amount is so recoverable if it is signed by a person authorised to do so by the Secretary of State or the Scottish Ministers (as the case may be).

(10)   For the purposes of subsection (9), a document purporting to be signed by a person authorised to do so by the Secretary of State or the Scottish Ministers (as the case may be) is to be treated as so signed unless the contrary is proved.

Miscellaneous and general

163   Regulations governing lump sums, periodical payments etc.

(1)   Regulations may make provision (including provision modifying this Part)—

   (a)   for cases to which section 150(2) applies in which two or more compensation payments in the form of lump sums are made by the same person in respect of the same injury,

   (b)   for cases to which section 150(2) applies in which an agreement is entered into for the making of—

      (i)   periodical compensation payments (whether of an income or capital nature), or

      (ii)   periodical compensation payments and lump sum compensation payments,

(c)   for cases in which the compensation payment to which section 150(2) applies is an interim payment of damages which a court orders to be repaid.

(2)   Regulations made by virtue of subsection (1)(a) may (among other things) provide—

(a)   for giving credit for amounts already paid, and

(b)   for the payment by any person of any balance or the recovery from any person of any excess.

(3)   Regulations may make provision modifying the application of this Part in relation to cases in which a payment into court is made and, in particular, may provide—

(a)   for the making of a payment into court to be treated in prescribed circumstances as the making of a compensation payment,

(b)   for application for, and issue of, certificates.

164   Liability of insurers

(1)   If a compensation payment is made in a case where—

(a)   a person is liable to any extent in respect of the injury, and

(b)   the liability is covered to any extent by a policy of insurance,

the policy is also to be treated as covering any liability of that person under section 150(2).

(2)   Liability imposed on the insurer by subsection (1) cannot be excluded or restricted.

(3)   For that purpose excluding or restricting liability includes—

(a)   making the liability or its enforcement subject to restrictive or onerous conditions,

(b)   excluding or restricting any right or remedy in respect of the liability, or subjecting a person to any prejudice in consequence of his pursuing any such right or remedy, or (c) excluding or restricting rules of evidence or procedure.

(4)   Regulations may in prescribed cases limit the amount of the liability imposed on the insurer by subsection (1).

(5)   This section applies in relation to policies of insurance issued before (as well as those issued after) the date on which it comes into force.

(6)   References in this section to policies of insurance and their issue include references to contracts of insurance and their making.

166   The Crown

This Part binds the Crown.

GAMBLING ACT 2005
(2005, c. 19)

335   Enforceability of gambling contracts

(1)   The fact that a contract relates to gambling shall not prevent its enforcement.

(2)   Subsection (1) is without prejudice to any rule of law preventing the enforcement of a contract on the grounds of unlawfulness (other than a rule relating specifically to gambling).

MENTAL CAPACITY ACT 2005
(2005, c. 9)

PART 1
PERSONS WHO LACK CAPACITY

The principles

1   The principles

(1)   The following principles apply for the purposes of this Act.

(2)   A person must be assumed to have capacity unless it is established that he lacks capacity.

(3)   A person is not to be treated as unable to make a decision unless all practicable steps to help him to do so have been taken without success.

(4) A person is not to be treated as unable to make a decision merely because he makes an unwise decision.

(5) An act done, or decision made, under this Act for or on behalf of a person who lacks capacity must be done, or made, in his best interests.

(6) Before the act is done, or the decision is made, regard must be had to whether the purpose for which it is needed can be as effectively achieved in a way that is less restrictive of the person's rights and freedom of action.

Preliminary

2   People who lack capacity

(1) For the purposes of this Act, a person lacks capacity in relation to a matter if at the material time he is unable to make a decision for himself in relation to the matter because of an impairment of, or a disturbance in the functioning of, the mind or brain.

(2) It does not matter whether the impairment or disturbance is permanent or temporary.

(3) A lack of capacity cannot be established merely by reference to—
(a) a person's age or appearance, or
(b) a condition of his, or an aspect of his behaviour, which might lead others to make unjustified assumptions about his capacity.

(4) In proceedings under this Act or any other enactment, any question whether a person lacks capacity within the meaning of this Act must be decided on the balance of probabilities.

(5) No power which a person ("D") may exercise under this Act—
(a) in relation to a person who lacks capacity, or
(b) where D reasonably thinks that a person lacks capacity, is exercisable in relation to a person under 16.

(6) Subsection (5) is subject to section 18(3).

3   Inability to make decisions

(1) For the purposes of section 2, a person is unable to make a decision for himself if he is unable—
(a) to understand the information relevant to the decision,
(b) to retain that information,
(c) to use or weigh that information as part of the process of making the decision, or
(d) to communicate his decision (whether by talking, using sign language or any other means).

(2) A person is not to be regarded as unable to understand the information relevant to a decision if he is able to understand an explanation of it given to him in a way that is appropriate to his circumstances (using simple language, visual aids or any other means).

(3) The fact that a person is able to retain the information relevant to a decision for a short period only does not prevent him from being regarded as able to make the decision.

(4) The information relevant to a decision includes information about the reasonably foreseeable consequences of—
(a) deciding one way or another, or
(b) failing to make the decision.

4   Best interests

(1) In determining for the purposes of this Act what is in a person's best interests, the person making the determination must not make it merely on the basis of—
(a) the person's age or appearance, or
(b) a condition of his, or an aspect of his behaviour, which might lead others to make unjustified assumptions about what might be in his best interests.

(2) The person making the determination must consider all the relevant circumstances and, in particular, take the following steps.

(3) He must consider—
(a) whether it is likely that the person will at some time have capacity in relation to the matter in question, and
(b) if it appears likely that he will, when that is likely to be.

(4) He must, so far as reasonably practicable, permit and encourage the person to participate, or to improve his ability to participate, as fully as possible in any act done for him and any decision affecting him.

(5) Where the determination relates to life-sustaining treatment he must not, in considering whether the treatment is in the best interests of the person concerned, be motivated by a desire to bring about his death.

(6) He must consider, so far as is reasonably ascertainable—
   (a) the person's past and present wishes and feelings (and, in particular, any relevant written statement made by him when he had capacity),
   (b) the beliefs and values that would be likely to influence his decision if he had capacity, and
   (c) the other factors that he would be likely to consider if he were able to do so.

(7) He must take into account, if it is practicable and appropriate to consult them, the views of—
   (a) anyone named by the person as someone to be consulted on the matter in question or on matters of that kind,
   (b) anyone engaged in caring for the person or interested in his welfare,
   (c) any donee of a lasting power of attorney granted by the person, and
   (d) any deputy appointed for the person by the court,
   as to what would be in the person's best interests and, in particular, as to the matters mentioned in subsection (6).

(8) The duties imposed by subsections (1) to (7) also apply in relation to the exercise of any powers which—
   (a) are exercisable under a lasting power of attorney, or
   (b) are exercisable by a person under this Act where he reasonably believes that another person lacks capacity.

(9) In the case of an act done, or a decision made, by a person other than the court, there is sufficient compliance with this section if (having complied with the requirements of subsections (1) to (7)) he reasonably believes that what he does or decides is in the best interests of the person concerned.

(10) "Life-sustaining treatment" means treatment which in the view of a person providing health care for the person concerned is necessary to sustain life.

(11) "Relevant circumstances" are those—
   (a) of which the person making the determination is aware, and
   (b) which it would be reasonable to regard as relevant.

4A Restriction on deprivation of liberty

(1) This Act does not authorise any person ("D") to deprive any person ("P") of his liberty.

(2) But that is subject to—
   (a) the following provisions of this section, and
   (b) section 4B.

(3) D may deprive P of his liberty, if by doing so, D is giving effect to a relevant decision of the court.

(4) A relevant decision of the court is a decision made by an order under section 16(2)(a) in relation to a matter concerning P's personal welfare.

(5) D may deprive P of his liberty if the deprivation is authorised by Schedule A1 (hospital and care home residents: deprivation of liberty).

4B Deprivation of liberty necessary for life-sustaining treatment etc.

(1) If the following conditions are met, D is authorised to deprive P of his liberty while a decision as respects any relevant issue is sought from the court.

(2) The first condition is that there is a question about whether D is authorised to deprive P of his liberty under section 4A.

(3) The second condition is that the deprivation of liberty—
   (a) is wholly or partly for the purpose of—
      (i) giving P life-sustaining treatment, or
      (ii) doing any vital act, or
   (b) consists wholly or partly of—
      (i) giving P life-sustaining treatment, or
      (ii) doing any vital act.

(4)   The third condition is that the deprivation of liberty is necessary in order to—
       (a)   give the life-sustaining treatment, or
       (b)   do the vital act.
(5)   A vital act is any act which the person doing it reasonably believes to be necessary to
       prevent a serious deterioration in P's condition.

Lasting powers of attorney

9   Lasting powers of attorney

(1)   A lasting power of attorney is a power of attorney under which the donor ("P") confers
       on the donee (or donees) authority to make decisions about all or any of the following—
       (a)   P's personal welfare or specified matters concerning P's personal welfare, and
       (b)   P's property and affairs or specified matters concerning P's property and affairs,
       and which includes authority to make such decisions in circumstances where P no
       longer has capacity.
(2)   A lasting power of attorney is not created unless—
       (a)   section 10 is complied with,
       (b)   an instrument conferring authority of the kind mentioned in subsection (1) is
              made and registered in accordance with Schedule 1, and
       (c)   at the time when P executes the instrument, P has reached 18 and has capacity
              to execute it.
(3)   An instrument which—
       (a)   purports to create a lasting power of attorney, but
       (b)   does not comply with this section, section 10 or Schedule 1, confers no authority.
(4)   The authority conferred by a lasting power of attorney is subject to—
       (a)   the provisions of this Act and, in particular, sections 1 (the principles) and 4 (best
              interests), and
       (b)   any conditions or restrictions specified in the instrument.

10   Appointment of donees

(1)   A donee of a lasting power of attorney must be—
       (a)   an individual who has reached 18, or
       (b)   if the power relates only to P's property and affairs, either such an individual or a
              trust corporation.
(2)   An individual who is bankrupt or is a person in relation to whom a debt relief order is
       made may not be appointed as donee of a lasting power of attorney in relation to P's
       property and affairs.
(3)   Subsections (4) to (7) apply in relation to an instrument under which two or more
       persons are to act as donees of a lasting power of attorney.
(4)   The instrument may appoint them to act—
       (a)   jointly,
       (b)   jointly and severally, or
       (c)   jointly in respect of some matters and jointly and severally in respect of others.
(5)   To the extent to which it does not specify whether they are to act jointly or jointly and
       severally, the instrument is to be assumed to appoint them to act jointly.
(6)   If they are to act jointly, a failure, as respects one of them, to comply with the
       requirements of subsection (1) or (2) or Part 1 or 2 of Schedule 1 prevents a lasting
       power of attorney from being created.
(7)   If they are to act jointly and severally, a failure, as respects one of them, to comply with
       the requirements of subsection (1) or (2) or Part 1 or 2 of Schedule 1—
       (a)   prevents the appointment taking effect in his case, but
       (b)   does not prevent a lasting power of attorney from being created in the case of
              the other or others.
(8)   An instrument used to create a lasting power of attorney—
       (a)   cannot give the donee (or, if more than one, any of them) power to appoint a
              substitute or successor, but
       (b)   may itself appoint a person to replace the donee (or, if more than one, any of
              them) on the occurrence of an event mentioned in section 13(6)(a) to (d) which
              has the effect of terminating the donee's appointment.

11   Lasting powers of attorney: restrictions

(1)   A lasting power of attorney does not authorise the donee (or, if more than one, any of them) to do an act that is intended to restrain P, unless three conditions are satisfied.

(2)   The first condition is that P lacks, or the donee reasonably believes that P lacks, capacity in relation to the matter in question.

(3)   The second is that the donee reasonably believes that it is necessary to do the act in order to prevent harm to P.

(4)   The third is that the act is a proportionate response to—
   (a)   the likelihood of P's suffering harm, and
   (b)   the seriousness of that harm.

(5)   For the purposes of this section, the donee restrains P if he—
   (a)   uses, or threatens to use, force to secure the doing of an act which P resists, or
   (b)   restricts P's liberty of movement, whether or not P resists, or if he authorises another person to do any of those things.

(6)   …

(7)   Where a lasting power of attorney authorises the donee (or, if more than one, any of them) to make decisions about P's personal welfare, the authority—
   (a)   does not extend to making such decisions in circumstances other than those where P lacks, or the donee reasonably believes that P lacks, capacity,
   (b)   is subject to sections 24 to 26 (advance decisions to refuse treatment), and
   (c)   extends to giving or refusing consent to the carrying out or continuation of a treatment by a person providing health care for P.

(8)   But subsection (7)(c)—
   (a)   does not authorise the giving or refusing of consent to the carrying out or continuation of life-sustaining treatment, unless the instrument contains express provision to that effect, and
   (b)   is subject to any conditions or restrictions in the instrument.

12   Scope of lasting powers of attorney: gifts

(1)   Where a lasting power of attorney confers authority to make decisions about P's property and affairs, it does not authorise a donee (or, if more than one, any of them) to dispose of the donor's property by making gifts except to the extent permitted by subsection (2).

(2)   The donee may make gifts—
   (a)   on customary occasions to persons (including himself) who are related to or connected with the donor, or
   (b)   to any charity to whom the donor made or might have been expected to make gifts, if the value of each such gift is not unreasonable having regard to all the circumstances and, in particular, the size of the donor's estate.

(3)   "Customary occasion" means—
   (a)   the occasion or anniversary of a birth, a marriage or the formation of a civil partnership, or
   (b)   any other occasion on which presents are customarily given within families or among friends or associates.

(4)   Subsection (2) is subject to any conditions or restrictions in the instrument.

13   Revocation of lasting powers of attorney etc.

(1)   This section applies if—
   (a)   P has executed an instrument with a view to creating a lasting power of attorney, or
   (b)   a lasting power of attorney is registered as having been conferred by P, and in this section references to revoking the power include revoking the instrument.

(2)   P may, at any time when he has capacity to do so, revoke the power.

(3)   P's bankruptcy, or the making of a debt relief order (under Part 7A of the Insolvency Act 1986) in respect of P, revokes the power so far as it relates to P's property and affairs.

(4)   But where P is bankrupt merely because an interim bankruptcy restrictions order has effect in respect of him or where P is subject to an interim debt relief restrictions order

(under Schedule 4ZB of the Insolvency Act 1986), the power is suspended, so far as it relates to P's property and affairs, for so long as the order has effect.

(5) The occurrence in relation to a donee of an event mentioned in subsection (6)—
    (a) terminates his appointment, and
    (b) except in the cases given in subsection (7), revokes the power.

(6) The events are—
    (a) the disclaimer of the appointment by the donee in accordance with such requirements as may be prescribed for the purposes of this section in regulations made by the Lord Chancellor,
    (b) subject to subsections (8) and (9), the death or bankruptcy of the donee or the making of a debt relief order (under Part 7A of the Insolvency Act 1986) in respect of the donee or, if the donee is a trust corporation, its winding-up or dissolution,
    (c) subject to subsection (11), the dissolution or annulment of a marriage or civil partnership between the donor and the donee,
    (d) the lack of capacity of the donee.

(7) The cases are—
    (a) the donee is replaced under the terms of the instrument,
    (b) he is one of two or more persons appointed to act as donees jointly and severally in respect of any matter and, after the event, there is at least one remaining donee.

(8) The bankruptcy of a donee or the making of a debt relief order (under Part 7A of the Insolvency Act 1986) in respect of a donee does not terminate his appointment, or revoke the power, in so far as his authority relates to P's personal welfare.

(9) Where the donee is bankrupt merely because an interim bankruptcy restrictions order has effect in respect of him or where the donee is subject to an interim debt relief restrictions order (under Schedule 4ZB of the Insolvency Act 1986), his appointment and the power are suspended, so far as they relate to P's property and affairs, for so long as the order has effect.

(10) Where the donee is one of two or more appointed to act jointly and severally under the power in respect of any matter, the reference in subsection (9) to the suspension of the power is to its suspension in so far as it relates to that donee.

(11) The dissolution or annulment of a marriage or civil partnership does not terminate the appointment of a donee, or revoke the power, if the instrument provided that it was not to do so.

14   Protection of donee and others if no power created or power revoked

(1) Subsections (2) and (3) apply if—
    (a) an instrument has been registered under Schedule 1 as a lasting power of attorney, but
    (b) a lasting power of attorney was not created,
whether or not the registration has been cancelled at the time of the act or transaction in question.

(2) A donee who acts in purported exercise of the power does not incur any liability (to P or any other person) because of the non-existence of the power unless at the time of acting he—
    (a) knows that a lasting power of attorney was not created, or
    (b) is aware of circumstances which, if a lasting power of attorney had been created, would have terminated his authority to act as a donee.

(3) Any transaction between the donee and another person is, in favour of that person, as valid as if the power had been in existence, unless at the time of the transaction that person has knowledge of a matter referred to in subsection (2).

(4) If the interest of a purchaser depends on whether a transaction between the donee and the other person was valid by virtue of subsection (3), it is conclusively presumed in favour of the purchaser that the transaction was valid if—
    (a) the transaction was completed within 12 months of the date on which the instrument was registered, or
    (b) the other person makes a statutory declaration, before or within 3 months after the completion of the purchase, that he had no reason at the time of the transaction to doubt that the donee had authority to dispose of the property which was the subject of the transaction.

(5)   In its application to a lasting power of attorney which relates to matters in addition to P's property and affairs, section 5 of the Powers of Attorney Act 1971 (c. 27) (protection where power is revoked) has effect as if references to revocation included the cessation of the power in relation to P's property and affairs.

(6)   Where two or more donees are appointed under a lasting power of attorney, this section applies as if references to the donee were to all or any of them.

Powers of the court in relation to lasting powers of attorney

22   Powers of court in relation to validity of lasting powers of attorney

(1)   This section and section 23 apply if —

   (a)   a person ("P") has executed or purported to execute an instrument with a view to creating a lasting power of attorney, or

   (b)   an instrument has been registered as a lasting power of attorney conferred by P.

(2)   The court may determine any question relating to—

   (a)   whether one or more of the requirements for the creation of a lasting power of attorney have been met;

   (b)   whether the power has been revoked or has otherwise come to an end.

(3)   Subsection (4) applies if the court is satisfied—

   (a)   that fraud or undue pressure was used to induce P—

      (i)   to execute an instrument for the purpose of creating a lasting power of attorney, or

      (ii)   to create a lasting power of attorney, or

   (b)   that the donee (or, if more than one, any of them) of a lasting power of attorney—

      (i)   has behaved, or is behaving, in a way that contravenes his authority or is not in P's best interests, or

      (ii)   proposes to behave in a way that would contravene his authority or would not be in P's best interests.

(4)   The court may—

   (a)   direct that an instrument purporting to create the lasting power of attorney is not to be registered, or

   (b)   if P lacks capacity to do so, revoke the instrument or the lasting power of attorney.

(5)   If there is more than one donee, the court may under subsection (4)(b) revoke the instrument or the lasting power of attorney so far as it relates to any of them.

(6)   "Donee" includes an intended donee.

23   Powers of court in relation to operation of lasting powers of attorney

(1)   The court may determine any question as to the meaning or effect of a lasting power of attorney or an instrument purporting to create one.

(2)   The court may—

   (a)   give directions with respect to decisions—

      (i)   which the donee of a lasting power of attorney has authority to make, and

      (ii)   which P lacks capacity to make;

   (b)   give any consent or authorisation to act which the donee would have to obtain from P if P had capacity to give it.

(3)   The court may, if P lacks capacity to do so—

   (a)   give directions to the donee with respect to the rendering by him of reports or accounts and the production of records kept by him for that purpose;

   (b)   require the donee to supply information or produce documents or things in his possession as donee;

   (c)   give directions with respect to the remuneration or expenses of the donee;

   (d)   relieve the donee wholly or partly from any liability which he has or may have incurred on account of a breach of his duties as donee.

(4)   The court may authorise the making of gifts which are not within section 12(2) (permitted gifts).

(5)   Where two or more donees are appointed under a lasting power of attorney, this section applies as if references to the donee were to all or any of them.

COMPANIES ACT 2006
(2006, c. 46)

33 Effect of company's constitution

(1) The provisions of a company's constitution bind the company and its members to the same extent as if there were covenants on the part of the company and of each member to observe those provisions.

(2) Money payable by a member to the company under its constitution is a debt due from him to the company.

In England and Wales and Northern Ireland it is of the nature of an ordinary contract debt.

39 A company's capacity

(1) The validity of an act done by a company shall not be called into question on the ground of lack of capacity by reason of anything in the company's constitution.

(2) This section has effect subject to section 42 (companies that are charities).

40 Power of directors to bind the company

(1) In favour of a person dealing with a company in good faith, the power of the directors to bind the company, or authorise others to do so, is deemed to be free of any limitation under the company's constitution.

(2) For this purpose—

    (a) a person "deals with" a company if he is a party to any transaction or other act to which the company is a party,

    (b) a person dealing with a company—

        (i) is not bound to enquire as to any limitation on the powers of the directors to bind the company or authorise others to do so,

        (ii) is presumed to have acted in good faith unless the contrary is proved, and

        (iii) is not to be regarded as acting in bad faith by reason only of his knowing that an act is beyond the powers of the directors under the company's constitution.

(3) The references above to limitations on the directors' powers under the company's constitution include limitations deriving—

    (a) from a resolution of the company or of any class of shareholders, or

    (b) from any agreement between the members of the company or of any class of shareholders.

(4) This section does not affect any right of a member of the company to bring proceedings to restrain the doing of an action that is beyond the powers of the directors.

But no such proceedings lie in respect of an act to be done in fulfilment of a legal obligation arising from a previous act of the company.

(5) This section does not affect any liability incurred by the directors, or any other person, by reason of the directors' exceeding their powers.

(6) This section has effect subject to— section 41 (transactions with directors or their associates), and section 42 (companies that are charities).

41 Constitutional limitations: transactions involving directors or their associates

(1) This section applies to a transaction if or to the extent that its validity depends on section 40 (power of directors deemed to be free of limitations under company's constitution in favour of person dealing with company in good faith).

Nothing in this section shall be read as excluding the operation of any other enactment or rule of law by virtue of which the transaction may be called in question or any liability to the company may arise.

(2) Where—

    (a) a company enters into such a transaction, and

    (b) the parties to the transaction include—

        (i) a director of the company or of its holding company, or

        (ii) a person connected with any such director, the transaction is voidable at the instance of the company.

(3) Whether or not it is avoided, any such party to the transaction as is mentioned in subsection (2)(b)(i) or (ii), and any director of the company who authorised the transaction, is liable—

    (a) to account to the company for any gain he has made directly or indirectly by the transaction, and

    (b) to indemnify the company for any loss or damage resulting from the transaction.

(4) The transaction ceases to be voidable if—

    (a) restitution of any money or other asset which was the subject matter of the transaction is no longer possible, or

    (b) the company is indemnified for any loss or damage resulting from the transaction, or

    (c) rights acquired bona fide for value and without actual notice of the directors' exceeding their powers by a person who is not party to the transaction would be affected by the avoidance, or

    (d) the transaction is affirmed by the company.

(5) A person other than a director of the company is not liable under subsection (3) if he shows that at the time the transaction was entered into he did not know that the directors were exceeding their powers.

(6) Nothing in the preceding provisions of this section affects the rights of any party to the transaction not within subsection (2)(b)(i) or (ii).

But the court may, on the application of the company or any such party, make an order affirming, severing or setting aside the transaction on such terms as appear to the court to be just.

(7) In this section—

    (a) "transaction" includes any act; and

    (b) the reference to a person connected with a director has the same meaning as in Part 10 (company directors).

43 Company contracts

(1) Under the law of England and Wales or Northern Ireland a contract may be made—

    (a) by a company, by writing under its common seal, or

    (b) on behalf of a company, by a person acting under its authority, express or implied.

(2) Any formalities required by law in the case of a contract made by an individual also apply, unless a contrary intention appears, to a contract made by or on behalf of a company.

51 Pre-incorporation contracts, deeds and obligations

(1) A contract that purports to be made by or on behalf of a company at a time when the company has not been formed has effect, subject to any agreement to the contrary, as one made with the person purporting to act for the company or as agent for it, and he is personally liable on the contract accordingly.

(2) Subsection (1) applies—

    (a) to the making of a deed under the law of England and Wales or Northern Ireland, and

    (b) to the undertaking of an obligation under the law of Scotland,

as it applies to the making of a contract.

COMPENSATION ACT 2006
(2006, c. 29)

1 Deterrent effect of potential liability

A court considering a claim in negligence or breach of statutory duty may, in determining whether the defendant should have taken particular steps to meet a standard of care (whether by taking precautions against a risk or otherwise), have regard to whether a requirement to take those steps might—

    (a) prevent a desirable activity from being undertaken at all, to a particular extent or in a particular way, or

    (b) discourage persons from undertaking functions in connection with a desirable activity.

2 Apologies, offers of treatment or other redress

An apology, an offer of treatment or other redress, shall not of itself amount to an admission of negligence or breach of statutory duty.

3 Mesothelioma: damages

(1) This section applies where—

  (a) a person ("the responsible person") has negligently or in breach of statutory duty caused or permitted another person ("the victim") to be exposed to asbestos,

  (b) the victim has contracted mesothelioma as a result of exposure to asbestos,

  (c) because of the nature of mesothelioma and the state of medical science, it is not possible to determine with certainty whether it was the exposure mentioned in paragraph (a) or another exposure which caused the victim to become ill, and

  (d) the responsible person is liable in tort, by virtue of the exposure mentioned in paragraph (a), in connection with damage caused to the victim by the disease (whether by reason of having materially increased a risk or for any other reason).

(2) The responsible person shall be liable—

  (a) in respect of the whole of the damage caused to the victim by the disease (irrespective of whether the victim was also exposed to asbestos—

    (i) other than by the responsible person, whether or not in circumstances in which another person has liability in tort, or

    (ii) by the responsible person in circumstances in which he has no liability in tort), and

  (b) jointly and severally with any other responsible person.

(3) Subsection (2) does not prevent—

  (a) one responsible person from claiming a contribution from another, or

  (b) a finding of contributory negligence.

(4) In determining the extent of contributions of different responsible persons in accordance with subsection (3)(a), a court shall have regard to the relative lengths of the periods of exposure for which each was responsible; but this subsection shall not apply—

  (a) if or to the extent that responsible persons agree to apportion responsibility amongst themselves on some other basis, or

  (b) if or to the extent that the court thinks that another basis for determining contributions is more appropriate in the circumstances of a particular case.

(5) In subsection (1) the reference to causing or permitting a person to be exposed to asbestos includes a reference to failing to protect a person from exposure to asbestos.

(6) In the application of this section to Scotland—

  (a) a reference to tort shall be taken as a reference to delict, and

  (b) a reference to a court shall be taken to include a reference to a jury.

(7) The Treasury may make regulations about the provision of compensation to a responsible person where—

  (a) he claims, or would claim, a contribution from another responsible person in accordance with subsection (3)(a), but

  (b) he is unable or likely to be unable to obtain the contribution, because an insurer of the other responsible person is unable or likely to be unable to satisfy the claim for a contribution.

(8) The regulations may, in particular—

  (a) ...

  (b) replicate or apply (with or without modification) a transitional compensation provision;

  (c) provide for a specified person to assess and pay compensation;

  (d) provide for expenses incurred (including the payment of compensation) to be met out of levies collected in accordance with section 213(3)(b) of the Financial Services and Markets Act 2000 (the Financial Services Compensation Scheme);

  (e) modify the effect of a transitional compensation provision;

  (f) enable the Financial Conduct Authority or the Prudential Regulation Authority to amend the Financial Services Compensation Scheme;

  (g) modify the Financial Services and Markets Act 2000 in its application to an amendment pursuant to paragraph (f);

    (h)   make, or require the making of, provision for the making of a claim by a responsible person for compensation whether or not he has already satisfied claims in tort against him;

    (i)   make, or require the making of, provision which has effect in relation to claims for contributions made on or after the date on which this Act is passed.

(10) In subsections (7) and (8)—

    (a)   a reference to a responsible person includes a reference to an insurer of a responsible person, and

    (b)   "transitional compensation provision" means a provision of an enactment which is made under the Financial Services and Markets Act 2000 and—

        (i)   preserves the effect of the Policyholders Protection Act 1975, or

        (ii)   applies the Financial Services Compensation Scheme in relation to matters arising before its establishment.

(11) Regulations under subsection (7)—

    (a)   may include consequential or incidental provison,

    (b)   may make provision which has effect generally or only in relation to specified cases or circumstances,

    (c)   may make different provision for different cases or circumstances,

    (d)   shall be made by statutory instrument, and

    (e)   may not be made unless a draft has been laid before and approved by resolution of each House of Parliament.

LEGAL SERVICES ACT 2007
(2007, c. 29)

PART 6
LEGAL COMPLAINTS

Defamation

154 Protection from defamation claims

For the purposes of the law of defamation—

    (a)   proceedings in relation to a complaint under the ombudsman scheme are to be treated as if they were proceedings before a court, and

    (b)   the publication of any matter by the OLC under this Part is absolutely privileged.

BANKING ACT 2009
(2009, c. 1)

PART 7
MISCELLANEOUS

Bank of England

244 Immunity

(1) The Bank of England has immunity in its capacity as a monetary authority.

(2) In this section—

    (a)   a reference to the Bank of England is a reference to the Bank and anyone who acts or purports to act as a director, officer, employee or agent of the Bank,

    (b)   "immunity" means immunity from liability in damages in respect of action or inaction, and

    (c)   a reference to the Bank's capacity as a monetary authority includes a reference to the exercise or purported exercise of the Bank's functions under the Financial

Services and Markets Act 2000, of its other regulatory functions or functions undertaken by the Bank for the purpose of or in connection with—
(i)   acting as the central bank of the United Kingdom, or
(ii)   protecting or enhancing the stability of the financial systems of the United Kingdom.

(2A) The Bank's functions under the Financial Services and Markets Act 2000 are to be taken to include any functions that it may exercise as a result of an appointment under any of sections 97, 166 to 169 and 284 of that Act.

(3) The immunity does not extend to action or inaction—
(a)   in bad faith, or
(b)   in contravention of section 6(1) of the Human Rights Act 1998.

EQUALITY ACT 2010
(2010, c. 15)

PART 2
EQUALITY: KEY CONCEPTS

CHAPTER 1
PROTECTED CHARACTERISTICS

4   The protected characteristics

The following characteristics are protected characteristics—
age;
disability;
gender reassignment;
marriage and civil partnership;
pregnancy and maternity;
race;
religion or belief; sex;
sexual orientation.

CHAPTER 2
PROHIBITED CONDUCT

Discrimination

13   Direct discrimination

(1) A person (A) discriminates against another (B) if, because of a protected characteristic, A treats B less favourably than A treats or would treat others.

(2) If the protected characteristic is age, A does not discriminate against B if A can show A's treatment of B to be a proportionate means of achieving a legitimate aim.

(3) If the protected characteristic is disability, and B is not a disabled person, A does not discriminate against B only because A treats or would treat disabled persons more favourably than A treats B.

(4) If the protected characteristic is marriage and civil partnership, this section applies to a contravention of Part 5 (work) only if the treatment is because it is B who is married or a civil partner.

(5) If the protected characteristic is race, less favourable treatment includes segregating B from others.

(6) If the protected characteristic is sex—
(a)   less favourable treatment of a woman includes less favourable treatment of her because she is breast-feeding;

(b)   in a case where B is a man, no account is to be taken of special treatment afforded to a woman in connection with pregnancy or childbirth.

(7)   Subsection (6)(a) does not apply for the purposes of Part 5 (work).

(8)   This section is subject to sections 17(6) and 18(7).

Other prohibited conduct

26   Harassment

(1)   A person (A) harasses another (B) if—
　　(a)   A engages in unwanted conduct related to a relevant protected characteristic, and
　　(b)   the conduct has the purpose or effect of—
　　　　(i)   violating B's dignity, or
　　　　(ii)   creating an intimidating, hostile, degrading, humiliating or offensive environment for B.

(2)   A also harasses B if—
　　(a)   A engages in unwanted conduct of a sexual nature, and
　　(b)   the conduct has the purpose or effect referred to in subsection (1)(b).

(3)   A also harasses B if—
　　(a)   A or another person engages in unwanted conduct of a sexual nature or that is related to gender reassignment or sex,
　　(b)   the conduct has the purpose or effect referred to in subsection (1)(b), and
　　(c)   because of B's rejection of or submission to the conduct, A treats B less favourably than A would treat B if B had not rejected or submitted to the conduct.

(4)   In deciding whether conduct has the effect referred to in subsection (1)(b), each of the following must be taken into account—
　　(a)   the perception of B;
　　(b)   the other circumstances of the case;
　　(c)   whether it is reasonable for the conduct to have that effect.

(5)   The relevant protected characteristics are—
　　age;
　　disability;
　　gender reassignment;
　　race;
　　religion or belief;
　　sex;
　　sexual orientation.

27   Victimisation

(1)   A person (A) victimises another person (B) if A subjects B to a detriment because—
　　(a)   B does a protected act, or
　　(b)   A believes that B has done, or may do, a protected act.

(2)   Each of the following is a protected act—
　　(a)   bringing proceedings under this Act;
　　(b)   giving evidence or information in connection with proceedings under this Act;
　　(c)   doing any other thing for the purposes of or in connection with this Act;
　　(d)   making an allegation (whether or not express) that A or another person has contravened this Act.

(3)   Giving false evidence or information, or making a false allegation, is not a protected act if the evidence or information is given, or the allegation is made, in bad faith.

(4)   This section applies only where the person subjected to a detriment is an individual.

(5)   The reference to contravening this Act includes a reference to committing a breach of an equality clause or rule.

PART 3
SERVICES AND PUBLIC FUNCTIONS

Preliminary

28 Application of this Part

(1) This Part does not apply to the protected characteristic of—

  (a) age, so far as relating to persons who have not attained the age of 18;

  (b) marriage and civil partnership.

(2) This Part does not apply to discrimination, harassment or victimisation—

  (a) that is prohibited by Part 4 (premises), 5 (work) or 6 (education), or

  (b) that would be so prohibited but for an express exception.

(3) This Part does not apply to—

  (a) a breach of an equality clause or rule;

  (b) anything that would be a breach of an equality clause or rule but for section 69 or Part 2 of Schedule 7;

  (c) a breach of a non-discrimination rule.

Provision of services, etc.

29 Provision of services, etc.

(1) A person (a "service-provider") concerned with the provision of a service to the public or a section of the public (for payment or not) must not discriminate against a person requiring the service by not providing the person with the service.

(2) A service-provider (A) must not, in providing the service, discriminate against a person (B)—

  (a) as to the terms on which A provides the service to B;

  (b) by terminating the provision of the service to B;

  (c) by subjecting B to any other detriment.

(3) A service-provider must not, in relation to the provision of the service, harass—

  (a) a person requiring the service, or

  (b) a person to whom the service-provider provides the service.

(4) A service-provider must not victimise a person requiring the service by not providing the person with the service.

(5) A service-provider (A) must not, in providing the service, victimise a person (B)—

  (a) as to the terms on which A provides the service to B;

  (b) by terminating the provision of the service to B;

  (c) by subjecting B to any other detriment.

(6) A person must not, in the exercise of a public function that is not the provision of a service to the public or a section of the public, do anything that constitutes discrimination, harassment or victimisation.

(7) A duty to make reasonable adjustments applies to—

  (a) a service-provider (and see also section 55(7));

  (b) a person who exercises a public function that is not the provision of a service to the public or a section of the public.

(8) In the application of section 26 for the purposes of subsection (3), and subsection (6) as it relates to harassment, neither of the following is a relevant protected characteristic—

  (a) religion or belief;

  (b) sexual orientation.

(9) In the application of this section, so far as relating to race or religion or belief, to the granting of entry clearance (within the meaning of the Immigration Act 1971), it does not matter whether an act is done within or outside the United Kingdom.

(10) Subsection (9) does not affect the application of any other provision of this Act to conduct outside England and Wales or Scotland.

Supplementary

31 Interpretation and exceptions

(1) This section applies for the purposes of this Part.

(2) A reference to the provision of a service includes a reference to the provision of goods or facilities.

(3) A reference to the provision of a service includes a reference to the provision of a service in the exercise of a public function.

(4) A public function is a function that is a function of a public nature for the purposes of the Human Rights Act 1998.

(5) Where an employer arranges for another person to provide a service only to the employer's employees—

    (a) the employer is not to be regarded as the service-provider, but

    (b) the employees are to be regarded as a section of the public.

(6) A reference to a person requiring a service includes a reference to a person who is seeking to obtain or use the service.

(7) A reference to a service-provider not providing a person with a service includes a reference to—

    (a) the service-provider not providing the person with a service of the quality that the service-provider usually provides to the public (or the section of it which includes the person), or

    (b) the service-provider not providing the person with the service in the manner in which, or on the terms on which, the service-provider usually provides the service to the public (or the section of it which includes the person).

(8) In relation to the provision of a service by either House of Parliament, the service-provider is the Corporate Officer of the House concerned; and if the service involves access to, or use of, a place in the Palace of Westminster which members of the public are allowed to enter, both Corporate Officers are jointly the service-provider.

(9) Schedule 2 (reasonable adjustments) has effect.

(10) Schedule 3 (exceptions) has effect.

PART 4

PREMISES

Preliminary

32 Application of this Part

(1) This Part does not apply to the following protected characteristics—

    (a) age;

    (b) marriage and civil partnership.

(2) This Part does not apply to discrimination, harassment or victimisation—

    (a) that is prohibited by Part 5 (work) or Part 6 (education), or

    (b) that would be so prohibited but for an express exception.

(3) This Part does not apply to the provision of accommodation if the provision—

    (a) is generally for the purpose of short stays by individuals who live elsewhere, or

    (b) is for the purpose only of exercising a public function or providing a service to the public or a section of the public.

(4) The reference to the exercise of a public function, and the reference to the provision of a service, are to be construed in accordance with Part 3.

(5) This Part does not apply to—

    (a) a breach of an equality clause or rule;

    (b) anything that would be a breach of an equality clause or rule but for section 69 or Part 2 of Schedule 7;

    (c) a breach of a non-discrimination rule.

Disposal and management

33   Disposals, etc.

(1)   A person (A) who has the right to dispose of premises must not discriminate against another (B)—

    (a)   as to the terms on which A offers to dispose of the premises to B;

    (b)   by not disposing of the premises to B;

    (c)   in A's treatment of B with respect to things done in relation to persons seeking premises.

(2)   Where an interest in a commonhold unit cannot be disposed of unless a particular person is a party to the disposal, that person must not discriminate against a person by not being a party to the disposal.

(3)   A person who has the right to dispose of premises must not, in connection with anything done in relation to their occupation or disposal, harass—

    (a)   a person who occupies them;

    (b)   a person who applies for them.

(4)   A person (A) who has the right to dispose of premises must not victimise another (B)—

    (a)   as to the terms on which A offers to dispose of the premises to B;

    (b)   by not disposing of the premises to B;

    (c)   in A's treatment of B with respect to things done in relation to persons seeking premises.

(5)   Where an interest in a commonhold unit cannot be disposed of unless a particular person is a party to the disposal, that person must not victimise a person by not being a party to the disposal.

(6)   In the application of section 26 for the purposes of subsection (3), neither of the following is a relevant protected characteristic—

    (a)   religion or belief;

    (b)   sexual orientation.

PART 5
WORK

CHAPTER 1
EMPLOYMENT, ETC.

Employees

39   Employees and applicants

(1)   An employer (A) must not discriminate against a person (B)—

    (a)   in the arrangements A makes for deciding to whom to offer employment;

    (b)   as to the terms on which A offers B employment;

    (c)   by not offering B employment.

(2)   An employer (A) must not discriminate against an employee of A's (B)—

    (a)   as to B's terms of employment;

    (b)   in the way A affords B access, or by not affording B access, to opportunities for promotion, transfer or training or for receiving any other benefit, facility or service;

    (c)   by dismissing B;

    (d)   by subjecting B to any other detriment.

(3)   An employer (A) must not victimise a person (B)—

    (a)   in the arrangements A makes for deciding to whom to offer employment;

    (b)   as to the terms on which A offers B employment;

    (c)   by not offering B employment.

(4)   An employer (A) must not victimise an employee of A's (B)—

    (a)   as to B's terms of employment;

    (b)   in the way A affords B access, or by not affording B access, to opportunities for promotion, transfer or training or for any other benefit, facility or service;

(c)   by dismissing B;

(d)   by subjecting B to any other detriment.

(5)   A duty to make reasonable adjustments applies to an employer.

(6)   Subsection (1)(b), so far as relating to sex or pregnancy and maternity, does not apply to a term that relates to pay—

(a)   unless, were B to accept the offer, an equality clause or rule would have effect in relation to the term, or

(b)   if paragraph (a) does not apply, except in so far as making an offer on terms including that term amounts to a contravention of subsection (1)(b) by virtue of section 13, 14 or 18.

(7)   In subsections (2)(c) and (4)(c), the reference to dismissing B includes a reference to the termination of B's employment—

(a)   by the expiry of a period (including a period expiring by reference to an event or circumstance);

(b)   by an act of B's (including giving notice) in circumstances such that B is entitled, because of A's conduct, to terminate the employment without notice.

(8)   Subsection (7)(a) does not apply if, immediately after the termination, the employment is renewed on the same terms.

CHAPTER 3
EQUALITY OF TERMS

Sex equality

66   Sex equality clause

(1)   If the terms of A's work do not (by whatever means) include a sex equality clause, they are to be treated as including one.

(2)   A sex equality clause is a provision that has the following effect—

(a)   if a term of A's is less favourable to A than a corresponding term of B's is to B, A's term is modified so as not to be less favourable;

(b)   if A does not have a term which corresponds to a term of B's that benefits B, A's terms are modified so as to include such a term.

(3)   Subsection (2)(a) applies to a term of A's relating to membership of or rights under an occupational pension scheme only in so far as a sex equality rule would have effect in relation to the term.

(4)   In the case of work within section 65(1)(b), a reference in subsection (2) above to a term includes a reference to such terms (if any) as have not been determined by the rating of the work (as well as those that have).

PART 9
ENFORCEMENT

CHAPTER 2
CIVIL COURTS

119   Remedies

(1)   This section applies if the county court or the sheriff finds that there has been a contravention of a provision referred to in section 114(1).

(2)   The county court has power to grant any remedy which could be granted by the High Court—

(a)   in proceedings in tort;

(b)   on a claim for judicial review.

(3)   The sheriff has power to make any order which could be made by the Court of Session—

(a)   in proceedings for reparation;

(b)   on a petition for judicial review.

(4) An award of damages may include compensation for injured feelings (whether or not it includes compensation on any other basis).

(5) Subsection (6) applies if the county court or sheriff—
     (a) finds that a contravention of a provision referred to in section 114(1) is established by virtue of section 19, but
     (b) is satisfied that the provision, criterion or practice was not applied with the intention of discriminating against the claimant or pursuer.

(6) The county court or sheriff must not make an award of damages unless it first considers whether to make any other disposal.

(7) The county court or sheriff must not grant a remedy other than an award of damages or the making of a declaration unless satisfied that no criminal matter would be prejudiced by doing so.

PART 10

CONTRACTS, ETC.

Contracts and other agreements

142 Unenforceable terms

(1) A term of a contract is unenforceable against a person in so far as it constitutes, promotes or provides for treatment of that or another person that is of a description prohibited by this Act.

(2) A relevant non-contractual term is unenforceable against a person in so far as it constitutes, promotes or provides for treatment of that or another person that is of a description prohibited by this Act, in so far as this Act relates to disability.

(3) A relevant non-contractual term is a term which—
     (a) is a term of an agreement that is not a contract, and
     (b) relates to the provision of an employment service within section 56(2)(a) to (e) or to the provision under a group insurance arrangement of facilities by way of insurance.

(4) A reference in subsection (1) or (2) to treatment of a description prohibited by this Act does not include—
     (a) a reference to the inclusion of a term in a contract referred to in section 70(2)(a) or 76(2), or
     (b) a reference to the failure to include a term in a contract as referred to in section 70(2)(b).

(5) Subsection (4) does not affect the application of section 148(2) to this section.

143 Removal or modification of unenforceable terms

(1) The county court or the sheriff may, on an application by a person who has an interest in a contract or other agreement which includes a term that is unenforceable as a result of section 142, make an order for the term to be removed or modified.

(2) An order under this section must not be made unless every person who would be affected by it—
     (a) has been given notice of the application (except where notice is dispensed with in accordance with rules of court), and
     (b) has been afforded an opportunity to make representations to the county court or sheriff.

(3) An order under this section may include provision in respect of a period before the making of the order.

144 Contracting out

(1) A term of a contract is unenforceable by a person in whose favour it would operate in so far as it purports to exclude or limit a provision of or made under this Act.

(2) A relevant non-contractual term (as defined by section 142) is unenforceable by a person in whose favour it would operate in so far as it purports to exclude or limit a provision of or made under this Act, in so far as the provision relates to disability.

(3) This section does not apply to a contract which settles a claim within section 114.

(4) This section does not apply to a contract which settles a complaint within section 120 if the contract—

    (a)   is made with the assistance of a conciliation officer, or

    (b)   is a qualifying settlement agreement.

(5) A contract within subsection (4) includes a contract which settles a complaint relating to a breach of an equality clause or rule or of a non-discrimination rule.

(6) A contract within subsection (4) includes an agreement by the parties to a dispute to submit the dispute to arbitration if—

    (a)   the dispute is covered by a scheme having effect by virtue of an order under section 212A of the Trade Union and Labour Relations (Consolidation) Act 1992, and

    (b)   the agreement is to submit the dispute to arbitration in accordance with the scheme.

Collective agreements and rules of undertakings

145 Void and unenforceable terms

(1) A term of a collective agreement is void in so far as it constitutes, promotes or provides for treatment of a description prohibited by this Act.

(2) A rule of an undertaking is unenforceable against a person in so far as it constitutes, promotes or provides for treatment of the person that is of a description prohibited by this Act.

146 Declaration in respect of void term, etc.

(1) A qualifying person (P) may make a complaint to an employment tribunal that a term is void, or that a rule is unenforceable, as a result of section 145.

(2) But subsection (1) applies only if—

    (a)   the term or rule may in the future have effect in relation to P, and

    (b)   where the complaint alleges that the term or rule provides for treatment of a description prohibited by this Act, P may in the future be subjected to treatment that would (if P were subjected to it in present circumstances) be of that description.

(3) If the tribunal finds that the complaint is well-founded, it must make an order declaring that the term is void or the rule is unenforceable.

(4) An order under this section may include provision in respect of a period before the making of the order.

(5) In the case of a complaint about a term of a collective agreement, where the term is one made by or on behalf of a person of a description specified in the first column of the table, a qualifying person is a person of a description specified in the second column.

Description of person who made collective agreement	Qualifying person
Employer	A person who is, or is seeking to be, an employee of that employer
Organisation of employers	A person who is, or is seeking to be, an employee of an employer who is a member of that organisation
Association of organisations of employers	A person who is, or is seeking to be, an employee of an employer who is a member of an organisation in that association

(6) In the case of a complaint about a rule of an undertaking, where the rule is one made by or on behalf of a person of a description specified in the first column of the table, a qualifying person is a person of a description specified in the second column.

Description of person who made rule of undertaking	Qualifying person
Employer	A person who is, or is seeking to be, an employee of that employer
Trade organisation or qualifications body	A person who is, or is seeking to be, a member of the organisation or body
	A person upon whom the body has conferred a relevant qualification
	A person seeking conferment by the body of a relevant qualification

THIRD PARTIES (RIGHTS AGAINST INSURERS) ACT 2010
(2010, c. 10)

1   Rights against insurer of insolvent person etc.

(1)   This section applies if—
   (a)   a relevant person incurs a liability against which that person is insured under a contract of insurance,or
   (b)   a person who is subject to such a liability becomes a relevant person.

(2)   The rights of the relevant person under the contract against the insurer in respect of the liability are transferred to and vest in the person to whom the liability is or was incurred (the"third party").

(3)   The third party may bring proceedings to enforce the rights against the insurer without having established the relevant person's liability; but the third party may not enforce those rights without having established that liability.

(4)   For the purposes of this Act, a liability is established only if its existence and amount are established; and, for that purpose, "establish" means establish—
   (a)   by virtue of a declaration under section 2 ...,
   (b)   by a judgment or decree,
   (c)   by an award in arbitral proceedings or by an arbitration, or
   (d)   by an enforceable agreement.

(5)   In this Act—
   (a)   references to an "insured" are to a person who incurs or who is subject to a liability to a third party against which that person is insured under a contract of insurance;
   (b)   references to a "relevant person" are to a person within sections 4 to 7;
   (c)   references to a "third party" are to be construed in accordance with subsection (2);
   (d)   references to "transferred rights" are to rights under a contract of insurance which are transferred under this section.

2   Establishing liability in England Wales and Northern Ireland

(1)   This section applies where a person (P)—
   (a)   claims to have rights under a contract of insurance by virtue of a transfer under section 1, but
   (b)   has not yet established the insured's liability which is insured under that contract.

(2)   P may bring proceedings against the insurer for either or both of the following—
   (a)   a declaration as to the insured's liability to P;
   (b)   a declaration as to the insurer's potential liability to P.

(3)   In such proceedings P is entitled, subject to any defence on which the insurer may rely, to a declaration under subsection (2)(a) or (b) on proof of the insured's liability to P or (as the case may be) the insurer's potential liability to P.

(4)   Where proceedings are brought under subsection (2)(a) the insurer may rely on any defence on which the insured could rely if those proceedings were proceedings brought against the insured in respect of the insured's liability to P.

(5) Subsection (4) is subject to section 12(1).

(6) Where the court makes a declaration under this section, the effect of which is that the insurer is liable to P, the court may give the appropriate judgment against the insurer.

(7) Where a person applying for a declaration under subsection (2)(b) is entitled or required, by virtue of the contract of insurance, to do so in arbitral proceedings, that person may also apply in the same proceedings for a declaration under subsection (2)(a).

(8) In the application of this section to arbitral proceedings, subsection (6) is to be read as if "tribunal" were substituted for "court" and "make the appropriate award" for "give the appropriate judgment".

(9) When bringing proceedings under subsection (2)(a), P may also make the insured a defendant to those proceedings.

(10) If (but only if) the insured is a defendant to proceedings under this section (whether by virtue of subsection (9) or otherwise), a declaration under subsection (2) binds the insured as well as the insurer.

(11) In this section, references to the insurer's potential liability to P are references to the insurer's liability in respect of the insured's liability to P, if established.

4 Individuals

(1) An individual is a relevant person if any of the following is in force in respect of that individual in England and Wales—

(a) ...

(b) an administration order made under Part 6 of the County Courts Act 1984,

(c) an enforcement restriction order made under Part 6A of that Act,

(d) subject to subsection (4), a debt relief order made under Part 7A of the Insolvency Act 1986.

(e) a voluntary arrangement approved in accordance with Part 8 of that Act, or

(f) a bankruptcy order made under Part 9 of that Act.

(4) If an individual is a relevant person by virtue of subsection (1)(d) ..., that person is a relevant person for the purposes of section 1(1)(b) only.

5 Individuals who die insolvent

(1) An individual who dies insolvent is a relevant person for the purpose of section 1(1)(b) only.

(2) For the purposes of this section an individual (D) is to be regarded as having died insolvent if, following D's death—

(a) D's estate falls to be administered under section 421 of the Insolvency Act 1986 ...

(3) Where a transfer of rights under section 1 takes place as a result of an insured person being a relevant person by virtue of this section, references in this Act to an insured are, where the context so requires, to be read as references to the insured's estate.

6 Corporate bodies etc.

(1) A body corporate or unincorporated body is a relevant person if a compromise or arrangement between the body and its creditors (or a class of them) is in force, having been sanctioned in accordance with section 899 of the Companies Act 2006.

(2) A body corporate or an unincorporated body is a relevant person if, in England and Wales ...—

(a) a voluntary arrangement approved in accordance with Part 1 of the Insolvency Act 1986 is in force in respect of it,

(b) the body is in administration under Schedule B1 to that Act,

(c) there is a person appointed in accordance with Part 3 of that Act who is acting as receiver or manager of the body's property (or there would be such a person so acting but for a temporary vacancy),

      (d)   the body is, or is being, wound up voluntarily in accordance with Chapter 2 of Part 4 of that Act,

      (e)   there is a person appointed under section 135 of that Act who is acting as provisional liquidator in respect of the body (or there would be such a person so acting but for a temporary vacancy),

      (f)   the body is, or is being, wound up by the court following the making of a winding-up order under Chapter 6 of Part 4 of that Act or Part 5 of that Act.

(3)   ...

(4)   ...

(5)   A body within subsection (1) is not a relevant person in relation to a liability that is transferred to another body by the order sanctioning the compromise or arrangement.

(6)   Where a body is a relevant person by virtue of subsection (1), section 1 has effect to transfer rights only to a person on whom the compromise or arrangement is binding.

8   Limit on rights transferred

Where the liability of an insured to a third party is less than the liability of the insurer to the insured (ignoring the effect of section 1), no rights are transferred under that section in respect of the difference.

10   Insurer's right of set off

(1)   This section applies if—

      (a)   rights of an insured under a contract of insurance have been transferred to a third party under section 1,

      (b)   the insured is under a liability to the insurer under the contract ("the insured's liability"), and

      (c)   if there had been no transfer, the insurer would have been entitled to set off the amount of the insured's liability against the amount of the insurer's own liability to the insured.

(2)   The insurer is entitled to set off the amount of the insured's liability against the amount of the insurer's own liability to the third party in relation to the transferred rights.

12   Limitation ...

(1)   Subsection (2) applies where a person brings proceedings for a declaration under section 2(2)(a), ... and the proceedings are started ...—

      (a)   after the expiry of a period of limitation applicable to an action against the insured to enforce the insured's liability ..., but

      (b)   while such action is in progress.

(2)   The insurer may not rely on the expiry of that period as a defence unless the insured is able to rely on it in the action against the insured.

(3)   For the purpose of subsection (1), an action is to be treated as no longer in progress if it has been concluded by a judgment or decree, or by an award, even if there is an appeal or a right of appeal.

(4)   Where a person who has already established an insured's liability to that person brings proceedings under this Act against the insurer, nothing in this Act is to be read as meaning—

      (a)   that, for the purpose of the law of limitation in England and Wales, that person's cause of action against the insurer arose otherwise than at the time when that person established the liability of the insured, ...

13   Jurisdiction within the United Kingdom

(1)   Where a person (P) domiciled in a part of the United Kingdom is entitled to bring proceedings under this Act against an insurer domiciled in another part, P may do so in the part where P is domiciled or in the part where the insurer is domiciled (whatever the contract of insurance may stipulate as to where proceedings are to be brought).

(2)   The following provisions of the Civil Jurisdiction and Judgments Act 1982 (relating to determination of domicile) apply for the purposes of subsection (1)—

      (a)   section 41(2), (3), (5) and (6) (individuals);

      (b)   section 42(1), (3), (4) and (8) (corporations and associations);

    (c)   section 45(2) and (3) (trusts)
    (d)   section 46(1), (3) and (7) (the Crown).

14   Effect of transfer on insured's liability

(1)   Where rights in respect of an insured's liability to a third party are transferred under section 1, the third party may enforce that liability against the insured only to the extent (if any) that it exceeds the amount recoverable from the insurer by virtue of the transfer.

(2)   Subsection (3) applies if a transfer of rights under section 1 occurs because the insured person is a relevant person by virtue of—
    (a)   section 4(1)(a) or (e), ...
    (b)   section 6(1)(a), (2)(a) ..., or
    (c)   ...

(3)   If the liability is subject to the arrangement, trust deed or compromise by virtue of which the insured is a relevant person, the liability is to be treated as subject to that arrangement, trust deed or compromise only to the extent that the liability exceeds the amount recoverable from the insurer by virtue of the transfer.

(4)   ...

(5)   ...

(6)   For the purposes of this section the amount recoverable from the insurer does not include any amount that the third party is unable to recover as a result of—
    (a)   a shortage of assets on the insurer's part, in a case where the insurer is a relevant person, or
    (b)   a limit set by the contract of insurance on the fund available to meet claims in respect of a particular description of liability of the insured.

(7)   Where a third party is eligible to make a claim in respect of the insurer's liability under or by virtue of rules made under Part 15 of the Financial Services and Markets Act 2000 (the Financial Services Compensation Scheme)—
    (a)   subsection (6)(a) applies only if the third party has made such a claim, and
    (b)   the third party is to be treated as being able to recover from the insurer any amount paid to, or due to, the third party as a result of the claim.

15   Reinsurance

This Act does not apply to a case where the liability referred to in section 1(1) is itself a liability incurred by an insurer under a contract of insurance.

16   Voluntarily-incurred liabilities

It is irrelevant for the purpose of section 1 whether or not the liability of the insured is or was incurred voluntarily.

17   Avoidance

(1)   A contract of insurance to which this section applies is of no effect in so far as it purports, whether directly or indirectly, to avoid or terminate the contract or alter the rights of the parties under it in the event of the insured—
    (a)   becoming a relevant person, or
    (b)   dying insolvent (within the meaning given by section 5(2)).

(2)   A contract of insurance is one to which this section applies if the insurer's rights under it are capable of being transferred under section 1.

18   Cases with a foreign element

Except as expressly provided, the application of this Act does not depend on whether there is a connection with a part of the United Kingdom; and in particular it does not depend on—
    (a)   whether or not the liability (or the alleged liability) of the insured to the third party was incurred in, or under the law of, England and Wales, Scotland or Northern Ireland;
    (b)   the place of residence or domicile of any of the parties;
    (c)   whether or not the contract of insurance (or a part of it) is governed by the law of England and Wales, Scotland or Northern Ireland;
    (d)   the place where sums due under the contract of insurance are payable.

DAMAGES (SCOTLAND) ACT 2011
(2011, asp 7)

1   Damages to injured person whose expectation of life is diminished

(1)   This section applies to an action for damages in respect of personal injuries suffered by a pursuer whose date of death is expected to be earlier than had the injuries not been suffered.

(2)   In assessing the amount of damages by way of solatium the court is, if the pursuer—

     (a)   was at any time,

     (b)   is, or

     (c)   is likely to become,

     aware of the reduced expectation of life, to have regard to the extent to which the pursuer, in consequence of that awareness, has suffered or is likely to suffer.

(3)   Subject to subsection (2), no damages by way of solatium are recoverable by the pursuer in respect of loss of expectation of life.

(4)   In making an award of damages by way of solatium, the court is not required to ascribe specifically any part of the award to loss of expectation of life.

(5)   In assessing the amount of any patrimonial loss in respect of the period after the date of decree the court is to assume that the pursuer will live until the date when death would have been expected had the injuries not been suffered (the "notional date of death").

(6)   Such part of that amount as is attributable to the period between the expected date of death and the notional date of death (the "lost period") is to be assessed as follows—

     (a)   the court is to estimate what (if anything) the pursuer would have earned during the lost period through the pursuer's own labour or own gainful activity had the injuries not been suffered,

     (b)   the court may, if it thinks fit, add to the amount so estimated (whether or not that amount is nil) an amount equivalent to all or part of what it estimates the pursuer would have received by way of relevant benefits during the lost period had the injuries not been suffered, and

     (c)   the court is then to deduct, from the total amount obtained by virtue of paragraphs (a) and (b), 25% of that amount (to represent what would have been the pursuer's living expenses during the lost period had the injuries not been suffered).

(7)   But, if satisfied that it is necessary to do so for the purpose of avoiding a manifestly and materially unfair result, the court may apply a different percentage to that specified in subsection (6)(c).

(8)   In paragraph (b) of subsection (6), "relevant benefits" means benefits in money or money's worth other than benefits—

     (a)   derived from the pursuer's own estate, or

     (b)   consisting of such earnings as are mentioned in paragraph (a) of that subsection.

2   Transmission of deceased's rights to executor

(1)   There are transmissible to a deceased person's executor ("E") the like rights to damages, including a right to damages for non-patrimonial loss, in respect of injuries suffered by the deceased ("A") and vested in A immediately before A's death, being—

     (a)   personal injuries, or

     (b)   injuries which, though not personal injuries, are—

         (i)   injuries to name or reputation, or

         (ii)   injuries resulting from harassment actionable under section 8 of the Protection from Harassment Act 1997.

(2)   The "like rights" mentioned in subsection (1) do not include any right to damages by way of compensation for patrimonial loss attributable to any period after the date of death; and in determining the amount of damages for non-patrimonial loss payable to E by virtue of this section, the only period to which the court is to have regard is that ending immediately before A's death.

(3)   In so far as a right to damages vested in A comprises a right to damages for nonpatrimonial loss in respect of such injuries as are mentioned in sub-paragraph (i) of subsection (1)(b), that right is transmissible to E only if an action to enforce the right is brought by A and is not concluded before A's death.

(4)   For the purposes of subsection (3) an action is not to be taken to be concluded—
    (a)   while an appeal is competent, or
    (b)   before any appeal taken is disposed of.

3   Application of sections 4 to 6

Sections 4 to 6 apply where a person ("A") dies in consequence of suffering personal injuries as the result of the act or omission of another person ("B") and the act or omission—
    (a)   gives rise to liability to pay damages to A (or to A's executor), or
    (b)   would have given rise to such liability but for A's death.

4   Sums of damages payable to relatives

(1)   B is liable under this subsection to pay—
    (a)   to any relative of A who is a member of A's immediate family, such sums of damages as are mentioned in paragraphs (a) and (b) of subsection (3),
    (b)   to any other relative of A, such sum of damages as is mentioned in paragraph (a) of that subsection.

(2)   But, except as provided for in section 5, no such liability arises if the liability to pay damages to A (or to A's executor) in respect of the act or omission—
    (a)   is excluded or discharged, whether by antecedent agreement or otherwise, by A before A's death, or
    (b)   is excluded by virtue of an enactment.

(3)   The sums of damages are—
    (a)   such sum as will compensate for any loss of support which as a result of the act or omission is sustained, or is likely to be sustained, by the relative after the date of A's death together with any reasonable expenses incurred by the relative in connection with A's funeral, and
    (b)   such sum, if any, as the court thinks just by way of compensation for all or any of the following—
        (i)   distress and anxiety endured by the relative in contemplation of the suffering of A before A's death,
        (ii)   grief and sorrow of the relative caused by A's death,
        (iii)   the loss of such non-patrimonial benefit as the relative might have been expected to derive from A's society and guidance if A had not died.

(4)   The court, in making an award under paragraph (b) of subsection (3) is not required to ascribe any part of the award specifically to any of the sub-paragraphs of that paragraph.

(5)   For the purpose of subsection (1)(a)—
    (a)   a relative of A is a member of A's immediate family if the relative falls within any of paragraphs (a) to (d) of the definition of "relative" in section 14(1), (b) paragraphs (a)(i) and
    (b)   of section 14(2) are to be disregarded.

5   Discharge of liability to pay damages: exception for mesothelioma

(1)   This section applies where—
    (a)   the liability to pay damages to A (or to A's executor) is discharged, whether by antecedent agreement or otherwise, by A before A's death,
    (b)   the personal injury in consequence of which A died is mesothelioma, and
    (c)   the discharge and the death each occurred on or after 20th December 2006.

(2)   Liability arises under section 4(1) but is limited to the payment of such sum of damages as is mentioned in paragraph (b) of section 4(3).

6   Relative's loss of personal services

(1)   A relative entitled to damages under paragraph (a) of section 4(3) is entitled to include, as a head of damages under that paragraph, a reasonable sum in respect of the loss to the relative of A's personal services as a result of the act or omission.

(2)   In subsection (1), "personal services" has the same meaning as in section 9(1) of the Administration of Justice Act 1982 (damages in respect of inability of injured person to render such services).

7 Assessment of compensation for loss of support

(1) Such part of an award under paragraph (a) of section 4(3) as consists of a sum in compensation for loss of support is to be assessed applying the following paragraphs—

    (a) the total amount to be available to support A's relatives is an amount equivalent to 75% of A's net income,

    (b) in the case of any other relative than—

        (i) a person described in paragraph (a) of the definition of "relative" in section 14(1), or

        (ii) a dependent child,

    the relative is not to be awarded more in compensation for loss of support than the actual amount of that loss,

    (c) if—

        (i) no such other relative is awarded a sum in compensation for loss of support, the total amount mentioned in paragraph (a) is to be taken to be spent by A in supporting such of A's relatives as are mentioned in subparagraphs (i) and (ii) of paragraph (b),

        (ii) any such other relative is awarded a sum in compensation for loss of support, the total amount mentioned in paragraph (a) is, after deduction of the amount of the sum so awarded, to be taken to be spent by A in supporting such of A's relatives as are mentioned in those sub-paragraphs, and

    (d) any multiplier applied by the court—

        (i) is to run from the date of the interlocutor awarding damages, and

        (ii) is to apply only in respect of future loss of support.

(2) But, if satisfied that it is necessary to do so for the purpose of avoiding a manifestly and materially unfair result, the court may apply a different percentage to that specified in subsection (1)(a).

(3) In subsection (1)(b)(ii), "dependent child" means a child who as at the date of A's death—

    (a) has not attained the age of 18 years, and

    (b) is owed an obligation of aliment by A.

8 Further provision as regards relative's entitlement to damages

(1) Subject to subsection (3), in assessing for the purposes of section 4 or 6 the amount of any loss of support sustained by a relative of A no account is to be taken of—

    (a) any patrimonial gain or advantage which has accrued or will or may accrue to the relative, by way of succession or settlement, from A or from any other person, or

    (b) any insurance money, benefit, pension or gratuity which has been, or will or may be, paid as a result of A's death.

(2) In subsection (1)—

"benefit" means benefit under the Social Security Contributions and Benefits Act 1992 or the Social Security Contributions and Benefits (Northern Ireland) Act 1992 and any payment by a friendly society or trade union for the relief or maintenance of a member's dependants,

"insurance money" includes a return of premiums, and

"pension" includes a return of contributions and any payment of a lump sum in respect of a person's employment.

(3) Where A has been awarded a provisional award of damages under section 12(2) of the Administration of Justice Act 1982, the making of that award does not prevent liability from arising under section 4(1); but in assessing for the purposes of section 4 or 6 the amount of any loss of support sustained by a relative the court is to take into account such part of the provisional award relating to future patrimonial loss as was intended to compensate A for a period beyond the date on which A died.

(4) In order to establish loss of support for the purposes of section 4 or 6, it is not essential for a relative to show that A was, or might have become, subject to a duty in law to provide support for, or contribute to the support of, the relative; but if any such fact is established it may be taken into account in determining whether, and if so to what extent, A would (had A not died) have been likely to provide, or contribute to, such support.

(5) Except as provided for in this Act or in any other enactment, no person is entitled by reason of relationship to damages in respect of the death of another person.

(6) In subsection (5), "damages" includes damages by way of solatium.

9 Transmission of relative's rights to executor

(1) This section applies where liability to pay damages to a relative ("R") has arisen under section 4 or 6 but R dies.

(2) If the right to damages is vested in R immediately before R's death that right is transmissible to R's executor ("E"); but in determining the amount of damages payable to E by virtue of this section, the only period to which the court is to have regard is the period ending immediately before R's death.

(3) In a case where—
   (a) section 5 applies, and
   (b) R died before 27th April 2007,
   any right of R to damages under that section is to be taken, for the purposes of subsection (2), to have vested in R on A's death.

10 Enforcement by executor of rights transmitted under section 2 or 9

(1) Where a right is transmitted by virtue of section 2 or 9, the executor in question is entitled—
   (a) to bring an action to enforce it, or
   (b) if an action to enforce it was brought by the deceased but not concluded before the date of death, to be sisted as pursuer in that action.

(2) For the purposes of subsection (1)(b) an action is not to be taken to be concluded—
   (a) while an appeal is competent, or
   (b) before any appeal taken is disposed of.

11 Executor's claim not excluded by relative's claim etc.

(1) A claim made by virtue of this Act by a deceased's executor is not excluded by a claim so made by a relative of the deceased (or by such a relative's executor).

(2) Nor is a claim so made by a such a relative (or by such a relative's executor) excluded by a claim so made by the deceased's executor.

12 Limitation of total amount of liability

(1) This section applies to an action directed against a defender ("B") in which, following the death of a person ("A") from personal injuries, damages are claimed—
   (a) in respect of those injuries, by A's executor, or
   (b) in respect of A's death, by any relative of A or by the executor of any relative of A.

(2) If it is shown that the liability arising in relation to B from the personal injuries in question—
   (a) had before A's death, by antecedent agreement or otherwise, been limited to damages of a specified or ascertainable amount, or
   (b) is so limited by virtue of an enactment,
   nothing in this Act makes B liable to pay damages exceeding that amount.

(3) Accordingly, where there are two or more pursuers, any damages to which they would (but for this section) respectively be entitled under this Act are, if necessary, to be reduced pro rata.

(4) And where two or more actions are conjoined the conjoined actions are to be treated, for the purposes of this section, as if they were a single action.

14 Interpretation

(1) In this Act, unless the context otherwise requires—
   "personal injuries" means—
   (a) any disease, and
   (b) any impairment of a person's physical or mental condition, and
   "relative", in relation to a person who has died, means a person who—
   (a) immediately before the death is the deceased's spouse or civil partner or is living with the deceased as if married to, or in civil partnership with, the deceased,

      (b)   is a parent or child of the deceased, accepted the deceased as a child of the person's family or was accepted by the deceased as a child of the deceased's family,

      (c)   is the brother or sister of the deceased or was brought up in the same household as the deceased and accepted as a child of the family in which the deceased was a child,

      (d)   is a grandparent or grandchild of the deceased, accepted the deceased as a grandchild of the person or was accepted by the deceased as a grandchild of the deceased,

      (e)   is an ascendant or descendant of the deceased (other than a parent or grandparent or a child or grandchild of the deceased),

      (f)   is an uncle or aunt of the deceased,

      (g)   is a child or other issue of—
          (i)   a brother or sister of the deceased, or
          (ii)   an uncle or aunt of the deceased, or

      (h)   is a former spouse or civil partner of the deceased having become so by virtue of divorce or (as the case may be) dissolution of the partnership.

(2)   In deducing a relationship for the purposes of the definition of "relative" in subsection (1)—

      (a)   any relationship—
          (i)   by affinity is to be treated as a relationship by consanguinity,
          (ii)   of the half blood is to be treated as a relationship of the whole blood,

      (b)   a stepchild of a person is to be treated as the person's child.

(3)   In any enactment passed or made before this Act, unless the context otherwise requires, any reference to—

      (a)   solatium in respect of the death of any person (however expressed), or

      (b)   a loss of society award, is to be construed as a reference to an award under paragraph (b) of section 4(3).

DEFAMATION ACT 2013
(2013, c. 26)

Requirement of serious harm

1   Serious harm

(1)   A statement is not defamatory unless its publication has caused or is likely to cause serious harm to the reputation of the claimant.

(2)   For the purposes of this section, harm to the reputation of a body that trades for profit is not "serious harm" unless it has caused or is likely to cause the body serious financial loss.

Defences

2   Truth

(1)   It is a defence to an action for defamation for the defendant to show that the imputation conveyed by the statement complained of is substantially true.

(2)   Subsection (3) applies in an action for defamation if the statement complained of conveys two or more distinct imputations.

(3)   If one or more of the imputations is not shown to be substantially true, the defence under this section does not fail if, having regard to the imputations which are shown to be substantially true, the imputations which are not shown to be substantially true do not seriously harm the claimant's reputation.

3   Honest opinion

(1)   It is a defence to an action for defamation for the defendant to show that the following conditions are met.

(2)   The first condition is that the statement complained of was a statement of opinion.

(3)   The second condition is that the statement complained of indicated, whether in general or specific terms, the basis of the opinion.

(4)   The third condition is that an honest person could have held the opinion on the basis of—

(a)   any fact which existed at the time the statement complained of was published;

(b)   anything asserted to be a fact in a privileged statement published before the statement complained of.

(5)   The defence is defeated if the claimant shows that the defendant did not hold the opinion.

(6)   Subsection (5) does not apply in a case where the statement complained of was published by the defendant but made by another person ("the author"); and in such a case the defence is defeated if the claimant shows that the defendant knew or ought to have known that the author did not hold the opinion.

(7)   For the purposes of subsection (4)(b) a statement is a "privileged statement" if the person responsible for its publication would have one or more of the following defences if an action for defamation were brought in respect of it—

(a)   a defence under section 4 (publication on matter of public interest);

(b)   a defence under section 6 (peer-reviewed statement in scientific or academic journal);

(c)   a defence under section 14 of the Defamation Act 1996 (reports of court proceedings protected by absolute privilege);

(d)   a defence under section 15 of that Act (other reports protected by qualified privilege).

4   Publication on matter of public interest

(1)   It is a defence to an action for defamation for the defendant to show that—

(a)   the statement complained of was, or formed part of, a statement on a matter of public interest; and

(b)   the defendant reasonably believed that publishing the statement complained of was in the public interest.

(2)   Subject to subsections (3) and (4), in determining whether the defendant has shown the matters mentioned in subsection (1), the court must have regard to all the circumstances of the case.

(3)   If the statement complained of was, or formed part of, an accurate and impartial account of a dispute to which the claimant was a party, the court must in determining whether it was reasonable for the defendant to believe that publishing the statement was in the public interest disregard any omission of the defendant to take steps to verify the truth of the imputation conveyed by it.

(4)   In determining whether it was reasonable for the defendant to believe that publishing the statement complained of was in the public interest, the court must make such allowance for editorial judgement as it considers appropriate.

(5)   For the avoidance of doubt, the defence under this section may be relied upon irrespective of whether the statement complained of is a statement of fact or a statement of opinion.

(6)   The common law defence known as the Reynolds defence is abolished.

5   Operators of websites

(1)   This section applies where an action for defamation is brought against the operator of a website in respect of a statement posted on the website.

(2)   It is a defence for the operator to show that it was not the operator who posted the statement on the website.

(3)   The defence is defeated if the claimant shows that—

(a)   it was not possible for the claimant to identify the person who posted the statement,

(b)   the claimant gave the operator a notice of complaint in relation to the statement, and

(c)   the operator failed to respond to the notice of complaint in accordance with any provision contained in regulations.

(4)   For the purposes of subsection (3)(a), it is possible for a claimant to "identify" a person only if the claimant has sufficient information to bring proceedings against the person.

(5)   Regulations may—
    (a)   make provision as to the action required to be taken by an operator of a website in response to a notice of complaint (which may in particular include action relating to the identity or contact details of the person who posted the statement and action relating to its removal);
    (b)   make provision specifying a time limit for the taking of any such action;
    (c)   make provision conferring on the court a discretion to treat action taken after the expiry of a time limit as having been taken before the expiry; (d) make any other provision for the purposes of this section.

(6)   Subject to any provision made by virtue of subsection (7), a notice of complaint is a notice which—
    (a)   specifies the complainant's name,
    (b)   sets out the statement concerned and explains why it is defamatory of the complainant,
    (c)   specifies where on the website the statement was posted, and
    (d)   contains such other information as may be specified in regulations.

(7)   Regulations may make provision about the circumstances in which a notice which is not a notice of complaint is to be treated as a notice of complaint for the purposes of this section or any provision made under it.

(8)   Regulations under this section—
    (a)   may make different provision for different circumstances;
    (b)   are to be made by statutory instrument.

(9)   A statutory instrument containing regulations under this section may not be made unless a draft of the instrument has been laid before, and approved by a resolution of, each House of Parliament.

(10)   In this section "regulations" means regulations made by the Secretary of State.

(11)   The defence under this section is defeated if the claimant shows that the operator of the website has acted with malice in relation to the posting of the statement concerned.

(12)   The defence under this section is not defeated by reason only of the fact that the operator of the website moderates the statements posted on it by others.

6   Peer-reviewed statement in scientific or academic journal etc.

(1)   The publication of a statement in a scientific or academic journal (whether published in electronic form or otherwise) is privileged if the following conditions are met.

(2)   The first condition is that the statement relates to a scientific or academic matter.

(3)   The second condition is that before the statement was published in the journal an independent review of the statement's scientific or academic merit was carried out by—
    (a)   the editor of the journal, and
    (b)   one or more persons with expertise in the scientific or academic matter concerned.

(4)   Where the publication of a statement in a scientific or academic journal is privileged by virtue of subsection (1), the publication in the same journal of any assessment of the statement's scientific or academic merit is also privileged if—
    (a)   the assessment was written by one or more of the persons who carried out the independent review of the statement; and
    (b)   the assessment was written in the course of that review.

(5)   Where the publication of a statement or assessment is privileged by virtue of this section, the publication of a fair and accurate copy of, extract from or summary of the statement or assessment is also privileged.

(6)   A publication is not privileged by virtue of this section if it is shown to be made with malice.

(7)   Nothing in this section is to be construed—
    (a)   as protecting the publication of matter the publication of which is prohibited by law;
    (b)   as limiting any privilege subsisting apart from this section.

(8) The reference in subsection (3)(a) to "the editor of the journal" is to be read, in the case of a journal with more than one editor, as a reference to the editor or editors who were responsible for deciding to publish the statement concerned.

Single publication rule

8 Single publication rule

(1) This section applies if a person—
   (a) publishes a statement to the public ("the first publication"), and
   (b) subsequently publishes (whether or not to the public) that statement or a statement which is substantially the same.
(2) In subsection (1) "publication to the public" includes publication to a section of the public.
(3) For the purposes of section 4A of the Limitation Act 1980 (time limit for actions for defamation etc.) any cause of action against the person for defamation in respect of the subsequent publication is to be treated as having accrued on the date of the first publication.
(4) This section does not apply in relation to the subsequent publication if the manner of that publication is materially different from the manner of the first publication.
(5) In determining whether the manner of a subsequent publication is materially different from the manner of the first publication, the matters to which the court may have regard include (amongst other matters)—
   (a) the level of prominence that a statement is given;
   (b) the extent of the subsequent publication.
(6) Where this section applies—
   (a) it does not affect the court's discretion under section 32A of the Limitation Act 1980 (discretionary exclusion of time limit for actions for defamation etc.), and
   (b) the reference in subsection (1)(a) of that section to the operation of section 4A of that Act is a reference to the operation of section 4A together with this section.

Jurisdiction

9 Action against a person not domiciled in the UK or a Member State etc.

(1) This section applies to an action for defamation against a person who is not domiciled—
   (a) in the United Kingdom;
   (b) in another Member State; or
   (c) in a state which is for the time being a contracting party to the Lugano Convention.
(2) A court does not have jurisdiction to hear and determine an action to which this section applies unless the court is satisfied that, of all the places in which the statement complained of has been published, England and Wales is clearly the most appropriate place in which to bring an action in respect of the statement.
(3) The references in subsection (2) to the statement complained of include references to any statement which conveys the same, or substantially the same, imputation as the statement complained of.
(4) For the purposes of this section—
   (a) a person is domiciled in the United Kingdom or in another Member State if the person is domiciled there for the purposes of the Brussels Regulation;
   (b) a person is domiciled in a state which is a contracting party to the Lugano Convention if the person is domiciled in the state for the purposes of that Convention.
(5) In this section—
   "the Brussels Regulation" means Council Regulation (EC) No 44/2001 of 22nd December 2000 on jurisdiction and the recognition and enforcement of judgments in civil and commercial matters, as amended from time to time and as applied by the Agreement made on 19th October 2005 between the European Community and the Kingdom of Denmark on jurisdiction and the recognition and enforcement of judgments in civil and commercial matters;

"the Lugano Convention" means the Convention on jurisdiction and the recognition and enforcement of judgments in civil and commercial matters, between the European Community and the Republic of Iceland, the Kingdom of Norway, the Swiss Confederation and the Kingdom of Denmark signed on behalf of the European Community on 30th October 2007.

10 Action against a person who was not the author, editor etc.

(1) A court does not have jurisdiction to hear and determine an action for defamation brought against a person who was not the author, editor or publisher of the statement complained of unless the court is satisfied that it is not reasonably practicable for an action to be brought against the author, editor or publisher.

(2) In this section "author", "editor" and "publisher" have the same meaning as in section 1 of the Defamation Act 1996.

Summary of court judgment

12 Power of court to order a summary of its judgment to be published

(1) Where a court gives judgment for the claimant in an action for defamation the court may order the defendant to publish a summary of the judgment.

(2) The wording of any summary and the time, manner, form and place of its publication are to be for the parties to agree.

(3) If the parties cannot agree on the wording, the wording is to be settled by the court.

(4) If the parties cannot agree on the time, manner, form or place of publication, the court may give such directions as to those matters as it considers reasonable and practicable in the circumstances.

(5) This section does not apply where the court gives judgment for the claimant under section 8(3) of the Defamation Act 1996 (summary disposal of claims).

Removal, etc. of statements

13 Order to remove statement or cease distribution etc.

(1) Where a court gives judgment for the claimant in an action for defamation the court may order—
   (a) the operator of a website on which the defamatory statement is posted to remove the statement, or
   (b) any person who was not the author, editor or publisher of the defamatory statement to stop distributing, selling or exhibiting material containing the statement.

(2) In this section "author", "editor" and "publisher" have the same meaning as in section 1 of the Defamation Act 1996.

(3) Subsection (1) does not affect the power of the court apart from that subsection.

Slander

14 Special damage

(2) The publication of a statement that conveys the imputation that a person has a contagious or infectious disease does not give rise to a cause of action for slander unless the publication causes the person special damage.

General provisions

15 Meaning of "publish" and "statement"

In this Act—
   "publish" and "publication", in relation to a statement, have the meaning they have for the purposes of the law of defamation generally;

"statement" means words, pictures, visual images, gestures or any other method of signifying meaning.

16 Consequential amendments and savings etc.

(4) Nothing in section 1 or 14 affects any cause of action accrued before the commencement of the section in question.

(5) Nothing in sections 2 to 7 or 10 has effect in relation to an action for defamation if the cause of action accrued before the commencement of the section in question.

(6) In determining whether section 8 applies, no account is to be taken of any publication made before the commencement of the section.

(7) Nothing in section 9 or 11 has effect in relation to an action for defamation begun before the commencement of the section in question.

(8) In determining for the purposes of subsection (7)(a) of section 3 whether a person would have a defence under section 4 to any action for defamation, the operation of subsection (5) of this section is to be ignored.

CONSUMER RIGHTS ACT 2015
(2015, c. 15)

PART 1
CONSUMER CONTRACTS FOR GOODS, DIGITAL CONTENT AND SERVICES

CHAPTER 1
INTRODUCTION

1 Where Part 1 applies

(1) This Part applies where there is an agreement between a trader and a consumer for the trader to supply goods, digital content or services, if the agreement is a contract.

(2) It applies whether the contract is written or oral or implied from the parties' conduct, or more than one of these combined.

(3) Any of Chapters 2, 3 and 4 may apply to a contract—
   (a)   if it is a contract for the trader to supply goods, see Chapter 2;
   (b)   if it is a contract for the trader to supply digital content, see Chapter 3 (also, subsection (6));
   (c)   if it is a contract for the trader to supply a service, see Chapter 4 (also, subsection (6)).

(4) In each case the Chapter applies even if the contract also covers something covered by another Chapter (a mixed contract).

(5) Two or all three of those Chapters may apply to a mixed contract.

(6) For provisions about particular mixed contracts, see—
   (a)   section 15 (goods and installation);
   (b)   section 16 (goods and digital content).

(7) For other provision applying to contracts to which this Part applies, see Part 2 (unfair terms).

2 Key definitions

(1) These definitions apply in this Part (as well as the definitions in section 59).

(2) "Trader" means a person acting for purposes relating to that person's trade, business, craft or profession, whether acting personally or through another person acting in the trader's name or on the trader's behalf.

(3) "Consumer" means an individual acting for purposes that are wholly or mainly outside that individual's trade, business, craft or profession.

(4) A trader claiming that an individual was not acting for purposes wholly or mainly outside the individual's trade, business, craft or profession must prove it.

(5) For the purposes of Chapter 2, except to the extent mentioned in subsection (6), a person is not a consumer in relation to a sales contract if—
    (a) the goods are second hand goods sold at public auction, and
    (b) individuals have the opportunity of attending the sale in person.

(6) A person is a consumer in relation to such a contract for the purposes of—
    (a) sections 11(4) and (5), 12, 28 and 29, and
    (b) the other provisions of Chapter 2 as they apply in relation to those sections.

(7) "Business" includes the activities of any government department or local or public authority.

(8) "Goods" means any tangible moveable items, but that includes water, gas and electricity if and only if they are put up for supply in a limited volume or set quantity.

(9) "Digital content" means data which are produced and supplied in digital form.

CHAPTER 2
GOODS

What goods contracts are covered?

3   Contracts covered by this Chapter

(1) This Chapter applies to a contract for a trader to supply goods to a consumer.

(2) It applies only if the contract is one of these (defined for the purposes of this Part in sections 5 to 8)—
    (a) a sales contract;
    (b) a contract for the hire of goods;
    (c) a hire-purchase agreement;
    (d) a contract for transfer of goods.

(3) It does not apply—
    (a) to a contract for a trader to supply coins or notes to a consumer for use as currency;
    (b) to a contract for goods to be sold by way of execution or otherwise by authority of law;
    (c) to a contract intended to operate as a mortgage, pledge, charge or other security;
    (d) in relation to England and Wales or Northern Ireland, to a contract made by deed and for which the only consideration is the presumed consideration imported by the deed;
    (e) in relation to Scotland, to a gratuitous contract.

(4) A contract to which this Chapter applies is referred to in this Part as a "contract to supply goods".

(5) Contracts to supply goods include—
    (a) contracts entered into between one part owner and another;
    (b) contracts for the transfer of an undivided share in goods;
    (c) contracts that are absolute and contracts that are conditional.

(6) Subsection (1) is subject to any provision of this Chapter that applies a section or part of a section to only some of the kinds of contracts listed in subsection (2).

(7) A mixed contract (see section 1(4)) may be a contract of any of those kinds.

4   Ownership of goods

(1) In this Chapter ownership of goods means the general property in goods, not merely a special property.

(2) For the time when ownership of goods is transferred, see in particular the following provisions of the Sale of Goods Act 1979 (which relate to contracts of sale)—
    section 16:   goods must be ascertained
    section 17:   property passes when intended to pass
    section 18:   rules for ascertaining intention
    section 19:   reservation of right of disposal
    section 20A: undivided shares in goods forming part of a bulk
    section 20B: deemed consent by co-owner to dealings in bulk goods

5   Sales contracts

(1)   A contract is a sales contract if under it—
  (a)   the trader transfers or agrees to transfer ownership of goods to the consumer, and
  (b)   the consumer pays or agrees to pay the price.

(2)   A contract is a sales contract (whether or not it would be one under subsection (1)) if under the contract—
  (a)   goods are to be manufactured or produced and the trader agrees to supply them to the consumer,
  (b)   on being supplied, the goods will be owned by the consumer, and
  (c)   the consumer pays or agrees to pay the price.

(3)   A sales contract may be conditional (see section 3(5)), but in this Part "conditional sales contract" means a sales contract under which—
  (a)   the price for the goods or part of it is payable by instalments, and
  (b)   the trader retains ownership of the goods until the conditions specified in the contract (for the payment of instalments or otherwise) are met;
  and it makes no difference whether or not the consumer possesses the goods.

6   Contracts for the hire of goods

(1)   A contract is for the hire of goods if under it the trader gives or agrees to give the consumer possession of the goods with the right to use them, subject to the terms of the contract, for a period determined in accordance with the contract.

(2)   But a contract is not for the hire of goods if it is a hire-purchase agreement.

7   Hire-purchase agreements

(1)   A contract is a hire-purchase agreement if it meets the two conditions set out below.

(2)   The first condition is that under the contract goods are hired by the trader in return for periodical payments by the consumer (and "hired" is to be read in accordance with section 6(1)).

(3)   The second condition is that under the contract ownership of the goods will transfer to the consumer if the terms of the contract are complied with and—
  (a)   the consumer exercises an option to buy the goods,
  (b)   any party to the contract does an act specified in it, or
  (c)   an event specified in the contract occurs.

(4)   But a contract is not a hire-purchase agreement if it is a conditional sales contract.

8   Contracts for transfer of goods

A contract to supply goods is a contract for transfer of goods if under it the trader transfers or agrees to transfer ownership of the goods to the consumer and—
  (a)   the consumer provides or agrees to provide consideration otherwise than by paying a price, or
  (b)   the contract is, for any other reason, not a sales contract or a hire-purchase agreement.

What statutory rights are there under a goods contract?

9   Goods to be of satisfactory quality

(1)   Every contract to supply goods is to be treated as including a term that the quality of the goods is satisfactory.

(2)   The quality of goods is satisfactory if they meet the standard that a reasonable person would consider satisfactory, taking account of—
  (a)   any description of the goods,
  (b)   the price or other consideration for the goods (if relevant), and
  (c)   all the other relevant circumstances (see subsection (5)).

(3)   The quality of goods includes their state and condition; and the following aspects (among others) are in appropriate cases aspects of the quality of goods—
  (a)   fitness for all the purposes for which goods of that kind are usually supplied;
  (b)   appearance and finish;

     (c)   freedom from minor defects;
     (d)   safety;
     (e)   durability.

(4)   The term mentioned in subsection (1) does not cover anything which makes the quality of the goods unsatisfactory—

     (a)   which is specifically drawn to the consumer's attention before the contract is made,

     (b)   where the consumer examines the goods before the contract is made, which that examination ought to reveal, or

     (c)   in the case of a contract to supply goods by sample, which would have been apparent on a reasonable examination of the sample.

(5)   The relevant circumstances mentioned in subsection (2)(c) include any public statement about the specific characteristics of the goods made by the trader, the producer or any representative of the trader or the producer.

(6)   That includes, in particular, any public statement made in advertising or labelling.

(7)   But a public statement is not a relevant circumstance for the purposes of subsection (2)(c) if the trader shows that—

     (a)   when the contract was made, the trader was not, and could not reasonably have been, aware of the statement,

     (b)   before the contract was made, the statement had been publicly withdrawn or, to the extent that it contained anything which was incorrect or misleading, it had been publicly corrected, or

     (c)   the consumer's decision to contract for the goods could not have been influenced by the statement.

(8)   In a contract to supply goods a term about the quality of the goods may be treated as included as a matter of custom.

(9)   See section 19 for a consumer's rights if the trader is in breach of a term that this section requires to be treated as included in a contract.

10   Goods to be fit for particular purpose

(1)   Subsection (3) applies to a contract to supply goods if before the contract is made the consumer makes known to the trader (expressly or by implication) any particular purpose for which the consumer is contracting for the goods.

(2)   Subsection (3) also applies to a contract to supply goods if—

     (a)   the goods were previously sold by a credit-broker to the trader,

     (b)   in the case of a sales contract or contract for transfer of goods, the consideration or part of it is a sum payable by instalments, and

     (c)   before the contract is made, the consumer makes known to the credit-broker (expressly or by implication) any particular purpose for which the consumer is contracting for the goods.

(3)   The contract is to be treated as including a term that the goods are reasonably fit for that purpose, whether or not that is a purpose for which goods of that kind are usually supplied.

(4)   Subsection (3) does not apply if the circumstances show that the consumer does not rely, or it is unreasonable for the consumer to rely, on the skill or judgment of the trader or credit-broker.

(5)   In a contract to supply goods a term about the fitness of the goods for a particular purpose may be treated as included as a matter of custom.

(6)   See section 19 for a consumer's rights if the trader is in breach of a term that this section requires to be treated as included in a contract.

11   Goods to be as described

(1)   Every contract to supply goods by description is to be treated as including a term that the goods will match the description.

(2)   If the supply is by sample as well as by description, it is not sufficient that the bulk of the goods matches the sample if the goods do not also match the description.

(3)   A supply of goods is not prevented from being a supply by description just because—

     (a)   the goods are exposed for supply, and

     (b)   they are selected by the consumer.

(4)   Any information that is provided by the trader about the goods and is information mentioned in paragraph (a) of Schedule 1 or 2 to the Consumer Contracts (Information, Cancellation and Additional Charges) Regulations 2013 (SI 2013/3134) (main characteristics of goods) is to be treated as included as a term of the contract.

(5)   A change to any of that information, made before entering into the contract or later, is not effective unless expressly agreed between the consumer and the trader.

(6)   See section 2(5) and (6) for the application of subsections (4) and (5) where goods are sold at public auction.

(7)   See section 19 for a consumer's rights if the trader is in breach of a term that this section requires to be treated as included in a contract.

12   Other pre-contract information included in contract

(1)   This section applies to any contract to supply goods.

(2)   Where regulation 9, 10 or 13 of the Consumer Contracts (Information, Cancellation and Additional Charges) Regulations 2013 (SI 2013/3134) required the trader to provide information to the consumer before the contract became binding, any of that information that was provided by the trader other than information about the goods and mentioned in paragraph (a) of Schedule 1 or 2 to the Regulations (main characteristics of goods) is to be treated as included as a term of the contract.

(3)   A change to any of that information, made before entering into the contract or later, is not effective unless expressly agreed between the consumer and the trader.

(4)   See section 2(5) and (6) for the application of this section where goods are sold at public auction.

(5)   See section 19 for a consumer's rights if the trader is in breach of a term that this section requires to be treated as included in the contract.

13   Goods to match a sample

(1)   This section applies to a contract to supply goods by reference to a sample of the goods that is seen or examined by the consumer before the contract is made.

(2)   Every contract to which this section applies is to be treated as including a term that—

    (a)   the goods will match the sample except to the extent that any differences between the sample and the goods are brought to the consumer's attention before the contract is made, and

    (b)   the goods will be free from any defect that makes their quality unsatisfactory and that would not be apparent on a reasonable examination of the sample.

(3)   See section 19 for a consumer's rights if the trader is in breach of a term that this section requires to be treated as included in a contract.

14   Goods to match a model seen or examined

(1)   This section applies to a contract to supply goods by reference to a model of the goods that is seen or examined by the consumer before entering into the contract.

(2)   Every contract to which this section applies is to be treated as including a term that the goods will match the model except to the extent that any differences between the model and the goods are brought to the consumer's attention before the consumer enters into the contract.

(3)   See section 19 for a consumer's rights if the trader is in breach of a term that this section requires to be treated as included in a contract.

15   Installation as part of conformity of the goods with the contract

(1)   Goods do not conform to a contract to supply goods if—

    (a)   installation of the goods forms part of the contract,

    (b)   the goods are installed by the trader or under the trader's responsibility, and

    (c)   the goods are installed incorrectly.

(2)   See section 19 for the effect of goods not conforming to the contract.

16   Goods not conforming to contract if digital content does not conform

(1)   Goods (whether or not they conform otherwise to a contract to supply goods) do not conform to it if—

    (a)   the goods are an item that includes digital content, and

    (b)   the digital content does not conform to the contract to supply that content (for which see section 42(1)).

(2)   See section 19 for the effect of goods not conforming to the contract.

17   Trader to have right to supply the goods etc.

(1)   Every contract to supply goods, except one within subsection (4), is to be treated as including a term—
    (a)   in the case of a contract for the hire of goods, that at the beginning of the period of hire the trader must have the right to transfer possession of the goods by way of hire for that period,
    (b)   in any other case, that the trader must have the right to sell or transfer the goods at the time when ownership of the goods is to be transferred.

(2)   Every contract to supply goods, except a contract for the hire of goods or a contract within subsection (4), is to be treated as including a term that—
    (a)   the goods are free from any charge or encumbrance not disclosed or known to the consumer before entering into the contract,
    (b)   the goods will remain free from any such charge or encumbrance until ownership of them is to be transferred, and
    (c)   the consumer will enjoy quiet possession of the goods except so far as it may be disturbed by the owner or other person entitled to the benefit of any charge or encumbrance so disclosed or known.

(3)   Every contract for the hire of goods is to be treated as including a term that the consumer will enjoy quiet possession of the goods for the period of the hire except so far as the possession may be disturbed by the owner or other person entitled to the benefit of any charge or encumbrance disclosed or known to the consumer before entering into the contract.

(4)   This subsection applies to a contract if the contract shows, or the circumstances when they enter into the contract imply, that the trader and the consumer intend the trader to transfer only—
    (a)   whatever title the trader has, even if it is limited, or
    (b)   whatever title a third person has, even if it is limited.

(5)   Every contract within subsection (4) is to be treated as including a term that all charges or encumbrances known to the trader and not known to the consumer were disclosed to the consumer before entering into the contract.

(6)   Every contract within subsection (4) is to be treated as including a term that the consumer's quiet possession of the goods—
    (a)   will not be disturbed by the trader, and
    (b)   will not be disturbed by a person claiming through or under the trader, unless that person is claiming under a charge or encumbrance that was disclosed or known to the consumer before entering into the contract.

(7)   If subsection (4)(b) applies (transfer of title that a third person has), the contract is also to be treated as including a term that the consumer's quiet possession of the goods—
    (a)   will not be disturbed by the third person, and
    (b)   will not be disturbed by a person claiming through or under the third person, unless the claim is under a charge or encumbrance that was disclosed or known to the consumer before entering into the contract.

(8)   In the case of a contract for the hire of goods, this section does not affect the right of the trader to repossess the goods where the contract provides or is to be treated as providing for this.

(9)   See section 19 for a consumer's rights if the trader is in breach of a term that this section requires to be treated as included in a contract.

18   No other requirement to treat term about quality or fitness as included

(1)   Except as provided by sections 9, 10, 13 and 16, a contract to supply goods is not to be treated as including any term about the quality of the goods or their fitness for any particular purpose, unless the term is expressly included in the contract.

(2)   Subsection (1) is subject to provision made by any other enactment (whenever passed or made).

What remedies are there if statutory rights under a goods contract are not met?

19   Consumer's rights to enforce terms about goods

(1)   In this section and sections 22 to 24 references to goods conforming to a contract are references to—

     (a)   the goods conforming to the terms described in sections 9, 10, 11, 13 and 14,

     (b)   the goods not failing to conform to the contract under section 15 or 16, and

     (c)   the goods conforming to requirements that are stated in the contract.

(2)   But, for the purposes of this section and sections 22 to 24, a failure to conform as mentioned in subsection (1)(a) to (c) is not a failure to conform to the contract if it has its origin in materials supplied by the consumer.

(3)   If the goods do not conform to the contract because of a breach of any of the terms described in sections 9, 10, 11, 13 and 14, or if they do not conform to the contract under section 16, the consumer's rights (and the provisions about them and when they are available) are—

     (a)   the short-term right to reject (sections 20 and 22);

     (b)   the right to repair or replacement (section 23); and

     (c)   the right to a price reduction or the final right to reject (sections 20 and 24).

(4)   If the goods do not conform to the contract under section 15 or because of a breach of requirements that are stated in the contract, the consumer's rights (and the provisions about them and when they are available) are—

     (a)   the right to repair or replacement (section 23); and

     (b)   the right to a price reduction or the final right to reject (sections 20 and 24).

(5)   If the trader is in breach of a term that section 12 requires to be treated as included in the contract, the consumer has the right to recover from the trader the amount of any costs incurred by the consumer as a result of the breach, up to the amount of the price paid or the value of other consideration given for the goods.

(6)   If the trader is in breach of the term that section 17(1) (right to supply etc.) requires to be treated as included in the contract, the consumer has a right to reject (see section 20 for provisions about that right and when it is available).

(7)   Subsections (3) to (6) are subject to section 25 and subsections (3)(a) and (6) are subject to section 26.

(8)   Section 28 makes provision about remedies for breach of a term about the time for delivery of goods.

(9)   This Chapter does not prevent the consumer seeking other remedies—

     (a)   for a breach of a term that this Chapter requires to be treated as included in the contract,

     (b)   on the grounds that, under section 15 or 16, goods do not conform to the contract, or

     (c)   for a breach of a requirement stated in the contract.

(10)   Those other remedies may be ones—

     (a)   in addition to a remedy referred to in subsections (3) to (6) (but not so as to recover twice for the same loss), or

     (b)   instead of such a remedy, or

     (c)   where no such remedy is provided for.

(11)   Those other remedies include any of the following that is open to the consumer in the circumstances—

     (a)   claiming damages;

     (b)   seeking specific performance;

     (c)   seeking an order for specific implement;

     (d)   relying on the breach against a claim by the trader for the price;

     (e)   for breach of an express term, exercising a right to treat the contract as at an end.

(12)   It is not open to the consumer to treat the contract as at an end for breach of a term that this Chapter requires to be treated as included in the contract, or on the grounds that, under section 15 or 16, goods do not conform to the contract, except as provided by subsections (3), (4) and (6).

(13)   In this Part, treating a contract as at an end means treating it as repudiated.

(14) For the purposes of subsections (3)(b) and (c) and (4), goods which do not conform to the contract at any time within the period of six months beginning with the day on which the goods were delivered to the consumer must be taken not to have conformed to it on that day.

(15) Subsection (14) does not apply if—
- (a) it is established that the goods did conform to the contract on that day, or
- (b) its application is incompatible with the nature of the goods or with how they fail to conform to the contract.

20   Right to reject

(1)   The short-term right to reject is subject to section 22.

(2)   The final right to reject is subject to section 24.

(3)   The right to reject under section 19(6) is not limited by those sections.

(4)   Each of these rights entitles the consumer to reject the goods and treat the contract as at an end, subject to subsections (20) and (21).

(5)   The right is exercised if the consumer indicates to the trader that the consumer is rejecting the goods and treating the contract as at an end.

(6)   The indication may be something the consumer says or does, but it must be clear enough to be understood by the trader.

(7)   From the time when the right is exercised—
- (a) the trader has a duty to give the consumer a refund, subject to subsection (18), and
- (b) the consumer has a duty to make the goods available for collection by the trader or (if there is an agreement for the consumer to return rejected goods) to return them as agreed.

(8)   Whether or not the consumer has a duty to return the rejected goods, the trader must bear any reasonable costs of returning them, other than any costs incurred by the consumer in returning the goods in person to the place where the consumer took physical possession of them.

(9)   The consumer's entitlement to receive a refund works as follows.

(10) To the extent that the consumer paid money under the contract, the consumer is entitled to receive back the same amount of money.

(11) To the extent that the consumer transferred anything else under the contract, the consumer is entitled to receive back the same amount of what the consumer transferred, unless subsection (12) applies.

(12) To the extent that the consumer transferred under the contract something for which the same amount of the same thing cannot be substituted, the consumer is entitled to receive back in its original state whatever the consumer transferred.

(13) If the contract is for the hire of goods, the entitlement to a refund extends only to anything paid or otherwise transferred for a period of hire that the consumer does not get because the contract is treated as at an end.

(14) If the contract is a hire-purchase agreement or a conditional sales contract and the contract is treated as at an end before the whole of the price has been paid, the entitlement to a refund extends only to the part of the price paid.

(15) A refund under this section must be given without undue delay, and in any event within 14 days beginning with the day on which the trader agrees that the consumer is entitled to a refund.

(16) If the consumer paid money under the contract, the trader must give the refund using the same means of payment as the consumer used, unless the consumer expressly agrees otherwise.

(17) The trader must not impose any fee on the consumer in respect of the refund.

(18) There is no entitlement to receive a refund—
- (a) if none of subsections (10) to (12) applies,
- (b) to the extent that anything to which subsection (12) applies cannot be given back in its original state, or
- (c) where subsection (13) applies, to the extent that anything the consumer transferred under the contract cannot be divided so as to give back only the amount, or part of the amount, to which the consumer is entitled.

(19) It may be open to a consumer to claim damages where there is no entitlement to receive a refund, or because of the limits of the entitlement, or instead of a refund.

(20) Subsection (21) qualifies the application in relation to England and Wales and Northern Ireland of the rights mentioned in subsections (1) to (3) where—

(a) the contract is a severable contract,

(b) in relation to the final right to reject, the contract is a contract for the hire of goods, a hire-purchase agreement or a contract for transfer of goods, and (c) section 26(3) does not apply.

(21) The consumer is entitled, depending on the terms of the contract and the circumstances of the case—

(a) to reject the goods to which a severable obligation relates and treat that obligation as at an end (so that the entitlement to a refund relates only to what the consumer paid or transferred in relation to that obligation), or

(b) to exercise any of the rights mentioned in subsections (1) to (3) in respect of the whole contract.

21 Partial rejection of goods

(1) If the consumer has any of the rights mentioned in section 20(1) to (3), but does not reject all of the goods and treat the contract as at an end, the consumer—

(a) may reject some or all of the goods that do not conform to the contract, but

(b) may not reject any goods that do conform to the contract.

(2) If the consumer is entitled to reject the goods in an instalment, but does not reject all of those goods, the consumer—

(a) may reject some or all of the goods in the instalment that do not conform to the contract, but

(b) may not reject any goods in the instalment that do conform to the contract.

(3) If any of the goods form a commercial unit, the consumer cannot reject some of those goods without also rejecting the rest of them.

(4) A unit is a "commercial unit" if division of the unit would materially impair the value of the goods or the character of the unit.

(5) The consumer rejects goods under this section by indicating to the trader that the consumer is rejecting the goods.

(6) The indication may be something the consumer says or does, but it must be clear enough to be understood by the trader.

(7) From the time when a consumer rejects goods under this section—

(a) the trader has a duty to give the consumer a refund in respect of those goods (subject to subsection (10)), and

(b) the consumer has a duty to make those goods available for collection by the trader or (if there is an agreement for the consumer to return rejected goods) to return them as agreed.

(8) Whether or not the consumer has a duty to return the rejected goods, the trader must bear any reasonable costs of returning them, other than any costs incurred by the consumer in returning those goods in person to the place where the consumer took physical possession of them.

(9) Section 20(10) to (17) apply to a consumer's right to receive a refund under this section (and in section 20(13) and (14) references to the contract being treated as at an end are to be read as references to goods being rejected).

(10) That right does not apply—

(a) if none of section 20(10) to (12) applies,

(b) to the extent that anything to which section 20(12) applies cannot be given back in its original state, or

(c) to the extent that anything the consumer transferred under the contract cannot be divided so as to give back only the amount, or part of the amount, to which the consumer is entitled.

(11) It may be open to a consumer to claim damages where there is no right to receive a refund, or because of the limits of the right, or instead of a refund.

(12) References in this section to goods conforming to a contract are to be read in accordance with section 19(1) and (2), but they also include the goods conforming to the terms described in section 17.

(13) Where section 20(21)(a) applies the reference in subsection (1) to the consumer treating the contract as at an end is to be read as a reference to the consumer treating the severable obligation as at an end.

22   Time limit for short-term right to reject

(1) A consumer who has the short-term right to reject loses it if the time limit for exercising it passes without the consumer exercising it, unless the trader and the consumer agree that it may be exercised later.

(2) An agreement under which the short-term right to reject would be lost before the time limit passes is not binding on the consumer.

(3) The time limit for exercising the short-term right to reject (unless subsection (4) applies) is the end of 30 days beginning with the first day after these have all happened—

   (a) ownership or (in the case of a contract for the hire of goods, a hire-purchase agreement or a conditional sales contract) possession of the goods has been transferred to the consumer,

   (b) the goods have been delivered, and

   (c) where the contract requires the trader to install the goods or take other action to enable the consumer to use them, the trader has notified the consumer that the action has been taken.

(4) If any of the goods are of a kind that can reasonably be expected to perish after a shorter period, the time limit for exercising the short-term right to reject in relation to those goods is the end of that shorter period (but without affecting the time limit in relation to goods that are not of that kind).

(5) Subsections (3) and (4) do not prevent the consumer exercising the short-term right to reject before something mentioned in subsection (3)(a), (b) or (c) has happened.

(6) If the consumer requests or agrees to the repair or replacement of goods, the period mentioned in subsection (3) or (4) stops running for the length of the waiting period.

(7) If goods supplied by the trader in response to that request or agreement do not conform to the contract, the time limit for exercising the short-term right to reject is then either—

   (a) 7 days after the waiting period ends, or

   (b) if later, the original time limit for exercising that right, extended by the waiting period.

(8) The waiting period—

   (a) begins with the day the consumer requests or agrees to the repair or replacement of the goods, and

   (b) ends with the day on which the consumer receives goods supplied by the trader in response to the request or agreement.

23   Right to repair or replacement

(1) This section applies if the consumer has the right to repair or replacement (see section 19(3) and (4)).

(2) If the consumer requires the trader to repair or replace the goods, the trader must—

   (a) do so within a reasonable time and without significant inconvenience to the consumer, and

   (b) bear any necessary costs incurred in doing so (including in particular the cost of any labour, materials or postage).

(3) The consumer cannot require the trader to repair or replace the goods if that remedy (the repair or the replacement)—

   (a) is impossible, or

   (b) is disproportionate compared to the other of those remedies.

(4) Either of those remedies is disproportionate compared to the other if it imposes costs on the trader which, compared to those imposed by the other, are unreasonable, taking into account—

   (a) the value which the goods would have if they conformed to the contract,

   (b) the significance of the lack of conformity, and

   (c) whether the other remedy could be effected without significant inconvenience to the consumer.

(5) Any question as to what is a reasonable time or significant inconvenience is to be determined taking account of—
   (a) the nature of the goods, and
   (b) the purpose for which the goods were acquired.

(6) A consumer who requires or agrees to the repair of goods cannot require the trader to replace them, or exercise the short-term right to reject, without giving the trader a reasonable time to repair them (unless giving the trader that time would cause significant inconvenience to the consumer).

(7) A consumer who requires or agrees to the replacement of goods cannot require the trader to repair them, or exercise the short-term right to reject, without giving the trader a reasonable time to replace them (unless giving the trader that time would cause significant inconvenience to the consumer).

(8) In this Chapter, "repair" in relation to goods that do not conform to a contract, means making them conform.

24 Right to price reduction or final right to reject

(1) The right to a price reduction is the right—
   (a) to require the trader to reduce by an appropriate amount the price the consumer is required to pay under the contract, or anything else the consumer is required to transfer under the contract, and
   (b) to receive a refund from the trader for anything already paid or otherwise transferred by the consumer above the reduced amount.

(2) The amount of the reduction may, where appropriate, be the full amount of the price or whatever the consumer is required to transfer.

(3) Section 20(10) to (17) applies to a consumer's right to receive a refund under subsection (1)(b).

(4) The right to a price reduction does not apply—
   (a) if what the consumer is (before the reduction) required to transfer under the contract, whether or not already transferred, cannot be divided up so as to enable the trader to receive or retain only the reduced amount, or
   (b) if anything to which section 20(12) applies cannot be given back in its original state.

(5) A consumer who has the right to a price reduction and the final right to reject may only exercise one (not both), and may only do so in one of these situations—
   (a) after one repair or one replacement, the goods do not conform to the contract;
   (b) because of section 23(3) the consumer can require neither repair nor replacement of the goods; or
   (c) the consumer has required the trader to repair or replace the goods, but the trader is in breach of the requirement of section 23(2)(a) to do so within a reasonable time and without significant inconvenience to the consumer.

(6) There has been a repair or replacement for the purposes of subsection (5)(a) if—
   (a) the consumer has requested or agreed to repair or replacement of the goods (whether in relation to one fault or more than one), and
   (b) the trader has delivered goods to the consumer, or made goods available to the consumer, in response to the request or agreement.

(7) For the purposes of subsection (6) goods that the trader arranges to repair at the consumer's premises are made available when the trader indicates that the repairs are finished.

(8) If the consumer exercises the final right to reject, any refund to the consumer may be reduced by a deduction for use, to take account of the use the consumer has had of the goods in the period since they were delivered, but this is subject to subsections (9) and (10).

(9) No deduction may be made to take account of use in any period when the consumer had the goods only because the trader failed to collect them at an agreed time.

(10) No deduction may be made if the final right to reject is exercised in the first 6 months (see subsection (11)), unless—
   (a) the goods consist of a motor vehicle, or
   (b) the goods are of a description specified by order made by the Secretary of State by statutory instrument.

(11) In subsection (10) the first 6 months means 6 months beginning with the first day after these have all happened—
  (a) ownership or (in the case of a contract for the hire of goods, a hire-purchase agreement or a conditional sales contract) possession of the goods has been transferred to the consumer,
  (b) the goods have been delivered, and
  (c) where the contract requires the trader to install the goods or take other action to enable the consumer to use them, the trader has notified the consumer that the action has been taken.

(12) In subsection (10)(a) "motor vehicle"—
  (a) in relation to Great Britain, has the same meaning as in the Road Traffic Act 1988 (see sections 185 to 194 of that Act);
  (b) in relation to Northern Ireland, has the same meaning as in the Road Traffic (Northern Ireland) Order 1995 (SI 1995/2994 (NI 18)) (see Parts I and V of that Order).

(13) But a vehicle is not a motor vehicle for the purposes of subsection (10)(a) if it is constructed or adapted—
  (a) for the use of a person suffering from some physical defect or disability, and
  (b) so that it may only be used by one such person at any one time.

(14) An order under subsection (10)(b)—
  (a) may be made only if the Secretary of State is satisfied that it is appropriate to do so because of significant detriment caused to traders as a result of the application of subsection (10) in relation to goods of the description specified by the order;
  (b) may contain transitional or transitory provision or savings.

(15) No order may be made under subsection (10)(b) unless a draft of the statutory instrument containing it has been laid before, and approved by a resolution of, each House of Parliament.

Other rules about remedies under goods contracts

25　Delivery of wrong quantity

(1) Where the trader delivers to the consumer a quantity of goods less than the trader contracted to supply, the consumer may reject them, but if the consumer accepts them the consumer must pay for them at the contract rate.

(2) Where the trader delivers to the consumer a quantity of goods larger than the trader contracted to supply, the consumer may accept the goods included in the contract and reject the rest, or may reject all of the goods.

(3) Where the trader delivers to the consumer a quantity of goods larger than the trader contracted to supply and the consumer accepts all of the goods delivered, the consumer must pay for them at the contract rate.

(4) Where the consumer is entitled to reject goods under this section, any entitlement for the consumer to treat the contract as at an end depends on the terms of the contract and the circumstances of the case.

(5) The consumer rejects goods under this section by indicating to the trader that the consumer is rejecting the goods.

(6) The indication may be something the consumer says or does, but it must be clear enough to be understood by the trader.

(7) Subsections (1) to (3) do not prevent the consumer claiming damages, where it is open to the consumer to do so.

(8) This section is subject to any usage of trade, special agreement, or course of dealing between the parties.

26　Instalment deliveries

(1) Under a contract to supply goods, the consumer is not bound to accept delivery of the goods by instalments, unless that has been agreed between the consumer and the trader.

(2)   The following provisions apply if the contract provides for the goods to be delivered by stated instalments, which are to be separately paid for.

(3)   If the trader makes defective deliveries in respect of one or more instalments, the consumer, apart from any entitlement to claim damages, may be (but is not necessarily) entitled—

(a)   to exercise the short-term right to reject or the right to reject under section 19(6) (as applicable) in respect of the whole contract, or

(b)   to reject the goods in an instalment.

(4)   Whether paragraph (a) or (b) of subsection (3) (or neither) applies to a consumer depends on the terms of the contract and the circumstances of the case.

(5)   In subsection (3), making defective deliveries does not include failing to make a delivery in accordance with section 28.

(6)   If the consumer neglects or refuses to take delivery of or pay for one or more instalments, the trader may—

(a)   be entitled to treat the whole contract as at an end, or

(b)   if it is a severable breach, have a claim for damages but not a right to treat the whole contract as at an end.

(7)   Whether paragraph (a) or (b) of subsection (6) (or neither) applies to a trader depends on the terms of the contract and the circumstances of the case.

27   Consignation, or payment into court, in Scotland

(1)   Subsection (2) applies where—

(a)   a consumer has not rejected goods which the consumer could have rejected for breach of a term mentioned in section 19(3) or (6),

(b)   the consumer has chosen to treat the breach as giving rise only to a claim for damages or to a right to rely on the breach against a claim by the trader for the price of the goods, and

(c)   the trader has begun proceedings in court to recover the price or has brought a counter-claim for the price.

(2)   The court may require the consumer—

(a)   to consign, or pay into court, the price of the goods, or part of the price, or

(b)   to provide some other reasonable security for payment of the price.

Other rules about goods contracts

28   Delivery of goods

(1)   This section applies to any sales contract.

(2)   Unless the trader and the consumer have agreed otherwise, the contract is to be treated as including a term that the trader must deliver the goods to the consumer.

(3)   Unless there is an agreed time or period, the contract is to be treated as including a term that the trader must deliver the goods—

(a)   without undue delay, and

(b)   in any event, not more than 30 days after the day on which the contract is entered into.

(4)   In this section—

(a)   an "agreed" time or period means a time or period agreed by the trader and the consumer for delivery of the goods;

(b)   if there is an obligation to deliver the goods at the time the contract is entered into, that time counts as the "agreed" time.

(5)   Subsections (6) and (7) apply if the trader does not deliver the goods in accordance with subsection (3) or at the agreed time or within the agreed period.

(6)   If the circumstances are that—

(a)   the trader has refused to deliver the goods,

(b)   delivery of the goods at the agreed time or within the agreed period is essential taking into account all the relevant circumstances at the time the contract was entered into, or

(c)   the consumer told the trader before the contract was entered into that delivery in accordance with subsection (3), or at the agreed time or within the agreed period, was essential,
then the consumer may treat the contract as at an end.

(7)   In any other circumstances, the consumer may specify a period that is appropriate in the circumstances and require the trader to deliver the goods before the end of that period.

(8)   If the consumer specifies a period under subsection (7) but the goods are not delivered within that period, then the consumer may treat the contract as at an end.

(9)   If the consumer treats the contract as at an end under subsection (6) or (8), the trader must without undue delay reimburse all payments made under the contract.

(10)   If subsection (6) or (8) applies but the consumer does not treat the contract as at an end—
(a)   that does not prevent the consumer from cancelling the order for any of the goods or rejecting goods that have been delivered, and
(b)   the trader must without undue delay reimburse all payments made under the contract in respect of any goods for which the consumer cancels the order or which the consumer rejects.

(11)   If any of the goods form a commercial unit, the consumer cannot reject or cancel the order for some of those goods without also rejecting or cancelling the order for the rest of them.

(12)   A unit is a "commercial unit" if division of the unit would materially impair the value of the goods or the character of the unit.

(13)   This section does not prevent the consumer seeking other remedies where it is open to the consumer to do so.

(14)   See section 2(5) and (6) for the application of this section where goods are sold at public auction.

29   Passing of risk

(1)   A sales contract is to be treated as including the following provisions as terms.

(2)   The goods remain at the trader's risk until they come into the physical possession of—
(a)   the consumer, or
(b)   a person identified by the consumer to take possession of the goods.

(3)   Subsection (2) does not apply if the goods are delivered to a carrier who—
(a)   is commissioned by the consumer to deliver the goods, and
(b)   is not a carrier the trader named as an option for the consumer.

(4)   In that case the goods are at the consumer's risk on and after delivery to the carrier.

(5)   Subsection (4) does not affect any liability of the carrier to the consumer in respect of the goods.

(6)   See section 2(5) and (6) for the application of this section where goods are sold at public auction.

30   Goods under guarantee

(1)   This section applies where—
(a)   there is a contract to supply goods, and
(b)   there is a guarantee in relation to the goods.

(2)   "Guarantee" here means an undertaking to the consumer given without extra charge by a person acting in the course of the person's business (the "guarantor") that, if the goods do not meet the specifications set out in the guarantee statement or in any associated advertising—
(a)   the consumer will be reimbursed for the price paid for the goods, or
(b)   the goods will be repaired, replaced or handled in any way.

(3)   The guarantee takes effect, at the time the goods are delivered, as a contractual obligation owed by the guarantor under the conditions set out in the guarantee statement and in any associated advertising.

(4)   The guarantor must ensure that—
(a)   the guarantee sets out in plain and intelligible language the contents of the guarantee and the essential particulars for making claims under the guarantee,

(b)   the guarantee states that the consumer has statutory rights in relation to the goods and that those rights are not affected by the guarantee, and

(c)   where the goods are offered within the territory of the United Kingdom, the guarantee is written in English.

(5)   The contents of the guarantee to be set out in it include, in particular—

(a)   the name and address of the guarantor, and

(b)   the duration and territorial scope of the guarantee.

(6)   The guarantor and any other person who offers to supply to consumers the goods which are the subject of the guarantee must, on request by the consumer, make the guarantee available to the consumer within a reasonable time, in writing and in a form accessible to the consumer.

(7)   What is a reasonable time is a question of fact.

(8)   If a person fails to comply with a requirement of this section, the enforcement authority may apply to the court for an injunction or (in Scotland) an order of specific implement against that person requiring that person to comply.

(9)   On an application the court may grant an injunction or (in Scotland) an order of specific implement on such terms as it thinks appropriate.

(10)   In this section—

"court" means—

(a)   in relation to England and Wales, the High Court or the county court,

(b)   in relation to Northern Ireland, the High Court or a county court, and

(c)   in relation to Scotland, the Court of Session or the sheriff;

"enforcement authority" means—

(a)   the Competition and Markets Authority,

(b)   a local weights and measures authority in Great Britain, and

(c)   the Department of Enterprise, Trade and Investment in Northern Ireland.

Can a trader contract out of statutory rights and remedies under a goods contract?

31   Liability that cannot be excluded or restricted

(1)   A term of a contract to supply goods is not binding on the consumer to the extent that it would exclude or restrict the trader's liability arising under any of these provisions—

(a)   section 9 (goods to be of satisfactory quality);

(b)   section 10 (goods to be fit for particular purpose);

(c)   section 11 (goods to be as described);

(d)   section 12 (other pre-contract information included in contract);

(e)   section 13 (goods to match a sample);

(f)   section 14 (goods to match a model seen or examined);

(g)   section 15 (installation as part of conformity of the goods with the contract);

(h)   section 16 (goods not conforming to contract if digital content does not conform);

(i)   section 17 (trader to have right to supply the goods etc.);

(j)   section 28 (delivery of goods);

(k)   section 29 (passing of risk).

(2)   That also means that a term of a contract to supply goods is not binding on the consumer to the extent that it would—

(a)   exclude or restrict a right or remedy in respect of a liability under a provision listed in subsection (1),

(b)   make such a right or remedy or its enforcement subject to a restrictive or onerous condition,

(c)   allow a trader to put a person at a disadvantage as a result of pursuing such a right or remedy, or

(d)   exclude or restrict rules of evidence or procedure.

(3)   The reference in subsection (1) to excluding or restricting a liability also includes preventing an obligation or duty arising or limiting its extent.

(4)   An agreement in writing to submit present or future differences to arbitration is not to be regarded as excluding or restricting any liability for the purposes of this section.

(5)   Subsection (1)(i), and subsection (2) so far as it relates to liability under section 17, do not apply to a term of a contract for the hire of goods.

(6)   But an express term of a contract for the hire of goods is not binding on the consumer to the extent that it would exclude or restrict a term that section 17 requires to be treated as included in the contract, unless it is inconsistent with that term (and see also section 62 (requirement for terms to be fair)).

(7)   See Schedule 3 for provision about the enforcement of this section.

32   Contracts applying law of non-EEA State

(1)   If—
   (a)   the law of a country or territory other than an EEA State is chosen by the parties to be applicable to a sales contract, but
   (b)   the sales contract has a close connection with the United Kingdom, this Chapter, except the provisions in subsection (2), applies despite that choice.

(2)   The exceptions are—
   (a)   sections 11(4) and (5) and 12;
   (b)   sections 28 and 29;
   (c)   section 31(1)(d), (j) and (k).

(3)   For cases where those provisions apply, or where the law applicable has not been chosen or the law of an EEA State is chosen, see Regulation (EC) No. 593/2008 of the European Parliament and of the Council of 17 June 2008 on the law applicable to contractual obligations.

CHAPTER 3
DIGITAL CONTENT

What digital content contracts are covered?

33   Contracts covered by this Chapter

(1)   This Chapter applies to a contract for a trader to supply digital content to a consumer, if it is supplied or to be supplied for a price paid by the consumer.

(2)   This Chapter also applies to a contract for a trader to supply digital content to a consumer, if—
   (a)   it is supplied free with goods or services or other digital content for which the consumer pays a price, and
   (b)   it is not generally available to consumers unless they have paid a price for it or for goods or services or other digital content.

(3)   The references in subsections (1) and (2) to the consumer paying a price include references to the consumer using, by way of payment, any facility for which money has been paid.

(4)   A trader does not supply digital content to a consumer for the purposes of this Part merely because the trader supplies a service by which digital content reaches the consumer.

(5)   The Secretary of State may by order provide for this Chapter to apply to other contracts for a trader to supply digital content to a consumer, if the Secretary of State is satisfied that it is appropriate to do so because of significant detriment caused to consumers under contracts of the kind to which the order relates.

(6)   An order under subsection (5)—
   (a)   may, in particular, amend this Act;
   (b)   may contain transitional or transitory provision or savings.

(7)   A contract to which this Chapter applies is referred to in this Part as a "contract to supply digital content".

(8)   This section, other than subsection (4), does not limit the application of section 46.

(9)   The power to make an order under subsection (5) is exercisable by statutory instrument.

(10) No order may be made under subsection (5) unless a draft of the statutory instrument containing it has been laid before, and approved by a resolution of, each House of Parliament.

What statutory rights are there under a digital content contract?

34   Digital content to be of satisfactory quality

(1)   Every contract to supply digital content is to be treated as including a term that the quality of the digital content is satisfactory.

(2)   The quality of digital content is satisfactory if it meets the standard that a reasonable person would consider satisfactory, taking account of—

    (a)   any description of the digital content,

    (b)   the price mentioned in section 33(1) or (2)(b) (if relevant), and

    (c)   all the other relevant circumstances (see subsection (5)).

(3)   The quality of digital content includes its state and condition; and the following aspects (among others) are in appropriate cases aspects of the quality of digital content—

    (a)   fitness for all the purposes for which digital content of that kind is usually supplied;

    (b)   freedom from minor defects;

    (c)   safety;

    (d)   durability.

(4)   The term mentioned in subsection (1) does not cover anything which makes the quality of the digital content unsatisfactory—

    (a)   which is specifically drawn to the consumer's attention before the contract is made,

    (b)   where the consumer examines the digital content before the contract is made, which that examination ought to reveal, or

    (c)   where the consumer examines a trial version before the contract is made, which would have been apparent on a reasonable examination of the trial version.

(5)   The relevant circumstances mentioned in subsection (2)(c) include any public statement about the specific characteristics of the digital content made by the trader, the producer or any representative of the trader or the producer.

(6)   That includes, in particular, any public statement made in advertising or labelling.

(7)   But a public statement is not a relevant circumstance for the purposes of subsection (2)(c) if the trader shows that—

    (a)   when the contract was made, the trader was not, and could not reasonably have been, aware of the statement,

    (b)   before the contract was made, the statement had been publicly withdrawn or, to the extent that it contained anything which was incorrect or misleading, it had been publicly corrected, or

    (c)   the consumer's decision to contract for the digital content could not have been influenced by the statement.

(8)   In a contract to supply digital content a term about the quality of the digital content may be treated as included as a matter of custom.

(9)   See section 42 for a consumer's rights if the trader is in breach of a term that this section requires to be treated as included in a contract.

35   Digital content to be fit for particular purpose

(1)   Subsection (3) applies to a contract to supply digital content if before the contract is made the consumer makes known to the trader (expressly or by implication) any particular purpose for which the consumer is contracting for the digital content.

(2)   Subsection (3) also applies to a contract to supply digital content if—

    (a)   the digital content was previously sold by a credit-broker to the trader,

    (b)   the consideration or part of it is a sum payable by instalments, and

    (c)   before the contract is made, the consumer makes known to the credit-broker (expressly or by implication) any particular purpose for which the consumer is contracting for the digital content.

(3)   The contract is to be treated as including a term that the digital content is reasonably fit for that purpose, whether or not that is a purpose for which digital content of that kind is usually supplied.

(4)   Subsection (3) does not apply if the circumstances show that the consumer does not rely, or it is unreasonable for the consumer to rely, on the skill or judgment of the trader or credit-broker.

(5)   A contract to supply digital content may be treated as making provision about the fitness of the digital content for a particular purpose as a matter of custom.

(6)   See section 42 for a consumer's rights if the trader is in breach of a term that this section requires to be treated as included in a contract.

36   Digital content to be as described

(1)   Every contract to supply digital content is to be treated as including a term that the digital content will match any description of it given by the trader to the consumer.

(2)   Where the consumer examines a trial version before the contract is made, it is not sufficient that the digital content matches (or is better than) the trial version if the digital content does not also match any description of it given by the trader to the consumer.

(3)   Any information that is provided by the trader about the digital content that is information mentioned in paragraph (a), (j) or (k) of Schedule 1 or paragraph (a), (v) or (w) of Schedule 2 (main characteristics, functionality and compatibility) to the Consumer Contracts (Information, Cancellation and Additional Charges) Regulations 2013 (SI 2013/3134) is to be treated as included as a term of the contract.

(4)   A change to any of that information, made before entering into the contract or later, is not effective unless expressly agreed between the consumer and the trader.

(5)   See section 42 for a consumer's rights if the trader is in breach of a term that this section requires to be treated as included in a contract.

37   Other pre-contract information included in contract

(1)   This section applies to any contract to supply digital content.

(2)   Where regulation 9, 10 or 13 of the Consumer Contracts (Information, Cancellation and Additional Charges) Regulations 2013 (SI 2013/3134) required the trader to provide information to the consumer before the contract became binding, any of that information that was provided by the trader other than information about the digital content and mentioned in paragraph (a), (j) or (k) of Schedule 1 or paragraph (a), (v) or (w) of Schedule 2 to the Regulations (main characteristics, functionality and compatibility) is to be treated as included as a term of the contract.

(3)   A change to any of that information, made before entering into the contract or later, is not effective unless expressly agreed between the consumer and the trader.

(4)   See section 42 for a consumer's rights if the trader is in breach of a term that this section requires to be treated as included in a contract.

38   No other requirement to treat term about quality or fitness as included

(1)   Except as provided by sections 34 and 35, a contract to supply digital content is not to be treated as including any term about the quality of the digital content or its fitness for any particular purpose, unless the term is expressly included in the contract.

(2)   Subsection (1) is subject to provision made by any other enactment, whenever passed or made.

39   Supply by transmission and facilities for continued transmission

(1)   Subsection (2) applies where there is a contract to supply digital content and the consumer's access to the content on a device requires its transmission to the device under arrangements initiated by the trader.

(2)   For the purposes of this Chapter, the digital content is supplied—
    (a)   when the content reaches the device, or
    (b)   if earlier, when the content reaches another trader chosen by the consumer to supply, under a contract with the consumer, a service by which digital content reaches the device.

(3)   Subsections (5) to (7) apply where—
    (a)   there is a contract to supply digital content, and
    (b)   after the trader (T) has supplied the digital content, the consumer is to have access under the contract to a processing facility under arrangements made by T.

(4)   A processing facility is a facility by which T or another trader will receive digital content from the consumer and transmit digital content to the consumer (whether or not other features are to be included under the contract).

(5)   The contract is to be treated as including a term that the processing facility (with any feature that the facility is to include under the contract) must be available to the consumer for a reasonable time, unless a time is specified in the contract.

(6)   The following provisions apply to all digital content transmitted to the consumer on each occasion under the facility, while it is provided under the contract, as they apply to the digital content first supplied—

(a)   section 34 (quality);

(b)   section 35 (fitness for a particular purpose);

(c)   section 36 (description).

(7)   Breach of a term treated as included under subsection (5) has the same effect as breach of a term treated as included under those sections (see section 42).

40   Quality, fitness and description of content supplied subject to modifications

(1)   Where under a contract a trader supplies digital content to a consumer subject to the right of the trader or a third party to modify the digital content, the following provisions apply in relation to the digital content as modified as they apply in relation to the digital content as supplied under the contract—

(a)   section 34 (quality);

(b)   section 35 (fitness for a particular purpose);

(c)   section 36 (description).

(2)   Subsection (1)(c) does not prevent the trader from improving the features of, or adding new features to, the digital content, as long as—

(a)   the digital content continues to match the description of it given by the trader to the consumer, and

(b)   the digital content continues to conform to the information provided by the trader as mentioned in subsection (3) of section 36, subject to any change to that information that has been agreed in accordance with subsection (4) of that section.

(3)   A claim on the grounds that digital content does not conform to a term described in any of the sections listed in subsection (1) as applied by that subsection is to be treated as arising at the time when the digital content was supplied under the contract and not the time when it is modified.

41   Trader's right to supply digital content

(1)   Every contract to supply digital content is to be treated as including a term—

(a)   in relation to any digital content which is supplied under the contract and which the consumer has paid for, that the trader has the right to supply that content to the consumer;

(b)   in relation to any digital content which the trader agrees to supply under the contract and which the consumer has paid for, that the trader will have the right to supply it to the consumer at the time when it is to be supplied.

(2)   See section 42 for a consumer's rights if the trader is in breach of a term that this section requires to be treated as included in a contract.

What remedies are there if statutory rights under a digital content contract are not met?

42   Consumer's rights to enforce terms about digital content

(1)   In this section and section 43 references to digital content conforming to a contract are references to the digital content conforming to the terms described in sections 34, 35 and 36.

(2)   If the digital content does not conform to the contract, the consumer's rights (and the provisions about them and when they are available) are—

(a)   the right to repair or replacement (see section 43);

(b)   the right to a price reduction (see section 44).

(3)   Section 16 also applies if an item including the digital content is supplied.

(4)   If the trader is in breach of a term that section 37 requires to be treated as included in the contract, the consumer has the right to recover from the trader the amount of any costs incurred by the consumer as a result of the breach, up to the amount of the price paid for the digital content or for any facility within section 33(3) used by the consumer.

(5)   If the trader is in breach of the term that section 41(1) (right to supply the content) requires to be treated as included in the contract, the consumer has the right to a refund (see section 45 for provisions about that right and when it is available).

(6)   This Chapter does not prevent the consumer seeking other remedies for a breach of a term to which any of subsections (2), (4) or (5) applies, instead of or in addition to a remedy referred to there (but not so as to recover twice for the same loss).

(7)   Those other remedies include any of the following that is open to the consumer in the circumstances—
     (a)   claiming damages;
     (b)   seeking to recover money paid where the consideration for payment of the money has failed;
     (c)   seeking specific performance;
     (d)   seeking an order for specific implement;
     (e)   relying on the breach against a claim by the trader for the price.

(8)   It is not open to the consumer to treat the contract as at an end for breach of a term to which any of subsections (2), (4) or (5) applies.

(9)   For the purposes of subsection (2), digital content which does not conform to the contract at any time within the period of six months beginning with the day on which it was supplied must be taken not to have conformed to the contract when it was supplied.

(10)   Subsection (9) does not apply if—
     (a)   it is established that the digital content did conform to the contract when it was supplied, or
     (b)   its application is incompatible with the nature of the digital content or with how it fails to conform to the contract.

43   Right to repair or replacement

(1)   This section applies if the consumer has the right to repair or replacement.

(2)   If the consumer requires the trader to repair or replace the digital content, the trader must—
     (a)   do so within a reasonable time and without significant inconvenience to the consumer; and
     (b)   bear any necessary costs incurred in doing so (including in particular the cost of any labour, materials or postage).

(3)   The consumer cannot require the trader to repair or replace the digital content if that remedy (the repair or the replacement)—
     (a)   is impossible, or
     (b)   is disproportionate compared to the other of those remedies.

(4)   Either of those remedies is disproportionate compared to the other if it imposes costs on the trader which, compared to those imposed by the other, are unreasonable, taking into account—
     (a)   the value which the digital content would have if it conformed to the contract,
     (b)   the significance of the lack of conformity, and
     (c)   whether the other remedy could be effected without significant inconvenience to the consumer.

(5)   Any question as to what is a reasonable time or significant inconvenience is to be determined taking account of—
     (a)   the nature of the digital content, and
     (b)   the purpose for which the digital content was obtained or accessed.

(6)   A consumer who requires or agrees to the repair of digital content cannot require the trader to replace it without giving the trader a reasonable time to repair it (unless giving the trader that time would cause significant inconvenience to the consumer).

(7)   A consumer who requires or agrees to the replacement of digital content cannot require the trader to repair it without giving the trader a reasonable time to replace it (unless giving the trader that time would cause significant inconvenience to the consumer).

(8) In this Chapter, "repair" in relation to digital content that does not conform to a contract, means making it conform.

44 Right to price reduction

(1) The right to a price reduction is the right to require the trader to reduce the price to the consumer by an appropriate amount (including the right to receive a refund for anything already paid above the reduced amount).

(2) The amount of the reduction may, where appropriate, be the full amount of the price.

(3) A consumer who has that right may only exercise it in one of these situations—

    (a) because of section 43(3)(a) the consumer can require neither repair nor replacement of the digital content, or

    (b) the consumer has required the trader to repair or replace the digital content, but the trader is in breach of the requirement of section 43(2)(a) to do so within a reasonable time and without significant inconvenience to the consumer.

(4) A refund under this section must be given without undue delay, and in any event within 14 days beginning with the day on which the trader agrees that the consumer is entitled to a refund.

(5) The trader must give the refund using the same means of payment as the consumer used to pay for the digital content, unless the consumer expressly agrees otherwise.

(6) The trader must not impose any fee on the consumer in respect of the refund.

45 Right to a refund

(1) The right to a refund gives the consumer the right to receive a refund from the trader of all money paid by the consumer for the digital content (subject to subsection (2)).

(2) If the breach giving the consumer the right to a refund affects only some of the digital content supplied under the contract, the right to a refund does not extend to any part of the price attributable to digital content that is not affected by the breach.

(3) A refund must be given without undue delay, and in any event within 14 days beginning with the day on which the trader agrees that the consumer is entitled to a refund.

(4) The trader must give the refund using the same means of payment as the consumer used to pay for the digital content, unless the consumer expressly agrees otherwise.

(5) The trader must not impose any fee on the consumer in respect of the refund.

Compensation for damage to device or to other digital content

46 Remedy for damage to device or to other digital content

(1) This section applies if—

    (a) a trader supplies digital content to a consumer under a contract,

    (b) the digital content causes damage to a device or to other digital content,

    (c) the device or digital content that is damaged belongs to the consumer, and

    (d) the damage is of a kind that would not have occurred if the trader had exercised reasonable care and skill.

(2) If the consumer requires the trader to provide a remedy under this section, the trader must either—

    (a) repair the damage in accordance with subsection (3), or

    (b) compensate the consumer for the damage with an appropriate payment.

(3) To repair the damage in accordance with this subsection, the trader must—

    (a) repair the damage within a reasonable time and without significant inconvenience to the consumer, and

    (b) bear any necessary costs incurred in repairing the damage (including in particular the cost of any labour, materials or postage).

(4) Any question as to what is a reasonable time or significant inconvenience is to be determined taking account of—

    (a) the nature of the device or digital content that is damaged, and

    (b) the purpose for which it is used by the consumer.

(5) A compensation payment under this section must be made without undue delay, and in any event within 14 days beginning with the day on which the trader agrees that the consumer is entitled to the payment.

(6) The trader must not impose any fee on the consumer in respect of the payment.

(7) A consumer with a right to a remedy under this section may bring a claim in civil proceedings to enforce that right.

(8) The Limitation Act 1980 and the Limitation (Northern Ireland) Order 1989 (SI 1989/1339 (NI 11)) apply to a claim under this section as if it were an action founded on simple contract.

(9) The Prescription and Limitation (Scotland) Act 1973 applies to a right to a remedy under this section as if it were an obligation to which section 6 of that Act applies.

Can a trader contract out of statutory rights and remedies under a digital content contract?

47   Liability that cannot be excluded or restricted

(1) A term of a contract to supply digital content is not binding on the consumer to the extent that it would exclude or restrict the trader's liability arising under any of these provisions—

   (a) section 34 (digital content to be of satisfactory quality),

   (b) section 35 (digital content to be fit for particular purpose),

   (c) section 36 (digital content to be as described),

   (d) section 37 (other pre-contract information included in contract), or

   (e) section 41 (trader's right to supply digital content).

(2) That also means that a term of a contract to supply digital content is not binding on the consumer to the extent that it would—

   (a) exclude or restrict a right or remedy in respect of a liability under a provision listed in subsection (1),

   (b) make such a right or remedy or its enforcement subject to a restrictive or onerous condition,

   (c) allow a trader to put a person at a disadvantage as a result of pursuing such a right or remedy, or

   (d) exclude or restrict rules of evidence or procedure.

(3) The reference in subsection (1) to excluding or restricting a liability also includes preventing an obligation or duty arising or limiting its extent.

(4) An agreement in writing to submit present or future differences to arbitration is not to be regarded as excluding or restricting any liability for the purposes of this section.

(5) See Schedule 3 for provision about the enforcement of this section.

(6) For provision limiting the ability of a trader under a contract within section 46 to exclude or restrict the trader's liability under that section, see section 62.

CHAPTER 4
SERVICES

What services contracts are covered?

48   Contracts covered by this Chapter

(1) This Chapter applies to a contract for a trader to supply a service to a consumer.

(2) That does not include a contract of employment or apprenticeship.

(3) In relation to Scotland, this Chapter does not apply to a gratuitous contract.

(4) A contract to which this Chapter applies is referred to in this Part as a "contract to supply a service".

(5) The Secretary of State may by order made by statutory instrument provide that a provision of this Chapter does not apply in relation to a service of a description specified in the order.

(6) The power in subsection (5) includes power to provide that a provision of this Chapter does not apply in relation to a service of a description specified in the order in the circumstances so specified.

(7) An order under subsection (5) may contain transitional or transitory provision or savings.

(8)   No order may be made under subsection (5) unless a draft of the statutory instrument containing it has been laid before, and approved by a resolution of, each House of Parliament.

What statutory rights are there under a services contract?

49   Service to be performed with reasonable care and skill

(1)   Every contract to supply a service is to be treated as including a term that the trader must perform the service with reasonable care and skill.

(2)   See section 54 for a consumer's rights if the trader is in breach of a term that this section requires to be treated as included in a contract.

50   Information about the trader or service to be binding

(1)   Every contract to supply a service is to be treated as including as a term of the contract anything that is said or written to the consumer, by or on behalf of the trader, about the trader or the service, if—

(a)   it is taken into account by the consumer when deciding to enter into the contract, or

(b)   it is taken into account by the consumer when making any decision about the service after entering into the contract.

(2)   Anything taken into account by the consumer as mentioned in subsection (1)(a) or (b) is subject to—

(a)   anything that qualified it and was said or written to the consumer by the trader on the same occasion, and

(b)   any change to it that has been expressly agreed between the consumer and the trader (before entering into the contract or later).

(3)   Without prejudice to subsection (1), any information provided by the trader in accordance with regulation 9, 10 or 13 of the Consumer Contracts (Information, Cancellation and Additional Charges) Regulations 2013 (SI 2013/3134) is to be treated as included as a term of the contract.

(4)   A change to any of the information mentioned in subsection (3), made before entering into the contract or later, is not effective unless expressly agreed between the consumer and the trader.

(5)   See section 54 for a consumer's rights if the trader is in breach of a term that this section requires to be treated as included in a contract.

51   Reasonable price to be paid for a service

(1)   This section applies to a contract to supply a service if—

(a)   the consumer has not paid a price or other consideration for the service,

(b)   the contract does not expressly fix a price or other consideration, and does not say how it is to be fixed, and

(c)   anything that is to be treated under section 50 as included in the contract does not fix a price or other consideration either.

(2)   In that case the contract is to be treated as including a term that the consumer must pay a reasonable price for the service, and no more.

(3)   What is a reasonable price is a question of fact.

52   Service to be performed within a reasonable time

(1)   This section applies to a contract to supply a service, if—

(a)   the contract does not expressly fix the time for the service to be performed, and does not say how it is to be fixed, and

(b)   information that is to be treated under section 50 as included in the contract does not fix the time either.

(2)   In that case the contract is to be treated as including a term that the trader must perform the service within a reasonable time.

(3)   What is a reasonable time is a question of fact.

(4)   See section 54 for a consumer's rights if the trader is in breach of a term that this section requires to be treated as included in a contract.

53   Relation to other law on contract terms

(1)   Nothing in this Chapter affects any enactment or rule of law that imposes a stricter duty on the trader.

(2)   This Chapter is subject to any other enactment which defines or restricts the rights, duties or liabilities arising in connection with a service of any description.

What remedies are there if statutory rights under a services contract are not met?

54   Consumer's rights to enforce terms about services

(1)   The consumer's rights under this section and sections 55 and 56 do not affect any rights that the contract provides for, if those are not inconsistent.

(2)   In this section and section 55 a reference to a service conforming to a contract is a reference to—

   (a)   the service being performed in accordance with section 49, or

   (b)   the service conforming to a term that section 50 requires to be treated as included in the contract and that relates to the performance of the service.

(3)   If the service does not conform to the contract, the consumer's rights (and the provisions about them and when they are available) are— (a) the right to require repeat performance (see section 55); (b) the right to a price reduction (see section 56).

(4)   If the trader is in breach of a term that section 50 requires to be treated as included in the contract but that does not relate to the service, the consumer has the right to a price reduction (see section 56 for provisions about that right and when it is available).

(5)   If the trader is in breach of what the contract requires under section 52 (performance within a reasonable time), the consumer has the right to a price reduction (see section 56 for provisions about that right and when it is available).

(6)   This section and sections 55 and 56 do not prevent the consumer seeking other remedies for a breach of a term to which any of subsections (3) to (5) applies, instead of or in addition to a remedy referred to there (but not so as to recover twice for the same loss).

(7)   Those other remedies include any of the following that is open to the consumer in the circumstances—

   (a)   claiming damages;

   (b)   seeking to recover money paid where the consideration for payment of the money has failed;

   (c)   seeking specific performance;

   (d)   seeking an order for specific implement;

   (e)   relying on the breach against a claim by the trader under the contract;

   (f)   exercising a right to treat the contract as at an end.

55   Right to repeat performance

(1)   The right to require repeat performance is a right to require the trader to perform the service again, to the extent necessary to complete its performance in conformity with the contract.

(2)   If the consumer requires such repeat performance, the trader—

   (a)   must provide it within a reasonable time and without significant inconvenience to the consumer; and

   (b)   must bear any necessary costs incurred in doing so (including in particular the cost of any labour or materials).

(3)   The consumer cannot require repeat performance if completing performance of the service in conformity with the contract is impossible.

(4)   Any question as to what is a reasonable time or significant inconvenience is to be determined taking account of—

   (a)   the nature of the service, and

   (b)   the purpose for which the service was to be performed.

56 Right to price reduction

(1) The right to a price reduction is the right to require the trader to reduce the price to the consumer by an appropriate amount (including the right to receive a refund for anything already paid above the reduced amount).

(2) The amount of the reduction may, where appropriate, be the full amount of the price.

(3) A consumer who has that right and the right to require repeat performance is only entitled to a price reduction in one of these situations—

    (a) because of section 55(3) the consumer cannot require repeat performance; or

    (b) the consumer has required repeat performance, but the trader is in breach of the requirement of section 55(2)(a) to do it within a reasonable time and without significant inconvenience to the consumer.

(4) A refund under this section must be given without undue delay, and in any event within 14 days beginning with the day on which the trader agrees that the consumer is entitled to a refund.

(5) The trader must give the refund using the same means of payment as the consumer used to pay for the service, unless the consumer expressly agrees otherwise.

(6) The trader must not impose any fee on the consumer in respect of the refund.

Can a trader contract out of statutory rights and remedies under a services contract?

57 Liability that cannot be excluded or restricted

(1) A term of a contract to supply services is not binding on the consumer to the extent that it would exclude the trader's liability arising under section 49 (service to be performed with reasonable care and skill).

(2) Subject to section 50(2), a term of a contract to supply services is not binding on the consumer to the extent that it would exclude the trader's liability arising under section 50 (information about trader or service to be binding).

(3) A term of a contract to supply services is not binding on the consumer to the extent that it would restrict the trader's liability arising under any of sections 49 and 50 and, where they apply, sections 51 and 52 (reasonable price and reasonable time), if it would prevent the consumer in an appropriate case from recovering the price paid or the value of any other consideration. (If it would not prevent the consumer from doing so, Part 2 (unfair terms) may apply.)

(4) That also means that a term of a contract to supply services is not binding on the consumer to the extent that it would —

    (a) exclude or restrict a right or remedy in respect of a liability under any of sections 49 to 52,

    (b) make such a right or remedy or its enforcement subject to a restrictive or onerous condition,

    (c) allow a trader to put a person at a disadvantage as a result of pursuing such a right or remedy, or

    (d) exclude or restrict rules of evidence or procedure.

(5) The references in subsections (1) to (3) to excluding or restricting a liability also include preventing an obligation or duty arising or limiting its extent.

(6) An agreement in writing to submit present or future differences to arbitration is not to be regarded as excluding or restricting any liability for the purposes of this section.

(7) See Schedule 3 for provision about the enforcement of this section.

CHAPTER 5
GENERAL AND SUPPLEMENTARY PROVISIONS

58 Powers of the court

(1) In any proceedings in which a remedy is sought by virtue of section 19(3) or (4), 42(2) or 54(3), the court, in addition to any other power it has, may act under this section.

(2) On the application of the consumer the court may make an order requiring specific performance or, in Scotland, specific implement by the trader of any obligation imposed on the trader by virtue of section 23, 43 or 55.

(3) Subsection (4) applies if—
  (a) the consumer claims to exercise a right under the relevant remedies provisions, but
  (b) the court decides that those provisions have the effect that exercise of another right is appropriate.

(4) The court may proceed as if the consumer had exercised that other right.

(5) If the consumer has claimed to exercise the final right to reject, the court may order that any reimbursement to the consumer is reduced by a deduction for use, to take account of the use the consumer has had of the goods in the period since they were delivered.

(6) Any deduction for use is limited as set out in section 24(9) and (10).

(7) The court may make an order under this section unconditionally or on such terms and conditions as to damages, payment of the price and otherwise as it thinks just.

(8) The "relevant remedies provisions" are—
  (a) where Chapter 2 applies, sections 23 and 24;
  (b) where Chapter 3 applies, sections 43 and 44;
  (c) where Chapter 4 applies, sections 55 and 56.

59   Interpretation

(1) These definitions apply in this Part (as well as the key definitions in section 2)—
  "conditional sales contract" has the meaning given in section 5(3);
  "Consumer Rights Directive" means Directive 2011/83/EU of the European Parliament and of the Council of 25 October 2011 on consumer rights, amending Council Directive 93/13/EEC and Directive 1999/44/EC of the European Parliament and of the Council and repealing Council Directive 85/577/EEC and Directive 97/7/EC of the European Parliament and of the Council;
  "credit-broker" means a person acting in the course of a business of credit brokerage carried on by that person;
  "credit brokerage" means—
  (a) introducing individuals who want to obtain credit to persons carrying on any business so far as it relates to the provision of credit,
  (b) introducing individuals who want to obtain goods on hire to persons carrying on a business which comprises or relates to supplying goods under a contract for the hire of goods, or
  (c) introducing individuals who want to obtain credit, or to obtain goods on hire, to other persons engaged in credit brokerage;
  "delivery" means voluntary transfer of possession from one person to another;
  "enactment" includes—
  (a) an enactment contained in subordinate legislation within the meaning of the Interpretation Act 1978,
  (b) an enactment contained in, or in an instrument made under, a Measure or Act of the National Assembly for Wales,
  (c) an enactment contained in, or in an instrument made under, an Act of the Scottish Parliament, and
  (d) an enactment contained in, or in an instrument made under, Northern Ireland legislation;
  "producer", in relation to goods or digital content, means—
  (a) the manufacturer,
  (b) the importer into the European Economic Area, or
  (c) any person who purports to be a producer by placing the person's name, trade mark or other distinctive sign on the goods or using it in connection with the digital content.

(2) References in this Part to treating a contract as at an end are to be read in accordance with section 19(13).

60   Changes to other legislation

Schedule 1 (amendments consequential on this Part) has effect.

PART 2

UNFAIR TERMS

What contracts and notices are covered by this Part?

61   Contracts and notices covered by this Part

(1)   This Part applies to a contract between a trader and a consumer.

(2)   This does not include a contract of employment or apprenticeship.

(3)   A contract to which this Part applies is referred to in this Part as a "consumer contract".

(4)   This Part applies to a notice to the extent that it—

     (a)   relates to rights or obligations as between a trader and a consumer, or

     (b)   purports to exclude or restrict a trader's liability to a consumer.

(5)   This does not include a notice relating to rights, obligations or liabilities as between an employer and an employee.

(6)   It does not matter for the purposes of subsection (4) whether the notice is expressed to apply to a consumer, as long as it is reasonable to assume it is intended to be seen or heard by a consumer.

(7)   A notice to which this Part applies is referred to in this Part as a "consumer notice".

(8)   In this section "notice" includes an announcement, whether or not in writing, and any other communication or purported communication.

What are the general rules about fairness of contract terms and notices?

62   Requirement for contract terms and notices to be fair

(1)   An unfair term of a consumer contract is not binding on the consumer.

(2)   An unfair consumer notice is not binding on the consumer.

(3)   This does not prevent the consumer from relying on the term or notice if the consumer chooses to do so.

(4)   A term is unfair if, contrary to the requirement of good faith, it causes a significant imbalance in the parties' rights and obligations under the contract to the detriment of the consumer.

(5)   Whether a term is fair is to be determined—

     (a)   taking into account the nature of the subject matter of the contract, and

     (b)   by reference to all the circumstances existing when the term was agreed and to all of the other terms of the contract or of any other contract on which it depends.

(6)   A notice is unfair if, contrary to the requirement of good faith, it causes a significant imbalance in the parties' rights and obligations to the detriment of the consumer.

(7)   Whether a notice is fair is to be determined—

     (a)   taking into account the nature of the subject matter of the notice, and

     (b)   by reference to all the circumstances existing when the rights or obligations to which it relates arose and to the terms of any contract on which it depends.

(8)   This section does not affect the operation of—

     (a)   section 31 (exclusion of liability: goods contracts),

     (b)   section 47 (exclusion of liability: digital content contracts),

     (c)   section 57 (exclusion of liability: services contracts), or

     (d)   section 65 (exclusion of negligence liability).

63   Contract terms which may or must be regarded as unfair

(1)   Part 1 of Schedule 2 contains an indicative and non-exhaustive list of terms of consumer contracts that may be regarded as unfair for the purposes of this Part.

(2)   Part 1 of Schedule 2 is subject to Part 2 of that Schedule; but a term listed in Part 2 of that Schedule may nevertheless be assessed for fairness under section 62 unless section 64 or 73 applies to it.

(3)　The Secretary of State may by order made by statutory instrument amend Schedule 2 so as to add, modify or remove an entry in Part 1 or Part 2 of that Schedule.

(4)　An order under subsection (3) may contain transitional or transitory provision or savings.

(5)　No order may be made under subsection (3) unless a draft of the statutory instrument containing it has been laid before, and approved by a resolution of, each House of Parliament.

(6)　A term of a consumer contract must be regarded as unfair if it has the effect that the consumer bears the burden of proof with respect to compliance by a distance supplier or an intermediary with an obligation under any enactment or rule implementing the Distance Marketing Directive.

(7)　In subsection (6)—

"the Distance Marketing Directive" means Directive 2002/65/EC of the European Parliament and of the Council of 23 September 2002 concerning the distance marketing of consumer financial services and amending Council Directive 90/619/EEC and Directives 97/7/EC and 98/27/EC;

"distance supplier" means—

(a)　a supplier under a distance contract within the meaning of the Financial Services (Distance Marketing) Regulations 2004 (SI 2004/2095), or

(b)　a supplier of unsolicited financial services within the meaning of regulation 15 of those regulations;

"enactment" includes an enactment contained in subordinate legislation within the meaning of the Interpretation Act 1978;

"intermediary" has the same meaning as in the Financial Services (Distance Marketing) Regulations 2004;

"rule" means a rule made by the Financial Conduct Authority or the Prudential Regulation Authority under the Financial Services and Markets Act 2000 or by a designated professional body within the meaning of section 326(2) of that Act.

64　Exclusion from assessment of fairness

(1)　A term of a consumer contract may not be assessed for fairness under section 62 to the extent that—

(a)　it specifies the main subject matter of the contract, or

(b)　the assessment is of the appropriateness of the price payable under the contract by comparison with the goods, digital content or services supplied under it.

(2)　Subsection (1) excludes a term from an assessment under section 62 only if it is transparent and prominent.

(3)　A term is transparent for the purposes of this Part if it is expressed in plain and intelligible language and (in the case of a written term) is legible.

(4)　A term is prominent for the purposes of this section if it is brought to the consumer's attention in such a way that an average consumer would be aware of the term.

(5)　In subsection (4) "average consumer" means a consumer who is reasonably wellinformed, observant and circumspect.

(6)　This section does not apply to a term of a contract listed in Part 1 of Schedule 2.

65　Bar on exclusion or restriction of negligence liability

(1)　A trader cannot by a term of a consumer contract or by a consumer notice exclude or restrict liability for death or personal injury resulting from negligence.

(2)　Where a term of a consumer contract, or a consumer notice, purports to exclude or restrict a trader's liability for negligence, a person is not to be taken to have voluntarily accepted any risk merely because the person agreed to or knew about the term or notice.

(3)　In this section "personal injury" includes any disease and any impairment of physical or mental condition.

(4)　In this section "negligence" means the breach of—

(a)　any obligation to take reasonable care or exercise reasonable skill in the performance of a contract where the obligation arises from an express or implied term of the contract,

(b)   a common law duty to take reasonable care or exercise reasonable skill,

(c)   the common duty of care imposed by the Occupiers' Liability Act 1957 or the Occupiers' Liability Act (Northern Ireland) 1957, or

(d)   the duty of reasonable care imposed by section 2(1) of the Occupiers' Liability (Scotland) Act 1960.

(5)   It is immaterial for the purposes of subsection (4)—

(a)   whether a breach of duty or obligation was inadvertent or intentional, or

(b)   whether liability for it arises directly or vicariously.

(6)   This section is subject to section 66 (which makes provision about the scope of this section).

66   Scope of section 65

(1)   Section 65 does not apply to—

(a)   any contract so far as it is a contract of insurance, including a contract to pay an annuity on human life, or

(b)   any contract so far as it relates to the creation or transfer of an interest in land.

(2)   Section 65 does not affect the validity of any discharge or indemnity given by a person in consideration of the receipt by that person of compensation in settlement of any claim the person has.

(3)   Section 65 does not—

(a)   apply to liability which is excluded or discharged as mentioned in section 4(2) (a) (exception to liability to pay damages to relatives) of the Damages (Scotland) Act 2011, or

(b)   affect the operation of section 5 (discharge of liability to pay damages: exception for mesothelioma) of that Act.

(4)   Section 65 does not apply to the liability of an occupier of premises to a person who obtains access to the premises for recreational purposes if—

(a)   the person suffers loss or damage because of the dangerous state of the premises, and

(b)   allowing the person access for those purposes is not within the purposes of the occupier's trade, business, craft or profession.

67   Effect of an unfair term on the rest of a contract

Where a term of a consumer contract is not binding on the consumer as a result of this Part, the contract continues, so far as practicable, to have effect in every other respect.

68   Requirement for transparency

(1)   A trader must ensure that a written term of a consumer contract, or a consumer notice in writing, is transparent.

(2)   A consumer notice is transparent for the purposes of subsection (1) if it is expressed in plain and intelligible language and it is legible.

69   Contract terms that may have different meanings

(1)   If a term in a consumer contract, or a consumer notice, could have different meanings, the meaning that is most favourable to the consumer is to prevail.

(2)   Subsection (1) does not apply to the construction of a term or a notice in proceedings on an application for an injunction or interdict under paragraph 3 of Schedule 3.

How are the general rules enforced?

70   Enforcement of the law on unfair contract terms

(1)   Schedule 3 confers functions on the Competition and Markets Authority and other regulators in relation to the enforcement of this Part.

(2)   For provision about the investigatory powers that are available to those regulators for the purposes of that Schedule, see Schedule 5.

Supplementary provisions

71   Duty of court to consider fairness of term

(1)   Subsection (2) applies to proceedings before a court which relate to a term of a consumer contract.

(2)   The court must consider whether the term is fair even if none of the parties to the proceedings has raised that issue or indicated that it intends to raise it.

(3)   But subsection (2) does not apply unless the court considers that it has before it sufficient legal and factual material to enable it to consider the fairness of the term.

72   Application of rules to secondary contracts

(1)   This section applies if a term of a contract ("the secondary contract") reduces the rights or remedies or increases the obligations of a person under another contract ("the main contract").

(2)   The term is subject to the provisions of this Part that would apply to the term if it were in the main contract.

(3)   It does not matter for the purposes of this section—
    (a)   whether the parties to the secondary contract are the same as the parties to the main contract, or
    (b)   whether the secondary contract is a consumer contract.

(4)   This section does not apply if the secondary contract is a settlement of a claim arising under the main contract.

73   Disapplication of rules to mandatory terms and notices

(1)   This Part does not apply to a term of a contract, or to a notice, to the extent that it reflects—
    (a)   mandatory statutory or regulatory provisions, or
    (b)   the provisions or principles of an international convention to which the United Kingdom or the EU is a party.

(2)   In subsection (1) "mandatory statutory or regulatory provisions" includes rules which, according to law, apply between the parties on the basis that no other arrangements have been established.

74   Contracts applying law of non-EEA State

(1)   If—
    (a)   the law of a country or territory other than an EEA State is chosen by the parties to be applicable to a consumer contract, but
    (b)   the consumer contract has a close connection with the United Kingdom, this Part applies despite that choice.

(2)   For cases where the law applicable has not been chosen or the law of an EEA State is chosen, see Regulation (EC) No. 593/2008 of the European Parliament and of the Council of 17 June 2008 on the law applicable to contractual obligations.

75   Changes to other legislation

Schedule 4 (amendments consequential on this Part) has effect.

76   Interpretation of Part 2

(1)   In this Part—
    "consumer contract" has the meaning given by section 61(3);
    "consumer notice" has the meaning given by section 61(7);
    "transparent" is to be construed in accordance with sections 64(3) and 68(2).

(2)   The following have the same meanings in this Part as they have in Part 1—
    "trader" (see section 2(2));
    "consumer" (see section 2(3));
    "goods" (see section 2(8));
    "digital content" (see section 2(9)).

(3)   Section 2(4) (trader who claims an individual is not a consumer must prove it) applies in relation to this Part as it applies in relation to Part 1.

Section 63   SCHEDULE 2
           CONSUMER CONTRACT TERMS WHICH MAY BE REGARDED AS UNFAIR

PART 1
LIST OF TERMS

1   A term which has the object or effect of excluding or limiting the trader's liability in the event of the death of or personal injury to the consumer resulting from an act or omission of the trader.

2   A term which has the object or effect of inappropriately excluding or limiting the legal rights of the consumer in relation to the trader or another party in the event of total or partial non-performance or inadequate performance by the trader of any of the contractual obligations, including the option of offsetting a debt owed to the trader against any claim which the consumer may have against the trader.

3   A term which has the object or effect of making an agreement binding on the consumer in a case where the provision of services by the trader is subject to a condition whose realisation depends on the trader's will alone.

4   A term which has the object or effect of permitting the trader to retain sums paid by the consumer where the consumer decides not to conclude or perform the contract, without providing for the consumer to receive compensation of an equivalent amount from the trader where the trader is the party cancelling the contract.

5   A term which has the object or effect of requiring that, where the consumer decides not to conclude or perform the contract, the consumer must pay the trader a disproportionately high sum in compensation or for services which have not been supplied.

6   A term which has the object or effect of requiring a consumer who fails to fulfil his obligations under the contract to pay a disproportionately high sum in compensation.

7   A term which has the object or effect of authorising the trader to dissolve the contract on a discretionary basis where the same facility is not granted to the consumer, or permitting the trader to retain the sums paid for services not yet supplied by the trader where it is the trader who dissolves the contract.

8   A term which has the object or effect of enabling the trader to terminate a contract of indeterminate duration without reasonable notice except where there are serious grounds for doing so.

9   A term which has the object or effect of automatically extending a contract of fixed duration where the consumer does not indicate otherwise, when the deadline fixed for the consumer to express a desire not to extend the contract is unreasonably early.

10   A term which has the object or effect of irrevocably binding the consumer to terms with which the consumer has had no real opportunity of becoming acquainted before the conclusion of the contract.

11   A term which has the object or effect of enabling the trader to alter the terms of the contract unilaterally without a valid reason which is specified in the contract.

12   A term which has the object or effect of permitting the trader to determine the characteristics of the subject matter of the contract after the consumer has become bound by it.

13   A term which has the object or effect of enabling the trader to alter unilaterally without a valid reason any characteristics of the goods, digital content or services to be provided.

14   A term which has the object or effect of giving the trader the discretion to decide the price payable under the contract after the consumer has become bound by it, where no price or method of determining the price is agreed when the consumer becomes bound.

15   A term which has the object or effect of permitting a trader to increase the price of goods, digital content or services without giving the consumer the right to cancel the contract if the final price is too high in relation to the price agreed when the contract was concluded.

16   A term which has the object or effect of giving the trader the right to determine whether the goods, digital content or services supplied are in conformity with the contract, or giving the trader the exclusive right to interpret any term of the contract.

17　A term which has the object or effect of limiting the trader's obligation to respect commitments undertaken by the trader's agents or making the trader's commitments subject to compliance with a particular formality.

18　A term which has the object or effect of obliging the consumer to fulfil all of the consumer's obligations where the trader does not perform the trader's obligations.

19　A term which has the object or effect of allowing the trader to transfer the trader's rights and obligations under the contract, where this may reduce the guarantees for the consumer, without the consumer's agreement.

20　A term which has the object or effect of excluding or hindering the consumer's right to take legal action or exercise any other legal remedy, in particular by—

(a) requiring the consumer to take disputes exclusively to arbitration not covered by legal provisions,

(b) unduly restricting the evidence available to the consumer, or

(c) imposing on the consumer a burden of proof which, according to the applicable law, should lie with another party to the contract.

PART 2
SCOPE OF PART 1

Financial services

21　Paragraph 8 (cancellation without reasonable notice) does not include a term by which a supplier of financial services reserves the right to terminate unilaterally a contract of indeterminate duration without notice where there is a valid reason, if the supplier is required to inform the consumer of the cancellation immediately.

22　Paragraph 11 (variation of contract without valid reason) does not include a term by which a supplier of financial services reserves the right to alter the rate of interest payable by or due to the consumer, or the amount of other charges for financial services without notice where there is a valid reason, if—

(a) the supplier is required to inform the consumer of the alteration at the earliest opportunity, and

(b) the consumer is free to dissolve the contract immediately.

Contracts which last indefinitely

23　Paragraphs 11 (variation of contract without valid reason), 12 (determination of characteristics of goods etc., after consumer bound) and 14 (determination of price after consumer bound) do not include a term under which a trader reserves the right to alter unilaterally the conditions of a contract of indeterminate duration if—

(a) the trader is required to inform the consumer with reasonable notice, and

(b) the consumer is free to dissolve the contract.

Sale of securities, foreign currency etc.

24　Paragraphs 8 (cancellation without reasonable notice), 11 (variation of contract without valid reason), 14 (determination of price after consumer bound) and 15 (increase in price) do not apply to—

(a) transactions in transferable securities, financial instruments and other products or services where the price is linked to fluctuations in a stock exchange quotation or index or a financial market rate that the trader does not control, and

(b) contracts for the purchase or sale of foreign currency, traveller's cheques or international money orders denominated in foreign currency.

Price index clauses

25　Paragraphs 14 (determination of price after consumer bound) and 15 (increase in price) do not include a term which is a price-indexation clause (where otherwise lawful), if the method by which prices vary is explicitly described.

Section 70   SCHEDULE 3
ENFORCEMENT OF THE LAW ON UNFAIR CONTRACT TERMS AND NOTICES

Application of Schedule

1   This Schedule applies to—
       (a)   a term of a consumer contract,
       (b)   a term proposed for use in a consumer contract,
       (c)   a term which a third party recommends for use in a consumer contract, or
       (d)   a consumer notice.

Consideration of complaints

2   (1)   A regulator may consider a complaint about a term or notice to which this Schedule
              applies (a "relevant complaint").
       (2)   If a regulator other than the CMA intends to consider a relevant complaint, it must
              notify the CMA that it intends to do so, and must then consider the complaint.
       (3)   If a regulator considers a relevant complaint, but decides not to make an application
              under paragraph 3 in relation to the complaint, it must give reasons for its decision to
              the person who made the complaint.

Application for injunction or interdict

3   (1)   A regulator may apply for an injunction or (in Scotland) an interdict against a person if
              the regulator thinks that—
              (a)   the person is using, or proposing or recommending the use of, a term or notice
                     to which this Schedule applies, and
              (b)   the term or notice falls within any one or more of sub-paragraphs (2), (3) or (5).
       (2)   A term or notice falls within this sub-paragraph if it purports to exclude or restrict
              liability of the kind mentioned in—
              (a)   section 31 (exclusion of liability: goods contracts),
              (b)   section 47 (exclusion of liability: digital content contracts),
              (c)   section 57 (exclusion of liability: services contracts), or
              (d)   section 65(1) (business liability for death or personal injury resulting from
                     negligence).
       (3)   A term or notice falls within this sub-paragraph if it is unfair to any extent.
       (4)   A term within paragraph 1(1)(b) or (c) (but not within paragraph 1(1)(a)) is to be treated
              for the purposes of section 62(4) and (5) (assessment of fairness) as if it were a term of
              a contract.
       (5)   A term or notice falls within this sub-paragraph if it breaches section 68 (requirement
              for transparency).
       (6)   A regulator may apply for an injunction or interdict under this paragraph in relation to
              a term or notice whether or not it has received a relevant complaint about the term or
              notice.

Notification of application

4   (1)   Before making an application under paragraph 3, a regulator other than the CMA must
              notify the CMA that it intends to do so.
       (2)   The regulator may make the application only if—
              (a)   the period of 14 days beginning with the day on which the regulator notified the
                     CMA has ended, or
              (b)   before the end of that period, the CMA agrees to the regulator making the
                     application.

Determination of application

5   (1)   On an application for an injunction under paragraph 3, the court may grant an injunction on such conditions, and against such of the respondents, as it thinks appropriate.

      (2)   On an application for an interdict under paragraph 3, the court may grant an interdict on such conditions, and against such of the defenders, as it thinks appropriate.

      (3)   The injunction or interdict may include provision about—

          (a)   a term or notice to which the application relates, or

          (b)   any term of a consumer contract, or any consumer notice, of a similar kind or with a similar effect.

      (4)   It is not a defence to an application under paragraph 3 to show that, because of a rule of law, a term to which the application relates is not, or could not be, an enforceable contract term.

      (5)   If a regulator other than the CMA makes the application, it must notify the CMA of—

          (a)   the outcome of the application, and

          (b)   if an injunction or interdict is granted, the conditions on which, and the persons against whom, it is granted.

Undertakings

6   (1)   A regulator may accept an undertaking from a person against whom it has applied, or thinks it is entitled to apply, for an injunction or interdict under paragraph 3.

      (2)   The undertaking may provide that the person will comply with the conditions that are agreed between the person and the regulator about the use of terms or notices, or terms or notices of a kind, specified in the undertaking.

      (3)   If a regulator other than the CMA accepts an undertaking, it must notify the CMA of—

          (a)   the conditions on which the undertaking is accepted, and

          (b)   the person who gave it.

Publication, information and advice

7   (1)   The CMA must arrange the publication of details of—

          (a)   any application it makes for an injunction or interdict under paragraph 3,

          (b)   any injunction or interdict under this Schedule, and

          (c)   any undertaking under this Schedule.

      (2)   The CMA must respond to a request whether a term or notice, or one of a similar kind or with a similar effect, is or has been the subject of an injunction, interdict or undertaking under this Schedule.

      (3)   Where the term or notice, or one of a similar kind or with a similar effect, is or has been the subject of an injunction or interdict under this Schedule, the CMA must give the person making the request a copy of the injunction or interdict.

      (4)   Where the term or notice, or one of a similar kind or with a similar effect, is or has been the subject of an undertaking under this Schedule, the CMA must give the person making the request—

          (a)   details of the undertaking, and

          (b)   if the person giving the undertaking has agreed to amend the term or notice, a copy of the amendments.

      (5)   The CMA may arrange the publication of advice and information about the provisions of this Part.

      (6)   In this paragraph—

          (a)   references to an injunction or interdict under this Schedule are to an injunction or interdict granted on an application by the CMA under paragraph 3 or notified to it under paragraph 5, and

          (b)   references to an undertaking are to an undertaking given to the CMA under paragraph 6 or notified to it under that paragraph.

Meaning of "regulator"

8   (1)   In this Schedule "regulator" means—
          (a)   the CMA,
          (b)   the Department of Enterprise, Trade and Investment in Northern Ireland,
          (c)   a local weights and measures authority in Great Britain,
          (d)   the Financial Conduct Authority,
          (e)   the Office of Communications,
          (f)   the Information Commissioner,
          (g)   the Gas and Electricity Markets Authority,
          (h)   the Water Services Regulation Authority,
          (i)   the Office of Rail Regulation,
          (j)   the Northern Ireland Authority for Utility Regulation, or
          (k)   the Consumers' Association.

     (2)   The Secretary of State may by order made by statutory instrument amend subparagraph (1) so as to add, modify or remove an entry.

     (3)   An order under sub-paragraph (2) may amend sub-paragraph (1) so as to add a body that is not a public authority only if the Secretary of State thinks that the body represents the interests of consumers (or consumers of a particular description).

     (4)   The Secretary of State must publish (and may from time to time vary) other criteria to be applied by the Secretary of State in deciding whether to add an entry to, or remove an entry from, sub-paragraph (1).

     (5)   An order under sub-paragraph (2) may make consequential amendments to this Schedule (including with the effect that any of its provisions apply differently, or do not apply, to a body added to sub-paragraph (1)).

     (6)   An order under sub-paragraph (2) may contain transitional or transitory provision or savings.

     (7)   No order may be made under sub-paragraph (2) unless a draft of the statutory instrument containing it has been laid before, and approved by a resolution of, each House of Parliament.

     (8)   In this paragraph "public authority" has the same meaning as in section 6 of the Human Rights Act 1998.

Other definitions

9   In this Schedule—
"the CMA" means the Competition and Markets Authority;
"injunction" includes an interim injunction;
"interdict" includes an interim interdict.

The Financial Conduct Authority

10   The functions of the Financial Conduct Authority under this Schedule are to be treated as functions of the Authority under the Financial Services and Markets Act 2000.

PACKAGE TRAVEL, PACKAGE HOLIDAYS AND PACKAGE TOURS REGULATIONS 1992
(SI 1992, No. 3288)

2   Interpretation

(1)   In these Regulations—

"brochure" means any brochure in which packages are offered for sale;

"contract" means the agreement linking the consumer to the organiser or to the retailer, or to both, as the case may be;

"the Directive" means Council Directive 90/314/EEC on package travel, package holidays and package tours;

"member State" means a member State of the European Community or another State in the European Economic Area;

"offer" includes an invitation to treat whether by means of advertising or otherwise, and cognate expressions shall be construed accordingly;

"organiser" means the person who, otherwise than occasionally, organises packages and sells or offers them for sale, whether directly or through a retailer;

"the other party to the contract" means the party, other than the consumer, to the contract, that is, the organiser or the retailer, or both, as the case may be;

"package" means the pre-arranged combination of at least two of the following components when sold or offered for sale at an inclusive price and when the service covers a period of more than twenty-four hours or includes overnight accommodation—

(a)   transport;

(b)   accommodation;

(c)   other tourist services not ancillary to transport or accommodation and accounting for a significant proportion of the package, and

(i)   the submission of separate accounts for different components shall not cause the arrangements to be other than a package;

(ii)   the fact that a combination is arranged at the request of the consumer and in accordance with his specific instructions (whether modified or not) shall not of itself cause it to be treated as other than pre-arranged; and

"retailer" means the person who sells or offers for sale the package put together by the organiser.

(2)   In the definition of "contract" in paragraph (1) above, "consumer" means the person who takes or agrees to take the package ("the principal contractor") and elsewhere in these Regulations "consumer" means, as the context requires, the principal contractor, any person on whose behalf the principal contractor agrees to purchase the package ("the other beneficiaries") or any person to whom the principal contractor or any of the other beneficiaries transfers the package ("the transferee").

3   Application of Regulations

(1)   These Regulations apply to packages sold or offered for sale in the territory of the United Kingdom.

4   Descriptive matter relating to packages must not be misleading

(1)   No organiser or retailer shall supply to a consumer any descriptive matter concerning a package, the price of a package or any other conditions applying to the contract which contains any misleading information.

(2)   If an organiser or retailer is in breach of paragraph (1) he shall be liable to compensate the consumer for any loss which the consumer suffers in consequence.

5   Requirements as to brochures

(1)   Subject to paragraph (4) below, no organiser shall make available a brochure to a possible consumer unless it indicates in a legible, comprehensive and accurate manner the price and adequate information about the matters specified in Schedule 1

to these Regulations in respect of the packages offered for sale in the brochure to the extent that those matters are relevant to the packages so offered.

(2) Subject to paragraph (4) below, no retailer shall make available to a possible consumer a brochure which he knows or has reasonable cause to believe does not comply with the requirements of paragraph (1).

(3) An organiser who contravenes paragraph (1) of this regulation and a retailer who contravenes paragraph (2) thereof shall be guilty of an offence and liable—
  (a) on summary conviction, to a fine not exceeding level 5 on the standard scale; and
  (b) on conviction on indictment, to a fine.

(4) Where a brochure was first made available to consumers generally before 31 December 1992 no liability shall arise under this regulation in respect of an identical brochure being made available to a consumer at any time.

6   Circumstances in which particulars in brochure are to be binding

(1) Subject to paragraphs (2) and (3) of this regulation, the particulars in the brochure (whether or not they are required by regulation 5(1) above to be included in the brochure) shall constitute implied warranties (or, as regards Scotland, implied terms) for the purposes of any contract to which the particulars relate.

(2) Paragraph (1) of this regulation does not apply—
  (a) in relation to information required to be included by virtue of paragraph 9 of Schedule 1 to these Regulations; or
  (b) where the brochure contains an express statement that changes may be made in the particulars contained in it before a contract is concluded and changes in the particulars so contained are clearly communicated to the consumer before a contract is concluded.

(3) Paragraph (1) of this regulation does not apply when the consumer and the other party to the contract agree after the contract has been made that the particulars in the brochure, or some of those particulars, should not form part of the contract.

7   Information to be provided before contract is concluded

(1) Before a contract is concluded, the other party to the contract shall provide the intending consumer with the information specified in paragraph (2) below in writing or in some other appropriate form.

(2) The information referred to in paragraph (1) is—
  (a) general information about passport and visa requirements which apply to nationals of the member State or States concerned who purchase the package in question, including information about the length of time it is likely to take to obtain the appropriate passports and visas;
  (b) information about health formalities required for the journey and the stay; and
  (c) the arrangements for security for the money paid over and (where applicable) for the repatriation of the consumer in the event of insolvency.

(3) If the intending consumer is not provided with the information required by paragraph (1) in accordance with that paragraph the other party to the contract shall be guilty of an offence and liable—
  (a) on summary conviction, to a fine not exceeding level 5 on the standard scale; and
  (b) on conviction on indictment, to a fine.

8   Information to be provided in good time

(1) The other party to the contract shall in good time before the start of the journey provide the consumer with the information specified in paragraph (2) below in writing or in some other appropriate form.

(2) The information referred to in paragraph (1) is the following—
  (a) the times and places of intermediate stops and transport connections and particulars of the place to be occupied by the traveller (for example, cabin or berth on ship, sleeper compartment on train);
  (b) the name, address and telephone number—
    (i) of the representative of the other party to the contract in the locality where the consumer is to stay, or, if there is no such representative,
    (ii) of an agency in that locality on whose assistance a consumer in difficulty would be able to call,

or, if there is no such representative or agency, a telephone number or other information which will enable the consumer to contact the other party to the contract during the stay; and

(c)   in the case of a journey or stay abroad by a child under the age of 16 on the day when the journey or stay is due to start, information enabling direct contact to be made with the child or the person responsible at the place where he is to stay; and

(d)   except where the consumer is required as a term of the contract to take out an insurance policy in order to cover the cost of cancellation by the consumer or the cost of assistance, including repatriation, in the event of accident or illness, information about an insurance policy which the consumer may, if he wishes, take out in respect of the risk of those costs being incurred.

(3)   If the consumer is not provided with the information required by paragraph (1) in accordance with that paragraph the other party to the contract shall be guilty of an offence and liable—

(a)   on summary conviction, to a fine not exceeding level 5 on the standard scale; and

(b)   on conviction on indictment, to a fine.

9   Contents and form of contract

(1)   The other party to the contract shall ensure that—

(a)   depending on the nature of the package being purchased, the contract contains at least the elements specified in Schedule 2 to these Regulations;

(b)   subject to paragraph (2) below, all the terms of the contract are set out in writing or such other form as is comprehensible and accessible to the consumer and are communicated to the consumer before the contract is made; and (c) a written copy of these terms is supplied to the consumer.

(2)   Paragraph (1)(b) above does not apply when the interval between the time when the consumer approaches the other party to the contract with a view to entering into a contract and the time of departure under the proposed contract is so short that it is impracticable to comply with the sub-paragraph.

(3)   It is an implied condition (or, as regards Scotland, an implied term) of the contract that the other party to the contract complies with the provisions of paragraph (1).

10   Transfer of bookings

(1)   In every contract there is an implied term that where the consumer is prevented from proceeding with the package the consumer may transfer his booking to a person who satisfies all the conditions applicable to the package, provided that the consumer gives reasonable notice to the other party to the contract of his intention to transfer before the date when departure is due to take place.

(2)   Where a transfer is made in accordance with the implied term set out in paragraph (1) above, the transferor and the transferee shall be jointly and severally liable to the other party to the contract for payment of the price of the package (or, if part of the price has been paid, for payment of the balance) and for any additional costs arising from such transfer.

11   Price revision

(1)   Any term in a contract to the effect that the prices laid down in the contract may be revised shall be void and of no effect unless the contract provides for the possibility of upward or downward revision and satisfies the conditions laid down in paragraph (2) below.

(2)   The conditions mentioned in paragraph (1) are that—

(a)   the contract states precisely how the revised price is to be calculated;

(b)   the contract provides that price revisions are to be made solely to allow for variations in—

(i)   transportation costs, including the cost of fuel,

(ii)   dues, taxes or fees chargeable for services such as landing taxes or embarkation or disembarkation fees at ports and airports, or

(iii)   the exchange rates applied to the particular package; and

(3)   Notwithstanding any terms of a contract,
    (i)   no price increase may be made in a specified period which may not be less than 30 days before the departure date stipulated; and
    (ii)   as against an individual consumer liable under the contract, no price increase may be made in respect of variations which would produce an increase of less than 2 per cent, or such greater percentage as the contract may specify ("non-eligible variations") and that the non-eligible variations shall be left out of account in the calculation.

12   Significant alterations to essential terms

In every contract there are implied terms to the effect that—

(a)   where the organiser is constrained before the departure to alter significantly an essential term of the contract, such as the price (so far as regulation 11 permits him to do so), he will notify the consumer as quickly as possible in order to enable him to take appropriate decisions and in particular to withdraw from the contract without penalty or to accept a rider to the contract specifying the alterations made and their impact on the price; and

(b)   the consumer will inform the organiser or the retailer of his decision as soon as possible.

13   Withdrawal by consumer pursuant to regulation 12 and cancellation by organiser

(1)   The terms set out in paragraphs (2) and (3) below are implied in every contract and apply where the consumer withdraws from the contract pursuant to the term in it implied by virtue of regulation 12(a), or where the organiser, for any reason other than the fault of the consumer, cancels the package before the agreed date of departure.

(2)   The consumer is entitled—

(a)   to take a substitute package of equivalent or superior quality if the other party to the contract is able to offer him such a substitute; or

(b)   to take a substitute package of lower quality if the other party to the contract is able to offer him one and to recover from the organiser the difference in price between the price of the package purchased and that of the substitute package; or

(c)   to have repaid to him as soon as possible all the monies paid by him under the contract.

(3)   The consumer is entitled, if appropriate, to be compensated by the organiser for nonperformance of the contract except where—

(a)   the package is cancelled because the number of persons who agree to take it is less than the minimum number required and the consumer is informed of the cancellation, in writing, within the period indicated in the description of the package; or

(b)   the package is cancelled by reason of unusual and unforeseeable circumstances beyond the control of the party by whom this exception is pleaded, the consequences of which could not have been avoided even if all due care had been exercised.

(4)   Overbooking shall not be regarded as a circumstance falling within the provisions of subparagraph (b) of paragraph (3) above.

14   Significant proportion of services not provided

(1)   The terms set out in paragraphs (2) and (3) below are implied in every contract and apply where, after departure, a significant proportion of the services contracted for is not provided or the organiser becomes aware that he will be unable to procure a significant proportion of the services to be provided.

(2)   The organiser will make suitable alternative arrangements, at no extra cost to the consumer, for the continuation of the package and will, where appropriate, compensate the consumer for the difference between the services to be supplied under the contract and those supplied.

(3)   If it is impossible to make arrangements as described in paragraph (2), or these are not accepted by the consumer for good reasons, the organiser will, where appropriate, provide the consumer with equivalent transport back to the place of departure or to another place to which the consumer has agreed and will, where appropriate, compensate the consumer.

15   Liability of other party to the contract for proper performance of obligations under contract

(1)   The other party to the contract is liable to the consumer for the proper performance of the obligations under the contract, irrespective of whether such obligations are to be performed by that other party or by other suppliers of services but this shall not affect any remedy or right of action which that other party may have against those other suppliers of services.

(2)   The other party to the contract is liable to the consumer for any damage caused to him by the failure to perform the contract or the improper performance of the contract unless the failure or the improper performance is due neither to any fault of that other party nor to that of another supplier of services, because—

    (a)   the failures which occur in the performance of the contract are attributable to the consumer;

    (b)   such failures are attributable to a third party unconnected with the provision of the services contracted for, and are unforeseeable or unavoidable; or

    (c)   such failures are due to—

        (i)   unusual and unforeseeable circumstances beyond the control of the party by whom this exception is pleaded, the consequences of which could not have been avoided even if all due care had been exercised; or

        (ii)   an event which the other party to the contract or the supplier of services, even with all due care, could not foresee or forestall.

(3)   In the case of damage arising from the non-performance or improper performance of the services involved in the package, the contract may provide for compensation to be limited in accordance with the international conventions which govern such services.

(4)   In the case of damage other than personal injury resulting from the nonperformance or improper performance of the services involved in the package, the contract may include a term limiting the amount of compensation which will be paid to the consumer, provided that the limitation is not unreasonable.

(5)   Without prejudice to paragraph (3) and paragraph (4) above, liability under paragraphs (1) and (2) above cannot be excluded by any contractual term.

(6)   The terms set out in paragraphs (7) and (8) below are implied in every contract.

(7)   In the circumstances described in paragraph (2)(b) and (c) of this regulation, the other party to the contract will give prompt assistance to a consumer in difficulty.

(8)   If the consumer complains about a defect in the performance of the contract, the other party to the contract, or his local representative, if there is one, will make prompt efforts to find appropriate solutions.

(9)   The contract must clearly and explicitly oblige the consumer to communicate at the earliest opportunity, in writing or any other appropriate form, to the supplier of the services concerned and to the other party to the contract any failure which he perceives at the place where the services concerned are supplied.

Regulation 5   SCHEDULE 1

INFORMATION TO BE INCLUDED (IN ADDITION TO THE PRICE) IN BROCHURES WHERE RELEVANT TO PACKAGES OFFERED

1.   The destination and the means, characteristics and categories of transport used.

2.   The type of accommodation, its location, category or degree of comfort and its main features and, where the accommodation is to be provided in a member State, its approval or tourist classification under the rules of that member State.

3.   The meals which are included in the package.
4.   The itinerary.
5.   General information about passport and visa requirements which apply for nationals of the member State or States in which the brochure is made available and health formalities required for the journey and the stay.
6.   Either the monetary amount or the percentage of the price which is to be paid on account and the timetable for payment of the balance.
7.   Whether a minimum number of persons is required for the package to take place and, if so, the deadline for informing the consumer in the event of cancellation.
8.   The arrangements (if any) which apply if consumers are delayed at the outward or homeward points of departure.
9.   The arrangements for security for money paid over and for the repatriation of the consumer in the event of insolvency.

Regulation 9   SCHEDULE 2

ELEMENTS TO BE INCLUDED IN THE CONTRACT IF RELEVANT
TO THE PARTICULAR PACKAGE

1.   The travel destination(s) and, where periods of stay are involved, the relevant periods, with dates.
2.   ...
3.   Where the package includes accommodation, its location, its tourist category of degree of comfort, its main features and, where the accommodation is to be provided in a member State, its compliance with the rules of that member State.
4.   The meals which are included in the package.
5.   Whether a minimum number of persons is required for the package to take place and, if so, the deadline for informing the consumer in the event of cancellation.
6.   The itinerary.
7.   Visits, excursions or other services which are included in the total price agreed for the package.
8.   The name and address of the organiser, the retailer and, where appropriate, the insurer.
9.   The price of the package, if the price may be revised in accordance with the term which may be included in the contract under regulation 11, an indication of the possibility of such price revisions, and an indication of any dues, taxes or fees chargeable for certain services (landing, embarkation or disembarkation fees at ports and airports and tourist taxes) where such costs are not included in the package.
10.   The payment schedule and method of payment.
11.   Special requirements which the consumer has communicated to the organiser or retailer when making the booking and which both have accepted.
12.   The periods within which the consumer must make any complaint about the failure to perform or the inadequate performance of the contract.

EMPLOYERS' LIABILITY (COMPULSORY INSURANCE)
REGULATIONS 1998
(SI 1998, No. 2573)

1   Citation, commencement and interpretation
(2)   In these Regulations—
        "the 1969 Act" means the Employers' Liability (Compulsory Insurance) Act 1969;
        ...

2   Prohibition of certain conditions in policies of insurance
(1)   For the purposes of the 1969 Act, there is prohibited in any contract of insurance any condition which provides (in whatever terms) that no liability (either generally or in

respect of a particular claim) shall arise under the policy, or that any such liability so arising shall cease, if—

(a)   some specified thing is done or omitted to be done after the happening of the event giving rise to a claim under the policy,

(b)   the policy holder does not take reasonable care to protect his employees against the risk of bodily injury or disease in the course of their employment;

(c)   the policy holder fails to comply with the requirements of any enactment for the protection of employees against the risk of bodily injury or disease in the course of their employment; or

(d)   the policy holder does not keep specified records or fails to provide the insurer with or make available to him information from such records.

(2)   For the purposes of the 1969 Act there is also prohibited in a policy of insurance any condition which requires—

(a)   a relevant employee to pay; or

(b)   an insured employer to pay the relevant employee, the first amount of any claim or any aggregation of claims.

(3)   Paragraphs (1) and (2) above do not prohibit for the purposes of the 1969 Act a condition in a policy of insurance which requires the employer to pay or contribute any sum to the insurer in respect of the satisfaction of any claim made under the contract of insurance by a relevant employee or any costs and expenses incurred in relation to any such claim.

3   Limit of amount of compulsory insurance

(1)   Subject to paragraph (2) below, the amount for which an employer is required by the 1969 Act to insure and maintain insurance in respect of relevant employees under one or more policies of insurance shall be, or shall in aggregate be not less than £5 million in respect of—

(a)   a claim relating to any one or more of those employees arising out of any one occurrence; and

(b)   any costs and expenses incurred in relation to any such claim.

PROVISION AND USE OF WORK EQUIPMENT REGULATIONS 1998
(SI 1998, No. 2306)

2   Interpretation

(1)   In these Regulations, unless the context otherwise requires— "the 1974 Act" means the Health and Safety at Work etc. Act 1974;

"employer" except in regulation 3(2) and (3) includes a person to whom the requirements imposed by the Regulations apply by virtue of regulation 3(3)(a) and (b);

"essential requirements" means requirements described in regulation 10(1);

"the Executive" means the Health and Safety Executive;

"inspection" in relation to an inspection under paragraph (1) or (2) of regulation 6—

(a)   means such visual or more rigorous inspection by a competent person as is appropriate for the purpose described in the paragraph;

(b)   where it is appropriate to carry out testing for the purpose, includes testing the nature and extent of which are appropriate for the purpose; "power press" means a press or press brake for the working of metal by means of tools, or for die proving, which is power driven and which embodies a flywheel and clutch;

"thorough examination" in relation to a thorough examination under paragraph (1), (2), (3) or (4) of regulation 32—

(a)   means a thorough examination by a competent person;

(b)   includes testing the nature and extent of which are appropriate for the purpose described in the paragraph;

"use" in relation to work equipment means any activity involving work equipment and includes starting, stopping, programming, setting, transporting, repairing, modifying, maintaining, servicing and cleaning;

"work equipment" means any machinery, appliance, apparatus, tool or installation for use at work (whether exclusively or not); and related expressions shall be construed accordingly.

4   Suitability of work equipment

(1)   Every employer shall ensure that work equipment is so constructed or adapted as to be suitable for the purpose for which it is used or provided.

(2)   In selecting work equipment, every employer shall have regard to the working conditions and to the risks to the health and safety of persons which exist in the premises or undertaking in which that work equipment is to be used and any additional risk posed by the use of that work equipment.

(3)   Every employer shall ensure that work equipment is used only for operations for which, and under conditions for which, it is suitable.

(4)   In this regulation "suitable"—

(a)   subject to paragraph (b), means suitable in any respect which it is reasonably foreseeable will affect the health and safety of any person;

...

5   Maintenance

(1)   Every employer shall ensure that work equipment is maintained in an efficient state, in efficient working order and in good repair.

(2)   Every employer shall ensure that where any machinery has a maintenance log, the log is kept up to date.

6   Inspection

(1)   Every employer shall ensure that, where the safety of work equipment depends on the installation conditions, it is inspected—

(a)   after installation and before being put into service for the first time; or

(b)   after assembly at a new site or in a new location,

to ensure that it has been installed correctly and is safe to operate.

(2)   Every employer shall ensure that work equipment exposed to conditions causing deterioration which is liable to result in dangerous situations is inspected—

(a)   at suitable intervals; and

(b)   each time that exceptional circumstances which are liable to jeopardise the safety of the work equipment have occurred,

to ensure that health and safety conditions are maintained and that any deterioration can be detected and remedied in good time.

(3)   Every employer shall ensure that the result of an inspection made under this regulation is recorded and kept until the next inspection under this regulation is recorded.

(4)   Every employer shall ensure that no work equipment—

(a)   leaves his undertaking; or

(b)   if obtained from the undertaking of another person, is used in his undertaking,

unless it is accompanied by physical evidence that the last inspection required to be carried out under this regulation has been carried out.

7   Specific risks

(1)   Where the use of work equipment is likely to involve a specific risk to health or safety, every employer shall ensure that—

(a)   the use of that work equipment is restricted to those persons given the task of using it; and

(b)   repairs, modifications, maintenance or servicing of that work equipment is restricted to those persons who have been specifically designated to perform operations of that description (whether or not also authorised to perform other operations).

(2)   The employer shall ensure that the persons designated for the purposes of sub-paragraph (b) of paragraph (1) have received adequate training related to any operations in respect of which they have been so designated.

8   Information and instructions

(1)   Every employer shall ensure that all persons who use work equipment have available to them adequate health and safety information and, where appropriate, written instructions pertaining to the use of the work equipment.

(2)   Every employer shall ensure that any of his employees who supervises or manages the use of work equipment has available to him adequate health and safety information and, where appropriate, written instructions pertaining to the use of the work equipment.

(3)   Without prejudice to the generality of paragraphs (1) or (2), the information and instructions required by either of those paragraphs shall include information and, where appropriate, written instructions on—

(a)   the conditions in which and the methods by which the work equipment may be used;

(b)   foreseeable abnormal situations and the action to be taken if such a situation were to occur; and

(c)   any conclusions to be drawn from experience in using the work equipment.

(4)   Information and instructions required by this regulation shall be readily comprehensive to those concerned.

9   Training

(1)   Every employer shall ensure that all persons who use work equipment have received adequate training for purposes of health and safety, including training in the methods which may be adopted when using the work equipment, any risks which such use may entail and precautions to be taken.

(2)   Every employer shall ensure that any of his employees who supervises or manages the use of work equipment has received adequate training for purposes of health and safety, including training in the methods which may be adopted when using the work equipment, any risks which such use may entail and precautions to be taken.

10   Conformity with Community requirements

(1)   Every employer shall ensure that an item of work equipment conforms at all times with any essential requirements, other than requirements which, at the time of its being first supplied or put into service in any place in which these Regulations apply, did not apply to work equipment of its type.

(2)   In this regulation "essential requirements", in relation to an item of work equipment, means requirements relating to the design and construction of work equipment of its type in any of the instruments listed in Schedule 1 (being instruments which give effect to Community directives concerning the safety of products).

(3)   This regulation applies to items of work equipment provided for use in the premises or undertaking of the employer for the first time after 31 December 1992.

11   Dangerous parts of machinery

(1)   Every employer shall ensure that measures are taken in accordance with paragraph (2) which are effective—

(a)   to prevent access to any dangerous part of machinery or to any rotating stock-bar; or

(b)   to stop the movement of any dangerous part of machinery or rotating stock-bar before any part of a person enters a danger zone.

(2)   The measures required by paragraph (1) shall consist of—

(a)   the provision of fixed guards enclosing every dangerous part or rotating stock-bar where and to the extent that it is practicable to do so, but where or to the extent that it is not, then

(b)   the provision of other guards or protection devices where and to the extent that it is practicable to do so, but where or to the extent that it is not, then

(c)   the provision of jigs, holders, push-sticks or similar protection appliances used in conjunction with the machinery where and to the extent that it is practicable to do so,

and the provision of information, instruction, training and supervision as is necessary.

(3)   All guards and protection devices provided under sub-paragraphs (a) or (b) of paragraphs (2) shall—

(a)   be suitable for the purpose for which they are provided;

(b)   be of good construction, sound material and adequate strength;

(c)   be maintained in an efficient state, in efficient working order and in good repair;

(d) not give rise to any increased risk to health or safety;

(e) not be easily bypassed or disabled;

(f) be situated at sufficient distance from the danger zone;

(g) not unduly restrict the view of the operating cycle of the machinery, where such a view is necessary;

(h) be so constructed or adapted that they allow operations necessary to fit or replace parts and for maintenance work, restricting access so that it is allowed only to the area where the work is to be carried out and, if possible, without having to dismantle the guard or protection device.

(4) All protection appliances provided under sub-paragraph (c) of paragraph (2) shall comply with sub-paragraphs (a) to (d) and (g) of paragraph (3).

(5) In this regulation—

"danger zone" means any zone in or around machinery in which a person is exposed to a risk to health or safety from contact with a dangerous part of machinery or a rotating stockbar;

"stock-bar" means any part of a stock-bar which projects beyond the head-stock of a lathe.

12 Protection against specified hazards

(1) Every employer shall take measures to ensure that the exposure of a person using work equipment to any risk to his health or safety from any hazard specified in paragraph (3) is either prevented, or, where that is not reasonably practicable, adequately controlled.

(2) The measures required by paragraph (1) shall—

(a) be measures other than the provision of personal protective equipment or of information, instruction, training and supervision, so far as is reasonably practicable; and

(b) include, where appropriate, measures to minimise the effects of the hazard as well as to reduce the likelihood of the hazard occurring.

(3) The hazards referred to in paragraph (1) are—

(a) any article or substance falling or being ejected from work equipment;

(b) rupture or disintegration of parts of work equipment;

(c) work equipment catching fire or overheating;

(d) the unintended or premature discharge of any article or of any gas, dust, liquid, vapour or other substance which, in each case, is produced, used or stored in the work equipment;

(e) the unintended or premature explosion of the work equipment or any article or substance produced, used or stored in it.

(4) For the purposes of this regulation "adequately" means adequately having regard only to the nature of the hazard and the nature and degree of exposure to the risk.

(5) This regulation shall not apply where any of the following Regulations apply in respect of any risk to a person's health or safety for which such Regulations require measures to be taken to prevent or control such risk, namely—

(a) the Ionising Radiations Regulations 1985;

(b) the Control of Asbestos Regulations 2012;

(c) the Control of Substances Hazardous to Health Regulations 1994;

(d) the Control of Noise at Work Regulations 2005;

(e) the Construction (Head Protection) Regulations 1989;

(f) the Control of Lead at Work Regulations 1998;

(g) the Control of Vibration at Work Regulations 2005.

13 High or very low temperature

Every employer shall ensure that work equipment, parts of work equipment and any article or substance produced, used or stored in work equipment which, in each case, is at a high or very low temperature shall have protection where appropriate so as to prevent injury to any person by burn, scald or sear.

14 Controls for starting or making a significant change in operating conditions

(1) Every employer shall ensure that, where appropriate, work equipment is provided with one or more controls for the purposes of—

(a)   starting the work equipment (including re-starting after a stoppage for any reason); or

(b)   controlling any change in the speed, pressure or other operating conditions of the work equipment where such conditions after the change result in risk to health and safety which is greater than or of a different nature from such risks before the change.

(2)   Subject to paragraph (3), every employer shall ensure that, where a control is required by paragraph (1), it shall not be possible to perform any operation mentioned in subparagraph (a) or (b) of that paragraph except by a deliberate action on such control.

(3)   Paragraph (1) shall not apply to re-starting or changing operating conditions as a result of the normal operating cycle of an automatic device.

15   Stop controls

(1)   Every employer shall ensure that, where appropriate, work equipment is provided with one or more readily accessible controls the operation of which will bring the work equipment to a safe condition in a safe manner.

(2)   Any control required by paragraph (1) shall bring the work equipment to a complete stop where necessary for reasons of health and safety.

(3)   Any control required by paragraph (1) shall, if necessary for reasons of health and safety, switch off all sources of energy after stopping the functioning of the work equipment.

(4)   Any control required by paragraph (1) shall operate in priority to any control which starts or changes the operating conditions of the work equipment.

16   Emergency stop controls

(1)   Every employer shall ensure that, where appropriate, work equipment is provided with one or more readily accessible emergency stop controls unless it is not necessary by reason of the nature of the hazards and the time taken for the work equipment to come to a complete stop as a result of the action of any control provided by virtue of regulation 15(1).

(2)   Any control required by paragraph (1) shall operate in priority to any control required by regulation 15(1).

17   Controls

(1)   Every employer shall ensure that all controls for work equipment are clearly visible and identifiable, including by appropriate marking where necessary.

(2)   Except where necessary, the employer shall ensure that no control for work equipment is in a position where any person operating the control is exposed to a risk to his health or safety.

(3)   Every employer shall ensure where appropriate—

(a)   that, so far as is reasonably practicable, the operator of any control is able to ensure from the position of that control that no person is in a place where he would be exposed to any risk to his health or safety as a result of the operation of that control, but where or to the extent that it is not reasonably practicable;

(b)   that, so far as is reasonably practicable, systems of work are effective to ensure that, when work equipment is about to start, no person is in a place where he would be exposed to a risk to his health or safety as a result of the work equipment starting, but where neither of these is reasonably practicable;

(c)   that an audible, visible or other suitable warning is given by virtue of regulation 24 whenever work equipment is about to start.

(4)   Every employer shall take appropriate measures to ensure that any person who is in a place where he would be exposed to a risk to his health or safety as a result of the starting or stopping of work equipment has sufficient time and suitable means to avoid that risk.

18   Control systems

(1)   Every employer shall ensure, so far as is reasonably practicable, that all control systems of work equipment—

(a)   are safe; and

(b)   are chosen making due allowance for the failures, faults and constraints to be expected in the planned circumstances of use.

(2) Without prejudice to the generality of paragraph (1), a control system shall not be safe unless—

   (a) its operation does not create any increased risk to health or safety;

   (b) it ensures, so far as is reasonably practicable, that any fault in or damage to any part of the control system or the loss of supply of any source of energy used by the work equipment cannot result in additional or increased risk to health or safety;

   (c) it does not impede the operation of any control required by regulation 15 or 16.

19 Isolation from sources of energy

(1) Every employer shall ensure that where appropriate work equipment is provided with suitable means to isolate it from all its sources of energy.

(2) Without prejudice to the generality of paragraph (1), the means mentioned in that paragraph shall not be suitable unless they are clearly identifiable and readily accessible.

(3) Every employer shall take appropriate measures to ensure that re-connection of any energy source to work equipment does not expose any person using the work equipment to any risk to his health or safety.

20 Stability

Every employer shall ensure that work equipment or any part of work equipment is stabilised by clamping or otherwise where necessary for purposes of health or safety.

21 Lighting

Every employer shall ensure that suitable and sufficient lighting, which takes account of the operations to be carried out, is provided at any place where a person uses work equipment.

22 Maintenance operations

Every employer shall take appropriate measures to ensure that work equipment is so constructed or adapted that, so far as is reasonably practicable, maintenance operations which involve a risk to health or safety can be carried out while the work equipment is shut down, or in other cases—

   (a) maintenance operations can be carried out without exposing the person carrying them out to a risk to his health or safety; or

   (b) appropriate measures can be taken for the protection of any person carrying out maintenance operations which involve a risk to his health or safety.

23 Markings

Every employer shall ensure that work equipment is marked in a clearly visible manner with any marking appropriate for reasons of health and safety.

24 Warnings

(1) Every employer shall ensure that work equipment incorporates any warnings or warning devices which are appropriate for reasons of health and safety.

(2) Without prejudice to the generality of paragraph (1), warnings given by warning devices on work equipment shall not be appropriate unless they are unambiguous, easily perceived and easily understood.

LATE PAYMENT OF COMMERCIAL DEBTS REGULATIONS 2002
(SI 2002, No. 1674)

3 Proceedings restraining use of grossly unfair terms

(1) In this regulation:

   (a) "small and medium-sized enterprises" means those enterprises defined in Annex 1 to Commission Regulation (EC) No 70/2001 of 12th January 2001 on the application of Articles 87 and 88 of the EC Treaty to State aid to small and medium sized enterprises;

(b)   "representative body" means an organisation established to represent the collective interests of small and medium-sized enterprises in general or in a particular sector or area.

(2)   This regulation applies where a person acting in the course of a business has written standard terms on which he enters (or intends to enter) as purchaser into contracts to which the Late Payment of Commercial Debts (Interest) Act 1998 applies which include a term purporting to oust or vary the right to statutory interest in relation to qualifying debts created by those contracts.

(3)   If it appears to the High Court that in all or any circumstances the purported use of such a term in a relevant contract would be void under the Late Payment of Commercial Debts (Interest) Act 1998, the court on the application of a representative body may grant an injunction against that person restraining him in those circumstances from using the offending term, on such terms as the court may think fit.

(4)   Only a representative body may apply to the High Court under this regulation.

ELECTRONIC COMMERCE (EC DIRECTIVE) REGULATIONS 2002 (SI 2002, No. 2013)

2   Interpretation

(1)   In these Regulations and in the Schedule—

"commercial communication" means a communication, in any form, designed to promote, directly or indirectly, the goods, services or image of any person pursuing a commercial, industrial or craft activity or exercising a regulated profession, other than a communication—

(a)   consisting only of information allowing direct access to the activity of that person including a geographic address, a domain name or an electronic mail address; or

(b)   relating to the goods, services or image of that person provided that the communication has been prepared independently of the person making it (and for this purpose, a communication prepared without financial consideration is to be taken to have been prepared independently unless the contrary is shown);

"the Commission" means the Commission of the European Communities;

"consumer" means any natural person who is acting for purposes other than those of his trade, business or profession;

"coordinated field" means requirements applicable to information society service providers or information society services, regardless of whether they are of a general nature or specifically designed for them, and covers requirements with which the service provider has to comply in respect of—

(a)   the taking up of the activity of an information society service, such as requirements concerning qualifications, authorisation or notification, and

(b)   the pursuit of the activity of an information society service, such as requirements concerning the behaviour of the service provider, requirements regarding the quality or content of the service including those applicable to advertising and contracts, or requirements concerning the liability of the service provider,

but does not cover requirements such as those applicable to goods as such, to the delivery of goods or to services not provided by electronic means;

"the Directive" means Directive 2000/31/EC of the European Parliament and of the Council of 8 June 2000 on certain legal aspects of information society services, in particular electronic commerce, in the Internal Market (Directive on electronic commerce);

"EEA Agreement" means the Agreement on the European Economic Area signed at Oporto on 2 May 1992 as adjusted by the Protocol signed at Brussels on 17 March 1993;

"enactment" includes an enactment comprised in Northern Ireland legislation and comprised in, or an instrument made under, an Act of the Scottish Parliament;

"enforcement action" means any form of enforcement action including, in particular—

(a)   in relation to any legal requirement imposed by or under any enactment, any action taken with a view to or in connection with imposing any sanction (whether criminal or otherwise) for failure to observe or comply with it; and

(b)   in relation to a permission or authorisation, anything done with a view to removing or restricting that permission or authorisation;

"enforcement authority" does not include courts but, subject to that, means any person who is authorised, whether by or under an enactment or otherwise, to take enforcement action;

"established service provider" means a service provider who is a national of a member State or a company or firm as mentioned in Article 54 of the Treaty and who effectively pursues an economic activity by virtue of which he is a service provider using a fixed establishment in a member State for an indefinite period, but the presence and use of the technical means and technologies required to provide the information society service do not, in themselves, constitute an establishment of the provider; in cases where it cannot be determined from which of a number of places of establishment a given service is provided, that service is to be regarded as provided from the place of establishment where the provider has the centre of his activities relating to that service; references to a service provider being established or to the establishment of a service provider shall be construed accordingly;

"information society services" (which is summarised in recital 17 of the Directive as covering "any service normally provided for remuneration, at a distance, by means of electronic equipment for the processing (including digital compression) and storage of data, and at the individual request of a recipient of a service") has the meaning set out in Article 2(a) of the Directive, (which refers to Article 1(2) of Directive 98/34/EC of the European Parliament and of the Council of 22 June 1998 laying down a procedure for the provision of information in the field of technical standards and regulations, as amended by Directive 98/48/EC of 20 July 1998);

"member State" includes a State which is a contracting party to the EEA Agreement;

"recipient of the service" means any person who, for professional ends or otherwise, uses an information society service, in particular for the purposes of seeking information or making it accessible;

"regulated profession" means any profession within the meaning of either Article 1(d) of Council Directive 89/48/EEC of 21 December 1988 on a general system for the recognition of higher-education diplomas awarded on completion of professional education and training of at least three years' duration or of Article 1(f) of Council Directive 92/51/EEC of 18 June 1992 on a second general system for the recognition of professional education and training to supplement Directive 89/48/EEC;

"service provider" means any person providing an information society service; "the Treaty" means the treaty establishing the European Community.

(2)   In regulation 4 and 5, "requirement" means any legal requirement under the law of the United Kingdom, or any part of it, imposed by or under any enactment or otherwise.

(3)   Terms used in the Directive other than those in paragraph (1) above shall have the same meaning as in the Directive.

9   Information to be provided where contracts are concluded by electronic means

(1)   Unless parties who are not consumers have agreed otherwise, where a contract is to be concluded by electronic means a service provider shall, prior to an order being placed by the recipient of a service, provide to that recipient in a clear, comprehensible and unambiguous manner the information set out in (a) to (d) below—

(a)   the different technical steps to follow to conclude the contract;

(b)   whether or not the concluded contract will be filed by the service provider and whether it will be accessible;

(c)   the technical means for identifying and correcting input errors prior to the placing of the order; and

(d)   the languages offered for the conclusion of the contract.

(2)   Unless parties who are not consumers have agreed otherwise, a service provider shall indicate which relevant codes of conduct he subscribes to and give information on how those codes can be consulted electronically.

(3)   Where the service provider provides terms and conditions applicable to the contract to the recipient, the service provider shall make them available to him in a way that allows him to store and reproduce them.

(4)   The requirements of paragraphs (1) and (2) above shall not apply to contracts concluded exclusively by exchange of electronic mail or by equivalent individual communications.

11   Placing of the order

(1)   Unless parties who are not consumers have agreed otherwise, where the recipient of the service places his order through technological means, a service provider shall—
  (a)   acknowledge receipt of the order to the recipient of the service without undue delay and by electronic means; and
  (b)   make available to the recipient of the service appropriate, effective and accessible technical means allowing him to identify and correct input errors prior to the placing of the order.
(2)   For the purposes of paragraph (1)(a) above—
  (a)   the order and the acknowledgement of receipt will be deemed to be received when the parties to whom they are addressed are able to access them; and
  (b)   the acknowledgement of receipt may take the form of the provision of the service paid for where that service is an information society service.
(3)   The requirements of paragraph (1) above shall not apply to contracts concluded exclusively by exchange of electronic mail or by equivalent individual communications.

12   Meaning of the term "order"

Except in relation to regulation 9(1)(c) and regulation 11(1)(b) where "order" shall be the contractual offer, "order" may be but need not be the contractual offer for the purposes of regulations 9 and 11.

13   Liability of the service provider

The duties imposed by regulations 6, 7, 8, 9(1) and 11(1)(a) shall be enforceable, at the suit of any recipient of a service, by an action against the service provider for damages for breach of statutory duty.

14   Compliance with regulation 9(3)

Where on request a service provider has failed to comply with the requirement in regulation 9(3), the recipient may seek an order from any court having jurisdiction in relation to the contract requiring that service provider to comply with that requirement.

15   Right to rescind contract

Where a person—
  (a)   has entered into a contract to which these Regulations apply, and
  (b)   the service provider has not made available means of allowing him to identify and correct input errors in compliance with regulation 11(1)(b),
he shall be entitled to rescind the contract unless any court having jurisdiction in relation to the contract in question orders otherwise on the application of the service provider.

RAILWAYS (CONVENTION ON INTERNATIONAL CARRIAGE BY RAIL) REGULATIONS 2005
(SI 2005, No. 2092)

3   Convention to have the force of law

(1)   The Convention shall have the force of law in the United Kingdom, and judicial notice shall be taken of it.
(2)   For the avoidance of doubt any question arising as to whether the Convention applies in the circumstances of a particular case falls to be determined in accordance with the provisions of paragraph 2 of Article 3.

5   Fatal accidents

(1)   Where by virtue of the Convention any person has a right of action in respect of the death of a passenger by reason of his being a person whom the passenger was under a legal duty to maintain—

(a)   subject to paragraph (2), no action in respect of the passenger's death shall be brought for the benefit of that person under the 1976 Act, but

(b)   nothing in section 2(3) of that Act (not more than one action in respect of the same subject matter of complaint) shall prevent an action being brought under that Act for the benefit of any other person.

(2)   Nothing in paragraph (1)(a) affects the right of any person to claim damages for bereavement under section 1A of the 1976 Act.

(3)   Section 4 of the 1976 Act (exclusion of certain benefits in assessment of damages) shall apply in relation to an action brought by any person under the Convention as it applies in relation to an action under that Act.

(4)   Where separate proceedings are brought under the Convention and under the 1976 Act in respect of the death of a passenger, a court, in awarding damages under that Act, shall take into account any damages awarded in the proceedings brought under the Convention and shall have jurisdiction to make any part of its award conditional on the result of those proceedings.

(5)   In the application of this regulation to Northern Ireland references to the 1976 Act and to sections 1A, 2(3) and 4 of that Act shall be construed as references to the Fatal Accidents (Northern Ireland) Order 1977 and Articles 3A, 4(3) and 6 of that Order.

(6)   The provisions of Schedule 1 to these Regulations shall, as respects Scotland, have effect in lieu of paragraphs (1) to (5).

CONSUMER CONTRACTS (INFORMATION, CANCELLATION AND ADDITIONAL CHARGES) REGULATIONS 2013 (SI 2013, No. 3134)

PART 1

General

1   Citation and commencement

(1)   These Regulations may be cited as the Consumer Contracts (Information, Cancellation and Additional Charges) Regulations 2013 and come into force on 13th June 2014.

(2)   These Regulations apply in relation to contracts entered into on or after that date.

2   Regulations superseded

The following do not apply in relation to contracts entered into on or after 13th June 2014—

(a)   the Consumer Protection (Distance Selling) Regulations 2000;

(b)   the Cancellation of Contracts made in a Consumer's Home or Place of Work etc., Regulations 2008.

4   "Consumer" and "trader"

In these Regulations—

"consumer" means an individual acting for purposes which are wholly or mainly outside that individual's trade, business, craft or profession;

"trader" means a person acting for purposes relating to that person's trade, business, craft or profession, whether acting personally or through another person acting in the trader's name or on the trader's behalf.

5   Other definitions

In these Regulations—

"business" includes the activities of any government department or local or public authority;

"business premises" in relation to a trader means—

(a)   any immovable retail premises where the activity of the trader is carried out on a permanent basis, or

(b)   any movable retail premises where the activity of the trader is carried out on a usual basis;

"CMA" means the Competition and Markets Authority;

"commercial guarantee", in relation to a contract, means any undertaking by the trader or producer to the consumer (in addition to the trader's duty to supply goods that are in conformity with the contract) to reimburse the price paid or to replace, repair or service goods in any way if they do not meet the specifications or any other requirements not related to conformity set out in the guarantee statement or in the relevant advertising available at the time of the contract or before it is entered into;

"court"—

(a)   in relation to England and Wales, means the county court or the High Court,

(b)   in relation to Northern Ireland, means a county court or the High Court, and

(c)   in relation to Scotland means the sheriff court or the Court of Session;

"delivery" means voluntary transfer of possession from one person to another; "digital content" means data which are produced and supplied in digital form;

"distance contract" means a contract concluded between a trader and a consumer under an organised distance sales or service-provision scheme without the simultaneous physical presence of the trader and the consumer, with the exclusive use of one or more means of distance communication up to and including the time at which the contract is concluded;

"district heating" means the supply of heat (in the form of steam or hot water or otherwise) from a central source of production through a transmission and distribution system to heat more than one building;

"durable medium" means paper or email, or any other medium that—

(a)   allows information to be addressed personally to the recipient,

(b)   enables the recipient to store the information in a way accessible for future reference for a period that is long enough for the purposes of the information, and

(c)   allows the unchanged reproduction of the information stored;

"functionality" in relation to digital content includes region coding, restrictions incorporated for the purposes of digital rights management, and other technical restrictions;

"goods" means any tangible moveable items, but that includes water, gas and electricity if and only if they are put up for sale in a limited volume or a set quantity;

"off-premises contract" means a contract between a trader and a consumer which is any of these—

(a)   a contract concluded in the simultaneous physical presence of the trader and the consumer, in a place which is not the business premises of the trader;

(b)   a contract for which an offer was made by the consumer in the simultaneous physical presence of the trader and the consumer, in a place which is not the business premises of the trader;

(c)   a contract concluded on the business premises of the trader or through any means of distance communication immediately after the consumer was personally and individually addressed in a place which is not the business premises of the trader in the simultaneous physical presence of the trader and the consumer;

(d)   a contract concluded during an excursion organised by the trader with the aim or effect of promoting and selling goods or services to the consumer;

"on-premises contract" means a contract between a trader and a consumer which is neither a distance contract nor an off-premises contract;

"public auction" means a method of sale where—

(a)   goods or services are offered by a trader to consumers through a transparent, competitive bidding procedure run by an auctioneer,

(b)   the consumers attend or are given the possibility to attend in person, and

(c)   the successful bidder is bound to purchase the goods or services;

"sales contract" means a contract under which a trader transfers or agrees to transfer the ownership of goods to a consumer and the consumer pays or agrees to pay the price, including any contract that has both goods and services as its object;

"service" includes—

(a)   the supply of water, gas or electricity if they are not put up for sale in a limited volume or a set quantity, and

(b)   the supply of district heating;

"service contract" means a contract, other than a sales contract, under which a trader supplies or agrees to supply a service to a consumer and the consumer pays or agrees to pay the price.

6   Limits of application: general

(1)   These Regulations do not apply to a contract, to the extent that it is—

    (a)   for—

        (i)   gambling within the meaning of the Gambling Act 2005 (which includes gaming, betting and participating in a lottery);

        (ii)   in relation to Northern Ireland, for betting, gaming or participating lawfully in a lottery within the meaning of the Betting, Gaming, Lotteries and Amusements (Northern Ireland) Order 1985; or

        (iii)   participating in a lottery which forms part of the National Lottery within the meaning of the National Lottery etc. Act 1993;

    (b)   for services of a banking, credit, insurance, personal pension, investment or payment nature;

    (c)   for the creation of immovable property or of rights in immovable property;

    (d)   for rental of accommodation for residential purposes;

    (e)   for the construction of new buildings, or the construction of substantially new buildings by the conversion of existing buildings;

    (f)   for the supply of foodstuffs, beverages or other goods intended for current consumption in the household and which are supplied by a trader on frequent and regular rounds to the consumer's home, residence or workplace;

    (g)   within the scope of Council Directive 90/314/EEC of 13 June 1990 on package travel, package holidays and package tours;

    (h)   within the scope of Directive 2008/122/EC of the European Parliament and of the Council on the protection of consumers in respect of certain aspects of timeshare, long-term holiday product, resale and exchange contracts.

(2)   These Regulations do not apply to contracts—

    (a)   concluded by means of automatic vending machines or automated commercial premises;

    (b)   concluded with a telecommunications operator through a public telephone for the use of the telephone;

    (c)   concluded for the use of one single connection, by telephone, internet or fax, established by a consumer;

    (d)   under which goods are sold by way of execution or otherwise by authority of law.

(3)   Paragraph (1)(b) is subject to regulations 38(4) (ancillary contracts) and 40(3) (additional payments).

PART 2

INFORMATION REQUIREMENTS

CHAPTER 1

PROVISION OF INFORMATION

7   Application of Part 2

(1)   This Part applies to on-premises, off-premises and distance contracts, subject to paragraphs (2), (3) and (4) and regulation 6.

(2)   This Part does not apply to contracts to the extent that they are—

    (a)   for the supply of a medicinal product by administration by a prescriber, or under a prescription or directions given by a prescriber;

    (b)   for the supply of a product by a health care professional or a person included in a relevant list, under arrangements for the supply of services as part of the health service, where the product is one that, at least in some circumstances is available under such arrangements free or on prescription.

(3) This Part, except for regulation 14(1) to (5), does not apply to contracts to the extent that they are for passenger transport services.

(4) This Part does not apply to off-premises contracts under which the payment to be made by the consumer is not more than £42.

(5) In paragraph (2)—

"health care professional" and "prescriber" have the meaning given by regulation 2(1) of the National Health Service (Pharmaceutical and Local Pharmaceutical Services) Regulations 2013;

"health service" means—

(a)   the health service as defined by section 275(1) of the National Health Service Act 2006 or section 206(1) of the National Health Service (Wales) Act 2006,

(b)   the health service as defined by section 108(1) of the National Health Service (Scotland) Act 1978, or

(c)   any of the health services under section 2(1)(a) of the Health and Social Care (Reform) Act (Northern Ireland) 2009;

"medicinal product" has the meaning given by regulation 2(1) of the Human Medicines Regulations 2012;

"relevant list" means—

(d)   a relevant list for the purposes of the National Health Service (Pharmaceutical and Local Pharmaceutical Services) Regulations 2013, or

(e)   a list maintained under those Regulations.

8   Making information etc. available to a consumer

For the purposes of this Part, something is made available to a consumer only if the consumer can reasonably be expected to know how to access it.

9   Information to be provided before making an on-premises contract

(1) Before the consumer is bound by an on-premises contract, the trader must give or make available to the consumer the information described in Schedule 1 in a clear and comprehensible manner, if that information is not already apparent from the context.

(2) Paragraph (1) does not apply to a contract which involves a day-to-day transaction and is performed immediately at the time when the contract is entered into.

(3) If the contract is for the supply of digital content other than a price paid by the consumer—

(a)   any information that the trader gives the consumer as required by this regulation is to be treated as a term of the contract, and

(b)   a change to any of that information, made before entering into the contract or later, is not effective unless expressly agreed between the consumer and the trader.

10   Information to be provided before making an off-premises contract

(1) Before the consumer is bound by an off-premises contract, the trader—

(a)   must give the consumer the information listed in Schedule 2 in a clear and comprehensible manner, and

(b)   if a right to cancel exists, must give the consumer a cancellation form as set out in part B of Schedule 3.

(2) The information and any cancellation form must be given on paper or, if the consumer agrees, on another durable medium and must be legible.

(3) The information referred to in paragraphs (l), (m) and (n) of Schedule 2 may be provided by means of the model instructions on cancellation set out in part A of Schedule 3; and a trader who has supplied those instructions to the consumer, correctly filled in, is to be treated as having complied with paragraph (1) in respect of those paragraphs.

(4) If the trader has not complied with paragraph (1) in respect of paragraph (g), (h) or (m) of Schedule 2, the consumer is not to bear the charges or costs referred to in those paragraphs.

(5) If the contract is for the supply of digital content other than the price paid by the consumer—

    (a)   any information that the trader gives the consumer as required by this regulation is to be treated as a term of the contract, and

    (b)   a change to any of that information, made before entering into the contract or later, is not effective unless expressly agreed between the consumer and the trader.

(6)   ...

(7)   This regulation is subject to regulation 11.

11 Provision of information in connection with repair or maintenance contracts

(1)   If the conditions in paragraphs (2), (3) and (4) are met, regulation 10(1) does not apply to an off-premises contract where –

    (a)   the contract is a service contract,

    (b)   the consumer has explicitly requested the trader to supply the service for the purpose of carrying out repairs or maintenance,

    (c)   the obligations of the trader and the consumer under the contract are to be performed immediately, and

    (d)   the payment to be made by the consumer is not more than £170.

(2)   The first condition is that, before the consumer is bound by the contract, the trader gives or makes available to the consumer on paper or, if the consumer expressly agrees, on another durable medium–

    (a)   the information referred to in paragraphs (b) to (d), (f) and (g) of Schedule 2,

    (b)   an estimate of the total price, where it cannot reasonably be calculated in advance, and

    (c)   where a right to cancel exists, a cancellation form as set out in part B of Schedule 3.

(3)   The second condition is that, before the consumer is bound by the contract, the trader gives or makes available to the consumer the information referred to in paragraphs (a), (l) and (o) of Schedule 2, either on paper or another durable medium or otherwise if the consumer expressly agrees.

(4)   The third condition is that the confirmation of the contract provided in accordance with regulation 12 contains the information required by regulation 10(1).

(5)   For the right to cancel where this regulation applies, see in particular–

    (a)   regulation 28(1)(e) and (2) (cases where cancellation excluded: visit requested for urgent work);

    (b)   regulation 36 (form of consumer's request, and consequences).

12 Provision of copy or confirmation of off-premises contracts

(1)   In the case of an off-premises contract, the trader must give the consumer–

    (a)   a copy of the signed contract, or

    (b)   confirmation of the contract.

(2)   The confirmation must include all the information referred to in Schedule 2 unless the trader has already provided that information to the consumer on a durable medium prior to the conclusion of the off-premises contract.

(3)   The copy or confirmation must be provided on paper or, if the consumer agrees, on another durable medium.

(4)   The copy or confirmation must be provided within a reasonable time after the conclusion of the contract, but in any event–

    (a)   not later than the time of the delivery of any goods supplied under the contract, and

    (b)   before performance begins of any service supplied under the contract.

(5)   If the contract is for the supply of digital content not on a tangible medium and the consumer has given the consent and acknowledgement referred to in regulation 37(1)(a) and (b), the copy or confirmation must include confirmation of the consent and acknowledgement.

13 Information to be provided before making a distance contract

(1)   Before the consumer is bound by a distance contract, the trader–

    (a)   must give or make available to the consumer the information listed in Schedule 2 in a clear and comprehensible manner, and in a way appropriate to the means of distance communication used, and

(b)   if a right to cancel exists, must give or make available to the consumer a cancellation form as set out in part B of Schedule 3.

(2)   In so far as the information is provided on a durable medium, it must be legible.

(3)   The information referred to in paragraphs (l), (m) and (n) of Schedule 2 may be provided by means of the model instructions on cancellation set out in part A of Schedule 3; and a trader who has supplied those instructions to the consumer, correctly filled in, is to be treated as having complied with paragraph (1) in respect of those paragraphs.

(4)   Where a distance contract is concluded through a means of distance communication which allows limited space or time to display the information—

     (a)   the information listed in paragraphs (a), (b), (f), (g), (h), (l) and (s) of Schedule 2 must be provided on that means of communication in accordance with paragraphs (1) and (2), but

     (b)   the other information required by paragraph (1) may be provided in another appropriate way.

(5)   If the trader has not complied with paragraph (1) in respect of paragraph (g), (h) or (m) of Schedule 2, the consumer is not to bear the charges or costs referred to in those paragraphs.

(6)   If the contract is for the supply of digital content other than the price paid by the consumer—

     (a)   any information that the trader gives the consumer as required by this regulation shall be treated as a term of the contract, and

     (b)   a change to any of that information made before entering into the contract or later, is not effective unless expressly agreed between the consumer and the trader.

14   Requirements for distance contracts concluded by electronic means

(1)   This regulation applies where a distance contract is concluded by electronic means.

(2)   If the contract places the consumer under an obligation to pay, the trader must make the consumer aware in a clear and prominent manner, and directly before the consumer places the order, of the information listed in paragraphs (a), (f), (g), (h), (s) and (t) of Schedule 2.

(3)   The trader must ensure that the consumer, when placing the order, explicitly acknowledges that the order implies an obligation to pay.

(4)   If placing an order entails activating a button or a similar function, the trader must ensure that the button or similar function is labelled in an easily legible manner only with the words 'order with obligation to pay' or a corresponding unambiguous formulation indicating that placing the order entails an obligation to pay the trader.

(5)   If the trader has not complied with paragraphs (3) and (4), the consumer is not bound by the contract or order.

(6)   The trader must ensure that any trading website through which the contract is concluded indicates clearly and legibly, at the latest at the beginning of the ordering process, whether any delivery restrictions apply and which means of payment are accepted.

15   Telephone calls to conclude a distance contract

If the trader makes a telephone call to the consumer with a view to concluding a distance contract, the trader must, at the beginning of the conversation with the consumer, disclose—

     (a)   the trader's identity,

     (b)   where applicable, the identity of the person on whose behalf the trader makes the call, and

     (c)   the commercial purpose of the call.

16   Confirmation of distance contracts

(1)   In the case of a distance contract the trader must give the consumer confirmation of the contract on a durable medium.

(2)   The confirmation must include all the information referred to in Schedule 2 unless the trader has already provided that information to the consumer on a durable medium prior to the conclusion of the distance contract.

(3) If the contract is for the supply of digital content not on a tangible medium and the consumer has given the consent and acknowledgment referred to in Regulation 37(1)(a) and (b), the confirmation must include confirmation of the consent and acknowledgement.

(4) The confirmation must be provided within a reasonable time after the conclusion of the contract, but in any event—
   (a) not later than the time of delivery of any goods supplied under the contract, and
   (b) before performance begins of any service supplied under the contract.

(5) For the purposes of paragraph (4), the confirmation is treated as provided as soon as the trader has sent it or done what is necessary to make it available to the consumer.

17 Burden of proof in relation to off-premises and distance contracts

(1) In case of dispute about the trader's compliance with any provision of regulations 10 to 16, it is for the trader to show that the provision was complied with.

(2) That does not apply to proceedings—
   (a) for an offence under regulation 19, or
   (b) relating to compliance with an injunction, interdict or order under regulation 45.

18 Effect on contract of failure to provide information

Every contract to which this Part applies is to be treated as including a term that the trader has complied with the provisions of—
   (a) regulations 9 to 14, and
   (b) regulation 16.

PART 3
RIGHT TO CANCEL

27 Application of Part 3

(1) This Part applies to distance and off-premises contracts between a trader and a consumer, subject to paragraphs (2) and (3) and regulations 6 and 28.

(2) This Part does not apply to contracts to the extent that they are—
   (a) for the supply of a medicinal product by administration by a prescriber, or under a prescription or directions given by a prescriber;
   (b) for the supply of a product by a health care professional or a person included in a relevant list, under arrangements for the supply of services as part of the health service, where the product is one that, at least in some circumstances is available under such arrangements free or on prescription;
   (c) for passenger transport services.

(3) This Part does not apply to off-premises contracts under which the payment to be made by the consumer is not more than £42.

(4) In paragraph (2)(a) and (b), expressions defined in regulation 7(5) have the meaning given there.

28 Limits of application: circumstances excluding cancellation

(1) This Part does not apply as regards the following—
   (a) the supply of—
      (i) goods, or
      (ii) services, other than supply of water, gas, electricity or district heating, for which the price is dependent on fluctuations in the financial market which cannot be controlled by the trader and which may occur within the cancellation period;
   (b) the supply of goods that are made to the consumer's specifications or are clearly personalised;
   (c) the supply of goods which are liable to deteriorate or expire rapidly;
   (d) the supply of alcoholic beverages, where—
      (i) their price has been agreed at the time of the conclusion of the sales contract,
      (ii) delivery of them can only take place after 30 days, and
      (iii) their value is dependent on fluctuations in the market which cannot be controlled by the trader;

(e) contracts where the consumer has specifically requested a visit from the trader for the purpose of carrying out urgent repairs or maintenance;

(f) the supply of a newspaper, periodical or magazine with the exception of subscription contracts for the supply of such publications;

(g) contracts concluded at a public auction;

(h) the supply of accommodation, transport of goods, vehicle rental services, catering or services related to leisure activities, if the contract provides for a specific date or period of performance.

(2) Sub-paragraph (e) of paragraph (1) does not prevent this Part applying to a contract for—

(a) services in addition to the urgent repairs or maintenance requested, or

(b) goods other than replacement parts necessarily used in making the repairs or carrying out the maintenance,

if the trader supplies them on the occasion of a visit such as is mentioned in that subparagraph.

(3) The rights conferred by this Part cease to be available in the following circumstances—

(a) in the case of a contract for the supply of sealed goods which are not suitable for return due to health protection or hygiene reasons, if they become unsealed after delivery;

(b) in the case of a contract for the supply of sealed audio or sealed video recordings or sealed computer software, if the goods become unsealed after delivery;

(c) in the case of any sales contract, if the goods become mixed inseparably (according to their nature) with other items after delivery.

29 Right to cancel

(1) The consumer may cancel a distance or off-premises contract at any time in the cancellation period without giving any reason, and without incurring any liability except under these provisions—

(a) regulation 34(3) (where enhanced delivery chosen by consumer);

(b) regulation 34(9) (where value of goods diminished by consumer handling);

(c) regulation 35(5) (where goods returned by consumer);

(d) regulation 36(4) (where consumer requests early supply of service).

(2) The cancellation period begins when the contract is entered into and ends in accordance with regulation 30 or 31.

(3) Paragraph (1) does not affect the consumer's right to withdraw an offer made by the consumer to enter into a distance or off-premises contract, at any time before the contract is entered into, without giving any reason and without incurring any liability.

30 Normal cancellation period

(1) The cancellation period ends as follows, unless regulation 31 applies.

(2) If the contract is—

(a) a service contract, or

(b) a contract for the supply of digital content which is not supplied on a tangible medium,

the cancellation period ends at the end of 14 days after the day on which the contract is entered into.

(3) If the contract is a sales contract and none of paragraphs (4) to (6) applies, the cancellation period ends at the end of 14 days after the day on which the goods come into the physical possession of—

(a) the consumer, or

(b) a person, other than the carrier, identified by the consumer to take possession of them.

(4) If the contract is a sales contract under which multiple goods are ordered by the consumer in one order but some are delivered on different days, the cancellation period ends at the end of 14 days after the day on which the last of the goods come into the physical possession of—

(a) the consumer, or

(b) a person, other than the carrier, identified by the consumer to take possession of them.

(5)   If the contract is a sales contract under which goods consisting of multiple lots or pieces of something are delivered on different days, the cancellation period ends at the end of 14 days after the day on which the last of the lots or pieces come into the physical possession of—
(a)   the consumer, or
(b)   a person, other than the carrier, identified by the consumer to take possession of them.

(6)   If the contract is a sales contract for regular delivery of goods during a defined period of more than one day, the cancellation period ends at the end of 14 days after the day on which the first of the goods come into the physical possession of—
(a)   the consumer, or
(b)   a person, other than the carrier, identified by the consumer to take possession of them.

31   Cancellation period extended for breach of information requirement

(1)   This regulation applies if the trader does not provide the consumer with the information on the right to cancel required by paragraph (l) of Schedule 2, in accordance with Part 2.

(2)   If the trader provides the consumer with that information in the period of 12 months beginning with the first day of the 14 days mentioned in regulation 30(2) to (6), but otherwise in accordance with Part 2, the cancellation period ends at the end of 14 days after the consumer receives the information.

(3)   Otherwise the cancellation period ends at the end of 12 months after the day on which it would have ended under regulation 30.

32   Exercise of the right to withdraw or cancel

(1)   To withdraw an offer to enter into a distance or off-premises contract, the consumer must inform the trader of the decision to withdraw it.

(2)   To cancel a contract under regulation 29(1), the consumer must inform the trader of the decision to cancel it.

(3)   To inform the trader under paragraph (2) the consumer may either—
(a)   use a form following the model cancellation form in part B of Schedule 3, or
(b)   make any other clear statement setting out the decision to cancel the contract.

(4)   If the trader gives the consumer the option of filling in and submitting such a form or other statement on the trader's website—
(a)   the consumer need not use it, but
(b)   if the consumer does, the trader must communicate to the consumer an acknowledgement of receipt of the cancellation on a durable medium without delay.

(5)   Where the consumer informs the trader under paragraph (2) by sending a communication, the consumer is to be treated as having cancelled the contract in the cancellation period if the communication is sent before the end of the period.

(6)   In case of dispute it is for the consumer to show that the contract was cancelled in the cancellation period in accordance with this regulation.

33   Effect of withdrawal or cancellation

(1)   If a contract is cancelled under regulation 29(1)—
(a)   the cancellation ends the obligations of the parties to perform the contract, and
(b)   regulations 34 to 38 apply.

(2)   Regulations 34 and 38 also apply if the consumer withdraws an offer to enter into a distance or off-premises contract.

34   Reimbursement by trader in the event of withdrawal or cancellation

(1)   The trader must reimburse all payments, other than payments for delivery, received from the consumer, subject to paragraph (10).

(2)   The trader must reimburse any payment for delivery received from the consumer, unless the consumer expressly chose a kind of delivery costing more than the least expensive common and generally acceptable kind of delivery offered by the trader.

(3) In that case, the trader must reimburse any payment for delivery received from the consumer up to the amount the consumer would have paid if the consumer had chosen the least expensive common and generally acceptable kind of delivery offered by the trader.

(4) Reimbursement must be without undue delay, and in any event not later than the time specified in paragraph (5) or (6).

(5) If the contract is a sales contract and the trader has not offered to collect the goods, the time is the end of 14 days after—
    (a) the day on which the trader receives the goods back, or
    (b) if earlier, the day on which the consumer supplies evidence of having sent the goods back.

(6) Otherwise, the time is the end of 14 days after the day on which the trader is informed of the consumer's decision to withdraw the offer or cancel the contract, in accordance with regulation 32.

(7) The trader must make the reimbursement using the same means of payment as the consumer used for the initial transaction, unless the consumer has expressly agreed otherwise.

(8) The trader must not impose any fee on the consumer in respect of the reimbursement.

(9) If (in the case of a sales contract) the value of the goods is diminished by any amount as a result of handling of the goods by the consumer beyond what is necessary to establish the nature, characteristics and functioning of the goods, the trader may recover that amount from the consumer, up to the contract price.

(10) An amount that may be recovered under paragraph (9)—
    (a) may be deducted from the amount to be reimbursed under paragraph (1);
    (b) otherwise, must be paid by the consumer to the trader.

(11) Paragraph (9) does not apply if the trader has failed to provide the consumer with the information on the right to cancel required by paragraph (l) of Schedule 2, in accordance with Part 2.

(12) For the purposes of paragraph (9) handling is beyond what is necessary to establish the nature, characteristics and functioning of the goods if, in particular, it goes beyond the sort of handling that might reasonably be allowed in a shop.

(13) Where the provisions of this regulation apply to cancellation of a contract, the contract is to be treated as including those provisions as terms.

35 Return of goods in the event of cancellation

(1) Where a sales contract is cancelled under regulation 29(1), it is the trader's responsibility to collect the goods if—
    (a) the trader has offered to collect them, or
    (b) in the case of an off-premises contract, the goods were delivered to the consumer's home when the contract was entered into and could not, by their nature, normally be returned by post.

(2) If it is not the trader's responsibility under paragraph (1) to collect the goods, the consumer must—
    (a) send them back, or
    (b) hand them over to the trader or to a person authorised by the trader to receive them.

(3) The address to which goods must be sent under paragraph (2)(a) is—
    (a) any address specified by the trader for sending the goods back;
    (b) if no address is specified for that purpose, any address specified by the trader for the consumer to contact the trader;
    (c) if no address is specified for either of those purposes, any place of business of the trader.

(4) The consumer must send off the goods under paragraph (2)(a), or hand them over under paragraph (2)(b), without undue delay and in any event not later than 14 days after the day on which the consumer informs the trader as required by regulation 32(2).

(5) The consumer must bear the direct cost of returning goods under paragraph (2), unless—
    (a) the trader has agreed to bear those costs, or

      (b)   the trader failed to provide the consumer with the information about the consumer bearing those costs, required by paragraph (m) of Schedule 2, in accordance with Part 2.

(6)   The contract is to be treated as including a term that the trader must bear the direct cost of the consumer returning goods under paragraph (2) where paragraph (5)(b) applies.

(7)   The consumer is not required to bear any other cost of returning goods under paragraph (2).

(8)   The consumer is not required to bear any cost of collecting goods under paragraph (1) unless the trade has offered to collect the goods and the consumer has agreed to bear the costs of the trader doing so.

36   Supply of service in cancellation period

(1)   The trader must not begin the supply of a service before the end of the cancellation period provided for in regulation 30(1) unless the consumer—

      (a)   has made an express request, and

      (b)   in the case of an off-premises contract, has made the request on a durable medium.

(2)   In the case of a service other than supply of water, gas, electricity or district heating, the consumer ceases to have the right to cancel a service contract under regulation 29(1) if the service has been fully performed, and performance of the service began—

      (a)   after a request by the consumer in accordance with paragraph (1), and

      (b)   with the acknowledgement that the consumer would lose that right once the contract had been fully performed by the trader.

(3)   Paragraphs (4) to (6) apply where a contract is cancelled under regulation 29(1) and a service has been supplied in the cancellation period.

(4)   Where the service is supplied in response to a request in accordance with paragraph (1), the consumer must (subject to paragraph (6)) pay to the trader an amount—

      (a)   for the supply of the service for the period for which it is supplied, ending with the time when the trader is informed of the consumer's decision to cancel the contract, in accordance with regulation 32(2), and

      (b)   which is in proportion to what has been supplied, in comparison with the full coverage of the contract.

(5)   The amount is to be calculated—

      (a)   on the basis of the total price agreed in the contract, or

      (b)   if the total price is excessive, on the basis of the market value of the service that has been supplied, calculated by comparing prices for equivalent services supplied by other traders.

(6)   The consumer bears no cost for supply of the service, in full or in part, in the cancellation period, if—

      (a)   the trader has failed to provide the consumer with the information on the right to cancel required by paragraph (l) of Schedule 2, or the information on payment of that cost required by paragraph (n) of that Schedule, in accordance with Part 2, or

      (b)   the service is not supplied in response to a request in accordance with paragraph (1).

37   Supply of digital content in cancellation period

(1)   Under a contract for the supply of digital content not on a tangible medium, the trader must not begin supply of the digital content before the end of the cancellation period provided for in regulation 30(1), unless—

      (a)   the consumer has given express consent, and

      (b)   the consumer has acknowledged that the right to cancel the contract under regulation 29(1) will be lost.

(2)   The consumer ceases to have the right to cancel such a contract under regulation 29(1) if, before the end of the cancellation period, supply of the digital content has begun after the consumer has given the consent and acknowledgement required by paragraph (1).

(3)   Paragraph (4) applies where a contract is cancelled under regulation 29(1) and digital content has been supplied, not on a tangible medium, in the cancellation period.

(4)   The consumer bears no cost for supply of the digital content, in full or in part, in the cancellation period, if—

(a)   the consumer has not given prior express consent to the beginning of the performance of the digital content before the end of the 14-day period referred to in regulation 30,

(b)   the consumer gave that consent but did not acknowledge when giving it that the right to cancel would be lost, or

(c)   the trader failed to provide confirmation required by regulation 12(5) or 16(3).

38   Effects of withdrawal or cancellation on ancillary contracts

(1)   If a consumer withdraws an offer to enter into a distance or off-premises contract, or cancels such a contract under regulation 29(1), any ancillary contracts are automatically terminated, without any costs for the consumer, other than any costs under these provisions—

(a)   regulation 34(3) (where enhanced delivery chosen by consumer);

(b)   regulation 34(9) (where value of goods diminished by consumer handling);

(c)   regulation 35(5) (where goods returned by consumer);

(d)   regulation 36(4) (where consumer requests early supply of service).

(2)   When a trader is informed by a consumer under regulation 32(1) or (2) of a decision to withdraw an offer or cancel a contract, the trader must inform any other trader with whom the consumer has an ancillary contract that is terminated by paragraph (1).

(3)   An "ancillary contract", in relation to a distance or off-premises contract (the "main contract"), means a contract by which the consumer acquires goods or services related to the main contract, where those goods or services are provided—

(a)   by the trader, or

(b)   by a third party on the basis of an arrangement between the third party and the trader.

(4)   Regulation 6(1)(b) (exclusion of financial services contracts) does not limit the contracts that are ancillary contracts for the purposes of this regulation.

PART 4
PROTECTION FROM ADDITIONAL CHARGES

40   Additional payments under a contract

(1)   Under a contract between a trader and a consumer, no payment is payable in addition to the remuneration agreed for the trader's main obligation unless, before the consumer became bound by the contract, the trader obtained the consumer's express consent.

(2)   There is no express consent (if there would otherwise be) for the purposes of this paragraph if consent is inferred from the consumer not changing a default option (such as a pre-ticked box on a website).

(3)   This regulation does not apply if the trader's main obligation is to supply services within regulation 6(1)(b), but in any other case it applies even if an additional payment is for such services.

(4)   Where a trader receives an additional payment which, under this regulation, is not payable under a contract, the contract is to be treated as providing for the trader to reimburse the payment to the consumer.

41   Help-line charges over basic rate

(1)   Where a trader operates a telephone line for the purpose of consumers contacting the trader by telephone in relation to contracts entered into with the trader, a consumer contacting the trader must not be bound to pay more than the basic rate.

(2)   If in those circumstances a consumer who contacts a trader in relation to a contract is bound to pay more than the basic rate, the contract is to be treated as providing for the trader to pay to the consumer any amount by which the charge paid by the consumer for the call is more than the basic rate.

SCHEDULE 1   **Regulation 9(1)**

INFORMATION RELATING TO ON-PREMISES CONTRACTS

The information referred to in regulation 9(1) is—

(a)   the main characteristics of the goods, services or digital content, to the extent appropriate to the medium of communication and to the goods, services or digital content;

(b)   the identity of the trader (such as the trader's trading name), the geographical address at which the trader is established and the trader's telephone number;

(c)   the total price of the goods or services inclusive of taxes, or where the nature of the goods, services or digital content is such that the price cannot reasonably be calculated in advance, the manner in which the price is to be calculated;

(d)   where applicable, all additional delivery charges or, where those charges cannot reasonably be calculated in advance, the fact that such additional charges may be payable;

(e)   where applicable, the arrangements for payment, delivery, performance, and the time by which the trader undertakes to deliver the goods, to perform the service or to supply the digital content;

(f)   where applicable, the trader's complaint handling policy;

(g)   in the case of a sales contract, a reminder that the trader is under a legal duty to supply goods that are in conformity with the contract;

(h)   where applicable, the existence and the conditions of after-sales services and commercial guarantees;

(i)   the duration of the contract, where applicable, or, if the contract is of indeterminate duration or is to be extended automatically, the conditions for terminating the contract;

(j)   where applicable, the functionality, including applicable technical protection measures, of digital content;

(k)   where applicable, any relevant compatibility of digital content with hardware and software that the trader is aware of or can reasonably be expected to have been aware of.

SCHEDULE 2   **Regulations 10(1) and 13(1)**

INFORMATION RELATING TO DISTANCE AND
OFF-PREMISES CONTRACTS

The information referred to in regulations 10(1) and 13(1) is (subject to the note at the end of this Schedule)—

(a)   the main characteristics of the goods, services or digital content, to the extent appropriate to the medium of communication and to the goods, services or digital content;

(b)   the identity of the trader (such as the trader's trading name);

(c)   the geographical address at which the trader is established and, where available, the trader's telephone number, fax number and e-mail address, to enable the consumer to contact the trader quickly and communicate efficiently;

(d)   where the trader is acting on behalf of another trader, the geographical address and identity of that other trader;

(e)   if different from the address provided in accordance with paragraph (c), the geographical address of the place of business of the trader, and, where the trader acts on behalf of another trader, the geographical address of the place of business of that other trader, where the consumer can address any complaints;

(f)   the total price of the goods, services or digital content inclusive of taxes, or where the nature of the goods, services or digital content is such that the price cannot reasonably be calculated in advance, the manner in which the price is to be calculated,

(g)   where applicable, all additional delivery charges and any other costs or, where those charges cannot reasonably be calculated in advance, the fact that such additional charges may be payable;

(h)   in the case of a contract of indeterminate duration or a contract containing a subscription, the total costs per billing period or (where such contracts are charged at a fixed rate) the total monthly costs;

(i)   the cost of using the means of distance communication for the conclusion of the contract where that cost is calculated other than at the basic rate;

(j)   the arrangements for payment, delivery, performance, and the time by which the trader undertakes to deliver the goods or supply the digital content to perform the services;

(k)   where applicable, the trader's complaint handling policy;

(l)   where a right to cancel exists, the conditions, time limit and procedures for exercising that right in accordance with regulations 27 to 38;

(m)   where applicable, that the consumer will have to bear the cost of returning the goods in case of cancellation and, for distance contracts, if the goods, by their nature, cannot normally be returned by post, the cost of returning the goods;

(n)   that, if the consumer exercises the right to cancel after having made a request in accordance with regulation 36(1), the consumer is to be liable to pay the trader reasonable costs in accordance with regulation 36(4);

(o)   where under regulation 28, 36 or 37 there is no right to cancel or the right to cancel may be lost, the information that the consumer will not benefit from a right to cancel, or the circumstances under which the consumer loses the right to cancel;

(p)   in the case of a sales contract, a reminder that the trader is under a legal duty to supply goods that are in conformity with the contract;

(q)   where applicable, the existence and the conditions of after-sale customer assistance, after- sales services and commercial guarantees;

(r)   the existence of relevant codes of conduct, as defined in regulation 5(3)(b) of the Consumer Protection from Unfair Trading Regulations 2008, and how copies of them can be obtained, where applicable;

(s)   the duration of the contract, where applicable, or, if the contract is of indeterminate duration or is to be extended automatically, the conditions for terminating the contract;

(t)   where applicable, the minimum duration of the consumer's obligations under the contract;

(u)   where applicable, the existence and the conditions of deposits or other financial guarantees to be paid or provided by the consumer at the request of the trader;

(v)   where applicable, the functionality, including applicable technical protection measures, of digital content;

(w)   where applicable, any relevant compatibility of digital content with hardware and software that the trader is aware of or can reasonably be expected to have been aware of;

(x)   where applicable, the possibility of having recourse to an out-of-court complaint and redress mechanism, to which the trader is subject, and the methods for having access to it.

Note: In the case of a public auction, the information listed in paragraphs (b) to (e) may be replaced with the equivalent details for the auctioneer.

PART III
EU LEGISLATION

COUNCIL DIRECTIVE
of 25 July 1985
on the approximation of the laws, regulations and administrative provisions of the Member States concerning liability for defective products
(85/374/EEC)

THE COUNCIL OF THE EUROPEAN COMMUNITIES,

Having regard to the Treaty establishing the European Economic Community, and in particular Article 100 thereof,

Having regard to the proposal from the Commission,

Having regard to the opinion of the European Parliament,

Having regard to the opinion of the Economic and Social Committee,

Whereas approximation of the laws of the Member States concerning the liability of the producer for damage caused by the defectiveness of his products is necessary because the existing divergences may distort competition and affect the movement of goods within the common market and entail a differing degree of protection of the consumer against damage caused by a defective product to his health or property;

Whereas liability without fault on the part of the producer is the sole means of adequately solving the problem, peculiar to our age of increasing technicality, of a fair apportionment of the risks inherent in modern technological production;

Whereas liability without fault should apply only to movables which have been industrially produced; whereas, as a result, it is appropriate to exclude liability for agricultural products and game, except where they have undergone a processing of an industrial nature which could cause a defect in these products; whereas the liability provided for in this Directive should also apply to movables which are used in the construction of immovables or are installed in immovables;

Whereas protection of the consumer requires that all producers involved in the production process should be made liable, in so far as their finished product, component part or any raw material supplied by them was defective; whereas, for the same reason, liability should extend to importers of products into the Community and to persons who present themselves as producers by affixing their name, trade mark or other distinguishing feature or who supply a product the producer of which cannot be identified;

Whereas, in situations where several persons are liable for the same damage, the protection of the consumer requires that the injured person should be able to claim full compensation for the damage from any one of them;

Whereas, to protect the physical well-being and property of the consumer, the defectiveness of the product should be determined by reference not to its fitness for use but to the lack of the safety which the public at large is entitled to expect; whereas the safety is assessed by excluding any misuse of the product not reasonable under the circumstances;

Whereas a fair apportionment of risk between the injured person and the producer implies that the producer should be able to free himself from liability if he furnishes proof as to the existence of certain exonerating circumstances;

Whereas the protection of the consumer requires that the liability of the producer remains unaffected by acts or omissions of other persons having contributed to cause the damage; whereas, however, the contributory negligence of the injured person may be taken into account to reduce or disallow such liability;

Whereas the protection of the consumer requires compensation for death and personal injury as well as compensation for damage to property; whereas the latter should nevertheless be limited to goods for private use or consumption and be subject to a deduction of a lower threshold of a fixed amount in order to avoid litigation in an excessive number of cases; whereas this Directive should not prejudice compensation for pain and suffering and other nonmaterial damages payable, where appropriate, under the law applicable to the case;

Whereas a uniform period of limitation for the bringing of action for compensation is in the interests both of the injured person and of the producer;

Whereas products age in the course of time, higher safety standards are developed and the state of science and technology progresses; whereas, therefore, it would not be reasonable to make the producer liable for an unlimited period for the defectiveness of his product; whereas, therefore, liability should expire after a reasonable length of time, without prejudice to claims pending at law;

Whereas, to achieve effective protection of consumers, no contractual derogation should be permitted as regards the liability of the producer in relation to the injured person;

Whereas under the legal systems of the Member States an injured party may have a claim for damages based on grounds of contractual liability or on grounds of non-contractual liability other than that provided for in this Directive; in so far as these provisions also serve to attain the objective of effective protection of consumers, they should remain unaffected by this Directive; whereas, in so far as effective protection of consumers in the sector of pharmaceutical products is already also attained in a Member State under a special liability system, claims based on this system should similarly remain possible;

Whereas, to the extent that liability for nuclear injury or damage is already covered in all Member States by adequate special rules, it has been possible to exclude damage of this type from the scope of this Directive;

Whereas, since the exclusion of primary agricultural products and game from the scope of this Directive may be felt, in certain Member States, in view of what is expected for the protection of consumers, to restrict unduly such protection, it should be possible for a Member State to extend liability to such products;

Whereas, for similar reasons, the possibility offered to a producer to free himself from liability if he proves that the state of scientific and technical knowledge at the time when he put the product into circulation was not such as to enable the existence of a defect to be discovered may be felt in certain Member States to restrict unduly the protection of the consumer; whereas it should therefore be possible for a Member State to maintain in its legislation or to provide by new legislation that this exonerating circumstance is not admitted; whereas, in the case of new legislation, making use of this derogation should, however, be subject to a Community standstill procedure, in order to raise, if possible, the level of protection in a uniform manner throughout the Community;

Whereas, taking into account the legal traditions in most of the Member States, it is inappropriate to set any financial ceiling on the producer's liability without fault; whereas, in so far as there are, however, differing traditions, it seems possible to admit that a Member State may derogate from the principle of unlimited liability by providing a limit for the total liability of the producer for damage resulting from a death or personal injury and caused by identical items with the same defect, provided that this limit is established at a level sufficiently high to guarantee adequate protection of the consumer and the correct functioning of the common market;

Whereas the harmonization resulting from this cannot be total at the present stage, but opens the way towards greater harmonization; whereas it is therefore necessary that the Council receive at regular intervals, reports from the Commission on the application of this Directive, accompanied, as the case may be, by appropriate proposals;

Whereas it is particularly important in this respect that a re-examination be carried out of those parts of the Directive relating to the derogations open to the Member States, at the expiry of a period of sufficient length to gather practical experience on the effects of these derogations on the protection of consumers and on the functioning of the common market,

HAS ADOPTED THIS DIRECTIVE:

Article 1

The producer shall be liable for damage caused by a defect in his product.

Article 2

For the purpose of this Directive 'product' means all movables, with the exception of primary agricultural products and game, even though incorporated into another movable or into an immovable. 'Primary agricultural products' means the products of the soil, of stock-farming and of fisheries, excluding products which have undergone initial processing. 'Product' includes electricity.

Article 3

1. 'Producer' means the manufacturer of a finished product, the producer of any raw material or the manufacturer of a component part and any person who, by putting his name, trade mark or other distinguishing feature on the product presents himself as its producer.
2. Without prejudice to the liability of the producer, any person who imports into the Community a product for sale, hire, leasing or any form of distribution in the course of his business shall be deemed to be a producer within the meaning of this Directive and shall be responsible as a producer.
3. Where the producer of the product cannot be identified, each supplier of the product shall be treated as its producer unless he informs the injured person, within a reasonable time, of the identity of the producer or of the person who supplied him with the product. The same shall apply, in the case of an imported product, if this product does not indicate the identity of the importer referred to in paragraph 2, even if the name of the producer is indicated.

Article 4

The injured person shall be required to prove the damage, the defect and the causal relationship between defect and damage.

Article 5

Where, as a result of the provisions of this Directive, two or more persons are liable for the same damage, they shall be liable jointly and severally, without prejudice to the provisions of national law concerning the rights of contribution or recourse.

Article 6

1. A product is defective when it does not provide the safety which a person is entitled to expect, taking all circumstances into account, including:
    (a) the presentation of the product;
    (b) the use to which it could reasonably be expected that the product would be put;
    (c) the time when the product was put into circulation.
2. A product shall not be considered defective for the sole reason that a better product is subsequently put into circulation.

Article 7

The producer shall not be liable as a result of this Directive if he proves:
(a) that he did not put the product into circulation; or
(b) that, having regard to the circumstances, it is probable that the defect which caused the damage did not exist at the time when the product was put into circulation by him or that this defect came into being afterwards; or
(c) that the product was neither manufactured by him for sale or any form of distribution for economic purpose nor manufactured or distributed by him in the course of his business; or
(d) that the defect is due to compliance of the product with mandatory regulations issued by the public authorities; or
(e) that the state of scientific and technical knowledge at the time when he put the product into circulation was not such as to enable the existence of the defect to be discovered; or
(f) in the case of a manufacturer of a component, that the defect is attributable to the design of the product in which the component has been fitted or to the instructions given by the manufacturer of the product.

Article 8

1. Without prejudice to the provisions of national law concerning the right of contribution or recourse, the liability of the producer shall not be reduced when the damage is caused both by a defect in product and by the act or omission of a third party.
2. The liability of the producer may be reduced or disallowed when, having regard to all the circumstances, the damage is caused both by a defect in the product and by the fault of the injured person or any person for whom the injured person is responsible.

Article 9

For the purpose of Article 1, 'damage' means:

    (a)   damage caused by death or by personal injuries;

    (b)   damage to, or destruction of, any item of property other than the defective product itself, with a lower threshold of 500 ECU, provided that the item of property:

        (i)   is of a type ordinarily intended for private use or consumption, and

        (ii)   was used by the injured person mainly for his own private use or consumption.

This Article shall be without prejudice to national provisions relating to non-material damage.

Article 10

1.   Member States shall provide in their legislation that a limitation period of three years shall apply to proceedings for the recovery of damages as provided for in this Directive. The limitation period shall begin to run from the day on which the plaintiff became aware, or should reasonably have become aware, of the damage, the defect and the identity of the producer.

2.   The laws of Member States regulating suspension or interruption of the limitation period shall not be affected by this Directive.

Article 11

Member States shall provide in their legislation that the rights conferred upon the injured person pursuant to this Directive shall be extinguished upon the expiry of a period of 10 years from the date on which the producer put into circulation the actual product which caused the damage, unless the injured person has in the meantime instituted proceedings against the producer.

Article 12

The liability of the producer arising from this Directive may not, in relation to the injured person, be limited or excluded by a provision limiting his liability or exempting him from liability.

Article 13

This Directive shall not affect any rights which an injured person may have according to the rules of the law of contractual or non-contractual liability or a special liability system existing at the moment when this Directive is notified.

Article 14

This Directive shall not apply to injury or damage arising from nuclear accidents and covered by international conventions ratified by the Member States.

Article 15

1.   Each Member State may:

    (a)   by way of derogation from Article 2, provide in its legislation that within the meaning of Article 1 of this Directive 'product' also means primary agricultural products and game;

    (b)   by way of derogation from Article 7(e), maintain or, subject to the procedure set out in paragraph 2 of this Article, provide in this legislation that the producer shall be liable even if he proves that the state of scientific and technical knowledge at the time when he put the product into circulation was not such as to enable the existence of a defect to be discovered.

2.   A Member State wishing to introduce the measure specified in paragraph 1(b) shall communicate the text of the proposed measure to the Commission. The Commission shall inform the other Member States thereof.

The Member State concerned shall hold the proposed measure in abeyance for nine months after the Commission is informed and provided that in the meantime the Commission has not submitted to the Council a proposal amending this Directive on the relevant matter. However, if within three months of receiving the said information, the Commission does not advise the Member State concerned that it intends submitting such a proposal to the Council, the Member State may take the proposed measure immediately. If the Commission does submit to the Council such a proposal amending this Directive within the aforementioned nine months, the Member State concerned shall hold the proposed measure in abeyance for a further period of 18 months from the date on which the proposal is submitted.

3. Ten years after the date of notification of this Directive, the Commission shall submit to the Council a report on the effect that rulings by the courts as to the application of Article 7(e) and of paragraph 1(b) of this Article have on consumer protection and the functioning of the common market. In the light of this report the Council, acting on a proposal from the Commission and pursuant to the terms of Article 100 of the Treaty, shall decide whether to repeal Article 7(e).

Article 16

1. Any Member State may provide that a producer's total liability for damage resulting from a death or personal injury and caused by identical items with the same defect shall be limited to an amount which may not be less than 70 million ECU.
2. Ten years after the date of notification of this Directive, the Commission shall submit to the Council a report on the effect on consumer protection and the functioning of the common market of the implementation of the financial limit on liability by those Member States which have used the option provided for in paragraph 1. In the light of this report the Council, acting on a proposal from the Commission and pursuant to the terms of Article 100 of the Treaty, shall decide whether to repeal paragraph 1.

Article 17

This Directive shall not apply to products put into circulation before the date on which the provisions referred to in Article 19 enter into force.

Article 18

1. For the purposes of this Directive, the ECU shall be that defined by Regulation (EEC) No 3180/78 (1), as amended by Regulation (EEC) No 2626/84 (2). The equivalent in national currency shall initially be calculated at the rate obtaining on the date of adoption of this Directive.
2. Every five years the Council, acting on a proposal from the Commission, shall examine and, if need be, revise the amounts in this Directive, in the light of economic and monetary trends in the Community.

Article 19

1. Member States shall bring into force, not later than three years from the date of notification of this Directive, the laws, regulations and administrative provisions necessary to comply with this Directive. They shall forthwith inform the Commission thereof.
2. The procedure set out in Article 15 shall apply from the date of notification of the Directive.

Article 20

Member States shall communicate to the Commission the texts of the main provisions of national law which they subsequently adopt in the field governed by this Directive.

Article 21

Every five years the Commission shall present a report to the Council on the application of this Directive and, if necessary, shall submit appropriate proposals to it.

Article 22

This Directive is addressed to the Member States.
    Done at Brussels, 25 July 1985.

COUNCIL DIRECTIVE
of 5 April 1993
on unfair terms in consumer contracts
(93/13/EEC)

THE COUNCIL OF THE EUROPEAN COMMUNITIES,

Having regard to the Treaty establishing the European Economic Community, and in particular Article 100A thereof,

Having regard to the proposal from the Commission,

In cooperation with the European Parliament,

Having regard to the opinion of the Economic and Social Committee,

Whereas it is necessary to adopt measures with the aim of progressively establishing the internal market before 31 December 1992; whereas the internal market comprises an area without internal frontiers in which goods, persons, services and capital move freely;

Whereas the laws of Member States relating to the terms of contract between the seller of goods or supplier of services, on the one hand, and the consumer of them, on the other hand, show many disparities, with the result that the national markets for the sale of goods and services to consumers differ from each other and that distortions of competition may arise amongst the sellers and suppliers, notably when they sell and supply in other Member States;

Whereas, in particular, the laws of Member States relating to unfair terms in consumer contracts show marked divergences;

Whereas it is the responsibility of the Member States to ensure that contracts concluded with consumers do not contain unfair terms;

Whereas, generally speaking, consumers do not know the rules of law which, in Member States other than their own, govern contracts for the sale of goods or services; whereas this lack of awareness may deter them from direct transactions for the purchase of goods or services in another Member State;

Whereas, in order to facilitate the establishment of the internal market and to safeguard the citizen in his role as consumer when acquiring goods and services under contracts which are governed by the laws of Member States other than his own, it is essential to remove unfair terms from those contracts;

Whereas sellers of goods and suppliers of services will thereby be helped in their task of selling goods and supplying services, both at home and throughout the internal market; whereas competition will thus be stimulated, so contributing to increased choice for Community citizens as consumers;

Whereas the two Community programmes for a consumer protection and information policy underlined the importance of safeguarding consumers in the matter of unfair terms of contract; whereas this protection ought to be provided by laws and regulations which are either harmonised at Community level or adopted directly at that level;

Whereas in accordance with the principle laid down under the heading "Protection of the economic interests of the consumers", as stated in those programmes: "acquirers of goods and services should be protected against the abuse of power by the seller or supplier, in particular against one-sided standard contracts and the unfair exclusion of essential rights in contracts";

Whereas more effective protection of the consumer can be achieved by adopting uniform rules of law in the matter of unfair terms; whereas those rules should apply to all contracts concluded between sellers or suppliers and consumers; whereas as a result inter alia contracts relating to employment, contracts relating to succession rights, contracts relating to rights under family law and contracts relating to the incorporation and organisation of companies or partnership agreements must be excluded from this Directive;

Whereas the consumer must receive equal protection under contracts concluded by word of mouth and written contracts regardless, in the latter case, of whether the terms of the contract are contained in one or more documents;

Whereas, however, as they now stand, national laws allow only partial harmonisation to be envisaged; whereas, in particular, only contractual terms which have not been individually negotiated are covered by this Directive; whereas Member States should have the option, with due regard for the Treaty, to afford consumers a higher level of protection through national provisions that are more stringent than those of this Directive;

Whereas the statutory or regulatory provisions of the Member States which directly or indirectly determine the terms of consumer contracts are presumed not to contain unfair terms; whereas, therefore, it does not appear to be necessary to subject the terms which reflect mandatory statutory or regulatory provisions and the principles or provisions of international contraventions to which the Member States or the Community are party; whereas in that respect the wording "mandatory statutory or regulatory provisions" in Article 1(2) also covers rules which, according to the law, shall apply between the contracting parties provided that no other arrangements have been established;

Whereas Member States must however ensure that unfair terms are not included, particularly because this Directive also applies to trades, business or professions of a public nature;

Whereas it is necessary to fix in a general way the criteria for assessing the unfair character of contract terms;

Whereas the assessment, according to the general criteria chosen, of the unfair character of terms, in particular in sale or supply activities of a public nature providing collective services which take account of solidarity among users, must be supplemented by a means of making an overall evaluation of the different interests involved; whereas this constitutes the requirement of good faith; whereas, in making an assessment of good faith, particular regard shall be had to the strength of the bargaining positions of the parties, whether the consumer had an inducement to agree to the term and whether the goods or services were sold or supplied to the special order of the consumer; whereas the requirement of good faith may be satisfied by the seller or supplier where he deals fairly and equitably with the other party whose legitimate interests he has to take into account;

Whereas, for the purposes of this Directive, the annexed list of terms can be of indicative value only and, because of the cause of the minimal character of the Directive, the scope of these terms may be the subject of amplification or more restrictive editing by the Member States in their national laws;

Whereas the nature of goods or services should have an influence on assessing the unfairness of contractual terms;

Whereas, for the purposes of this Directive, assessment of unfair character shall not be made of terms which describe the main subject matter of the contract nor the quality/price ratio of the goods or services supplied; whereas the main subject matter of the contract and the price/quality ratio may nevertheless be taken into account in assessing the fairness of other terms; whereas it follows, *inter alia*, that in insurance contracts, the terms which clearly define or circumscribe the insured risk and the insurer's liability shall not be subject to such assessment since these restrictions are taken into account in calculating the premium paid by the consumer;

Whereas contracts should be drafted in plain, intelligible language, the consumer should actually be given an opportunity to examine all the terms and, if in doubt, the interpretation most favourable to the consumer should prevail;

Whereas Member States should ensure that unfair terms are not used in contracts concluded with consumers by a seller or supplier and that if, nevertheless, such terms are so used, they will not bind the consumer, and the contract will continue to bind the parties upon those terms if it is capable of continuing in existence without the unfair provisions;

Whereas there is a risk that, in certain cases, the consumer may be deprived of protection under this Directive by designating the law of a non-Member country as the law applicable to the contract; whereas provisions should therefore be included in this Directive designed to avert this risk;

Whereas persons or organisations, if regarded under the law of a Member State as having a legitimate interest in the matter, must have facilities for initiating proceedings concerning terms of contract drawn up for general use in contracts concluded with consumers, and in particular unfair terms, either before a court or before an administrative authority competent to decide upon complaints or to initiate appropriate legal proceedings; whereas this possibility does not, however, entail prior verification of the general conditions obtaining in individual economic sectors;

Whereas the courts or administrative authorities of the Member States must have at their disposal adequate and effective means of preventing the continued application of unfair terms in consumer contracts,

HAS ADOPTED THIS DIRECTIVE:

Article 1

1. The purpose of this Directive is to approximate the laws, regulations and administrative provisions of the Member States relating to unfair terms in contracts concluded between a seller or supplier and a consumer.

2. The contractual terms which reflect mandatory statutory or regulatory provisions and the provisions or principles of international conventions to which the Member States or the Community are party, particularly in the transport area, shall not be subject to the provisions of this Directive.

Article 2

For the purposes of this Directive:

(a) "unfair terms" means the contractual terms defined in Article 3;

(b) "consumer" means any natural person who, in contracts covered by this Directive, is acting for purposes which are outside his trade, business or profession;

(c) "seller or supplier" means any natural or legal person who, in contracts covered by this Directive, is acting for purposes relating to his trade, business or profession, whether publicly owned or privately owned.

Article 3

1. A contractual term which has not been individually negotiated shall be regarded as unfair if, contrary to the requirement of good faith, it causes a significant imbalance in the parties' rights and obligations arising under the contract, to the detriment of the consumer.

2. A term shall always be regarded as not individually negotiated where it has been drafted in advance and the consumer has therefore not been able to influence the substance of the term, particularly in the context of a pre-formulated standard contract.

   The fact that certain aspects of a term or one specific term have been individually negotiated shall not exclude the application of this Article to the rest of a contract if an overall assessment of the contract indicates that it is nevertheless a pre-formulated standard contract.

   Where any seller or supplier claims that a standard term has been individually negotiated, the burden of proof in this respect shall be incumbent on him.

3. The Annex shall contain an indicative and non-exhaustive list of the terms which may be regarded as unfair.

Article 4

1. Without prejudice to Article 7, the unfairness of a contractual term shall be assessed, taking into account the nature of the goods or services for which the contract was concluded and by referring, at the time of conclusion of the contract, to all the circumstances attending the conclusion of the contract and to all the other terms of the contract or of another contract on which it is dependent.

2. Assessment of the unfair nature of the terms shall relate neither to the definition of the main subject matter of the contract nor to the adequacy of the price and remuneration, on the one hand, as against the services or goods supplied in exchange, on the other, in so far as these terms are in plain intelligible language.

Article 5

In the case of contracts where all or certain terms offered to the consumer are in writing, these terms must always be drafted in plain, intelligible language.

Where there is doubt about the meaning of a term, the interpretation most favourable to the consumer shall prevail. This rule on interpretation shall not apply in the context of the procedures laid down in Article 7(2).

Article 6

1. Member States shall lay down that unfair terms used in a contract concluded with a consumer by a seller or supplier shall, as provided for under their national law, not be binding on the consumer and that the contract shall continue to bind the parties upon those terms if it is capable of continuing in existence without the unfair terms.

2.   Member States shall take the necessary measures to ensure that the consumer does not lose the protection granted by this Directive by virtue of the choice of the law of a nonMember country as the law applicable to the contract if the latter has a close connection with the territory of the Member States.

Article 7

1.   Member States shall ensure that, in the interests of consumers and of competitors, adequate and effective means exist to prevent the continued use of unfair terms in contracts concluded with consumers by sellers or suppliers.

2.   The means referred to in paragraph 1 shall include provisions whereby persons or organisations, having a legitimate interest under national law in protecting consumers, may take action according to the national law concerned before the courts or before competent administrative bodies for a decision as to whether contractual terms drawn up for general use are unfair, so that they can apply appropriate and effective means to prevent the continued use of such terms.

3.   With due regard for national laws, the legal remedies referred to in paragraph 2 may be directed separately or jointly against a number of sellers or suppliers from the same economic sector or their associations which use or recommend the use of the same general contractual terms or similar terms.

Article 8

Member States may adopt or retain the most stringent provisions compatible with the Treaty in the area covered by this Directive, to ensure a maximum degree of protection for the consumer.

Article 9

The Commission shall present a report to the European Parliament and to the Council concerning the application of this Directive five years at the latest after the date in Article 10(1).

Article 10

1.   Member States shall bring into force the laws, regulations and administrative provisions necessary to comply with this Directive no later than 31 Deccember 1994. They shall forthwith inform the Commission thereof.
      These provisions shall be applicable to all contracts concluded after 31 December 1994.

2.   When Member States adopt these measures, they shall contain a reference to this Directive or shall be accompanied by such reference on the occasion of their official publication. The methods of making such a reference shall be laid down by the Member States.

3.   Member States shall communicate the main provisions of national law which they adopt in the field covered by this Directive to the Commission.

Article 11

This Directive is addressed to the Member States.
      Done at Luxembourg, 5 April 1993.

ANNEX
TERMS REFERRED TO IN ARTICLE 3(3)

1.   Terms which have the object or effect of:
      (a)   excluding or limiting the legal liability of a seller or supplier in the event of the death of a consumer or personal injury to the latter resulting from an act or omission of that seller or supplier;
      (b)   inappropriately excluding or limiting the legal rights of the consumer vis-à-vis the seller or supplier or another party in the event of total or partial non-performance or inadequate performance by the seller or supplier of any of the contractual obligations, including the option of offsetting a debt owed to the seller or supplier against any claim which the consumer may have against him;

(c)   making an agreement binding on the consumer whereas provision of services by the seller or supplier is subject to a condition whose realisation depends on his own will alone;

(d)   permitting the seller or supplier to retain sums paid by the consumer where the latter decides not to conclude or perform the contract, without providing for the consumer to receive compensation of an equivalent amount from the seller or supplier where the latter is the party cancelling the contract;

(e)   requiring any consumer who fails to fulfil his obligation to pay a disproportionately high sum in compensation;

(f)   authorising the seller or supplier to dissolve the contract on a discretionary basis where the same facility is not granted to the consumer, or permitting the seller or supplier to retain the sums paid for services not yet supplied by him where it is the seller or supplier himself who dissolves the contract;

(g)   enabling the seller or supplier to terminate a contract of indeterminate duration without reasonable notice except where there are serious grounds for doing so;

(h)   automatically extending a contract of fixed duration where the consumer does not indicate otherwise, when the deadline fixed for the consumer to express this desire not to extend the contract is unreasonably early;

(i)   irrevocably binding the consumer to terms with which he had no real opportunity of becoming acquainted before the conclusion of the contract;

(j)   enabling the seller or supplier to alter the terms of the contract unilaterally without a valid reason which is specified in the contract;

(k)   enabling the seller or supplier to alter unilaterally without a valid reason any characteristics of the product or service to be provided;

(l)   providing for the price of goods to be determined at the time of delivery or allowing a seller of goods or supplier of services to increase their price without in both cases giving the consumer the corresponding right to cancel the contract if the final price is too high in relation to the price agreed when the contract was concluded;

(m)   giving the seller or supplier the right to determine whether the goods or services supplied are in conformity with the contract, or giving him the exclusive right to interpret any term of the contract;

(n)   limiting the seller's or supplier's obligation to respect commitments undertaken by his agents or making his commitments subject to compliance with a particular formality;

(o)   obliging the consumer to fulfil all his obligations where the seller or supplier does not perform his;

(p)   giving the seller or supplier the possibility of transferring his rights and obligations under the contract, where this may serve to reduce the guarantees for the consumer, without the latter's agreement;

(q)   excluding or hindering the consumer's right to take legal action or exercise any other legal remedy, particularly by requiring the consumer to take disputes exclusively to arbitration not covered by legal provisions, unduly restricting the evidence available to him or imposing on him a burden of proof which, according to the applicable law, should lie with another party to the contract.

2. Scope of subparagraphs (g), (j) and (l)

(a)   Subparagraph (g) is without hindrance to terms by which a supplier of financial services reserves the right to terminate unilaterally a contract of indeterminate duration without notice where there is a valid reason, provided that the supplier is required to inform the other contracting party or parties thereof immediately.

(b)   Subparagraph (j) is without hindrance to terms under which a supplier of financial services reserves the right to alter the rate of interest payable by the consumer or due to the latter, or the amount of other charges for financial services without notice where there is a valid reason, provided that the supplier is required to inform the other contracting party or parties thereof at the earliest opportunity and that the latter are free to dissolve the contract immediately.

Subparagraph (j) is also without hindrance to terms under which a seller or supplier reserves the right to alter unilaterally the conditions of a contract of indeterminate duration, provided that he is required to inform the consumer with reasonable notice and that the consumer is free to dissolve the contract.

(c) Subparagraphs (g), (j) and (l) do not apply to:
- transactions in transferable securities, financial instruments and other products
- or services where the price is linked to fluctuations in a stock exchange quotation or index or a financial market rate that the seller or supplier does not control;
- contracts for the purchase or sale of foreign currency, traveller's cheques or nternational money orders denominated in foreign currency;

(d) Subparagraph (l) is without hindrance to price-indexation clauses, where lawful, provided that the method by which prices vary is explicitly described.

DIRECTIVE OF THE EUROPEAN PARLIAMENT AND OF THE COUNCIL
of 8 June 2000
on certain legal aspects of information society services, in particular electronic commerce, in the Internal Market
(Directive on electronic commerce)
(2000/31/EC)

CHAPTER II
PRINCIPLES

Section 3: Contracts concluded by electronic means

Article 9   Treatment of contracts

1. Member States shall ensure that their legal system allows contracts to be concluded by electronic means. Member States shall in particular ensure that the legal requirements applicable to the contractual process neither create obstacles for the use of electronic contracts nor result in such contracts being deprived of legal effectiveness and validity on account of their having been made by electronic means.

2. Member States may lay down that paragraph 1 shall not apply to all or certain contracts falling into one of the following categories:
   (a) contracts that create or transfer rights in real estate, except for rental rights;
   (b) contracts requiring by law the involvement of courts, public authorities or professions exercising public authority;
   (c) contracts of suretyship granted and on collateral securities furnished by persons acting for purposes outside their trade, business or profession; (d) contracts governed by family law or by the law of succession.

3. Member States shall indicate to the Commission the categories referred to in paragraph 2 to which they do not apply paragraph 1. Member States shall submit to the Commission every five years a report on the application of paragraph 2 explaining the reasons why they consider it necessary to maintain the category referred to in paragraph 2(b) to which they do not apply paragraph 1.

Article 10   Information to be provided

1. In addition to other information requirements established by Community law, Member States shall ensure, except when otherwise agreed by parties who are not consumers, that at least the following information is given by the service provider clearly, comprehensibly and unambiguously and prior to the order being placed by the recipient of the service:
   (a) the different technical steps to follow to conclude the contract;
   (b) whether or not the concluded contract will be filed by the service provider and whether it will be accessible;

    (c)   the technical means for identifying and correcting input errors prior to the placing of the order;

    (d)   the languages offered for the conclusion of the contract.

2.   Member States shall ensure that, except when otherwise agreed by parties who are not consumers, the service provider indicates any relevant codes of conduct to which he subscribes and information on how those codes can be consulted electronically.

3.   Contract terms and general conditions provided to the recipient must be made available in a way that allows him to store and reproduce them.

4.   Paragraphs 1 and 2 shall not apply to contracts concluded exclusively by exchange of electronic mail or by equivalent individual communications.

Article 11 Placing of the order

1.   Member States shall ensure, except when otherwise agreed by parties who are not consumers, that in cases where the recipient of the service places his order through technological means, the following principles apply:

    — the service provider has to acknowledge the receipt of the recipient's order without undue delay and by electronic means,

    — the order and the acknowledgement of receipt are deemed to be received when the parties to whom they are addressed are able to access them.

2.   Member States shall ensure that, except when otherwise agreed by parties who are not consumers, the service provider makes available to the recipient of the service appropriate, effective and accessible technical means allowing him to identify and correct input errors, prior to the placing of the order.

3.   Paragraph 1, first indent, and paragraph 2 shall not apply to contracts concluded exclusively by exchange of electronic mail or by equivalent individual communications.

INDEX